*PLANNING
AND MARKETS:
Modern Trends
in Various
Economic Systems*

PLANNING AND MARKETS:
Modern Trends in Various Economic Systems

JOHN T. DUNLOP
Professor of Economics
Harvard University

NIKOLAY P. FEDORENKO
Director of the Central Economical
*   and Mathematical Institute*
Academy of Sciences, USSR

McGRAW-HILL
BOOK COMPANY
New York
St. Louis
San Francisco
London
Sydney
Toronto
Mexico
Panama

INTRODUCTION

A Conference on *Planning and Markets: Modern Trends in Various Economic Systems* was held at Nice, France, August 31 to September 7, 1966. Almost 40 economists, equally divided between Western and Eastern countries, participated in these sessions held under the auspices of the International Economic Association. The planning and arrangements for the conference were made by a Program Committee, originally appointed by the Association. The Nice meetings were the fourth conference organized by the Labor Productivity Committee of the International Economic Association first established in 1960.

In order to prepare for the Nice conference, a preliminary meeting with 20 participants from 10 countries, both Eastern and Western, was held at the beautiful Villa Serbelloni, Bellagio, Italy, September 5 to 10, 1965. The major topics for the subsequent conference and a tentative allocation of papers was established. The discussions at the Villa Serbelloni identified problems of mutual scientific interest and led to suggestions for papers and topics for reports which were to make the Nice meetings the more productive. In the selection of conference participants and authors, it was also suggested that promising young scholars be included who may be known within their own country but who are not so well known to scholars of other countries.

At Nice the conference participants stayed at the Hotel Ruhl, and the meetings were held a pleasant walk away at the Centre Universitaire Méditerranéen, whose facilities were graciously made available to the Conference by the mayor. The simultaneous translation in Russian and English, the official languages of the Conference, materially facilitated free discussion. There was also considerable opportunity for fruitful informal conversations.

The International Economic Association acknowledges the financial assistance of The Ford Foundation in meeting the expenses of the Conference at Nice and the financial assistance of the Rockefeller Foundation and The Ford Foundation for the preliminary meetings at the Villa Serbelloni. In the publication of the English edition, financial assistance is acknowledged to the Wertheim Committee in Industrial Relations, Harvard University.

The members of the Program Committee at the Nice Conference were as follows:

> Professor Eugene Mateev, Bulgaria
> Dr. Bedřich Levčík, Czechoslovakia
> Dr. Istvan Friss, Hungary
> Professor Bronislaw Minc, Poland
> Professor Maksimilian Pohorille, Poland
> Dr. Yu. M. Pavlov, Soviet Union
> Dr. Aubrey Silberston, Great Britain
> Professor Pieter De Wolff, Netherlands
> Professor Walter Galenson, United States
> Professor John T. Dunlop, Chairman, United States

NICE CONFERENCE
ON PLANNING
AND MARKETS

PARTICIPANTS

Almon, Clopper, USA Professor, University of Maryland

Augustinovics, M., HUNGARY Institute of Economic Planning, Budapest

Bergson, Abram, USA Professor, Harvard University

Cazes, M. Bernard, FRANCE Commissariat Général du Plan, Paris

De Wolff, Pieter, THE NETHERLANDS Director, The Netherlands Central Planning Bureau, Amsterdam

Dolgu, Gheorghe, RUMANIA Assistant Director of Economics, University of Bucharest

Dumitru, Dimitriu, RUMANIA Professor, Economic Institute of the Rumanian Academy

Dunlop, John T., USA Professor, Harvard University

Ekstrom, Tord, SWEDEN Research Director, Wood and Paper Workers' Union, Stockholm

Fedorenko, Nikolay P., USSR Director, Central Economical and Mathematical Institute, Academy of Sciences, Moscow

Filkus, R., CZECHOSLOVAKIA Professor, Institute of Economics, Czechoslovak Academy of Sciences, Bratislava

Friss, Istvan, HUNGARY Professor, Institute of Economics, Hungarian Institute of Sciences, Budapest

Galenson, Walter, USA Professor, Harvard University

Gliński, Bohdan, POLAND Director, Economic Institute of The Polish Academy of Sciences, Warsaw

Harcourt, G. C., ENGLAND University Lecturer, Cambridge University

Kapustin, E. I., USSR Professor, Research Labor Institute, Moscow

Kouba, Karel, CZECHOSLOVAKIA Professor, Institute of Economics, Czechoslovak Academy of Sciences, Prague

Leontief, Wassily, USA Professor, Harvard University

Levčík, Bedřich, CZECHOSLOVAKIA Professor, Institute of Economics, Czechoslovak Academy of Sciences, Prague

Mateev, Eugene, BULGARIA Professor, Bulgarian Academy of Sciences, Sofia

McKean, Roland N., USA Professor, University of California at Los Angeles

Mileusnić, Nenad, YUGOSLAVIA Professor, Yugoslav Institute of Economic Research, Belgrade

Minc, Bronislaw, POLAND Director, Economic Institute of the Polish Academy of Sciences, Warsaw

Mirrlees, J. A., ENGLAND University Lecturer, Trinity College, Cambridge

Pavlov, Yu. M., USSR Professor, Central Economical and Mathematical Institute, Academy of Sciences, Moscow

Pohorille, Maksymilian, POLAND Professor, Central School of Planning, Warsaw

Pyatt, F. G. ENGLAND Professor, University of Warwick, Warwickshire

Ruffolo, Giorgio, ITALY   Ministry of Finance, Rome

Sevaldson, Per, NORWAY   Central Bureau of Statistics, Oslo

Šik, Ota, CZECHOSLOVAKIA   Director, Institute of Economics of The Czechoslovak Academy of Sciences, Prague

Silbertson, Aubrey, ENGLAND   Professor, University of Cambridge

Stanescu, Maria, RUMANIA   Professor, Economic Institute of the Rumanian Academy

Szikszai, B., HUNGARY   Professor, Karl Marx University, Budapest

Waelbroeck, Jean, BELGIUM   Professor, Free University of Brussels

Weinberg, Robert, USA   Director of Analytic Research, International Business Machines Corporation

CONTENTS

xi

TABLES

FIGURES

*PLANNING
AND MARKETS:
Modern Trends
in Various
Economic Systems*

PART ONE

PLANNING OF THE NATIONAL ECONOMY

Chapter 1

CENTRAL ECONOMIC PLANNING IN THE NETHERLANDS[1]

PIETER DE WOLFF

The Netherlands' Central Planning Bureau, Amsterdam

INTRODUCTION

The theory of quantitative economic planning as it has developed up to now, as well as its practical application to current Dutch economic planning, owes a great deal to the imagination and scientific activities of Jan Tinbergen. Although his ideas on economic policy took a more definite shape during and after the Second World War, he had as far back as 1936 constructed an econometric policy model[2] to study the effectiveness of various measures considered as possible instruments to cope with the depression of the thirties which in particular hit the Netherlands. In 1945, immediately after the war, when it was decided to found the Central Planning Bureau (CPB), he was appointed its first director, and in a few years, starting from scratch, he succeeded in extending it to a size and level which has not considerably changed. During his directorate he stimulated the construction of the first postwar policy model.

---

[1] This paper is an abbreviated and up-to-date version of an article under the same title published by the author in *Weltwirtschaftliches Archiv*, 1964.

[2] "Is a recovery in the domestic situation of this country possible, with or without action on the part of the government, even without an improvement in our export position? What can be learned about this problem from the experience of other countries?" Paper read before the Dutch Economic Association, 1936.

It is essential to begin with a brief account of the conceptual framework of his theory. For a more detailed exposition the reader is referred to Tinbergen's works.[3]

The starting point of his considerations is a model of the economy for which policy has to be formulated. It consists of a number of equations representing the interdependencies existing between the economic quantities entering into it. These quantities—usually called variables—are more or less broad aggregates. They can be classified as endogenous and exogenous. The former quantities, in number equal to the number of equations of the model, are determined by the economic relationships, symbolized in the model. The latter, as their name indicates, are determined by outside forces.

The endogenous variables again can be subdivided into two groups—the target variables and the rest (those in Tinbergen's terminology termed irrelevant). The target variables are very important from the policy point of view. It is their size and/or rate of change one wants to influence by adequate policy measures. Their choice again depends very much on the problem to be solved. The exogenous variables, too, can be broken down into two important groups—external variables and instruments. External variables are those playing an important role in the economy which are not themselves subject to reactions from the economy. The instruments are very important for policy purposes. The variables in this category are those which, to a certain extent, can be changed by the policy-makers.

For the present, we shall consider the model as given, and then economic policy can be described as the study of the ways and the extent to which it is possible for the policy-maker to reach certain targets through an adequate use of the available instruments—obviously within their own limits.

It will not always be possible to reach a given set of aims; this is particularly the case when their number surpasses the number of available instruments. The way out of this difficulty can be found through a social welfare function, indicating the combinations of target values which are equally satisfactory to the policy-maker. Such a function, which in practice can only be approached crudely, makes it possible to weigh the disadvantages ensuing from deviations of the target values against their optimal ones.

[3] A very good introduction is presented in *Economic Policy: Principles and Design* (Amsterdam, 1956).

CHARACTERISTICS OF SHORT-TERM
ECONOMIC PLANNING IN THE NETHERLANDS

The Dutch concept of planning. From the concept of quantitative economic policy, it is not far to the definition of central economic planning in current use in the Netherlands. As I have explained, this theory consists of two principal elements. First, there is the model, describing the connection between variables considered as aims of economic policy and instrument-variables through which it is possible to influence the aims. Second, there is a valuation of the aims which enables the policy-maker to make an optimal choice from the policy alternatives open to him. Only one step is needed to arrive at planning. We are not living in a static world, and the results of certain policy measures may be impaired by developments outside the control of the policy-maker. Therefore one must make forecasts. This is done on the basis of estimates of the expected changes of the external variables. In the first instance, a forecast is usually made assuming unchanged policy (that is, leaving the instruments unchanged). Its result is compared to the goals, and, when this confrontation leads to unsatisfactory results, a study is made of the implications of various policy changes. Each of these will lead to an alternative forecast, and, in principle, the one will be chosen that yields optimal (expected) results. This is the designated procedure when central economic planning is mentioned in our country. It will be clear that it is purely neutral. Apart from the fact that it might also be applied to planning at the enterprise level, it is equally applicable to short-term planning. Moreover, it is politically neutral. It can be used in mixed economies where governments have only limited powers to influence the economic process (that is, where their set of instruments is very restricted), where entrepreneurs enjoy a large degree of freedom, and where the market mechanism plays an important role. But it is also relevant to cases where the central government is strongly equipped and where entrepreneurs have no freedom (or hardly any) to set their own policies. Only in the virtually nonexistent case of a completely liberal economy, where government cannot exert any economic power, the scope of planning, defined above, would be reduced to a purely unconditional forecast. This might still be very important for informative purposes. However, it would no longer contain the most essential element of planning—choice of the values of targets and instruments.

In the Netherlands, the economic system belongs to the mixed economy type, and it does not differ very much from the types found in several other Western countries. Only a few generally adopted over-all economic goals are targeted; they are: a high degree of employment, a satisfactory rate of growth of the national product balance-of-payments equilibrium, a stable price level, and a fair distribution of income between wages and other incomes. These general targets will be found among the policy aims of several other countries. Apart from the general aims, there are a few more specific ones, referring to regional development, agricultural incomes, and so forth. They are, however, less relevant in the present context.

The instruments, too, are to a large extent familiar: budgetary policy (including both fiscal and expenditure), monetary policy, and licensing policy in construction. The less common group is formed by wage and price policies.

Going into detail, one may of course find special traits of minor importance. For example, in addition to discount, open-market, and cash-reserve policies, the central bank has the power to impose credit ceilings on the commercial banks when circumstances appear to require such a measure. There are special investment incentives; apart from a system of accelerated depreciation familiar to many countries there is the less generally applied possibility of investment deductions according to which entrepreneurs are entitled to charge a certain fraction of investment costs to their current account. The government, though subject to subsequent approval by parliament, is entitled to manipulate the tariffs of these incentives in accordance with the economic conditions, and so forth. It would be going too far to give a detailed description of the various instruments. Reference may be made to existing literature.[4] Due to its special character, however, it will be useful to give a brief account of the wage and price policies.

Shortly after the war, the bipartite Foundation of Labor was established (which is still in existence). It is made up of representatives of the boards of the three biggest federations of trade unions—Socialist, Roman-Catholic and Protestant—of the three most important employers' federations—liberal, Roman Catholic and Protestant. The employers' representation is in accordance with the fact that their organizations separately cover the fields of industry, commerce and agriculture. Soon it was officially recognized by the government in its Extraordinary Decree on Labor Conditions of October 1945 as an advisory body to the government board of mediators, instituted by the same decree as the central authority in the field of wage formation and labor conditions. The board derived its name from an official prewar

[4] *The Problem of Rising Prices,* report of a group of experts, published by the OECD, May 1961; in particular appendix 4, pp. 359–390; *Policies for Price Stability,* report of the Working Party on Costs of Production and Prices of the Economic Policy Committee of the OECD, November 1962, in particular p. 45.

institution established to mediate in labor disputes. As previously decreed, its members are appointed by the Minister of Social Affairs, but much greater powers are entrusted to the new board. In practice, it has full responsibility for the administration of the government's wage policy and receives general instructions from the minister as guidelines for its task. Under the decree it has powers to: 1) establish wage rates and make other regulations on its own initiative or at the suggestion of organized labor or management; 2) accept, reject or modify collective agreements submitted to it for approval; 3) extend the provisions of collective agreements to parties outside the bargaining unit; 4) permit a changing of the terms of collective agreements in specific cases; 5) obtain compliance with its regulations through the courts.

In considering these powers, two points still have to be taken into account. In the first place, wage contracts concluded after the war have always stipulated precisely fixed wage increases and not minima or maxima. Therefore, they resulted in exact pay levels (apart from variations due to tariff earnings, overtime, and so on), and employers are neither allowed to pay more or less. Second, before the war a law had been passed to the effect that the results of a collective agreement could be made binding for parties outside the bargaining unit—usually to all employers and workers in the same trade. Thus, power, transferred to the board, has been used extensively (which can be illustrated by the fact that in recent years approximately 80 per cent of all workers were covered by collective agreements and related arrangements, whereas the coverage of the union movement is roughly half as big).

Another interesting aspect is the role played by the Foundation of Labor. The advisory role attributed to it by the Extraordinary Decree has been taken very seriously. Every contract negotiated between parties was checked by the wage committee of the foundation, and renegotiated if it proved to be inconsistent with the general guidelines valid at that moment, before it was submitted to the board for approval together with the advice of the foundation. Only in rare cases has the advice of the foundation not been followed by the board. The checking procedure was abolished by 1965 in connection with an institutional change in the whole set-up of the wage policy (which we will discuss later).

The wage policy has from the very beginning been seconded by a price policy, again of a rather stringent nature. No doubt, reasons of equity were among the arguments in favor of such a policy. It will always be difficult to win the support of the workers for a policy of restraint as far as their own incomes are concerned, where this policy is not supplemented by one which will limit effectively the possibilities of their counterparts. But there were also very important direct reasons. Notwithstanding a rather successful monetary purge shortly after the war, the liquidity situation remained very easy, and risks of demand inflation were still very high. Therefore, the government wanted to have direct control on the price level. It derived its authority in this field from an emergency Act Against Price Raising and Hoarding, passed during the mobilization period before May 1940, strengthening the hands of the government in advance against possible abuses of the economic situation in later stages of the war, and was reenforced through additional decrees issued during the war. According to this law, price increases needed authorization by the Minister of Economic Affairs, and, in principle, permission was only given when the firm could explain that the intended rise was justified by a price rise of its material inputs. Wage increases were not considered as legal reasons for claims to raise prices. Increases surpassing the use in labor productivity, and consequently leading to cost increases, were not to be made. As the price rules were valid for all firms, virtually the only acceptable reasons for price rises were those having to do with imported commodities used in production. Such acceptable cost increases could only be passed on to the buyer, but the mark-up had to be kept constant in absolute terms (not as a percentage). Moreover, the minister had the right to issue price decrees, usually fixing the price level of a group of commodities for a certain period. In view of what has been said on the required absorption of the effect of wage increases, this would seem only logical.

The wage and price policies described so far have been in operation, with a number of important modifications, up to the present time. The price policy has been applied with varying intensity at particular phases of the postwar period, depending on the requirements of the moment, but it has not undergone essential changes. The wage policy, however, has been changed several times, and in general there has been a tendency to replace the strict system introduced immediately after the war with a more flexible one, leaving more room for negotiations at the branch or factory levels.

The most important phases may be summarized briefly. Up to 1959, wages were mainly changed through so-called wage rounds, that is, equal changes of all wages. In addition to these, adaptations took place in branches where levels were considered to be lagging. During that period an effort was made to arrive at a system where wages, through job classification and merit-rating, depended only on the characteristics of the jobs.

The period may be split into two parts: during the years of reconstruction up to 1950, the policy aimed at keeping real wages constant; in the second, when foreign assistance was no longer needed, and the real national income continued to rise rapidly, wages were raised *pari passu* with the growth of the national income per capita.

Gradually, the rigid system not allowing for any differentiation of wages caused dissatisfaction, and in 1959 it was replaced with a more flexible one. As the main goal was still to arrive at an average increase in wages consistent with the general policy aims, the possibilities for differentiation were made dependent on the trend of productivity in the various branches. The system was not very satisfactory. It rested on a rather dubious theoretical basis, and, as it was introduced during a period of great tension in the labor market, the government felt obliged to supplement the rates with several restrictive indications leading to much irritation among the negotiating parties. Therefore, in 1963 the system was altered once more, and other and more reasonable criteria for differentiation (profitability, labor demand, and so forth) were introduced, together with a rather elaborate system of coordinating indications worked out by the Foundation of Labor for the negotiating parties which envisaged an average wage increase not surpassing the macro-economic possibilities. These possibilities were to be assessed in semi-annual reports of the Social Economic Council and to be based on analyses by the Central Planning Bureau. The important role of this council, set up in 1950, will be described later. Very soon the new system was threatened—this time through an unplanned and rather explosive rise in wages which only with great difficulty could be contained. A completely satisfactory solution has not yet been found, and at present even the checking procedure of the Foundation of Labor has the power, in the hands of the government, to impose a wage stop or a restricted increase along the lines of the old wage rounds if such a step is deemed necessary.

At present, therefore, the wage policy can hardly be considered a regular instrument of economic policy. It has played an important role in the past and no doubt facilitated the development of the Dutch export position and also contributed to restoring equilibrium after the depressions of 1950 and 1957. But now it fulfills at best only the role of a safeguard to which recourse may be taken in case of emergency (which is still considerably more than can be said about other countries in similar positions).

Planning in the sense described can be applied to long- as well as short-term economic developments, but the models used will be different. Up to now, however, the latter received the greatest attention. During the reconstruction period, which ended roughly around 1950, there were few opportunities for a general economic policy. The very limited resources of foreign currency, to a large extent depending on the size of the available foreign aid, entirely determined the scope of the policy during these years. A more deliberately chosen policy could only be built up after the reconstruction period, when the restrictions stemming from the war were gradually removed. Taking into account that the economic development of the Netherlands (being a relatively small country) is strongly dependent on the growth of its exports, it is not difficult to understand that this policy particularly stressed the importance of a balanced development. Several measures were taken to foster growth. In this connection, we may point to the development of infrastructure and energy production, to the extension of facilities for advanced education, to investment stimuli and to the main aim of the wage and price policies—to maintain a competitive export price level. But growth was not formally planned, and no definite growth targets were set. The actual outcome was considered to be the result of a great number of forces largely outside the sphere of governmental influence. Great attention, on the other hand, was attributed to the term "balanced." It was realized that the development might be disturbed by influences from abroad or by inflationary or deflationary forces at home, and, therefore, a short-term economic policy was drawn up which deliberately planned for as smooth a development as possible. Therefore annual forecasts were made to find out whether in the short run the main policy aims would be satisfied, and when the results were not satisfactory, corrective measures were designed.

In order to avoid misunderstanding, it should be made clear that the description given up to now refers to the ideal situation. It has not always been possible to avoid serious difficulties, and planning has therefore not precluded problems but has taken measures to correct them as quickly and efficiently as possible, once they arose. Moreover, it would be going too far to state that there is a generally accepted welfare function which should be maximized by adequate policy measures. The weight to be given to a more or less complete realization of the different aims still remains a difficult problem. However, it may be concluded that great importance has always been attached to a high degree of employment and a balance-of-payments equilibrium. The priority given to the other aims has been different according to circumstances. But even with respect to employment and balance-of-payments equilibrium, no dogmatic attitude has been adopted.

The strong wage increase in 1964 was agreed upon as a step to reduce the gap between the internal and external price levels. It was acknowledged that this move would be connected with a considerable deterioration of the balance of payments and a marked rise in prices, leaving only a moderate improvement in the real income of the workers. Its effects on the tension of the labor market (if any) were not assessed to be very high. The loss of foreign currency was acceptable in view of the available resources. The price rise had to be accepted as a penalty for the adaption. As a matter of fact, up to now tension in the labor market has not been reduced at all, mainly as a consequence of inflationary processes abroad. Consequently, wage pressure has been maintained leading to problems which have not yet been satisfactorily solved.

METHODOLOGY AND RESULTS OF THE DUTCH SHORT-TERM ECONOMIC PLANNING

The institutional framework. The over-all macro-economic aspect of the general Dutch economic policy has already been stressed. The responsibility for the formulation and execution of this policy is borne by the government which is answerable on this as well as on all other questions to parliament.

However, in the preparation of this policy, the Central Planning Bureau has an important task. It was founded in 1945, but it acquired a definitive statutory basis, when on April 21, 1947, parliament unanimously enacted the Central Economic Plan. According to this law, the plan has to be set up annually, and it was interpreted as "a balanced system of forecasts and directives in relation to the economy of the Netherlands."

The CPB comes formally under the Minister of Economic Affairs, although its activities are interdepartmental. In virtue of the same act, a Central Planning Committee (CPC) was set up to advise the Central Planning Bureau. This implies, in accordance with the general principles of constitutional law in the Netherlands, that parliament can call the minister to account for the activities of the CPB and in particular may discuss with him any plans or proposals published by the bureau. The members of the CPC are appointed by the Minister of Economic Affairs and chosen from trade union officials, representatives of entrepreneurial organizations, scientific circles, and so forth.

The budget year in the Netherlands coincides with the calendar year, and thus it is understandable that the plans which have been regularly designed by the CPB, from 1946 onward, also refer to a calendar year. They are usually published in the early months of the year after having gone through the following procedure. A first draft is prepared shortly after the opening of the parliamentary session on the third Tuesday in September during which the next year's budget is presented. This draft is discussed with so-called contact persons—high officials representing the various ministries. They supply relevant information with respect to the intended policy of their ministries, in particular on points which have not already been fixed in the budget itself. Their comments which are advisory are taken into account in the second draft that will be confidentially presented to the members of the CPC. The advice of this body is given during a special meeting attended by the board of directors of the CPB. On the basis of this information, a third draft is prepared to be discussed at the governmental level. It is submitted to the Council of Economic Affairs (CEA), a subcommittee of the cabinet whose ministers have strong economic influence. Its meetings are attended by the president of the Central Bank and the director of the CPB. During one of its meetings, usually shortly before the end of the year, the final draft is approved and released for publication.

From the preceding description, it is clear that the plan is set up at a moment when the most important economic decisions, in particular those embodied in the state budget, have already been made. It is therefore not surprising that the plans tend to be forecasts for the coming years. Only occasionally are they written in more conditionally—either when strong feelings of uncertainty with respect to the rate of change of one or more of the external variables may give rise to a so-called "datum alternative," or when there is a real choice left open at the policy level which leads to a "policy alternative." Examples may be found in recent plans.

In 1962 the prospects for the development of foreign trade were considered to be rather uncertain, and, therefore, in addition to the central alternative of a 4 per cent increase of the volume of exports, the consequences of a 1 per cent higher or lower result were investigated (the actual outcome was 7 per cent). In 1961 the Minister of Finance announced a reduction of the income tax rate to be operative July 1, 1962, but won the approval of parliament for his proposal to postpone the introduction if the prevailing boom would be reinforced, making a tax reduction inadequate from a business cycle point of view. Consequently the 1961 Plan contained two forecasts—one based on the assumed reduction, and the other referring to "no change" (actually the introduction was postponed by one year).

The tendency of the plans to change into forecasts was allied with the desire of the government to leave the responsibility for these forecasts with the CPB. On several occasions the government has expressed this opinion in parliamentary discussion. The development is obvious. Pure forecasts have informative value only, and the purpose is best served when their users feel that the results are not biased by political influences. As a consequence, the plan procedure has lost some of its importance. Nevertheless it still fulfills a useful function. In the first place it guarantees that the policies of the various ministries have been correctly interpreted in the final document. Secondly, it sometimes leads to important information which otherwise might be overlooked, and it offers several opportunities for discussions on the main aspects of the forecast which may lead to improvements.

The information contained in the plans is generally appreciated by those who benefit—mainly the staff officials of the larger enterprise and, in general, by circles which for professional or other interests want to be kept informed about the economic development, including several international organizations.[5]

At the same time it is clear that the CPB can only perform a task in the process of policy formulation when its results are available at a time when the process is still in full swing. Therefore, several years ago, the CPB started to produce reports twice or three times a year in which it gives an analysis of recent trends together with a forecast for the following three or four quarters. In these reports, policy recommendations can be made if appropriate, and these reports receive attention at the governmental level at the same time they are being discussed at a CEA meeting. When recommendations are made and accepted by the CEA, the appropriate member will make a corresponding proposal to the cabinet, to which the final decision is left. It is clear that policy recommendations need not always originate within the CPB. The CEA or one of its members can make suggestions, and the CPB may be charged with the task of studying the probable effects and to report on them to the CEA.

In addition it should be stressed that gradually informal relations have been established between the CPB and representatives of various ministries. These contacts are very valuable to the coordination of the work of the CPB with the activities going on in the ministries. In this way, a practical consensus of opinion is attained between the Ministry of Finance and the CPB about the future development of the state revenue.

[5] This was clearly brought out at the conference organized by the Netherlands' Institute for Efficiency in 1961.

The two informal (in the sense of not legally prescribed) types of of exchange of thought have proved very effective for a smooth functioning of the CPB's advisory task.

In 1961, the CPB started publishing preliminary forecasts appearing simultaneously with the state budget. These Macro-Economic Estimates (ME) are made at the request of parliament which expressed the desire to be informed about the economic prospects at the moment it starts the most important part of its legislative task. The procedure followed in this case is much simpler than with the plans. A draft is prepared for the CEA and discussed, but the content of the forecast proper is again left to the CPB. Obviously the ME constitute rather ambitious forecasting activity. They have to be completed at a moment when only statistical material for the current year is available. This comes to an actual forecasting period not far from two years. Nevertheless, the effort is made, not only in order to comply with the request from parliament but also because the Minister of Finance needs similar data as background for his state budget.

A new function has been attributed to the ME in connection with the recent change in the Dutch wage policy, briefly indicated above. Before elucidating, it is necessary to describe the relation of the CPB to the Social Economic Council. This council was established in accordance with the 1950 Act of the Industrial Organization. It is a tripartite body, at present consisting of 45 members. One third of its members are appointed by the federations of trade unions, one third by the federations of entrepreneurial organizations, and the remaining third by the government. These "crown members" are called upon to take care of the general interest. Like the other members, they perform their task without consultation with or instruction from the bodies by which they are appointed. The council plays an important role in the public industrial organization, set up in accordance with the 1950 Act, but in this connection its advisory task is most important. According to the law, government is obliged to ask the council's advice on important social and economic problems, particularly on those which have a bearing on industrial life. For instance, the changes in the wage policy have all been prepared on the advice of the council. Unlike the CPB, the council is political, and the numerous pieces of advice given since its founding have had a great influence on the development of the social and economic policy. The council has a secretariat at its disposal, but its task is mainly administrative. For the economic analyses on which the council bases its advisory work, it usually calls upon the CPB. Consequently, the CPB acts as technical adviser. The link between the two is strengthened by the fact that the director of the CPB is usually appointed as one of the crown members. It is therefore quite natural that the council recently decided to take ME in a given year as the starting point for its discussions on the economic situation.

Short-term economic planning experience in the Netherlands. It is not possible at this time to give a complete account of the experiences of the planning system during the postwar period. Such an evaluation would be rather lengthy as it would have to include many aspects, such as the quality of the different models, the changes performed and the reasons why, their effect upon the results and the reliability of the forecasts, the relations between forecasts and policy measures, the role of structural and other factors interfering with the short-term policy consideration in the final choice of measures, and so forth. Much research has been done on these views, and some of the results have been published. As to the policy aspects, interesting information will be found in a recent CPB monograph about developments since 1950. We shall restrict ourselves to the description of one particular case—the revaluation of the Dutch guilder in 1961.

The revaluation of the German Reichsmark in March 1961 forced the Dutch government to make an urgent decision. The business situation was such, both with respect to balance-of-payments surpluses as well as to employment of factors of production, that a revaluation was a consideration. However, it was unlikely that a small country like the Netherlands would make such a move on its own account. But, when on Saturday morning, March 11, the decision of the German authorities was announced, opinion in financial circles was that the Netherlands very well might take a similar step. Dr. Blessing, the president of the Reichsbank, in a press conference on the same day, said that in his eyes the Netherlands was the only country that might follow the German example. This illustrates how important it was for the Dutch government to announce its decision, whether positive or negative, before the reopening of the money exchanges on the next Monday, in order to prevent undesirable speculation against the guilder. Obviously, the date of the German step could not have been foreseen, but the step itself was by no means a surprise. On the contrary, the German situation showed clearer signs of a fundamental disequilibrium than did the Dutch, and for a long time the German authorities had been advised (by the OECD) to increase the external value of the Deutsche mark in order to counteract the continuing and strong accumulation of foreign reserves resulting from balance-of-payments surpluses. The possibility of a revaluation of the Deutsche mark had to be taken into account, and, therefore, in 1960, the CPB studied the consequences of such a step. It started with the assumption that the Deutsche mark would be revalued by 10 per cent, and inferred that only three realistic alternatives would be open to the Dutch authorities—to follow the German example even with respect to the size of the change, to refrain from any action, and to take an intermediate position by revaluing at 5 per cent. The result of this study strongly facilitated the decision of the Dutch government. They could easily be adapted to the actual revaluation of the Deutsche mark by 5 per cent, and clearly the number of realistic alternatives was reduced to two.

The effects of these alternatives have been derived from the model normally used for forecasting purposes and evaluation of the consequences of policy alternatives (although some changes had to be made to take account of the special characteristics of the problem). For example, the import price level appears as an explanatory variable in the equations describing the formation of stocks. It reflects the speculative movements usually connected with a change of this variable. Obviously such consequences need not be expected from a change called forth by a revaluation. A complication results from the fact that the model, due to its over-all character, does not contain import or export price levels for different countries. The effect of a revaluation of the Deutsche mark separately therefore had to be computed as a weighted average of price changes as far as Germany was concerned, and constant prices for all other countries. The German shares along with the other countries in the Dutch import and export trade, were used as weights. A similar system was followed for the alternative. The effects have been computed for two consecutive years starting from the hypothetical moment of the revaluation. The main results are given in Table 1 (for the revaluation of the guilder they have been taken from the 1962 Central Economic Plan; for the Deutsche mark revaluation they have been borrowed from international reports).

Obviously they try to reflect the consequences of a revaluation *ceteris paribus,* that is, without simultaneous changes of other external variables.

A comparison of the first- and second-year effects shows, as might be expected, that the adaption is not restricted to the first year only. It is even probable that the move may make itself felt during a much longer period, but the results of a corresponding extrapolation were considered to be too inaccurate.

The figures in Table 1 point out that following the German example would have an unfavorable effect on four variables representing important Dutch national aims—balance of payments, volume of production, employment, volume of investment—and only a favorable result for the

Table 1. Short-term economic consequences of a 5 per cent revaluation for a number of basic data concerning the Dutch economy.

Variable	Unit	Deutsche mark only		Dutch guilder only	
		1st year[a]	2nd year[a]	1st year[a]	2nd year[a]
Surplus of the balance of payments on current account	mln glds	40	100	−170	−60
Volume of production	mln glds	−20	45	−90	−375
Volume of investment	per cent	−0.3	−0.3	0.2	−3.0
Registered unemployment	1000	0	0.6	4	8
Consumption price level	per cent	−0.1	−0.1	−1.5	−1.5

[a] Changes with respect to the initial situation.

consumer-price level. These results, however, cannot be evaluated independent of the initial situation. By the beginning of 1961 there was tension in the labor market, leading to losses in efficiency and all sorts of disturbances, and particularly to a considerable cost push. A decrease of this tension and a (*ceteris paribus*) downward effect on the price level were therefore appreciated, and the only question was how large the deterioration of the balance of payments would be. The relative mild effect resulting from the table—partly due to the fact that the foreign demand could not completely be satisfied as a consequence of the pull of the home market—was an important argument in favor of the decision finally reached, to follow the German example.

The question of how far the subsequent development confirmed the forecasts may be asked. It is not possible to give an exact answer, as it is a very delicate task to disentangle the effects of revaluation and other changes occurring almost simultaneously, of which a considerable reduction in working hours (about 6 per cent) was one of the most spectacular. However, as far as conclusions are possible, they show that the main results have satisfactorily been predicted.

LONG-TERM ECONOMIC PLANNING

As we have discussed, it has been said that central economic planning in the Netherlands is mainly of short-term character. However, various circles have recently expressed their interest in planning for longer periods, and, in order to give as complete a description of the Dutch situation as possible, a brief account of this changing attitude is presented.

Several of the larger firms, using more or less refined methods of planning for their own activities, and using the CPB forecasts as part of their external information, have expressed the desire for similar results for periods of four to five years (as this corresponds to the length of time they use to draw up their own plans). In addition, official spokesmen of the employers' organizations have expressed a similar interest, and, finally, the federations of trade unions have mentioned long-term planning as one of the important items in their recently formulated program of action. The interpretation of long-term planning is not the same in all these cases. The entrepreneurs and their organizations are mainly interested in the informative value of consistent long-term forecasts, broken down to a certain number of important sectors of industry, whereas the trade unions in addition to this also put strong emphasis on the possible use of such forecasts for central economic-policy purposes.

Government, too, was not entirely averse to long-term planning ideas. Attention has already been directed to long-term planning methods applied to various sectors of public administration, such as education, infrastructure, land improvement, and so forth.

The changing attitude toward long-term planning stems from various causes. The postwar experience of a rather smooth development disturbed only by a few relatively mild recessions strengthened the conviction that such a process might be expected to continue. Moreover, the view is held that, in such circumstances, long-term economic forecasts may help to prevent bottlenecks in the labor market, to improve the allocation of capital, and to reduce the fluctuations in the volume of investments, which at present still show rather strong sensitivity to cyclical influences. Such effects might by themselves already be conducive to growth, but the positive effects are obviously advocated more strongly by those who are in favor of a special, central growth-policy based on long-term forecasts.

The example of other countries has undoubtedly also been influential. Some, like France and Norway, have been applying long-term economic planning methods, and the same is true for Sweden, although the emphasis there has mainly been on forecasting for informative purposes only. But the fact that countries like Belgium and the U.K. have proceeded to long-term economic planning to speed up their growth ratio has probably also influenced opinion in the Netherlands. Recently a committee for medium-term policy was instituted by the European Economic Community to undertake a study of the economic development till 1970 of the member countries as a whole.

Finally, it is understood that the claims on the national means continuously and increasingly put forward by different pressure groups can only be realized in a reasonable span of time when the growth rate can be maintained at or even somewhat raised above the 4 to 5 per cent average of the postwar period.

In a speech from the throne, September 1963, a more definite approach of long-term planning was announced. "For the sake of economic development, an investigation will be made in close consultation with industry into the medium-term perspectives of the economy as a whole and of different sectors in particular."

The Central Planning Bureau is charged with the drafting of these perspectives. As in the case of the annual forecasts, it will assume responsibility for the methodology. The essential policy decisions will obviously be made by the government, but, in order to facilitate the problem of choice, several alternatives will be worked out—particularly with respect to the budgetary policy.

The first investigation will span the period 1965–1970, and for the subsequent ones a revolving procedure will be applied.

In order to assist the CPB in its study of the trends of the various sectors, a number of advisory committees have been set up. These are presided over by a staff member of the bureau, and their members are experts from management and trade union circles. In a few committees dealing with branches for which government assumes a special responsibility (agriculture, construction, energy, and so forth), it will be represented through a number of senior officials, At present, five committees have been installed, but in the future similar bodies will be set up for all major economic sectors. Moreover, an interdepartmental Central Economic Commission, which in the past acted as an advisory body to the government in designing short-term economic policy measures, will now also be called upon to fulfill this role in the medium-term field. In particular, it will assist in the elaboration and coordination of the plans of the various governmental sectors. Apart from these special aspects the medium-term planning procedure does not differ very much from the annual one already described. The plan will be submitted to the CPC for advice and to the CEA for final decision.

In conclusion, it is hardly necessary to add that the medium-term plan will not be binding for the private sector. In this respect it is purely indicative. As far as the government is concerned, it will of course have a more decisive character. But, even at this level, for various reasons it cannot be compared to the annual budget approved by parliament. In the first place it may be possible that the first publications will contain alternatives in order to stimulate public discussions, and these alternatives will correspond to different choices of governmental policy. Moreover, the period up to 1970 extends beyond the term of office of the present cabinet, and a newly elected cabinet may have different opinions. And, of course there is the possibility that unforseen short-run developments may interfere with the plans.

Chapter 2

FRENCH PLANNING

BERNARD CAZES

Commissariat Général du Plan

INTRODUCTION

The object of this paper is not to give a complete description of the procedures and techniques characteristic of French planning, but to demonstrate the extent to which the Fifth Plan for economic and social development (1966–1970) differs from preceding plans both from the point of view of its formulation (which is now an accomplished fact) and from the point of view of its application (or, more exactly, the strategy chosen to make its success more probable).

Before indicating the new aspects in French planning, it should be borne in mind that the Fifth Plan still conforms to the initial model worked out on an empiric basis nearly twenty years ago under the pressure of the circumstances then prevailing; this model's basic characteristics are: 1) an attempt to bring some coherence to public and private decisions likely to influence the middle-term future, and this by framing them into middle-term demographic, economic and financial projections; 2) an attempt to insure public discussion and inclusion into the democratic process of national targets regarding economic and social development and to associate the representatives of organized private interests with the definition of those aims.

One last point must be made concerning the reasons for all the changes described below. To an extent that would be difficult to determine with any precision, these reasons arise on the one hand from the existence of new conditions of growth, which increase the uncertainty of the future, and, on the other hand, from a keener appreciation of this uncertainty by French economic opinion. These new conditions are themselves linked to France's closer integration into the European Common Market and world trade and to the rising standard of living, which make future trends in economic development less discernible.[1]

PART ONE: INNOVATIONS IN
THE FORMULATION OF THE PLAN

Formulation procedure on the national and regional scale. A long time was necessary before the inclusion of parliament in the planning procedure began to show relatively satisfactory results. The First Plan (1947–1953) was published as a government decree, and parliament, which had not in any case asked to be consulted, supervised the application of the plan through its annual vote on budget appropriations alone. The Second Plan (1954–1957) was approved by parliament, but after a delay of more than two years after its coming into effect. Because of the political situation, the Third Plan (1958–1961) was published as a governmental decree.

The Fourth Plan marked a change with regard to the past, in that it was put before parliament and was passed as the law of August 4, 1962, which was drawn up very succinctly:

> The Fourth Plan, known as the Plan for social and economic development, annexed to this present law, has been passed as a framework for investment programs for the period 1962–1965 and as the instrument by means of which economic expansion and social progress may be oriented.
>
> In this latter field, its object is:
>
> On the one hand, to improve conditions for the nation's least favored classes, notably, old people, those with families at their charge, the repatriates, farmers, craftsmen, and the lower wage scales;

---

[1] It may be added that at least one of the innovations introduced in the Fifth Plan, and which concerns the drafting procedures, does not depend on the new conditions of growth to which allusion has just been made, but is the result of the aforementioned permanent characteristics of French planning (the second, to be precise).

On the other hand, acceleration of economic and social progress in under-developed areas.

But this same law included a very important article (Article 2) which introduced a significant change in the organization of the political discussion of the plan. This article said: "Before issuing its instructions to the General Commissioner for Planning, the Government will put a bill before Parliament; this bill will approve a report on the main options of the Plan and mainly: economic expansion, distribution of the gross domestic production between investment and consumption; a desirable structure for the final demand; orientation of social policy as well as that of regional policy."

To understand the significance of this change in procedure it should be remembered that, for the Fourth Plan, the plan's formulation was divided into two stages: analysis of its general targets by the planners, and the government's decision on these targets (which was confirmed by the issuing of instructions to the Commissariat Général du Plan); then translation of these objects into detailed programs and forecasts for each sector, synthesis by the planners and presentation of the resulting draft plan to parliament, for its approval.

Parliament was then faced with a fully elaborated document giving quantitative expression to the basic economic choices which had already been made and which had not been the object of any public discussion (except for a consultation with the Economic and Social Council). Thus, there was no alternative but to pass *en bloc* or to reject the whole bill presented, with the additional inconvenience that the margins left open and the terms of choice between alternative objects were not always clear.

The novelty was in the insertion of an intermediary stage between the two others, to be known as the stage of options, where the government set down in a report all the elements which led to its suggesting a certain growth target and a certain distribution of the results of this growth among the various items of final demand; the same report also pointed out the problems of economic policy which would arise from the implementation of the recommended objectives, as well as the probable consequences of the different options. Thus only the "broad outlines" were submitted for discussion and not the execution of any individual program.

Such an experiment is encouraging in that it demonstrates the possibility of putting the problems of choice among objectives, and economic policies before a political assembly—problems which, up to now, were thought to be solvable only by experts. It was also of pedagogical value in that those participating in the political discussion were obliged to take as their point of departure a common conceptual framework—that is, the framework provided by a prospective national accounts system; thus the interdependence of apparently unrelated problems may be demonstrated, as well as the long-term implications of a sequence of marginal decisions.[2]

It must, however, be admitted that the establishment of a formalized discussion on the main options of the plan cannot bring with it any rapid transformation of the political conditions under which the plan is formulated in a society which is at once pluralist and divided. First of all, differences of attitudes on certain main policies falling outside the plan (for instance, national defense) cannot be eliminated. In addition, the evaluation of the changes of and the risks entailed by one variant opposed to another is to some extent subjective on calculated odds; the politician will react differently, depending on whether he is in the government or belongs to the opposition, on whether he is sensitive to the dangers of unemployment or of inflation. Finally, there is a sort of technical limit in the value of this kind of experiment: first, five years is after all a relatively short span of time which does not allow for any very extensive variation in marginal decisions (if these are extremely important it may be argued that the results should then be calculated over a longer period); second, the concepts employed in the discussion about options are aggregate and abstract, and their significance is thus limited for the nonspecialists who understand concrete debates on topics of a more direct relevance.

It may be added that this procedural modification concerning the discussion of the plan in parliament has had two consequences for the organizational aspects of the planning system: first, the options of the Fifth Plan were put before the Economic and Social Council before being presented in parliament (so that the council, like parliament, was called upon to take two votes on the plan's content: at the stage of the main options and then on the final plan); second, the preparation of a government report on the options in the Fifth Plan entailed a meeting of the modernization committees at an earlier stage than before, since, instead of working within a previously established framework provided by government instructions, the committees had to answer "open" questions on the probability of past trends being continued or, conversely, the possibilities of discontinuities

---

[2] For a discussion of the way the planning outlook enriches politics, see Pierre Avril, *Un President, pour quoi faire?* (Le Seuil, 1965), chap. X.

in these trends and the defining of the needs which will have to be satisfied between now and 1970 in the field of social overhead equipment.

The decentralization of the preparatory work on the plan was systematically organized for the Fifth Plan only, with the creation in 1964 of regional economic development committees which were to be the spokesmen for the different regions before the national plan was translated in terms of regional forecasts and programs.

These committees are made up as follows: a quarter of the members are chosen by the government from among the most competent people; the other members are nominated by local authorities (*conseils généraux*), the chambers of commerce, employers' organizations and trade unions.

Their role is consultative and will be exercised twice while the plan is under preparation: the committees have first of all given their advice on the general report prepared by the prefect of each region on the possibilities for economic development in each region and the desirable characteristics of public investment in social overhead equipment; at the beginning of 1966 they gave a second opinion on the various "regional divisions" of the Fifth Plan (in the preliminary draft of each of these "sections," the prefect of the region suggests priorities for public investment to the national authorities).

Long-term prospects of the Fifth Plan. For the Third Plan and for the Fourth Plan (1958–1961 and 1962–1965 respectively), long-term projections were formulated for the appraisal of future needs to be satisfied by slow-maturing investments (energy, transport and human). For the Fifth Plan, the National Institute for Statistics also made up a projection for 1969–1985; it was broken down in three sectors and assumed constant prices; but the exploration of the distant future was carried out more systematically by an ad hoc group composed of certain persons with quite different backgrounds. In addition to its chairman, P. Guillaumat, former Minister of Defense and now Chairman of the Ste Nationale des Pétroles d'Aquitaine, it included four economists, a physician, a former minister of housing, two specialists in agricultural problems, a trade union leader, and an industrialist. In addition, a group of *rapporteurs* comprising young engineers and civil servants was put at the disposal of Groupe 1985.

Their object, defined by the General Planning Commissioner, was to bring into focus all facts which may be significant in the long-range future and to identify the probable features in 1985 which should be taken into account while drafting the Fifth Plan. The group therefore selected a certain number of themes which appeared important for the future—scientific research, leisure, economic growth, transport—and proceeded to obtain the opinion of competent experts on each of these subjects; then, in the course of a series of very free discussions, the conjectures outlined by these experts were commented upon and criticized. The *rapporteurs* sifted the elements for a synthesizing report from all this material and published *Reflections for 1985*.

To what extent has the image of France outlined for 1985 influenced the content of the Fifth Plan?

It appeared necessary first of all to look for more information about the factors and conditions for economic growth, the resulting social tensions and the economic imbalances which would hinder a continuing of growth. *Reflections for 1985* refrains from any recommendations as to increasing production to its maximum as an end in itself, but, noting the intensity of the propensity to consume and the collective needs which continue to grow (see, for example, the Buchanan report *Traffic in Towns*), the authors of the report came to the inevitable conclusion that in twenty-five years we will probably not be able to consider growth as an end that has been achieved, but that we will still have to make a difficult choice between more productive effort and more leisure.

Another conclusion drawn immediately from the 1985 report was the value of the creation within certain ministries of a "cell for predictive reflection" charged with analyzing long-term trends which may influence domains coming under the scope of government action.

It was also decided to include in the Fifth Plan three major themes of research which correspond to three particularly crucial problems for the future; this would prolong the task of the 1985 group.

The first concerns the *periodical bringing up to date of education*, which, in a rapidly changing world has become a necessity which can no longer be satisfied through the prolongation of compulsory schooling: it is probable that completely new methods will have to be developed, bringing enterprises, trade unions and universities into collaboration. On the completion of this evolution, one may perhaps foresee the realization of a Utopian dream, the elimination of the age-old division of man's existence into three parts: education, work, retirement—which would no longer follow one another irrevocably in fixed stages, but would become complementary ways of life.

The second theme, closely related to the first, deals with the organization of the way of living and working life of the *third age*. It is in fact important to bear in mind the consequences of medical research in geriatrics (which prolongs man's active life), the psychological effects of the sudden change to complete inactivity, and, finally, the collective cost of an ambitious policy of social transfers to the benefit of the aged. It would be necessary to reshape careers in a way which, by mutual agreement, would prolong the activity of those over retirement age in suitable jobs (*Report on the Orientation of the Fifth Plan*, p. 135).

The last theme for research concerns the place of social overhead equipment (and collective consumption) in tomorrow's society, and the financing thereof. The industrial society is a society (where men work, travel and relax *together*), while the administrative structures and means of financing were conceived in an era where the way of life implied a very much more limited "consumption" of collective services. The aforementioned projection of the French economy in 1985 has shown that if recent trends were to be prolonged in a reasoned way, the total growth in production would rise to a coefficient of 3.15 in comparison with 1960; household consumption would reach a coefficient of 3, while social overhead equipment and social transfers would reach a coefficient of 7, which would create crucial financial problems. Thus, with the Fifth Plan, the accent has been on the necessity of using tariff more systematically than in the past as a means of liberating financial resources which would be psychologically more acceptable in so far as the link between payment and services rendered would be more visible.

This method of working has allowed, with great economy of means, the bringing to the forefront of a certain number of problems for the future and the awakening of public opinion to the constraints and openness which characterize the long-range future. However, there is no doubt that the use of prospective analysis, to determine the decisions to be included (or not to be included) in medium-term plans, is still in its infancy and should be the object of profound methodological research not only by the economists but also by other social scientists and even the philosophers, so that the validity of "future" research may be more rigorously assessed. A second observation would be that this first experience in prediction carried out for the Fifth Plan resulted in the establishment of a relatively complete picture[3] of the more plausible characteristics of French economy and society during the 1980's. But, besides the fact that this picture included some parts that had been less thoroughly explored than others (problems of

[3] Within the limits Groupe 1985 first set itself, which excluded changes in the international environment and the relationship between France and this environment from its field of study.

work, education, scientific and technical research), the conclusions to which it leads have not always been the subject of sufficiently profound discussions which may have called these same conclusions into question or qualified their implications—a limitation which is in any case inevitable, bearing in mind the immensity of the subject. Thus, for future plans, it would without doubt be more suitable to make research on a more limited scale, but more profoundly—on the subject, for example, of demographic behavior or the economic impact of the main technological innovations about to be introduced—so that future syntheses would be constructed on a more solid basis. A third trend it would seem desirable to follow would be the organization of public discussions on the hypothetical prospects such reports would have shown as probable. In this respect television would play an important role in that it would allow the visual translation of alternative patterns of life; these images would be sufficiently different to arouse the interest of the audience and to prompt them to a choice.[4] A less ambitious solution would be to institute one or more "predictive forums" where every prediction on the distant future would be presented for discussion by specialists.

Study of variants. The formulation of a single projection is not the best way to bring to light the decisions which the political authorities will have to take regarding the main orientations of the plan, as such a projection will describe and discuss one single "path" alone that the economy could take. It would evidently be preferable to explore several alternative directions which would be defined by assumptions different from those characterizing the initial project.[5] It is for this reason that the programming division of the INSEE has prepared a certain number of decision variants, each implying a different economic policy.

Two types of variants were distinguished: variants relative to production factors and economic growth; variants relative to the alternative uses of growth results, taking the growth rate as constant.

Three determinants of growth were studied: labor, investment, and policies influencing the economic structures.

As to labor, the availability of manpower and a change in the number of hours worked were studied separately.

[4] To my knowledge, the only experiment in this field is that of Paul and Percival Goodman, who, in their book *Communitas,* outlined three "paradigms" of institutional and material arrangements based on clearly differentiated socio-economic scales of values.
[5] Called hereafter "central outline," "central projection" or "reference projection," this is characterized by a certain rate of growth and a "physical" balance of goods and services, plus a "balance in value terms" (notably between savings and investments) compatible with the physical balance. This central outline does not differ significantly from that finally proposed by the government as the options of the Fifth Plan.

Available manpower can be increased either by more immigration or by a rise in the rate of activity in the population. It would seem unrealistic to expect much result from increased immigration, taking into account the low training of the foreign workers prepared to emigrate to France. As for the rate of activity, it is in the female element of the population that it is most likely to increase. Taking as maximum and minimum limits for increase between now and 1970 the present percentage for female participation in Russia (predicted to be equalled by France in 1985) on the one hand, and the ratio envisaged for the USA by 1970 on the other (which France will presumably attain by 1970), there will be an additional 500,000 female workers—that is, 400,000 in the full-time equivalent. The gain in rate of growth is estimated at 0.3 per cent per year between 1966 and 1970; but part of this gain would be absorbed by the concomitant investment (plants and equipment, housing, outlay for training). Of course, we only took into account the properly economic effects of increased female employment; the social effects of this option have not been brought into the picture.

The option dealing with hours worked could scarcely discuss the possibility of an increase in the working week, annual holidays or the legal retirement age. Thus a reduction has been envisaged in each of these three areas. For the last two possibilities (where the public authorities can take the initiative) the economic effects on the rate of growth are quite limited— 0.3 to 0.4 per cent per year for an extra week's holiday and even less for an earlier retirement age from sixty-five to sixty years. The effects of a reduction in the working week are more marked: one point of growth per year if the 43-hour week were brought down to 40 hours.

The variant on investment applied only to the so-called productive investments (business investments), since the social overhead equipment are dealt with *à propos* of the distribution of the results of growth. The margin of choice as to productive investments appeared very limited because the rate of indebtedness of French firms is already very high, so that any increase in investments must correspond to a concomitant increase in the rate of self-financing. Now under the assumption of rather stable prices and the rate of productivity, the increase in self-financing should imply a slower increase in labor costs. Thus the assumed growth of investments has been limited to 1 per cent per annum. The effect on the general rate of growth would be about 0.2 to 0.3 per cent per year, and this additional production would be available for consumption only after 1970.

The structural variant could theoretically give rise to a great number of research studies to assess the net effect on growth of: reforms in "administered" prices, incentives for occupational mobility of manpower, and elimination of obstacles to free competition.[6] In fact, for practical reasons, only the shifts of agricultural workers to nonagricultural jobs have been investigated. The assumption was an additional reduction in the working population in agriculture by 370,000 in five years, a little less than two-thirds of whom would resume activity in a nonagricultural sector. It has been assumed that agricultural production would not be affected by this, while the added value per head ascribed to the additional labor would be the same as for workers already employed in the same industry (with a reduction to take their lower productivity into account). The growth gain for the period of the plan is modest (0.2 per cent per year at the maximum), while the assumed shift of labor is quite large. The public outlays implied by this alternative would mean that the benefit in terms of consumption would not be felt till after 1970, and would weigh heavily on the budget. In addition, it may be asked whether the margin for manipulation left open by EEC agricultural policies would allow a voluntarist policy on this scale (moreover, the social implications of this variant should not be underestimated).

If an attempt is made to consolidate all these measures according to their respective impacts, it will be found that they have one of these two opposing results: a higher rate of expansion than in the central projection; or a lower rate of expansion in what can be called the "leisure variant."

The "high" variant would above all result from an increase in available manpower (annual expected rise: 1 to 1.5 per cent), while other sorts of measures would be more expensive to bring into effect and would bring results after a much longer term (this is particularly true of structural reforms). In addition, the risk of inflationary tension (formerly only evaluated qualitatively) now increases. Altogether, a policy aiming at an extension in growth potential can only leave hope for an increase of not more than 1 per cent per year compared with the central projection.

The "low" variant is linked to a more or less significant reduction in working hours. The return to an actual working week of 40 hours which entails a reduction by one point of the annual growth rate shows that the leisure-consumption option would still be a premature step in France, at least in the drastic form proposed in this study.

[6] An important structural policy recommended in the Fifth Plan—the creation within a certain number of industries of production units of "international dimensions"—was decided on the basis of qualitative judgments through international comparisons, without any attempt being made to assess in quantitative terms the benefits to be expected in terms of growth.

Here, there is no change in the rate of growth; in the same way, those elements coming under the heading "technical allocation of production" (productive investments, net changes in inventories, foreign trade balance) are taken as given. It is thus assumed that any change in other components of the final demand have no significant impact on the rate of growth.

Here again the possible variants are very high in number, since the distribution of resources may be envisaged under various forms, either among categories of economic agents (households, enterprises, government and local authorities), or within each of these categories. Actually, only three variants were envisaged: two regarding the structure of the final demand and one concerning the distribution of income.

The variant concerning "social overhead equipment and housing" implies more rapid progress in these two items of final demand; this is quite admissible when the wide range of needs to be satisfied is taken into account, but seems rather unrealistic from the point of view of the difficulties it entails. These difficulties have nothing to do with the maintenance of a physical balance between resources and expenditure: considering the great difference of weight between household consumption and the two items "housing plus social overhead equipment," a very limited slowing down in the growth of the first will allow for a very substantial rise in the second.[7] The most difficult problems are to be found in the maintaining of the financial balance.

With a given rate of growth, an increase in the gross fixed capital formation inherent to this variant (an increase estimated at 8 billion francs) should bring with it an equivalent increase in savings. How would this additional saving be distributed among the economic agents (public authorities, enterprises and households)?

The share of additional investments made by the authorities (5 billion) should entail an equivalent savings drive, as long as it is admitted that to maintain stability of prices there would be no change in the budget deficit (thus no increase in the "financial needs" of the authorities, that is, the difference between their investments and their own savings). The remainder will find its counterbalance in an increase in household savings to an equivalent amount—that is, 3 milliards; this implies a rate of savings for households of 12.5 per cent (as opposed to 11.5 per cent in the central projection); this rate is very high in comparison with previous years and taking into account the fact that consumption will rise a little less quickly.

To bring the savings of the authorities up to 5 milliards it would be

[7] The impact on household consumption would only be four tenths of a point per year.

possible either to increase receipts from taxes, or to reduce certain running expenses (administrative consumption, salaries, transfers). From the point of view of tax returns, there are two possibilities: taxes on enterprises and taxes on households. These possibilities are limited on the one hand by the necessity of encouraging households to save, and on the other hand because of the depressive effect of too great an increase of the tax burden on business investment. The maximum of additional receipts has been estimated at 2 billion, divided equally between the two kinds of taxes.[8]

The remainder—3 billion—should be obtained by a reduction in running expenses by the authorities. The only domain where cuts would be conceivable would be in social transfers; in effect, the consumption in the civil authorities could not be reduced as its scope is determined by the amplitude of the social overhead equipment which one is trying to increase; outlays for the aid to developing countries and national defense are prerequisites; government employees' salaries cannot be restricted in order to avoid distortion in relation to wage-earners of the business sector.

In addition to all this, there would evidently be problems concerning the "transformation" of short-term saving into long-term saving; they would arise especially in the area of household savings in so far as these savings would tend to take on a more or less liquid character.

In conclusion, it is possible to determine, at the level of goods and services and at the level of income, an *ex post* equilibrium between resources and expenditure which would integrate a more rapid increase in social overhead equipment and housing during the course of the plan. The reduction in household consumption by 8 billion francs would be brought about by means of a series of convergent moves: a slower increase of wages and salaries, income of individual businesses (−1 billion) and social transfers (−3 billion); a higher increase in direct taxes (+1 billion) and household savings (+3 billion). But the probability of this new financial equilibrium[9] is subject to the possibility of stimulating the propensity of households to save under conditions that are not very favorable, and to slow down the growth of social transfers to an appreciable extent.

The second variant is classified under the heading "variants relative to

[8] To avoid reduction in business savings, it was assumed that the increase of 1 billion in business taxes would be compensated by an equivalent reduction in the income of wage- and salary-earners and individual businessmen; this would obviously entail a particularly dynamic income policy, where this reduction would be represented as the price to pay for more social overhead equipment.

[9] "Financial balance" covers here the set of hypotheses and results concerning: 1) distribution among various incomes categories of the production counterparts; 2) the use that is made of these incomes for the purpose of consumption or saving.

final demand," rather arbitrarily, it would seem, as it is in fact a question of studying the implications of a policy that would tend to reduce by half the size of spontaneous migration from the west of France to the Paris region—that is, to induce 125,000 active persons to remain in the west instead of migrating to Paris. It has been estimated that a little over half these jobs —that is, 70,000 persons—would be in industry; this figure has been increased by 30,000 to take into account the additional agricultural workers who may be incited to leave their farms if there were jobs available in their own region —that would mean a total of 100,000 additional industrial jobs to be created.

The economic cost of the decision is defined in terms of the additional transport costs and the differences in productivity between the regions. An indirect evaluation of this cost has been made on the basis of the differences in labor costs between regions and of the subsidies granted to enterprises setting up in underdeveloped areas. Another element in the cost is constituted by the outlays for social overhead equipment and housing to be created in the west; this would be added to the programs concerning the Paris region (in effect, a hypothesis was formulated whereby these programs would be maintained at the same level in spite of the increased effort toward regional industrialization). The expenses involved by the transfer of the active agricultural population to other sectors must also be borne in mind. From this total, one has to deduce the saving in social costs due to the reduction in interregional population shifts.

The total, about 2 billion francs, represents a comparatively low burden in comparison with national production, but it weighs very heavily on the state budget, the balance of which is already very precarious in the central projection. We may add that, as with other variants already mentioned, the positive sides of such a policy will not be felt until after 1970.

The policy studied concerned raising the growth rate for social transfers to a higher level than that provided for in the central projection (+45 per cent instead of +38–40 per cent in five years). One assumed that the physical balance remained unchanged; the exercise thus was completing this physical balance with a financial balance including more social transfers.

The process followed is similar to that described for the previous variant and implies the use of the same accounting framework, the so-called over-all economic table. Ruling out an increase in the indebtedness of the authorities because of the necessity for a budgetary equilibrium, the financing of social transfers requires an increase in tax receipts and welfare compulsory contribution, the burden of which is distributed between firms (3/5) and households (2/5). So that business savings will not be compromised, the additional financial burden falling to them should be compensated by a reduction in the direct income they pay to the households (wage-earners and individual businesses).

From this exercise it may be concluded that: 1) household savings could hardly increase at the rate envisaged due to the increase in taxes and the higher indirect income accruing to households; 2) there is the risk that business savings will be jeopardized if wage-earners do not accept the redistributive effect implied by this more active transfers policy; 3) if the increase in the tax burden does not reach the necessary level, the additional expenditure of the authorities will possibly exceed their additional receipts, which would entail a reduction in their savings. It would thus seem unrealistic to look for higher social transfers within the framework of an unmodified rate of growth.

The programming in value terms. Up to and including the Fifth Plan, French planning was based on projections outlining *ex post* balances between "physical" quantities: level of the gross domestic production, production factors and outlets for this production—the evolution of these quantities being described "in volume" (that is, at constant prices). The balance was calculated first at the aggregate level, then by sectors through an input-output table.

This kind of projection brings out on the one hand the problems connected with the implementation of a given target for expansion, and on the other hand the choices which must be made in the distribution of the results of this expansion. But it is inadequate in that the social targets of the plan cannot be expressed clearly (in so far as these targets correspond to transfers of income), nor can the aim of stability (which is also strongly influenced by changes in income).

Thus, in the preparation of the Fifth Plan, an attempt was made to complete the projection of goods and services with a projection in value terms, the aim of which would be to study how far: 1) the mechanisms through which income are distributed and employed by the economic agents would create the amount of savings required for the financing of the investments in the plan; 2) financial channels (banks, treasury, and so forth) would be able to transfer savings from the economic agents with a "financial capacity" (whose resources in savings are in excess of investment needs) toward the economic agents with "financial needs."

The accounts system used for this programming in value terms is based on the over-all economic table (OET)[10] for the problems of balance between income distributed and employed, and the financial transactions table (FTT) showing the balance between "financial capacity" and "financial needs."

The work consists of filling in the successive cells of the OET through successive approximations: the "floor" n[0] 1 (transactions on goods and services) where the physical balance should be recalculated by taking in account the movements in relative prices; then the "floors" n[0] 2 (distributive operations) and 3 (balance between financial capacity and financial needs). In order to do this, one determines the spontaneous "financial" propensities of the economic agents from the basis of past trends; then these propensities are modified "on paper" in order to obtain a financial balance compatible with the predetermined constraints (stability of prices, budgetary balance, growth in social overhead equipment and social transfers greater than in production) and with certain criteria of plausibility (the admissible tax burden of ratio of business indebtedness, rates of saving for households, minimum growth rate of wages per capita); and finally an attempt is made to find what measures would in reality bring about the desired modifications (A).

Once the over-all balance between savings and investment has been calculated, it would still have to be shown that the financial channels would ensure sufficient communication between areas of excess and of insufficient saving (B).

The operations are presented in a logical order which simplifies the description of the facts, but in reality the very principle of the method of successive approximations makes necessary frequent iterations between the different cells of the OET.

The balance between production and its uses as described by the projection in volume (that is, with 1962 prices) is recalculated on the basis of "real value"—in other words, taking into account the variations in the relative prices of goods and services in the gross domestic output and in the final demand, while assuming that the general level of prices remains stable.

The assumptions formulated about relative prices take into account the growing integration of France into the world market and a number of orientations indicated in the Fifth Plan (effects of the EEC agricultural

---

[10] The over-all economic table is a consolidation in a synthetic form of all the economic accounts by types of agents (in columns) and by types of operations (in-lines).

The table of financial transactions describes the financial transactions affected by the various economic agents, and allows for checking whether there are satisfying adjustments between net demands and net supplies of capital.

policy, rise in rent, more rational prices in public enterprises, and so forth).
From production prices, one obtains through an input-output table a set
of relative prices for the main aggregates of final domestic demand. The
relative prices obtained thereby hardly differ from the trend observed between 1960 and 1965, except for housing (because of the rise in productivity
anticipated in the building trade) and foreign trade (less rapid rise than
in the past in the general level of domestic prices).

By applying to the figures of the projection in volume the aforementioned
variations in relative prices, a new balance is obtained, in real terms, between production and uses of goods and services.

The two following paragraphs concern "distributive operations";[11] the
first regards the evolution of income of domestic economic agents up to
1970; the second concerns income and expenditure from abroad.

Evolution of income of domestic economic agents between now and 1970.
The change in income was examined from two points of view: in the primary stage, distribution of income in direct provenance from production;
in the final stage, distribution of income from various sources accruing to
households (after transfers). Income and expenditure for public authorities
involved were also studied thoroughly.

The table for primary income paid out by firms gives the distribution
of the added value produced by each sector among the various recipients of
this added value: wages and salaries plus welfare contributions, indirect
taxes, income of the individual agricultural and nonagricultural firms,
gross corporate savings, other types of income (rents, interests, and so
forth). In comparison with past trends, the headings "gross corporate
savings," "gross income of agricultural enterprises," and "other types of
income" are shown as increasing more rapidly, thus conforming to the
plan's option in favor of a growth in self-financing, the revaluing of agricultural income and the continuation of the rise in rents for the older
houses. On the other hand, wages and salaries and indirect taxation are
advancing less quickly than in the past because of a lower increase in household consumption, which is also one of the options included in the plan.

The table for incomes received by households is obtained after a series
of transfers such as welfare benefits, payment of rents by tenants and
farmers, interest on capital, and so forth (not forgetting direct taxation on
passing from gross income to the net income of households). The main
characteristic of this table is the difference between the growth in the gross

[11] In national accounts terminology, these are the operations (transactions?) which make for
the distribution between economic agents of the added value accruing from gross domestic
production and imports.

household income (5.1 per cent per year), and on the other hand the growth of the average per capita wages and the average income of the individual businessman (3.3 per cent in both cases). This discrepancy can be explained by the rise in the active population and by a certain number of disparities in the development of different types of income received by households: welfare benefits and agricultural income in particular are advancing more rapidly than the average income, so that the *direct* income of *nonagricultural* members of the labor force should advance less quickly than the average.

We turn now to the projected balance of administrative expenditure and receipts.[12] The development of expenditures is linked to the political choices stipulated in the plan's targets concerning: social overhead equipment, consumption of civil and military administration, welfare benefits, foreign aid, the "realistic price" policy (implying a reduction in budget subsidies to public enterprises). These choices had to be elaborated by means of complementary hypotheses dealing with two kinds of expenditure: the purchase of land by the authorities and the salaries of government employees (which would rise in the same way as wages and salaries in private sectors). The growth in administrative expenditure (5.9 per cent per year) is a little higher than that of gross domestic production but appreciably lower than that for the years 1960–1965 (7.8 per cent). This difference of two points implied quite a sharp application of restrictions, which will apply mainly to transfer expenditure (welfare benefits, subsidies).

Receipts increase a little less quickly than expenditure (5.6 per cent), with the result that the authorities exhibit "financial needs." As for the structure of the receipts, the advance of indirect taxation has to be somewhat modified for a whole series of reasons,[13] so that, in order to strike a balance within the authorities account, a more rapid increase in household taxation than in the GDP had to be accepted.

External receipts and expenditure. At present our balance-of-payments structure is characterized by an excess of capital inflows movement and a tendency to an unbalance in the goods and services. It would not be desirable to have this situation continue: thus, one of the plan's aims is to correct long-range capital movements, commercial balance, and the invisible balance, so that a healthier balance-of-payments situation will result. This means, in practice: that it would be desirable for France to become pro-

---

[12] Central and local authorities *plus* the social security agencies.
[13] The elimination of tariffs makes for a decrease in customs receipts; harmonization of tax regulations within the EEC prevents a too great reliance on the added-value tax; business competition would be hampered by a too rapid progression of their welfare contributions.

gressively a net exporter of capital; that the deficit of the invisible balance should be reduced (particularly from the point of view of tourism and maritime transport); and finally that the commercial balance should be favorable. These different developments should result in a "financial capacity" of the foreign economic agents (or to a negative balance for current operations) much more limited in comparison with 1965 (0.6 per cent of the GDP as against 1.2 per cent).

Schematically speaking, the savings/investment balance is a plausible approximate equality between:

Resources	*Uses*
Business savings (including the financing of investment by individual businesses)	Investment and business inventories
Household savings	Household investment
Administrative savings	Administrative investment
Financial capacity of foreign economic agents	Capital formation of financial institutions (for a negligible amount)
Savings by financial institutions[14]	

The uses of savings are determined by the targets of the plan; among the resources the financial capacity for foreign agents is determined by the forecasts and the normative targets for foreign trade. The over-all level of domestic savings in 1970 results from these preliminary assumptions. It would represent about 25 per cent of the GDP, a rate that has never previously been achieved. Its breadth may be explained by the great increase in productive investment and social investment and the aimed-at reduction in the negative balance of current operations. It could still be considered insufficient if the 1970 level of productive investment proved to have been too closely calculated.

How would the distribution of this saving among the three categories of domestic agents—that is, mainly business firms, household and the authorities—be brought about?

Business saving was calculated on the basis of the necessity of raising the rate of self-financing to 70 per cent, as this had declined over previous years.

Household saving is difficult to project in the future as the relationship

---

[14] Or negative of the current transactions balance when the balance is positive (corresponding to a financial need from the "foreign" agents account and it appears in the "uses" column).

of savings to consumption is strongly influenced by short-term considerations. The ratio chosen for 1970—12.5 per cent—corresponds to the trends
developed after 1950. Truthfully, the problem does not really lie in the level
to be reached, but in the desirable structure of household savings; it is in
effect probable that the spontaneous savings from this source will include
an insufficient proportion of long-term capital.

The savings made by authorities are formed by the differences between
their taxes and other resources on the one hand and their running expenses
(consumption, salaries, economic and social transfers, consequently exclusive of investments) on the other. Their extent is determined first by the
requirements for a total balance between savings and investment (that is,
by the proportion of the total domestic savings composed from other
sources), and then by government attitude toward the budgetary balance.
The final figure corresponds to quite a limited net indebtedness for the
authorities; this covers the local communities' need for exogenous capital
and financing capacity (for a lower amount) on the part of the state.

The balance between savings and investments shows the part to be supplied by the savings of each of the categories of agents, but also the savings
transfers between these agents. By 1970, the financing of investments will
thus be insured by the transfer of an increased volume of savings from
household and financial institutions to business enterprises and the authorities (local communities).

We will pass quickly over this second part of the predictive analysis of
the financial balance for 1970, as many of the problems raised are meaningless without reference to French organization in financial channels. The
only question with any general interest is the study of the balance between
offer and demand for saving from the point of view of the length of im-
mobilization. The extrapolation of recent trends would in effect lead to a
situation in 1970 which would be characterized by a structural discordance:
the supply of capital in 1970 would be two-thirds short-term and one-third
long-term, while demand for capital envisaged for business, households and
the authorities would be about three-fourths long-term and one-fourth short-
term. Banks and other financing institutions would thus have an important
part to play in the "transformation" of liquid or short-term savings into
long-term savings.

Employing the terminology suggested by Mr. Pierre Massé,[15] two types
of planning may be distinguished from the point of view of the technique
used: these are discretionary planning and formalized planning.

[15] Notably in his communication to the IEA Congress in Vienna, August 1962.

Discretionary planning is based on the existence of a national accounts system which would allow for verification of the coherence of figures of which the plan is composed, and on the procedures of iteration between the planning body and the experts in the different fields (notably those working on the modernization committees). The passage from data to unknown facts being by no means an automatic process, it would always be possible to introduce on the way any corrections recommended by experience or common sense. Inversely, such a process is complicated and difficult to explain to the layman (and its results are thus difficult to deal with in public discussion); in addition, after a certain amount of iteration, the reason for such and such a figure becomes obscure, so that while a plan obtained in this way may be considered practicable (or coherent), it may not always be the best one possible.

Formalized planning differs from the above in that the arbitrary element in the formulation of the plan comes into evidence at the beginning of the process (that is, in the choice of a model and discussion of assumptions), while the rest of the process assumes an automatic nature. For reasons pertaining mainly to the lack of economic information and to the absence of a theory that would take into account the interaction of physical balance (GDP, consumption, and so forth) and balance in value terms, formalization in the establishment of the Fifth Plan was limited to the exploration of the variants modifying the length of the working week, distribution of manpower among the different branches and production techniques.[16] The model employed is a physical one, which consists of twelve branches with linear constraints only, and in two periods: in the first the capital is a "given" that cannot be changed; in the second period the capital depends on the investment made during the first period. On the other hand, this capital may be constituted through two techniques (which only come into existence for the second period), one of them "classical" and the other "recent" (that is more capitalistic). Finally, in this model, the objective-function was determined as the consumption of the second period plus the assets recuperated from equipment built up during the first period and not completely amortized at the end of the second.

PART TWO: INNOVATIONS AS REGARDS THE APPLICATION OF THE PLAN

It is evidently a little premature to discuss the application of the Fifth Plan when this has just entered its first year of effectiveness. However,

---

[16] The model is described in the appendix to the report on the Main Options to the Fifth Plan (*Journaux Officials*, 1964).

its formulation already threw advance light on the main difficulties which would be met with the bringing into effect of the plan, and the measures—already taken or under study—which would remove these difficulties. These measures are dealing with the four following types of problem: 1) the significance of uncertainty; 2) growth policies; 3) influence on volume and structure of demand; 4) financing of investments.

The uncertainty of the future is by no means a radically new element to the Fifth Plan, but was felt more keenly than previously, for a whole series of reasons: uncertainty concerning work participation rates of certain categories of people (youngsters, women, the elderly) while the labor market should be slackening (the participation rates of the recent period on the contrary were influenced by labor shortages on the market); uncertainty as to consumer behavior in an economy reaching a level of relative abundance; uncertainty about the behavior of individual savers and the propensity of business firms to invest in a less inflationary environment; finally, uncertainty regarding foreign trade: the bringing into being of the Common Market; increased international competition.

In the face of this uncertainty, there is the desire on the part of the public authorities to "accept hard facts, but without fatalism" (P. Massé); this calls for a clearer definition of those of the plan's targets which would be "upheld," [17] and those elements which constitute assumptions or forecasts to be revised yearly; this has also led to a more systematic link between medium-term targets and their day-by-day application through a system of "alarm signals."

The targets of the Fifth Plan. At the most general level, the aims of the Fifth Plan are defined in the introduction of the general report in the following manner: "to set the competitive capacity of our economy on a solid basis with a view to preserving its independence, to insure its balanced expansion and to make it the stay of real and lasting social advance."

The following may thus be considered as intermediate or "instrumental" targets; among which three groups may be distinguished: 1) the targets to which the "alarm signals" apply movement of the general level of prices; foreign trade balance; growth of over-all production and industrial production; growth of productive investment; employment situation; 2) the targets outside the "alarm signals" system. Some of these aims depend on public decisions, and their inclusion in the plan, according to the "Report on the Options of the Fifth Plan," constitutes "an engagement to attain them excluding any serious miscalculation objectively assessed within the

---

[17] Or to be revised by a policy decision if the difference between aim(s) and implementation is considered insuperable.

over-all economic development": outlays for aid and defense; social over-head equipment; social housing. Others may, on the contrary, be influenced by government incentives, but their bringing into effect depends, in the last analysis, on the behavior of business heads. This is the case for what the plan calls "structural targets," an idea expressed in the following terms: "The Fifth Plan proposes as an aim, the constitution or, where they already exist, the strengthening, of a small number of enterprises or of groups of international dimensions capable of facing foreign groups in those fields where competition arises"; 3) finally, in so far as the development of income determines to a large extent the behavior of certain alarm signals (notably those relative to prices and foreign exchange), indications[18] on this subject are: agricultural income, wages and salaries, income of nonagricultural individual businessmen, gross corporate savings, welfare benefits.

Alarm signals. As Pr Svennilson[19] says, "under conditions of uncertainty, planning may be developed to a higher level of sophistication. The possibility of alternative events may be *anticipated,* and the planner may *plan to adjust his action to the events that actually occur.* We may call his type of plan a *strategy.*" An attempt has been made to define just this strategy for the Fifth Plan. The adjustment to events takes the form of a possibility to revise the aims and forecasts mentioned above. But the nature of the "events" that may occur must also be agreed upon, events which will bring about the application of countermeasures of a discretionary nature (in the sense that they have not been previously defined). This is the reason for the "alarm signals" (or "blinkers") described in the Fifth Plan.

This is a method which "consists of 1) choosing the most important economic magnitudes, for which the plan stipulates norms of development, 2) of determining the size of variations which may be tolerated for each one on the basis of the norms and 3) of defining the indicator for each of these dimensions as well as the threshold limit permitted in each variation. The alarm—that is, the crossing of one of these thresholds—would entail either the bringing into effect of corrective measures or the express alteration of one of the Plan's aims."

Five alarm signals were agreed upon for the Fifth Plan. 1) General price

[18] This word is used in the text of the Fifth Plan to stress that the estimated magnitudes defining prospective change in prices and incomes do not imply any contractual engagement on the part of the government of both parts of industry. We may add that the "indicative" nature of an economic magnitude depends more on the possibility of influencing it than on the intrinsic importance of this magnitude. The forecasts on consumption trends per product are also indicative, but are less essential for the maintenance of a balanced growth, than the movements of prices and incomes.

[19] "Planning in a Market Economy," 27.4 1965, mimeographed document, p. 4.

level (monthly indicator): alarm will be given when, for three consecutive months, the difference between the monthly growth of the retail price index for France and the corresponding growth of our six main associates (the United States, the United Kingdom, the Federal German Republic, Belgium, Italy, the Netherlands) is more than 1 per cent. 2) Foreign trade balance (monthly indicator): the alarm will be given when the rate of imports covered by exports for the previous three months (calculated over 12 months on a moving average) drops below 90 per cent. At present a balance is represented by a rate of 92 per cent. 3) Growth in gross domestic production (yearly indicator) and in industrial production (monthly indicator). In the first case the alarm will be given if the National Accounts Commission should discover, at its autumn session, that the annual growth rate (in volume) of the GDP for the current year is lower than 2 per cent. In the second case, the indicator warns if the industrial production calculated over the last twelve months drops below 2 per cent for three consecutive months. 4) Productive investment (annual indicator): the threshold for alarm is a growth rate lower than 2.5 per cent found by the National Accounts Commission in the spring of the following year. 5) Employment situation (monthly indicator): the usual indicators were not considered satisfactory: the first—unemployed drawing unemployment benefits—because its development is influenced by extra-economical factors (legal conditions set for the right to draw any benefit, number and geographical situation of the local public agencies dealing with unemployment compensation); the second—applications for unavailable jobs registered by the Department of Labor local agencies—either because the information about jobs within the labor agencies is sometimes inadequate or because the privilege of registering as out-of-work varies according to age, sex and the social category.

Therefore another criterion was chosen: the number of unemployed persons who declare they are looking for work. Alarm is given if, for three consecutive months, this number rises above 2.5 per cent of the active population. The exact proportion will only be known directly on the occasion of a population census or an employment survey; during the intermediate periods one of the two above criteria will be used: the number of applications for unavailable employment; this criterion will be modified by a coefficient which will be brought up to date by the Statistical Institute at the beginning of each year.

It may be seen that these are alarm signals of an official nature, intended to set in motion corrective measures or a revision of the plan, which explains their restricted number and the rather broad definition of the thresholds for alarm, as well as their comparatively retarded nature (intended to reduce to the minimum any dispute about the correctness of the diagnosis). These would have to be supplemented by early cyclical indicators which would sound the alert before the warning signals.

Growth policies. The aim of these policies would be to improve incentive in production capacities and to place the problems of adjustment between potential growth and actual growth at a higher level of expansion. There are three main fields of action: manpower training and retraining, encouragement for research-development (in particular through a system of advance payments to firms which would be reimbursed only in the case of success), and, finally, the reorganization of production structures with a view to greater specialization and concentration.

The problem would be to obtain expansion in internal demand and of exports which would respect the proportions determined in the plan. The problem posed by investments and savings will be dealt with last; here it is a matter simply of export promotion policy and income policy.

The first point gives little rise to comment because of its classical nature: a question of measures tending to encourage tourism and develop commercial networks abroad, as well as a reform in the system of credit for exports.

The second point, on the other hand, is worth going into a little more, because of the unusual nature of its subject—experience in this field extends only over an extremely modest scale limited by the many difficulties which arise here.

In purely rational terms, an income policy is justified both from the economic and from the social points of view. For the regulation of the growth in demand it would, economically speaking, seem necessary to avoid using only the traditional instruments embodied in the monetary and fiscal policy, as it is difficult to assess their impact with any precision. Taxation has, certainly, a stabilizing effect, but its influence is purely *a posteriori* and does not cure cost inflation. The conclusion is that the only measure whose influence would be both early and sufficiently selective has to deal with the totality of primary incomes distributed by firms and involves an attempt to adjust their progression to the guidelines arrived at by the programming in value terms.

On the other hand, from the social point of view a neutral policy with regard to distribution of income will allow certain disparities to continue and perhaps grow, while their elimination or reduction is in any case regarded as desirable. But, in practice, a corrective policy, to be noninflationary, would assume that the incomes which do not benefit from this policy would not try to maintain their relatively favored position—in other words, the extra distributed to some must be deducted from the others (or even better, should not be paid out to them so that production costs will therefore not go up).

But if the practical possibilities of an income policy are examined, it will be seen that they are, for the moment, limited because of the political context and the nature of the relationship between unions and employers, and because the norms governing the progression of incomes both in their absolute and relative values imply, in certain cases, an appreciable change in rhythm in comparison with past trends,[20] as shown by the following figures (annual rates): Real net wage and salary per active person was 4.9 per cent in 1960–1961, and 3.3 per cent in 1965–1970; gross corporate savings were 4.4 per cent in the earlier period and 6.4 per cent in the latter period; welfare benefits were 10.2 per cent and 6.2 per cent; and direct taxes paid by households (in per cent of consumption) were 7.2 per cent and 1970 8.7 per cent.

Therefore, the income policy outlined in the Fifth Plan is only an indicative one, exclusive of any contractual agreement from both parts of industry. The following three points serve as its basis:

1) The existence of a programming in value terms which supplements planning in volume and shows the interrelations between production targets and the uses of goods and services on the one hand and the various price and incomes developments on the other.

2) Yearly adaptations by the government of the norms concerning the development of prices and incomes as indicated in the plan. This adaptation will be made with the establishment of the annual economic budget. After consulting employers' organizations and trade unions, the government will announce its recommendations with regard to incomes and prices and the attitude it will take in fields under direct governmental authority (incomes in public and semipublic agencies and firms, agricultural prices, public tariffs, welfare benefits and contributions).

3) The implementation of these recommendations will be followed up by a special body, the Research Center for Costs and Incomes, the mission of which will be not to observe the development of prices and incomes

---

[20] This inflection in the rate of growth is even more marked if one considers the trends in nominal terms.

permanently but to study, at the government's request, such and such a particular situation and to demonstrate how, in a given sector, subsector or enterprise, the added value of the entity under examination is formed and distributed. Such demonstrations will be published under conditions to be determined, and the center will prepare an annual report on its activities.

Financial measures already included in the plan or under preparation are intended to stimulate saving and to adapt financial channels to the needs of the investors. The measures to increase savings will vary according to each category of economic agents: reductions in taxes on profits made by private companies, rise in tariffs for public enterprises, reforms in the methods of financing the purchase of houses and establishment of "long-term savings plans" for householders, a revision of the bases of local taxation and the setting of prices on certain free services provided by local authorities.

As concerns financial channels, here the offer of capital (where, as has been seen, short-term capital tends to predominate) has to be adapted to the demand, which is mainly for long-term savings. The banks will have to play the part of "transformer" to a greater extent (right now, joint stock banks can extend their credit above five years), but during the transition period the treasury should be ready to offset any insufficiency in the financial channels.

Chapter 3

FRENCH AND BELGIAN PLANNING

JEAN WAELBROECK

Free University of Brussels

French planning is the offshoot of one of the numerous post-World War II experiments in economic planning. In many countries, these experiments were given up when opinion was against close control of economic life by the government. French planning proved able to adapt to the changing methods of running the economy and preserving a leading role in policy-making.

France's success in renovating her economy at a relatively low cost in investment has been widely noted. While the roots of economic growth are no easier to discern in France than anywhere else, it is clear that a possible explanation is the existence of its original planning system. The prospect of reaping an extra 1 or 2 per cent of annual rate of growth at the low price of the French type of planning apparatus was surely most tempting, and it is not surprising that several other countries were inspired or decided to try planning.

One of these was Belgium, which set up its Economic Programming Bureau in 1959. There was at the time widespread concern over persistent unemployment and low rate of growth, as well as over the difficulties in the coal mines and the economic consequences of the loss of the Congo.

French planning, with its emphasis on dealing with the structural problems of the economy, seemed well suited to deal with these problems, and the newly created Programming Bureau patterned its activities closely after the French model.

In the spirit of the title of the paper, French planning will thus be taken as an original and apparently effective technique of coordination of long-term economic policies of the authorities of a country; and Belgian planning as an attempt to import the "French formula" into a country with different political and administrative traditions and a far more open economy.

THE FRENCH PLANNING EXPERIMENT

The best way to describe the institutions on which the French system of planning is based is to explain how they influence the process of plan-making and enforcement. (The description applies to the Fourth Plan.)

The first stage is drawing up "sketches" (*esquisses*)—describing alternative patterns of development in the economy. These take the form initially of highly aggregated dynamic input-output tables, which are progressively disaggregated to give increasing insight into economic prospects. The "sketches" and the more detailed interindustry tables are built up by the Institut de Statistique et d'Etudes Economiques, which undertakes much of the basic research on which the plan is based, together with the Plan Commissariat and the *rapporteurs* of the Modernization Commissions (the commissions responsible for advising the Plan Commissariat on specific aspects of the plan).

After preliminary research, the advice of the government is sought on the general lines of development strategy. A version of the plan corresponding to the decisions of the government is then transmitted by the Plan Commissariat to the Modernization Commissions, made up of civil servants and people from the business world and trade unions.

Commissions may be set up to study the prospects and problems of specific industries (vertical commissions), or aspects of over-all economic balance such as foreign payments, financing investments, and so on (horizontal commissions). Altogether, the apparatus of the commissions and their working groups is cumbersome, and it has been estimated that they bring some three thousand persons in some way or other into the sphere of planning. A major task of the Plan Commissariat, with a staff of some hundred civil servants, is to guide the whole process and to prevent its getting out of hand.

As may be guessed, the output of the work of the Modernization Commissions is of varying quality and is far from being thoroughly satisfactory. The commissions arrive at decisions without voting, so that their reports are strongly influenced by the preconceptions of their advisers. While the final version of the plan will reflect the findings of these groups, the Plan Commissariat does use a good deal of common sense in arriving at the conclusive details.

Next comes the time-consuming and awkward procedure of consulting organs representing public opinion. These are the Economic and Social Council (a board representing social groups) and the Superior Planning Council (a body of some 50 highly qualified persons) and finally parliament itself. These contacts are useful in insuring publicity for the main features of the plan, but probably do little to improve it from a technical point of view or to achieve the democratic control over technocrats which many feel is desirable. The process of plan-making is so complicated that by the time the plan is submitted, it cannot be changed in any essential way.

The plan is, in any case, only a statement of intentions which are loosely related to action. Of the real policy decisions, some are bound to come under parliamentary control as the laws inspired by the plan are voted upon. Much of the implementation of the plan takes place at the administrative level and does not normally come under parliamentary scrutiny. These decisions are influenced by momentary political forces and pressures at the time they are taken, but it is doubtful that they are much influenced by debate over the plan itself.

Economic techniques used in drawing up the plan. The techniques used in plan-making are essentially pragmatic. There is no true general model of the French economy; the only econometrics involved in the final synthesis is the requirement of input-output consistency. In other words, the choice of figures is based on the "best judgment" of the planners, subject only to the constraint that the sums of inputs and outputs be in balance.

This approach to plan-making does find a justification in the desire to rely as much as possible on the commission work. Certainly, it does not seem possible to bring together several thousand experts to cooperate closely in the construction of a sophisticated econometric model. To this common-sense justification may be added a definite distrust of econometrics which is widespread among French planners.

This description of plan-making techniques would be misleading if it did not give due recognition to the considerable volume of applied economic research often highly original and imaginative, which is undertaken under the aegis of the planning bodies. Only part of the work is done in the Plan Commissariat and in the INSEE. A considerable amount is carried on in a number of independent research institutes, often directed by former officials of the plan. This independent research is only loosely connected to the task of constructing the four-year plans; it serves rather as a substratum of creative thinking which helps the whole planning system evolve and adapt to the challenge of changing problems.

Enforcement of the plan. The means of enforcement are rather weak and have been becoming weaker through the years.

A first and important method is the voice given to the Plan Commissar in the decisions of the FDES (Fund for Economic and Social Development). About half of government investment funds are spent via the fund—the rest taking the form of direct budget appropriations. Those government funds go mainly to public investment, housing, and the investment of nationalized industries. What the fund staff coordinates therefore is mainly public investment in a broad sense.

Planners are also able to offer a variety of incentives to private enterprises for investing in particular industries or regions. The range of incentives and their scope have decreased over time, but there is still enough to give by cooperating with the administration to persuade enterprises to adapt to a certain extent the details of their investments to the preferences of planners. The main incentives are interest subsidies, investment allowances, and tax relief. Firms must obtain building permits to invest and to enlarge their facilities in the Paris region. Authorization is also necessary for certain capital issues.

As noted, the trend has been toward weakening the means by which planners are able to influence the private economy. Historically, it is possible to trace the disappearance or near disappearance of specific incentives to particular events. In some cases, means of discrimination have had to be given up as a result of international agreements in OECD or of the ECSC and Rome treaties. Special techniques like the vote of *lois-cadre,* specifying details of aid to individual industries over a period of years, proved awkward as they reduced the freedom of action of the administration; the so-called quasi-contracts committing the administration to give specific benefits to enterprises in exchange for a commitment by the latter to undertake specific programs do not seem to have proved to be as convenient as had been hoped.

That available incentives are not very strong does not mean that planners are powerless to direct investments. Their ability to persuade entrepreneurs to invest in particular regions or industries depends on whether or not a sufficient number of projects can be amended to suit planners' wishes without much change in their expected profitability. To what extent investment projects of enterprises do press such flexibility can be decided only on the basis of broader experience than the author of this paper possesses.

THE BELGIAN PLANNING EXPERIMENT

The Economic Programming Bureau was set up in Belgium in 1959 in a troubled period. The Congo had just become independent. A severe crisis was forcing the closing of a large number of coal mines in the French-speaking part of the country, triggering off a general strike a short time after. There were also latent doubts about the ability of the Belgian economy to adapt to Common Market competition.

It is usual in Belgium to arrive at political decisions only after prolonged squabbling between whichever two of the three great parties happen to form the government, and the founding of the Programming Bureau was no exception as the Liberal members of the government had to overcome their distrust of planning.

The Programming Bureau, with a staff of five economists, was functionally responsible to the Prime Minister, but administratively dependent on the Minister of Economic Affairs. Its staff—of five economists—was recruited with one exception from outside the administration, on the basis of special contracts which placed it outside the normal civil service hierarchy.

The bureau had a double mission. First it was asked to establish a program of economic development. Establishment of this program, as with the French plans, was to involve founding coordinated investment plans by ministries and public enterprises, as well as projections of growth of the private sector established in cooperation with representatives of business and of trade unionists. Its second and no less important mission was to assist five newly created expert committees entrusted with the task of proposing legal and organizational reforms in the fields of short- and medium-term finance; regional policy and planning; public investments and housing; employment; and small and medium enterprises.

It is clear that with its tiny staff (even when this was later somewhat increased) the Programming Bureau found itself in the situation of an inexperienced elephant boy expected to climb on an untrained elephant and guide it by mere pressure of the feet. Looking back, it can be said that the elephant was on the whole willing to do its best, but not very clear on what was expected of it.

In carrying out the complicated and time-consuming task of building up the development program, the bureau relied as much as possible on research undertaken at its request in other public administrations and, to a limited extent, in employer federations and similar bodies. This was a deliberate policy and not a makeshift device imposed by lack of staff, as it seemed that exchanges of facts and statistical information might be an effective way of bringing outsiders within the planning process. Quantitative data which could not be obtained in this way was supplied by university research units.

The five expert committees which were to study institutional problems proved to be useless from the point of view of long-term economic planning. The Financial Commission gave its attention to banking and short-term credit problems and left aside the more important question (from the planners' point of view) of better coordination of the public credit organizations which in Belgium account for most of medium- and long-term investment credits. The proposals for establishing appropriate institutions for regional policy and planning foundered in interministerial and interparty bickering. With the deterioration of Flemish Walloon relations, this problem has become very much of a political hot potato, and there is little hope that any useful action will be taken in this field now. The work of other committees did not lead to significant conclusions or results.

In its attempt to coordinate public investments, the Programming Bureau encountered the same obstacle of autonomy in reaching greater cooperation among public medium-term credit institutions. It did not prove possible to make all public investors communicate meaningful investment plans or to obtain the establishment of clear priorities by the government, and planning failed on the whole to achieve a real improvement in the public investment process.

In their relations with the private sector, the experience of Belgian planners parallels that of France. On the labor side, there was lack of interest or understanding of the details of the plan. Underlying the labor attitude was a nagging (and probably justified) suspicion that because of their concern with the promotion of investment and with the international competition of the economy, planners are biased in favor of wage restraint. On the employer's side, however, the reaction was quite favorable. There was satisfaction that the government was interested in consulting businessmen on policy, and the hope that through the consultation procedures of the plan the government might be induced to take the needs and problems of business more into account. Due to the size of the staff of the Programming Bureau and lack of time, it proved impossible however to establish a comprehensive network of commissions and working groups of the French type to give institutional expression to contacts with the private sector. A number of groups were set up, however, and functioned.

On the government side, the original intention to have the Programming Bureau directly dependent for instructions on the Prime Minister was not adhered to, and the bureau came to be more and more an organ of the Ministry of Economic Affairs. This undoubtedly impaired its ability to play a coordinating role in the administration, by making it appear as an instrument for extending the authority of a ministry whose tendency to expand its sphere of influence has traditionally been resented by other administrations.

The close connection with the Ministry of Economic Affairs did have an advantage insofar as the ministry has the most influence over the granting of credits and other incentives to enterprises. The instruments available to the Belgian government to guide investment are at last as strong as they are in France, including: guarantees and substantial interest subsidies to credit for approved investments in regions deemed to be underdeveloped (in practice scattered all over the country); public participation in financing applied research and preparation of prototypes of new products; construction of industrial estates and of the infrastructure facilities required by private industries; authorization for foreign firms to establish factories in Belgium.

In France, therefore, probably as in many industrial countries, investors have good reason to show willingness to adapt their investment projects to the preferences of the administration in exchange for valuable advantages.

In practice, such negotiations have in most cases not directly involved the experts of the Programming Bureau. The program did serve however as background information in the decision-making process, and as a means of making the preferences of the government known to entrepreneurs.

The bureau was consulted directly on a small number of exceptionally important decisions—in particular, the creation of two large steel plants near Liège and on the coast, on the long-term plans for procuring an adequate supply of fresh water, and on the import of Dutch natural gas.

Influenced by the very lively debate among French economists and politicians on planning and democracy at that time, great care was taken to consult organs representing public opinion at all stages of the planmaking process. A highly preliminary version of the program—hardly more than one of the French *esquisses*—was submitted early in 1960 to the Central Council for the Economy, a broad body which serves as a discussion forum for economic and social problems. The Programming Bureau also reported regularly to the National Council for Economic Expansion, which provides for discussions of economic issues by ministers, and trade union and employers' federation leaders. The final version of the program was submitted to parliament. The usefulness of the elaborate procedure is a little doubtful, and the organs consulted found it difficult to come to grips with the substance of the program and to discover exactly in what way it was relevant to their problems and interests.

Chapter 4

THE CREATION OF THE NATIONAL ECONOMIC PLANNING SYSTEM AND THE MAIN STAGES OF ITS DEVELOPMENT

NIKOLAY P. FEDORENKO
Academy of Sciences of the USSR

The first stage in the development of planning in the USSR (1918–1921) focused on determining the respective scopes and interrelations between the central and local planning bodies. The grave conditions prevailing in Russia after World War I called for the establishment of a single body for planning the allocation of resources. The state electrification plan laid a foundation for a national economic plan by bringing together separate blocks of the economy and defining scientific principles for regional location and specialization.

The second stage (1921–1927) was marked by sharp debates over the roles of the market and the plan. The essence of the problem was what should be the determining factor in the transition period—planning by directives or projections of the market demand?

The Marxist-Leninist economists voted for changing the pattern along the lines of industrialization and controlled development of the national economy.

The period of coexistence of the state and the private sectors ended in ultimate victory for the state sector. However, the situation called for great flexibility in economic policy. A brilliant example of this was the introduction of the New Economic Policy (NEP).

It was at this point that the construction of balances was begun (1923–1924). Later it developed into a universal method of balance calculations used for determining economic ratios and variables and the coordination of interrelationships between particular production sectors. The feasibility of a general perspective plan and current production plans was also the subject of study.

In the middle of the 1920's work was begun to establish and update the control figures for annual economic plans. The accumulation of experience in the process of establishment and implementation of control figures appeared indispensable later for the transition from the electrification plan to the first Five-Year Plan.

During the third stage, the main problems were solved (1927–1932) concerning expanded reproduction on a progressive scale under the predominance of the state sector in mining-manufacturing and public utilities (gas, water, electricity supplies, and transportation) and the switchover of the Soviet farmer to full-scale collectivization. At the present time, the well-balanced coordination of every aspect of the national economy, especially a more rapid development of the production-means sectors, has become the basic tool of national economic planning.

The balance method constitutes the foundation of planning in the USSR and other Socialist countries. Essentially, this is to balance the supply and demand of material, financial and labor resources. The main variables are computed by a system of balances.

The computing operations used in the planning work fall into two groups: 1) balances reflecting the more general process in the economy, such as GNP, national income, and labor resources (balances of capital stock, money income, and expenditures of the population also belong in this category); 2) the system of material balances for particular commodities and the balance of productive capacities.

The planning system comprises two constituent components: the perspective (long-term) plans and the current (short-term) plans. The latter are usually drawn up on the basis of the former which generally mean a five-year period.

The main task of a perspective plan is to determine the ratio of each production sector in the economic development and the amount of capital investment with its distribution among the particular production sectors.

This central idea serves as criterion for setting the control figures, that is, the basic plan variables. The latter includes: the volume of the national income; the rates of development in the production of the basic commodities (by production sectors); the capital investment (by production sectors); and the variables in the growth of the living standard.

The determination of the pattern of the national economy in the period covered by the plan is a major task of a perspective plan. To meet this aim, structural shifts are investigated, and volume of production figures is evaluated for every production sector. The next step is to plan the modernization of industries. This is done by experience and scientific research.

The regional location of new enterprises and improvement in the economic patterns of particular regions are important.

Planning the economy of a union republic is of special importance. The complex development is planned in a way which takes into account its natural and labor resources, its climate, and geographic conditions. A continuous growth in the wealth and cultural level of the nations living in the corresponding republic is a *sine qua non* in the planning of its economy. The planning agencies of the republics are extremely competent and provide harmonious and efficient development and make rational use of local materials, finances and labor resources.

Thus, the perspective plans built by the State Planning Committee of the USSR (GOSPLAN) have two concerns: first, the separate production sectors (production and technical progress), and, second, the regions (the comprehensibility of economic growth, employment, and the living standards).

The control figures of the perspective plan are sent to the union ministries (and agencies) and to the state planning committees of the union republics. These bodies draw up their plans within the framework of the control figures and then set their own control figures for the individual enterprises.

Each enterprise makes up its own plan for the development of production based on the directives received. This plan determines the lines of development for the period covered. A plan of this kind is being continuously updated, while experience is accumulated and technology progresses.

Current plans determine the economic development for the year to come. They include: production; plans of material and technical supply; managing the commodity circulation between enterprises; wholesale-trade plans determining the flow of goods from the enterprises into commerce; and the state budget that determines the source of the funds formation by the government.

Current plans are prepared for variables listed by the perspective plans.

Their elaboration is effectuated simultaneously from the top (from GOS-PLAN down to individual enterprises) and from the bottom (from the individual enterprises up to GOSPLAN).

Each enterprise draws up its plan within the framework of the perspective plan and on the basis of the orders received for the forthcoming year.

The finance and production plans of the enterprises are then examined by the higher agencies that approve the plans after certain corrections ensuing from the plan assignments set by GOSPLAN.

In 1966, the introduction of a new system of planning and economic stimulation was started at a number of enterprises and in some industries. The new system is to give incentive to the staff of the enterprises and the higher agencies and thus to raise efficiency of production. The principle of self-support is introduced in all phases of the structure of industrial production. Simultaneously, centralized planning is being transformed. Centralized planning provides for optimal decisions on a national scale and therefore cannot be reduced. However, the principle of self-support changes the scope and the methods of this system, transforming centralized planning into the supreme synthesis of proportionalities combined with powerful material levers.

Under conditions of ideal self-support, centralized planning will concentrate primarily on the improvement of the basic ratios and on better location for production and harmonious development of the economic regions. The state will be able to supervise the effectuation of a uniform policy in the fields of technical progress, capital investment, wages, prices, rate of return, finance and credits.

According to the new system the directives for the enterprises comprise eight variables: 1) total sales; 2) the major commodities in terms of kind; 3) the total wage fund; 4) total profits and profit ratio; 5) budget payments and allocations; 6) capital stock investment from the centralized investment funds; 7) assignments concerning the introduction of new kinds of commodities and new techniques as well as all-round mechanization and automation of principal importance for the industry in question; 8) the volume of raw materials and machinery supplied to the enterprise from the funds distributed by the higher agencies.

The enterprises plan their costs, net and gross outputs as well as the average wages, the number of personal staff, the utilization of equipment and capacities, rate of return and distribution of working capital among components, and so forth. All this is done by the enterprises independently, using their own judgment with a view to their goals. The top-level agencies will use these variables for calculations only. The flexible system of economic levers that will regulate the operations of the enterprises along the lines dictated by the interests of society include prices, standard payments on production funds, rental payments, maneuvering the centralized resources of capital investment, and balancing disproportions with the help of a comprehensive network of reserves.

These are factors creating the conditions necessary for perfect self-support in the industry. The main criterion in testing an enterprise is whether it is paying its own way.

Parallel to the innovations in industry, the system of prices is being modernized to make it adequate for the new conditions.

While emphasizing the advantages of the Socialist system, we must realize that it possesses vast reserves the utilization of which will promote efficiency in social production and its growth rates, thus raising the living standard.

The grandiose goals of Communist construction generate essentially new requirements in planning and management of the economy. The growth of the scale of production, the accelerated rates of technological progress and the continuous complication of economic relations make it impossible to optimize the economy by means of traditional planning methods—that is, to maximize the results of rational utilization of the resources available in the periods covered by the plan and thus to provide for the full reaping of the advantages of the Socialist mode of production. This is a goal achieved by basing the planning operations on the many uses of modern scientific techniques and equipment—namely, mathematical methods which allow the choice of optimal variant plans and the electronic computers able to process the masses of data indispensable for an effective management of the processes of production, distribution and consumption.

The present development phase and the achievements of the social and natural sciences have pushed into the foreground as a major element of the economic policy the task of creating an optimal planning and management system for the Soviet economy which would perfectly match its political organization.

Every decision undertaken by an authoritative body should be substantiated by calculations of the optimal variants and determination of the consequences this decision is liable to produce in the perspective development of the economy.

The science of planning and management must become an exact science in the full sense and hence an effective tool for building and running a unified optimal planning and management system, based on all-round applications of mathematical economics and computers. The creation of such a system presupposes a thorough research into a wide range of economic, technical and social problems.

The result of this research must be a practical scheme of the aggregate dynamic model of the economy that would make it possible to solve the actual problems of unified optimal planning, recording and operational management. The technical basis of this system will be provided by a unified network of state computing centers.

The following main divisions of the field of research should be distinguished and developed simultaneously for the quickest possible results: 1) the theoretical foundations of optimal planning and management; 2) a system of economic information providing for the needs of optimal planning and efficient management by automation of the collection, transfer and processing of the primary economic data; 3) the mathematical backgrounds of optimal planning—namely, elaboration of the computing methods for solving the planning and management problems at all levels with the aid of computers; 4) the creation of a unified network of state computing centers that would be the bases for optimal planning and effective management of the national economy; 5) the elaboration of specific management and planning systems for the particular links of the economy from individual enterprises up to the central bodies of scientific planning; all these systems will be based on mathematical schemes and use computers.

Economic levers helping to bring into effect the optimal plans and subjective psychological and material incentives stimulating the creation of the plans and development in their implementation will also constitute an inherent part of the system of optimal planning and management.

The choice and substantiation of the optimal test must be determined by, and account for, the basic economic law of socialism—that is, maximal satisfaction with the growing requirements of the members of a Socialist society. For meeting its goal of satisfying the requirements at every stage, the society has a definite (limited) amount of material, labor, natural resources, and scientific and technical capacities. These constitute the productive capacities of the society.

Evidently, allocation of a given resource for any sphere would in a certain way affect the efficiency of some other sphere and eventually the whole of the economy. Hence, there is the task of finding the best way to reach society's goal considering the available resources.

Along with the optimal plan, the system of prices should be defined, since it is a lever stimulating the implementation of the plan; a rate of investment return and employee income should be evaluated as well as a number of other variables playing a part in the dynamics of Socialist reproduction on a progressive scale.

The definition of the duration of the planning period and the ratios of consumption and capital formation play an important role in the optimal test of economic development.

The commensurability of social utilities of the particular commodities and resources is a basic assumption in the theory of optimal planning. The theory assumes that the utility corresponding with the highest possible level of satisfaction can be realistically evaluated. Utility is expressed in terms of price resulting from the optimal plan. In economic terms, the price of a commodity (a resource) corresponds to the money expression of the contribution made by the increase of the given item to the attainment of the goal. The main difficulty lies in finding the ways for an individual enterprise to harmonize the conflicting trends in the growth of output and the changing structure of its costs in order to balance the interests of the enterprise and those of the society.

A successful solution to this problem is attainable, only if all the economic units have the same test for evaluating their efficiency compatible with the optimal test of the national economy. This optimal test can be derived only in case the prices of the commodities produced and consumed correspond to the prices of the optimal plan. Since these prices reflect the possible effect of an increase in the output of a certain commodity or the possible losses that would result from nonfulfillment, an individual economic body can judge its own activities from the national standpoint using the data on rates of return. Thanks to these prices, it will know what gains the national economy will achieve if this or that resource is saved, or what losses at the other sectors of the economy will arise due to an overexpenditure of the resource.

Under the above conditions, the specific test can be formulated as maximum return. It shows what ultimate increase in utility is introduced by the given economic unit into the value of the general optimal test as a result of its actions affecting the amount and quality of product and the costs. Hence, it follows that the conditions of optimal planning under socialism—the tendency to raise an enterprise's rate of return—is in harmony with the main goal of the society.

Orienting their activities along the lines of maximization of return by the prices of the optimal plan, the staff of the enterprises working on the principle of self-support will be able to establish the optimal policy providing for maximization of the general criterion of the national economy. The new schemes of development of production in the enterprises along with the predetermined system of prices will serve as the basis for the calculations of a new version of the national economic plan until the optimal has been reached. The system of prices of this plan will, in its turn, further stimulate the enterprises to improve the plan for better meeting the optimal test of the national economy.

This provides for intricate interrelations of planning in kind and in money terms.

The principle of democratic centralism receives its highest form of development in the system of optimal planning and management of the economy. In fact, the national economy is controlled by scientific and centralized planning serving the interests of the state, while at the same time competence of the economic units is enlarged in all the spheres where benefits of a unit or a single worker stand in harmony with the interests of the state.

Also, along with continuous elaboration and adjustment of the five-year plans, a perspective long-term plan for a period of ten to twenty years and more is to be developed using aggregate variables. This work must be repeated every year or two in order to specify the society's actual needs and capacities and to update the system with data on the current state of economic development, technological progress and research achievements. Continuous planning will allow the merging of planning and managerial activities in a single process based on regular feedback between plans and the results of their implementation.

Any actual social and economic system is so complex that in principle its exhaustive description is unfeasible, and therefore a system of direct administrative control is doomed to be relatively weak and inadequate. The limited capacities of the administrative channels exclude the possibility of foreseeing and planning all the factors and trends in economic development. These limits are explained both by technical deficiencies and by considerations of reasonable costs of management. In other words, a complete formal description of the operations of the economy and creation of a fully automated centralized planning and management system would be unjustified.

Hence, with conditions prevailing in the USSR, and especially with future growth in the scope and complexity of social production, improvement in management efficiency will call for a much more complex and flexible scheme combining the method of centralized optimal planning with decentralized management.

The combined use of these mutually complementary management instruments is possible thanks to the interactions of the variables of the optimal plan expressed in terms of kind and in terms of money—that is, a money system bringing into motion a system of economic levers and incentives.

This twofold scheme provides for the combination of a scientific program of a centralized system and highly flexible and adjustable systems of economic management levers.

The mathematical branch of Soviet economic science will give flesh to these ideas, reflecting the regularities and interrelations of the particular links of the economy in a complex mathematical scheme of interdependencies. This aggregated model should incorporate not only the structure of the controlling agencies and the actual technical relations between industries and their input and output but also the interactions of the various methods of management in the national economy.

Thus, a system of optimal management is neither overcentralized nor spontaneous. It is a new form of management that provides for a harmonious interaction of central planning and the autonomy of every individual economic cell.

However, the point should be made that centralization would be feasible and efficient but only in a clear-cut, liberal frame of centralized planning.

The basis for this harmony of centralization and decentralization will be provided by a system of optimal planning that would integrate the optimality criterion of the economy on a national scale with the specific tests for the individual industries and also interrelate the plan variables expressed in money with those expressed in terms of kind at all levels of the national economy.

Chapter 5

THE MARKET AND THE PLAN IN THE LIGHT OF ECONOMIC REFORM IN POLAND

BOHDAN GLIŃSKI AND JÓZEF PAJESTKA

The Polish Academy of Sciences

The period when there was some sense in setting the plan against the market is beginning to fade into the past. In socialism, these two institutions could have been set against each other when it was necessary to pull the economy out of a state of stagnation equilibrium. It should be remembered that in Socialist countries of the present day, the market economy prevailed before they turned to socialism. This did not insure dynamic growth and kept them in a state of economic backwardness. Therefore, their road to economic development not only had to eliminate exploitation and social inequalities, but also to counteract the market forces which had a negative influence both on social relations and on economic growth.

The strategy of speeding up industrialization chosen by the Socialist countries was changing the structure of the economy into a more dynamic one and in utilizing, to the greatest possible extent, existing economic resources, particularly the available labor power. This was accomplished by abolishing the principle of enterprise profitability and reducing the role of the market to a minimum. The development of the new economic structure proceeded against market traditions. For this reason, it was necessary to eliminate or, at least, to minimize the impact of market forces. The effects of this strategy were quite impressive. They manifested themselves in a high rate of growth of the social product and in desirable transformations in the socio-economic structure. The question could be raised today whether these effects could not have been achieved by preserving, to a greater degree, the market mechanism. At present, however, this would be a rather irrelevant and purely theoretical question.

The rapid rate of growth in industry has produced, after a number of years, a very different situation. The methods of centralized management were becoming less and less suited to the developed industry characterized by various complex relations among the enterprises, and, consequently, factors hampering economic growth began to appear. It was becoming more and more obvious that both the methods and the instruments should be changed. It has been widely recognized that the new instruments, first of all, should be better suited to satisfying social needs, should create better conditions for the development of individual initiative, should facilitate the inclusion of the national economy in international trade and cooperation, and should induce a more rational management of the enterprise. This need was felt with varying degrees of intensity in different Socialist countries, but it was felt in all of them, and especially in the more developed.

In these new conditions, created by a higher stage of development, the setting of the plan against the market has begun to be meaningless, and the need to search for and develop new methods and forms of harmonizing planning with the market forces has begun to be felt more and more intensely. The targets set in the plan and the market forces should supplement each other. The plan should satisfy the requirements of the market, and the latter should facilitate the implementation of the planned policy of growth.

An enhancement of the role played by the market in a Socialist economy is intended to insure a better adaptation of production to demand. This is of particular importance in conditions of a very rapid growth in production of goods which are now within reach of practically every consumer because of a tremendous, almost fantastic, rate of technical progress. A better adaptation of production to existing demand is tantamount to raising the efficiency of management because production not properly geared to needs inevitably results in social losses.

The enhanced role of the market is also a condition of decentralized management and, thus, of a more active and dynamic participation of individuals in the economic processes. It is also conducive to a more rational management of the enterprise. National planning is a basic instrument of rationality in macro-economic terms. The combination of planning with market forces results in the preservation of rationality in macro-economic terms and in supplementing it with the mechanism of rationality in micro-economic terms.

The combining of planning with the market in the economic reforms now taking place in Poland (and this seems also to be true in other Socialist countries) is characterized by one general but most essential feature. The market is being used primarily as a mechanism for a short-run mutual adaptation of activities of various economic units. In this function the market is to serve, first of all, the purpose of a better adaptation of production to social demand as well as the related purpose of a better allocation of the factors of production, albeit in the short run only.

On the other hand, it is assumed that the market mechanism does not provide a sufficient foundation for choosing long-term directions of development and, thus, of the allocation of investments. To support this kind of solution of the relationship between market and plan, a number of theoretical arguments can be found. Thus, for instance, it can be argued that the market prices are determined *ex post* by economic conditions and cannot provide a satisfactory basis for a long-run choice.

This problem can also be considered from a more practical point of view. It should be noted that a sudden and far-reaching introduction of market mechanisms into the existing system would result in all sorts of perturbations, would change the priorities of development, and so forth. Various repercussions would arise because no sufficiently effective instruments and forces for controlling the market in the name of social interest would have been immediately developed. For this reason, it seems logical to introduce the market mechanism gradually and to learn, in the process, how to use and control it.

It is difficult to say now in which direction this evolution will go. For the road chosen for our reform does not allow for substituting one theoretical concept for another, but for changing the instruments that have turned out to be inadequate and in introducing new ones on the basis of experience gained. These instruments must be effective and must be consistent with the basic principles of socialism.

The process of introducing new mechanisms and instruments is, thus, rather one of trial and experiment. Not all solutions are consistent and fully prepared theoretically.

Many Polish economists worked on a theoretical formulation of a model of decentralized management of the economy on the basis of the use of the market mechanism. The general conclusion of their work is that the use of the market mechanism does not contradict the principles of a planned economy and that there are no valid arguments for treating the institution of the market as a foreign body in socialism.

The theoretical justification for using the market mechanism assumes the necessity of working out many particular solutions in which the functioning of the market mechanism would insure consistency between the influence of market and plan.

To do this, the following problems, in particular, should be solved: 1) price policy must be made much more elastic if the market mechanism is to function properly; and 2) conditions must be created which would enable the producer to adjust quickly to market requirements and to adapt the methods of planning to the possibility of utilizing the market mechanism.

The problem of setting prices has always been of great interest to both theoretical and applied economists in their discussions on the use of the market mechanism in a Socialist economy.

The importance of this problem is as evident as the difficulty in finding a solution. It is particularly clear that the role played by prices must be completely different from the one they play in a system of centralized management.

In a centralized system, prices were primarily tools for recording production and aggregating indicators. They did not play an active part in the allocation of labor power and material resources. While prices performed this function, serious shortcomings of a practical nature have developed in price policy. Tools not frequently used become dull. This happened to prices. For this reason, there are now serious difficulties in using them as an active instrument of economic policy. These difficulties constitute one of the greatest obstacles in introducing an effective market mechanism.

In defining the principles of the market mechanism the basic problem is: who determines prices? The two possible extreme solutions are well known. One is that prices are set by the government, and, the other, that they are determined in the market. Compromise solutions are, of course, also possible: certain prices can be set by the government, and others may be left to a free play of market forces. In Poland there is a tendency toward government price-setting. The emphasis is on this solution. It is being justified by arguing that decentralization in management consists of departing from the setting of production targets, from allocating resources, and so forth, and in influencing economic units by economic instruments, the foremost being prices.

Many theoretical arguments could be found to support this solution. It is interesting to note that a theoretical model was worked out by Professor Oskar Lange. However, practical considerations are of great importance here, and there are two basic ones. One is the awareness that under the circumstances prevailing in this country, and particularly considering the necessary limitations in foreign trade, conditions are not suitable for sufficiently broad competition that would insure that prices determined on the market would not be monopolistic. The other and very important one is the awareness of the consequences of the redistributive function of prices. Considerations of this kind favor leaving the function of controlling prices in the hands of the government.

If it is assumed that the government sets the prices, there arises the problem of price flexibility and of economic grounds for setting them. The experience of the Polish economy in the field of price policy is very interesting. In agriculture, private ownership plays a predominant role, and the prices of practically all agricultural products are set by the government. In spite of this, these prices in a number of cases are quite elastic, and they correspond to relations prevailing on the market.

The market for agricultural products is dealt with in the paper presented by Professor Pohorille, and, therefore, we shall concentrate primarily on manufactured goods.

THE WAYS OF INCREASING THE ELASTICITY OF THE PRICES OF MANUFACTURED GOODS

It has been generally felt in Poland that at the beginning of the period of decentralization the following changes should be introduced in order to make price policy more flexible and realistic: a) to define precisely the principles of determining initial prices; b) to determine the principles of, and the criteria for, deviations in sales prices of the means of production from the initial prices; c) to define the principles of increasing the elasticity of market prices maintaining, at the same time, the parametric nature of prices in relation to the enterprises.

The concept of initial prices is somewhat theoretical. The point is to decide on what the price should be based: the average cost in a given industry, or the average cost of high-cost producers, if they supply a major portion of the total production of a given commodity?

Consideration has also been given to the problem of whether the ratios of initial prices should be based only on the ratios of direct outlays, or whether the interest on capital, the land rent and certain costs of social benefits for the workers, included in the government budget, should also be taken into account.

The importance of the methods for expediting the price system mentioned above stems mainly from the fact that the prices of the means of production had been set for a number of years at a level lower than their value. They were supposed to cover the cost of production and to provide a minimum of profit. The guiding principle was simplicity in calculations and the need to facilitate and encourage investments. It is now generally regarded that these practices are not advisable, especially while striving for a balanced growth of the economy.

The recognition of the need to make the initial prices reflect labor outlays does not eliminate situations in which there are differences in the degree of scarcity of various commodities. These differences are often long-lasting and result from the structure of production apparatus or from balance-of-payments considerations. In such cases, deviations in sales prices of the means of production from the prices reflecting actual outlays may be permanent. This problem is controversial, and therefore little progress has so far been achieved in finding a theoretical solution. In practice, the process of gradually raising prices of the means of production is noticeable, and thus they are getting closer to the level at which they will fully reflect the actual outlays.

For a proper functioning of the market mechanism, the problem of increasing the elasticity of market prices is of particular importance. Under prevailing conditions, the easiest method was to change the practice in relation to prices of the products traded directly among the Socialist enterprises, that is, the prices of what we call "cooperation" commodities. With respect to these prices, the accepted principle is to let the supplier and the buyer determine the contract price as they see fit. A similar principle has been accepted with respect to export goods when the quality of export production differs from the quality of goods sold at home. A similar principle has also been applied to fruits and vegetables which are also determined in direct negotiations between the buyer and the seller. The prices are also set freely for what we call nonstandard products.

It was much more difficult to increase the elasticity of the prices of staple manufactured consumer goods. The level of their prices plays an essential part in determining the cost of living. A Socialist government, as a defender of the interests of the consumers, counteracts tendencies toward raising the prices of staple consumer goods. All the more so that seasonal increases in the prices of fruits and vegetables contributed in part to an increase in the cost-of-living index. And, as decentralization progresses, interest in raising enterprise profitability grows, creating the danger of price increases by enterprises enjoying a monopolistic position on the market.

In this situation it was necessary to seek solutions that, on the one hand, would permit preserving the present price structure and, on the other, would provide instruments for influencing the enterprises in a way similar to the functioning of the market mechanism. The object was to increase the interest of the producers in turning out goods for which there is demand—newer and more useful goods with aesthetic value.

It has been decided to use factory prices for this purpose. The factory price differs from the retail price in that it does not include the commercial profit margin or the turnover tax.

Factory prices were in use previously in consumer goods industries. In 1965 the decision was made to expand their use to the whole industry, changing at the same time the method of their application.

The factory price includes the average cost of production for the whole industry plus a specified profit margin. In practice so far, factory prices were usually determined on the basis of the average cost for the industry plus 5 per cent of profit calculated in relation to enterprise costs. The prices determined in this way were seldom changed, although, because of differences in lowering enterprise costs, the profitability of producing different commodities varied considerably.

In the reform introduced last year the following assumptions have been made: In most industries profit is to be determined in relation to the cost of manufacturing—the cost of production minus the cost of materials used; The superior unit may set a higher margin of profit for the following products: a) those granted a quality mark, b) newer ones of a high technical standard, c) commodities in short supply on the market for which there is a great demand. Corrections in factory prices should be made periodically especially in the following situations: a) in cases of changes in production preferences, b) in cases of essential differences in profits, not corresponding to planned preferences and resulting from various degrees of lowering unit costs, c) in cases when the rate of profit achieved on the average by a given amalgamation of enterprises exceeds the rate recognized as the upper limit and d) if, in consequence of changes in the prices of materials, the cost of production of a given commodity is higher than the factory price.

In this way factory prices will, to some extent, play the role of market prices inducing the producer to improve the quality of his products and to adapt them to the requirements of the consumers, without the necessity of changing prevailing market prices.

One can hardly fail to see that this kind of reform goes only halfway. There is a clear danger of severing the tie between factory price and retail price (which is the real market price). This, in turn, may have negative consequences for market prices by making them more rigid and by maintaining improper relations among the prices of different products. A conflict may also arise between a factory price (discouraging, for example, the production of a given commodity) and a relatively attractive market price (maintaining the demand for the obsolete product). Therefore, studies are now under way to develop a method of tying factory prices to sales prices and, thus, to market prices by a proper manipulation of the turnover tax. The simplest solution would be to apply the turnover tax in the form of a specified percentage addition to the factory price.[1] This percentage could be differentiated for various industries, and would thus become an economic instrument. This method of determining the turnover tax has been used for several years in certain branches of the textile industry (the cotton, wool and silk industries). This applies, of course, to the prices of new products launched on the market.

On the basis of the experience gained in the textile industry, it is now possible to set in motion a peculiar sort of price mechanism. The price calculated on the basis of the cost of manufacturing and material norms, and increased by a specified profit is, in turn, increased by a specified percentage of the turnover tax and by the profit margin. In this way we arrive at the retail price. Thus calculated, the retail price could be subject to change in a way similar to changes in factory prices.

This kind of market mechanism can function even without determining prices of particular products by the Government Price Committee. A future evolution in price policy will undoubtedly head in this direction.

THE PROBLEM OF THE ADJUSTMENT OF THE ENTERPRISE TO THE MARKET

When there exists a market in which prices are determined with a sufficient degree of elasticity, thus serving notice to the producers about consumer requirements, it is of essential importance whether the producer is

---

[1] Until now the turnover tax has usually been determined as a difference between the sales price and the factory price.

interested in adjusting his production to the requirements of the market and whether it is possible for him to make such adjustments. In particular, the following conditions must be satisfied: First of all, there must be freedom in determining the range of goods to be produced by the enterprise; second, there must be freedom in purchasing raw materials and other production materials as well as in using the direct labor necessary for implementing a given production program; third, it must be possible to increase productive capacity and to modernize the production processes.

The problem of increasing the material interest of the enterprise has been solved by increasing the variable part of management remuneration and by relating it to the operating results. Since 1960, the size of the management bonus fund has been directly or indirectly related to increases in profit compared with the preceding year. With respect to the employees, a similar role is played by the factory fund which is part of the profit earmarked for individual bonuses for employees and for various social and cultural benefits as well as for housing.

The possibilities of the adaptation of the enterprise to the requirements of the market have been increased because of reforms in the system of management. First of all, the extent of setting administrative directives for the enterprise concerning the range of products has been considerably decreased. A great majority of enterprises now determine their own range of products, in consultation with their customers. In a number of branches of light industry the range of products is set only for quarterly production plans in order to better adjust production to rapidly changing market requirements.

Greater difficulties are encountered in creating for the enterprise the possibilities of its adjustment to the market.

First of all, this depends upon material and nonmaterial reserves in the economy. In a period of a far-advanced centralization of management, however, a Socialist economy was supposed to function with a bare minimum of reserves. The period of decentralization initiated some changes in this respect, but the actual state of affairs is, at present, far removed from a situation in which one could speak of the existence of substantial reserves.

Second, in a Socialist economy the entrenched practice has been to limit the wage fund. The reasons are relatively complex. In the period of centralized management, the limitation of the wage fund with a simultaneous setting of high production targets was a means of speeding up the rate of growth. This provided, at the same time, a guarantee of government control over the ratio between the wage fund and the total value of goods available on the market; this control was needed to prevent inflation. At the same time, it follows from the principles of the Socialist system that every citizen has a right to work. This, in turn, reduces the elasticity of substitution between labor and material outlays, makes it difficult to lay off employees, even if they are superfluous in one enterprise but needed in another. At the same time, the right to work is conducive to hiring an excessive number of workers. It can be said that the right to work was sometimes used not exactly in accordance with the social interest, and this brought about the control of the wage fund and employment in the enterprises.

There are, of course, various ways of adjusting the wage fund properly to the labor intensity of the production program in order to insure that the additional wage fund will be used to produce goods for which there is demand, not only without disturbing the relations between the amount of money and the amount of goods, but even improving them.

In Polish industry, studies have been conducted for some years on the creation of instruments that would enable changes in the wage fund of the enterprise depending upon the increases in labor outlays necessary for carrying out the production program and upon increases in labor productivity. Similar studies are being conducted in other Socialist countries, and in some of them (particularly Yugoslavia), attempts are being made to tie changes in the wage fund to changes in the income of the enterprise.

Work on developing economic tools proceeds slowly, and, therefore, it is essential to bring to light the factors that slow down the process.

The use of economic instruments implies the necessity of cost-accounting, of calculating the work and material norms, of preparing programs for utilizing productive capacity, of calculating the cost of production. This is easy in mass production industries, especially in textiles and foodstuffs. It is much more difficult in various branches of the machinery industry in which the range of products varies frequently. On the other hand, to make cost-accounting more precise it is often necessary to hire additional administrative personnel or to increase the number of office machines. These matters continue to be troublesome in Polish industry.

The most decisive progress has been achieved in making available to the enterprise the means necessary for the modernization of production, for the purchase of new machinery and equipment, and so forth. While in the period of centralization the enterprises had practically no resources for these purposes, today they have at their disposal considerable investment means accumulated from profits and surpluses from working capital, not counting the fund earmarked for major repairs and formed from depreciation allowances.

In the initial period of decentralization (1956–1959), the funds for what is known as "decentralized" investments were at the disposal of the enterprises. In recent years the role of industrial amalgamations (of enterprises) has increased in this respect.

Amalgamations in Polish industry are organizations in which the enterprises of a given branch of industry are included. For instance, the Amalgamation of the Tobacco Industry includes all the enterprises of the industry; the Amalgamation of the Pharmaceutical Industry—all major factories producing drugs (only small cooperative plants are not included). At the beginning, amalgamations played the role of administrative bodies controlling the enterprises, and were intermediaries between the central planning and management authorities on the one hand and the enterprises on the other. Now they are undergoing transformations with a view to becoming economic rather than administrative bodies. Among other tasks, the amalgamations are responsible for directing the development of branches of industry controlled by them. For this reason, the majority of the means for modernization or for renovation investments are now at the disposal of amalgamations. In 1961–1965, they controlled 19 per cent of all investments envisaged in the central plan, and together with the enterprises they controlled 30.9 per cent. In the next five-year period (1966–1970) the share of amalgamation control should increase to 26.4 per cent (and together with the enterprises to 35.3 per cent). Investments are financed almost exclusively from the income of their enterprises: 1) from the profits; 2) from depreciation—a major part of the depreciation fund is earmarked for financing investments; 3) from bank credit.

In addition to the means for financing investments, the amalgamations have separate funds for technical progress (for outlays for mastering new production techniques, for scientific research work, and so forth). They also have at their disposal a reserve fund which can be used for helping enterprises in overcoming temporary difficulties. All these funds come from the income or revenues of the enterprises. Thus the principle of self-financing of economic units is being implemented, and, at the same time, management and employees of the amalgamation are interested in improving operating results since the development of the given branch of industry depends on them. Their interest is strengthened by a system of incentives which relates the bonuses for management and for the whole administrative staff of the amalgamation to the operating results of all associated enterprises. Thus the amalgamations are becoming more and more active in providing assistance to enterprises in solving technical, organizational and supply difficulties and in adjusting production to market requirements. In many amalgamations market research units have been set up.

Other changes in the system of management are indirectly related to the role of the market, but are primarily intended to expedite the planning procedure. Particularly worth mentioning is an extension of the planning period and the introduction of the principle of providing for reserves in planning.

Experience has shown that plans stretched over several fields are difficult to implement, and in case of a breakdown in one spot a chain reaction sets in. Difficulties in one sector which cannot be overcome because of the lack of reserves result in difficulties in other sectors. Lack of reserves does not leave room for economic maneuver and reduces the effects of development. For these reasons it has been decided to provide for reserves in planning. This process has partly begun in the current five-year period and will be developed both in annual and in five-year planning.

The system comprises the following main reserves: investment; the wage fund; the balance sheet of personal income and expenditures; raw materials and other materials; and foreign exchange.

These reserves are of basic importance to the implementation of the five-year plan and are intended to insure the fulfillment of the plan in situations where unexpected difficulties arise.

All the changes described above considerably increase the role of the market, but do not reduce the decisive part played by the central plan. The point is that the market mechanism cannot function spontaneously in our type of economy; it is steered by the government which controls all the basic tools of economic policy. Second, government authorities not only can analyze and control the operations of economic units, but also are informed, through the system of planning, of long-run and short-run expansion plans for all economic organizations. For the limitation of the scope of the directive targets set in the plan does not mean that planning is being limited and that the central authorities are not being informed of the plans of economic organizations. Thus, the central authorities can always interfere in cases where the directions of activities of economic organisms are not consistent with the general premises of the economic development of the country or with the public interest. Third, it should not be forgotten that comprehensive and effective means of social and political influence are well developed.

All these factors indicate that there is no question of allowing spontaneous and uncontrolled forces to take over.

The essence of the introduction of a well-controlled market mechanism in our specific conditions is not a departure from the principle of central planning and management, but an attempt to use in the implementation of this principle more sensitive, precise and elastic instruments that can be reconciled with greater social initiative and can create better conditions for a rational behavior in the enterprise.

PART TWO

PLANNING AT THE INDUSTRY AND ENTERPRISE LEVEL

Chapter 6

PLANNING AT THE INDUSTRY LEVEL IN THE UNITED KINGDOM

AUBREY SILBERTSON

Cambridge University

INTRODUCTION

In recent years there has been a revival of interest in planning at the industry level in Britain. This has been closely associated with the moves that have been made to plan the economy more closely in order to insure steady growth without inflation and to avoid balance-of-payments difficulties. In this paper I shall not be concerned with planning at the national level since this has been discussed elsewhere, but I shall of course be concerned with the implications of national planning for planning at the industry level.

Before I describe recent developments, it may be as well to say that there has been a long history of governmental intervention in industry in the United Kingdom. Apart from general legislation regulating hours of work, minimum wages, the rights of trade unions, the financial structure of companies, and so forth, the government has been much concerned with legislative and other activities directed toward particular industries. By the time of the First World War, for example, the state had intervened to regulate the growth of the railways and to control prices and profits in railways, gas and electricity supply. In the interwar period there was further legislation regarding particular industries—for example, coal and cotton. During the Second World War, government intervention at the industrial level was, of course, very great. Partly as a result of this, the links between government and industry have been a good deal closer since the Second World War than before it. During the postwar period, the government has intervened considerably in private industry, and in addition a number of industries have been taken into public ownership.

PLANNING IN THE PERIOD 1930–1945

During the 1930's great problems were, of course, posed by the Great Depression and the slow recovery from it. At the same time, in the United Kingdom, there was the additional problem of a long-term decline in demand for the products of certain industries, notably cotton-textile manufacturing, coal mining and shipbuilding. The combined effect of these factors was that many industries found themselves in a very weak condition, and governmental action was taken to strengthen them in order to prevent their further decline, or, at the very least, to see that their decline was regulated in the least harmful way. Much stress was placed on rationalization. Already in the early 1920's, the government had brought about an amalgamation of the main-line railway companies into four large groups by Act of Parliament. In 1930, an Act was passed to rationalize the coal industry and to reduce competition in it. Just before the Second World War a similar Act was passed for the cotton-textile industry. Attempts were also made to help the steel companies. A heavy import duty was imposed in 1932 to protect the industry from strong foreign competition, and a government committee was given the task of insuring that the steel industry used the opportunity given to it by the tariff to reorganize itself and to carry out new investment. Agricultural marketing acts were passed in 1931 and 1933 to rationalize marketing and to control prices. Subsidies were given to agriculture, and imports of agricultural commodities were restricted over a wide range. In addition to these direct governmental attempts to rationalize industries and control competition in them, there were private schemes which received official support—for example, a scheme to reduce the capacity of the shipbuilding industry.

During the Second World War, the shortage of materials and manpower and the need to divert resources to war production led to very stringent controls over private industry. Industry was controlled partly through raw materials and partly through control of labor. In addition, government departments were given responsibility for the over-all control of industry, including power to concentrate industries into fewer manufacturing units. Members of the industries concerned played a considerable part in implementing these controls, either because they were seconded to government departments, or because existing trade associations were used by the government as instruments of control.

When the war came to an end, controls on industry were dismantled gradually, but by the mid-1950's virtually all the wartime controls had disappeared. Nevertheless, the system to which industry had become accustomed during the war—of having a particular government department as "sponsor" or "production" department for each major industry—remained in the postwar period. Under this system, every industry looks to a particular government department as the one that is primarily concerned with it and which examines its problems and potentialities. These sponsoring government departments are consulted by other parts of the government when any problem concerning one of their industries is involved, and the industries turn to their departments when they wish the government to change its policy (for example, on taxation) in order to help them. Industries also call on their sponsoring departments when they wish the government to intervene on their behalf in matters of overseas trade (for example, when they would like a tariff in an export market to be lowered or a discriminatory tax overseas to be removed).

PLANNING IN THE NATIONALIZED INDUSTRIES

Following the Second World War, the Labor Government nationalized the coal industry, the railways, the airlines, and the gas and electricity industries, among others. It also nationalized the iron and steel industry in 1949, but the industry was denationalized by the Conservative Government in 1953.

The pattern of government control over nationalized industries has followed that which had been set in previous cases of public ownership of utilities, such as the British Broadcasting Corporation and the London Passenger Transport Board. Government control over these industries is not direct. Each industry is administered by a board appointed by the government. The board is given a broad directive to provide an efficient and adequate service and to break even financially, taking one year with another, and is then left to run its industry. The minister has legal powers to give general directions to nationalized industries, but it is envisaged that he should only exercise these powers in the last resort. As to financial matters, however, the government has considerable power over the way the nationalized industries raise their funds for investment. It may also be called upon to subsidize losses in the nationalized industries, such as those that have been incurred on the railways. This financial control, together with the ultimate authority to give policy directions to the industry, gives the government, in practice, a good deal of influence over nationalized industries. The appropriate government department is always in close touch with its industry, and is given full information about its plans. Government departments are likely to be closely involved in decisions about new investment, and are also likely to be involved, especially at the present time, in decisions about prices, wages, and so on.

Having said this, one must not exaggerate the extent of government control over the nationalized industries. Their boards have a considerable degree of autonomy, and, when these industries have had strong chairmen, they have often managed to persuade the government not to oppose policies that the industries wished to adopt.

Government control of a fairly direct nature has not been confined to nationalized industries. Even after the iron and steel industry was denationalized, there was a government-appointed body, the Iron and Steel Board, which has had the task of supervising the investment and price policies of the industry. It has powers to delay investment, and it still lays down a maximum price for steel. It also has considerable influence on the size and pattern of new investment in the industry, and has pressed at different times for more expansion or more rationalization than the industry itself has wanted, with some measure of success.

Government control over nationalized or seminationalized industries is more direct and powerful than its control over private industry because of its influence in financial matters. When, for example, financial crises in the affairs of the country have occurred, the government has often decreed that the nationalized industries cut back their investment programs and, when the crisis has passed, has relaxed its control. In this way it has been able to exercise considerable influence over the total scale of investment in these industries, as well as on the type of investment carried out.

One should perhaps add that the government directly runs certain important sectors of the economy, such as education, the building of major roads, the post office, and the health service, through various central ministries and through local government authorities. Control over the investment and other policies of these sectors is very close—a good deal closer than that over the nationalized industries. In total, the annual investment of public authorities and nationalized industries is very substantial. It amounts to 45 to 50 per cent of gross domestic fixed capital formation in the United Kingdom.

PLANNING IN THE PRIVATE SECTOR

Direct government control over private industry is, as has been said, a good deal less strong than over nationalized industries. The "sponsoring" government departments of individual industries exert a certain amount of pressure, but their primary role is to act as channels of communication between their industries and the government. Even though sponsoring departments are now staffed by career civil servants, rather than by individuals seconded from industry, what seems to happen almost inevitably is that sponsoring departments become, to some extent at least, allies of their industries. They are critical allies, to be sure, but they normally consider it their role to foster good relations with their industries, and to take a sympathetic view of representations put forward by them. In a few industries (for example automobiles), formal committees have been set up, consisting of representatives of employers and workers in the industry, of members of various government departments, and also of independent members, but these committees also act primarily as channels of communication rather than as a means of government pressure or control.

I should perhaps say at this stage that there is one private industry—aircraft—which has, throughout its history, been subject to very considerable government control, and has rationalized its structure considerably as a result of governmental pressure. This industry, however, is in a unique position, both because of the military implications of decisions to manufacture aircraft, and of the degree of financial support that it has needed from the government.

To return to normal private industries—there was an attempt after the war to set up development councils for the major private industries. These councils included representatives of management and trade unions and also independent members, but the government was not represented. Their object was to provide for the internal coordination of their industries as much as for liaison between government and industry. These councils were not successful. Only two remain, one of them being the Cotton Board, which was first set up in 1939.

Throughout the postwar period a great deal of government money has been made available to finance research in industry, including private industry. In particular, the Department of Scientific and Industrial Research has shared the financing of some forty research associations, in specific industries, with the firms in those industries. Much of the work of the department in sponsoring research has now been taken over and extended by the newly formed Ministry of Technology. In addition to these industrial research associations, there are a number of research institutions, financed entirely by the government, which do work of interest to private industry. The government has also set up and financed the National Research Development Corporation, since the Second World War, to exploit inventions made in government and government-aided research establishments, and to exploit important inventions not taken up by private industry: of these Hovercraft is perhaps the best known. In total, the government provides 60 per cent of the funds used for research in the United Kingdom, including approximately 50 per cent of the funds used for research in private industry.

A new departure of great importance occurred in 1962. This was the setting up of the National Economic Development Council (NEDC), and the attempt to use it as an instrument for planning the growth of the economy. This has led, in my opinion, to a substantial change in the relationship between government and private industry.

The original role of the NEDC was to examine the performance and plans of industry, to consider obstacles to faster growth, and to seek agreement on ways to improve national competitive power and efficiency. The NEDC consists of representatives of the government, of industry, and of the trade unions. It has no executive power, but it was hoped that it would exert influence because of the eminence of its members and the fact that the chairman of the NEDC was originally the Chancellor of the Exchequer (the minister in charge of finance).

One of the first actions of the NEDC was to produce a report on growth in the economy of the United Kingdom during the period 1961–1966. A rate of growth of 4 per cent per annum for the economy as a whole was taken as a target, and the implications of this for investment, manpower, balance of payments, and so on, were considered. In the course of drawing up this plan a number of industries were consulted by the NEDC to discover what their investment and output plans for the period 1961–1966 were, and to consider whether these plans were consistent with the general national plan for growth.

Following this consultation between the NEDC and industry, it was agreed that it would be desirable to establish consultation on a more permanent basis. Steps were therefore taken to secure the establishment of consultative bodies for a wide range of industries, in order to insure that future work on the growth of the economy could be carried out in cooperation with the industries concerned. As a result, a number of Economic Development Committees of "Little Neddies," as they are often called, were set up, and their number is still growing. The first was set up in 1964, and, by mid-1966, there will be approximately twenty-five in existence.

Since the EDC's were first set up there has been a change in governmental organization, and the Department of Economic Affairs has come into being. This department is now responsible for national planning, and produced "The National Plan" in September 1965, to review the growth of the economy during the period to 1970. The National Economic Development Council (together with its Office) remains, however, and is responsible for the EDC's for particular industries. The chairman of the NEDC is now the minister in charge of the Department of Economic Affairs.

When the National Plan was being drawn up in 1965, the sections on particular industries were referred to the relevant EDC's, and the EDC's helped, to some extent, to shape the projections for their industries. The main role of the EDC's, however, is to improve the efficiency of the industries for which they are responsible, and to see that their industries contribute toward the achievement of the national growth target. If obstacles to the achievement of the growth target are seen to arise in their industries, it is the task of the EDC's to see what can be done to remove them. The EDC's have, therefore, a more positive role to play in coordinating the plans of government and industry than most previous committees or councils for particular industries that have been set up.

The membership of the EDC's is not, at first sight, particularly unusual. The EDC for any particular industry consists of industrialists and trade unionists drawn from that industry, together with representatives of the Department of Economic Affairs and of the NEDC office. There is also a representative of the sponsoring government department for the industry and a few independent members—economists, management experts, and so on. The most unusual feature of the membership of the EDC's, however, is the fact that their chairmen are independent. They are normally very senior men from industry or commerce, who have no connection with the particular industry with which their EDC is dealing. The independent chairmen give the EDC's a flavor quite unlike that of committees which have ministers or civil servants in the chair. Because of their eminence, the chairmen are respected by the representatives of industry, and, at the same time, they have the confidence to act independently of the government machine. They are in a powerful position, therefore, to speak frankly both to representatives of the industry and to government officials. The independent members also have a somewhat unusual role to play, in that they are virtually encouraged, by the whole circumstances of the EDC's, to be critical of industries in the presence of their management and union representatives.

The EDC's were, as has been said, consulted in the course of drawing up the National Plan which was published in 1965. As they establish themselves, it is likely that they will have more influence on the plan's industrial targets than they have so far had. However, their most important role is to see what can be done to help their industries to improve their efficiency. For this purpose, EDC's carry out investigations and make recommendations both to their industries and to the government. The EDC, with which I am connected as an independent member, for instance, has working parties, as they are called, on manpower, imports, exports, technological development, and financial control. These working parties have already commissioned studies of comparative labor productivity in industry, and of the optimum scale of production in different sections of the industry. Attention is also being paid by the EDC to the possibilities of rationalization, of import saving, and of improving the flow of exports.

Another EDC has recommended that the government stimulate innovation in the machine tool industry through the purchase of "prototype" advanced machine tools, and has carried out detailed studies of the imports of machine tools, to find out to what extent these imports can be replaced by machine tools manufactured in Britain. The EDC concerned with electrical engineering has brought about an agreement to reduce the types of electrical distribution cables from 250 to 50, and attempts are now being made to achieve greater standardization in the manufacture of electrical transformers. Yet another EDC has improved cooperation between chemical manufacturers and the manufacturers of chemical plant, with the object of improving the availability of plant for the investment program of the chemical industry.

EDC's are not left simply to pursue their own devices. From time to time, the responsible minister asks the EDC's for advice on particular problems, for example, on import saving in their industries, and makes requests for investigations to be carried out and a report sent to him within a relatively short time.

In all these ways, therefore, the EDC's are very active, and the critical spirit toward their industries which their activity has engendered is something relatively new in British industry.

When all this has been said, it has to be recognized that the planning activities of the government in relation to private industry are still of an "indicative" nature. The government draws up plans for the growth of investment, output, and productivity in various industries, with the help both of mathematical models of the economy and of consultation with industry. But the implementation of these plans is not made mandatory on private industry in any way. Taxation and other indirect methods are used to push industries in the directions that the government would like to see, and pressure is exerted through the EDC's and other channels, but that is all.

In what sense then is there planning in private industry in Britain? There is certainly very little in any strict sense of the word. However, the very process of producing a national plan has given rise to an atmosphere in which the government appears committed to the growth of the economy. Because of this, there is perhaps rather more assurance for private firms, when formulating their investment plans, that the government will not allow growth to be held back, and the profitability of investment to be seriously prejudiced. In addition, the formulation and discussion of investment plans for individual industries probably leads to greater coordination of investment than would otherwise be the case. The effect of this is beneficial in saving resources which might otherwise be duplicated, although one could of course argue that a certain amount of competitive over-investment is not without its advantages. Finally, the activities of the EDC's in stimulating their industries to achieve the targets of the national plan, and to improve their efficiency generally, must not be underrated. It is, however, still early to assess at all fully the effectiveness of the EDC's.

OTHER GOVERNMENT MEASURES

The activities of the government affect industry in so many ways that it is impossible to list them all. Obviously taxation of a general character is very important, whether it is taxation on commodities sold to the public or on the profits of companies. The government also uses taxation in a directional manner, to stimulate investment, for example, in particular industries. Recently there has been instituted a system of investment cash grants which are available for manufacturing industry, for example, but not for investment in the distribution of goods or the provision of services.

The government also makes loans and grants to particular industries when they are in difficulty, or when it is considered that the national interest requires their expansion or rationalization.

Financial measures have also been used to deal with regional problems. Certain areas of the United Kingdom, notably Scotland, South Wales, Northern Ireland and the North East coast, have been less prosperous in the past than the rest of the country. This is mainly because of the fact that there is concentration of "old" industries in these areas. Since the end of the Second World War, the government has pursued a policy of inducing new industries to go to these parts of the country. It has provided grants and loans, new factory premises, helped with the retraining of workers, and so on. It has also imposed restraint on factory and office building in the more prosperous parts of the country. Perhaps its most striking activity in the regional sphere has been the bulding of new towns, although these new towns have been built to help with congestion problems as well as to improve the prosperity of depressed areas. Recently regional planning boards and advisory councils have been set up in all regions in a further attempt to plan rationally at the regional level.

The government has been very active in quite another sphere—that of the control of monopoly and restrictive practices. Before the Second World War there was virtually no legal restraint on these practices. Since the war, there have been a succession of laws which have progressively tightened up control over monopolistic practices. In 1948, the Monopolies Commission was set up, and in 1956, the Restrictive Practices Court. The Monopolies Commission is now concerned with cases of single-firm monopoly (including the prices charged by these monopolies), with restrictive practices in the supply of services, and with the investigation of mergers between companies. The Restrictive Practices Court is concerned with restrictive agreements in the supply of goods and with the investigation of resale price maintenance on the part of individual manufacturers. The enforcement of collective resale price maintenance was declared illegal in 1956. The impact of all these measures has been growing, especially since 1956 when the Restrictive Practices Court was set up. A very large number of restrictive agreements have been abandoned, and competition in British industry has undoubtedly increased. Mergers also are being looked at with a more critical eye, and resale price maintenance appears to be crumbling. In the sphere of mergers there appears to be some divergence of view between different government departments. Those concerned with the national plan tend to favor mergers, because they can lead to economies of large-scale production and to rationalization. The department concerned with the control of monopoly is more suspicious of mergers, although it has in fact not held up the great majority of mergers referred to it. Now, a new government body, the Industrial Reorganization Corporation, is being set up to bring about industrial rationalization and reorganization. This body will undoubtedly encourage mergers, but it will also provide a means of acquiring for the government shares in private firms, and thus of strengthening its influence over them.

Finally, I should mention the attempt to control prices and incomes which the Labor Government has pursued since 1964. A new advisory board was set up to review cases of increased wages and prices, and to make recommendations to the government. Now an Act is to be passed requiring projected wage and price increases to be notified to the government, and this is already being done on a voluntary basis. No mandatory powers are being sought, and the government is continuing to rely on influence and pressure to moderate the rate of increase of wages and prices. The advisory board is, however, very active and is attempting to see that increases in wages above the norm are linked with increases in efficiency. In this way it is bringing pressure to bear on both unions and employers to revise working practices and save resources.

CONCLUSION

It is obvious from what I have said that planning at the industry level, in the normally accepted sense of that term, is not extensively employed in the United Kingdom today. However, governmental control and influence over industry is exercised in a very large number of ways, and the tendency is for this control and influence to grow. If the iron and steel industry, and perhaps other industries, are nationalized, the sphere within which the government will have a direct influence will widen, but it is by no means clear that government influence over private industry is notably less than its influence over nationalized industry. It has, indeed, been argued that government influence is at its height when the government threatens to nationalize an industry but does not actually do so! Whatever the truth of this, it is certain that Britain is now far from being a privately owned and controlled "free enterprise" economy in the textbook sense of the phrase.

Chapter 7

STRATEGIC PLANNING IN AMERICAN INDUSTRY

ROBERT S. WEINBERG

International Business Machines Corporation

During the past decade, and particularly the last five years, there has been a series of subtle changes in the business environment in the United States. Four significant ones have taken place: 1) the increased availability of timely and accurate data describing the business environment itself; 2) the increased availability of computers (most larger companies now have their own, and small companies are able to make use of the largest computer at a data center or service bureau); 3) the increased availability of powerful, new analytical techniques developed in the fields of mathematical model-building, operations research, and management science; 4) the increased need for sound evaluations of the business situation, as well as for more accurate and consistent operating and long-range plans. The structure of the economy itself is changing; new marketing opportunities will disappear; business will be more competitive, and customers will be more demanding. The large expenditures required to take advantage of new marketing opportunities and the long "lead-time" required to open and penetrate new markets will underscore the need for integrated market planning. The stakes are becoming too high to allow for a short-term, hit-or-miss strategy.

The first three changes in the business environment have created a situation where the *logistical support* necessary to sustain a "managerial revolution" is, for the first time, available. The fourth change—and possibly the most significant—creates the *incentive* for the "revolution." Our old tools are no longer good enough—we need new tools. Business problems are becoming too complicated, and the risks of a wrong solution too great, to allow us not to use the most advanced techniques available for business problem-solving.

Out of these changes has come a great interest in various concepts of business planning—particularly long-term strategic planning. To understand the nature of the long-term strategic planning process, we must first understand the top-management process itself. Much has been written on the subject of what top executives do. Through the years various authors and researchers have surveyed the upper ranks of American management. The results have been published in leading business periodicals, university and association research reports, and books on management. Care must be taken in interpreting these surveys. In many cases the results are too general or theoretical to be useful, and in other cases the survey shows how management would like to spend its time rather than how it actually does spend it. Based on an analysis of published surveys and on my own discussions with company board chairmen, presidents, and other key executives throughout the United States and in Europe, I conclude that most top executives are concerned with seven broad management activities: 1) setting the company's short- and long-term objectives; 2) determining the company's over-all prices; 3) making or approving decisions that will have a significant impact on the company's profits or future operations; 4) coordinating several major corporate functions; 5) developing and maintaining an organization of qualified subordinates; 6) delegating responsibility and authority to the organization; and 7) controlling performance and results through at least one level of supervision.

It is interesting to note that most top executives appear to regard working toward the achievement of their company's over-all objective as their own number-one objective. The activity of planning and setting the company's policies and objectives rates second as a universal top-management activity. Indeed, it is this activity that is probably most uniquely reserved for top management. The final approval of company objectives, over-all policies, and corporate strategies is a prerogative that few managers are willing to share with their subordinates. Strategic planning, therefore, is one of the most potentially important and useful tools for top management. Speaking quite frankly, however, relatively few companies are taking full advantage of this tool. Only a small fraction of the total resources that companies are allocating to the planning function are being spent on the development and operation of a meaningful strategic planning system. There are four major reasons for this situation: 1) the concept of strategic planning in business is relatively new; 2) the real need to develop a strategic planning system is relatively recent; 3) the development of a meaningful strategic planning system requires top-management support, understanding, and participation; 4) there is too great a temptation to be preoccupied with immediate answers to immediate problems at the expense of true long-range planning.

As indicated, the general environment of business is changing, and at the same time new management planning and control concepts and tools are becoming available. The new tools and concepts provide the "logistical base" from which a strategic planning system may be developed. The changing business environment has created a need for strategic planning. In the past (particularly in the immediate postwar period, and for many companies even through the late 1950's) the business environment was stable or was changing in a systematic, predictable manner, and major decisions could be made on the basis of immediate past experience (trend following) or intuition alone. In the rapidly changing environment of the past five years, however, old rules of thumb no longer seem to work as well. Management can no longer afford to set its objectives and establish its strategies by guess work. Most thoughtful managers realize this and are deeply concerned. They recognize the need to develop a system that will allow their staff executives to gather and analyze meaningful facts and develop an objective, factual picture of the company's operating environment. They realize that they must learn to manage by analysis and not by consensus alone. The groundwork for strategic planning has been laid.

Consider now the nature of strategic planning and the distinction between it, tactical planning, and operating or budget planning. There are three different approaches to planning. Each approach represents an important and useful tool for management.

1) *Strategic planning* is concerned with the determination of objectives and with the selection of the most attractive (profitable) combination of available alternatives for achieving these objectives. 2) *Tactical planning* is concerned with determining the most efficient use of the resources that have been allocated for achieving an already specified objective. 3) *Operating or budget planning* is concerned with the development of a control mechanism

to assure the effective implementation of the actions specified in the strategic and tactical plans and for providing a basis for the measurement of actual performances relative to plan.

Top management will, of course, be interested in all three approaches to planning, but, of the three, only the strategic planning process is concerned with top management's most crucial problem—setting corporate objectives and determining the company's over-all strategies. The purpose of a strategic planning system is to assist corporate management in making better and faster decisions in a rapidly changing business environment. This planning system must provide a logical and accurate quantitative (factual) basis for considering nine basic problems: 1) preparing a program of alternative, feasible corporate objectives and the resources and strategies required to attain them (this will assist management in objective setting); 2) focusing management's attention and judgment on major problem areas or, more important, potential future problem areas (one of the most important uses for a planning system is to allow management to anticipate future problem areas and to take the corrective action necessary to avoid a problem situation before it becomes a problem); 3) evaluating many different alternative strategies (with the use of mathematical planning models and computers it becomes practical to consider literally millions of possible strategy alternatives); 4) evaluating specific proposals or opportunities (the use of mathematical planning models and computers allows the planner to consider the company as a whole or as a collection of specific markets or opportunities; it is therefore possible to superimpose the impact of any specific proposal or new opportunity development effort on the total operations of the company to perform a before and after analysis); 5) conducting feasibility analyses (here we are concerned with resource requirements and availability and with the time phasing or scheduling of resource "producing" and "consuming" activities); 6) diagnostic evaluation of the company's current performance (here we are concerned with developing an objective appraisal of the company's current operations); for example, finding out to what extent a change in profits represents a change (a) in the level of economic activity; (b) the relationship between the industry and the economy; (c) the level of competition within the industry; (d) a change in the company's sales/profits relation (cost structure), and so forth; 7) discovering new areas of opportunity or advance warning of the possible deterioration of existing areas of opportunities (in this area market research must play an important part in measuring market potential and in determining the rate at which new markets can be expected to open or new products will displace older existing products); 8) measuring the impact of a possible change in the company's operating environment on its performance (here we are concerned with developing a kind of "min-max" approach to determining future strategy—that is, to determine a strategy that will produce a maximum result even under the most adverse possible future circumstances); 9) establishing action priorities and action timetables (in addition to knowing *what* action should be taken it is often more important to know *when* this action should be taken).

To provide solutions to these problems, the strategic planning system must be designed with certain specific technical or methodological needs in mind. The system must provide a basis for carrying out analyses and evaluations in marginal or incremental terms rather than in terms of averages. This is an extremely important point. In the absence of information, there is a strong tendency to consider average cost or expenditure productivity factors. Such a practice can easily lead to a misallocation of resources. Consider the following example. A company markets two products, Product A and Product B. For the first six months of 1965, marketing and profit performance of these products can be seen in Table 2.

From Table 2, it will be noted that Products A and B contributed 1,100 thousand and 1,625 thousand dollars respectively to the company's total pre-tax profits. The company spent 400 thousand dollars promoting Product A, and 500 thousand dollars promoting Product B. *On the average* a dollar's worth of promotional expense allocated to Product A produced 2.75 dollars in pre-tax net profits. Similarly, a dollar's worth of promotional expense allocated to Product B produced 3.25 dollars in pre-tax net profits.

Table 2. Marketing and profit performance of Products A and B (6 mos. of 1965).

Category	Product A	Product B
Sales (units)	100,000	85,000
Profit per unit excluding promotional expenses (dollars)	15	25
Total profit, excluding promotional expenses (dollars)	1,500,000	2,125,000
Promotional effort (dollars)	400,000	500,000
Pre-tax net profits (dollars)	1,100,000	1,625,000
Sales per dollar of promotional expense (units)	0.25	0.17
Net profit per dollar of promotional expense (dollars)	2.75	3.25

In June 1965, the company discovered that as a result of exceeding its original sales forecasts for other products it could afford to increase its promotional expenditures by 100 thousand dollars. (For the sake of simplicity we will assume that the company has already committed 400 thousand and 500 thousand dollars respectively for promotional expenditures for Products A and B, and that these commitments cannot be changed. We will also assume that all of the 100 thousand-dollar increment of additional promotional expenditures must be allocated to a single product.) On the basis of the *average* profit return per dollar of promotional expense estimates shown in Table 2, the company's management decided to allocate the additional 100 thousand dollars to Product B. On the basis of these *average rate of return* factors, it appeared that a dollar spent promoting Product B produced 18.1 per cent more profit than a dollar spent promoting Product A (that is, 3.25/2.75 = 1.181). The mistake the company made in arriving at this decision was ignoring the *marginal productivity* of the additional 100 thousand dollars of promotional effort. It turned out that an additional 100 thousand dollars spent promoting Product B would not yield 17,000 additional units in sales, but only 11,333 units (the marginal productivity of the incremental promotional expenditures was not 0.17, but only 0.1133). The marginal productivity of an additional 100 thousand dollars of promotional expenditures allocated to Product A, however, would have been 0.2875 instead of the average rate of 0.25. In the case of Product B, the level of promotional effort expended by the company and its competitors had reached a saturation point yielding sharply diminishing returns on any additional promotional expenditure. The Product A market, however, was still sufficiently undeveloped so that any increase in promotional effort would produce increasing returns. The company using *average productivity factors* as a basis for its decision produced the results shown in Table 3.

The company's total pre-tax net profit during the second half of the year was 2,908,325 dollars, up 183,325 dollars over the first half of the year. However, had the company been using a *marginal* or *incremental analysis* in determining its promotional resource allocation, it would have committed the additional 100 thousand dollars to Product A, producing the results in Table 4.

The company's total pre-tax net profits from Products A and B would be 3,056,250 million dollars, 147,925 dollars greater than the profits the company realized as a result of the misallocation, and a 331,250 dollar increase over the first half of the year. Had the company been thinking in marginal or incremental terms rather than in terms of averages, the 100

Table 3. Marketing and profit performance of Products A and B using average productivity factors (6 mos. of 1965).

Category	Product A	Product B
Sales (units)	100,000	96,333
Profit per unit excluding promotional expenses (dollars)	15	25
Total profit, excluding promotional expenses (dollars)	1,500,000	2,408,325
Promotional effort (dollars)	400,000	600,000
Pre-tax net profits (dollars)	1,100,000	1,808,325
Sales per dollar of promotional expense (units)	0.25	0.161
Net profit per dollar of promotional expense (dollars)	2.75	3.01

thousand dollars in additional promotional expenditures would have produced 331,250 dollars in additional profits instead of only 183,325 dollars. It could have increased its incremental gain by almost 81 per cent by using the correct allocation procedure. I cite this example in detail because it illustrates one of the most common mistakes made by management in handling resource allocation problems.

The strategic planning system must be designed to allow any analysis to be carried out at the most meaningful level of aggregation. If too much detail is considered, the system becomes too cumbersome. If, however, the analysis is too aggregate, important structural interrelationships will be lost

Table 4. Marketing and profit performance of Products A and B using marginal (or incremental) analysis (6 mos. of 1965).

Category	Product A	Product B
Sales (units)	128,750	85,000
Profit per unit, excluding promotional expenses (dollars)	15	25
Total profit, excluding promotional expenses (dollars)	1,931,250	2,125,000
Promotional effort (dollars)	500,000	500,000
Pre-tax net profits (dollars)	1,431,250	1,625,000
Sales per dollar of promotional expenses (units)	0.2575	0.17
Net profit per dollar of promotional expense (dollars)	2.86	3.25

in the aggregation process. The aggregation problem becomes important when several different individual products or market sectors are added together to develop a product or market group total. For example, it is possible for a company marketing in two or more submarkets to observe a completely different picture of its operations if an evaluation of its performance is made on a total market rather than a submarket basis. The competitive performance of the American Tobacco Company from 1950 through 1959 offers a dramatic example of this phenomenon. (The cigarette market is one of the few markets for which company sales and brand sales data are published. The estimates were prepared by H. M. Wooten, and were published in *Printers' Ink* magazine).

From Table 5 we would draw the conclusion that American Tobacco's competitive performance was favorable during the first half of the decade and highly unfavorable during the second half. In the absence of any further data, we might reach the conclusion that something went wrong with the company's marketing programs. If, however, instead of considering the cigarette market as a whole (a high level of analytical aggregation), we disaggregated the market into four submarkets representing the four types of cigarettes being marketed, a completely different picture emerges. (See Tables 6–9.)

Tables 7 through 9 correspond to Table 5, but instead of analyzing the

Table 5. Competitive performance of the American Tobacco Company (1950–1959).

Years	Total industry cigarette sales[a]	American Tobacco cigarette sales	American Tobacco Company	
			Share of the market	Net change in share of the market
	(billions of cigarettes)		(per cent)	
1950	361.4	113.0	31.27	—
1951	377.4	121.0	32.06	+0.79
1952	391.7	128.5	32.81	+0.75
1953	391.0	127.8	32.69	−0.12
1954	367.1	123.0	33.51	+0.82
1955	377.8	124.0	32.82	−0.69
1956	388.5	122.3	31.48	−1.34
1957	407.5	119.0	29.20	−2.28
1958	433.5	115.5	26.64	−2.56
1959	460.2	120.6	26.21	−0.43

[a] Big six manufacturers.

Table 6. Total industry cigarette sales, by product class (1950–1959).

Year	Regular	King	Filter	Mentholated	Total
			(billions of cigarettes)		
1950	314.7	35.3	2.2	9.2	361.4
1951	315.7	48.0	3.2	10.5	377.4
1952	305.0	70.3	4.9	11.5	391.7
1953	264.8	102.4	12.3	11.5	391.0
1954	215.8	102.0	37.2	12.1	367.1
1955	193.4	97.7	74.0	12.7	377.8
1956	172.4	91.2	108.6	16.3	388.5
1957	154.5	84.3	142.3	26.4	407.5
1958	142.7	86.2	167.5	37.1	433.5
1959	136.8	86.4	185.3	51.7	460.2

total cigarette market we have broken the market into four broad product classes, regular cigarettes, king-size, filter-tip, and mentholated. From Table 9 the following significant trends in American Tobacco's share of the market are evident: 1) In 1951 the company's share of a major submarket (regular cigarettes) was down, but the increase in its share of the king-size market (and the increased importance of this market) created a situation where its share of the total market increased. 2) In 1952 the company's share of both markets in which it operated decreased, yet its share of the total market increased. 3) In 1953 the company suffered a major loss in the king-size market and a slight gain in the regular market yielding a slight decline in the total market. 4) In 1954 the company made substantial gains in all three submarkets but registered only a slight gain in its share of the

Table 7. American Tobacco Company cigarette sales, by product class (1950–1959).

Year	Regular	King	Filter	Mentholated	Total
			(billions of cigarettes)		
1950	82.5	30.5	—	—	113.0
1951	79.0	42.0	—	—	121.0
1952	73.5	55.0	—	—	128.5
1953	66.3	61.5	—	—	127.8
1954	58.5	63.0	1.5	—	123.0
1955	57.5	63.0	3.5	—	124.0
1956	55.5	61.4	5.4	—	122.3
1957	51.5	59.4	8.1	—	119.0
1958	47.2	61.5	6.8	—	115.5
1959	44.5	66.2	9.7	0.2	120.6

Table 8. American Tobacco Company share of the market, by product class (1950–1959).

Year	Regular	King	Filter	Mentholated	Total
			(per cent)		
1950	26.22	86.40	—	—	31.27
1951	25.02	87.50	—	—	32.06
1952	24.10	78.23	—	—	32.81
1953	25.04	60.06	—	—	32.69
1954	27.11	61.77	4.03	—	33.51
1955	29.73	64.48	4.73	—	32.82
1956	32.19	67.32	4.97	—	31.48
1957	33.33	70.46	5.69	—	29.20
1958	33.08	71.35	4.06	—	26.64
1959	32.53	76.62	5.23	0.39	26.21

total market. 5) In 1955, 1956, and 1957, the company increased its share in each submarket in which it operated, but its share of the total market declined. 6) In 1958 and 1959, the company's performance in each of its submarkets was significantly better than its total market performance (this was particularly true in 1959).

It is interesting to note that in four of the nine years studied (1952, 1955, 1956, and 1957), American Tobacco's market performance in each of its submarkets was exactly the opposite of its performance in the total market. How is it possible for a company to increase its market share in every market in which it operates and still suffer from a declining share of the total market? The answer lies in the fact that there were significant shifts

Table 9. American Tobacco Company net change in share of the market, by product class (1951–1959).

Year	Regular	King	Filter	Mentholated	Total
			(per cent)		
1951	−1.20	+1.10	—	—	+0.79
1952	−0.92	−9.27	—	—	+0.75
1953	+0.94	−18.17	—	—	−0.12
1954	+2.07	+1.71	+4.03	—	+0.82
1955	+2.62	+2.71	+0.70	—	−0.69
1956	+2.46	+2.84	+0.24	—	−1.34
1957	+1.14	+3.14	+0.72	—	−2.28
1958	−0.25	+0.89	−1.63	—	−2.56
1959	−0.55	+5.27	+1.17	+0.39	−0.43

Table 10. The structure of the cigarette market (1950–1959).

Year	Regular	King	Filter	Mentholated	Total
		(percentage of total market)			
1950	87.08	9.77	0.61	2.54	100.00
1951	83.65	12.72	0.85	2.78	100.00
1952	77.87	17.95	1.24	2.94	100.00
1953	67.72	26.19	3.15	2.94	100.00
1954	58.78	27.79	10.13	3.30	100.00
1955	51.19	25.86	19.59	3.36	100.00
1956	44.38	23.47	27.95	4.20	100.00
1957	37.91	20.69	34.92	6.48	100.00
1958	32.92	19.86	38.64	8.56	100.00
1959	29.73	18.77	40.27	11.23	100.00

in the structure of the total market. Table 10 shows the percentage distribution of total industry cigarette sales.

If we examine the changing structure of the market, we can easily see the reason for the paradoxical behavior of American Tobacco's share in 1952, 1955, 1956, and 1957. In 1952 the company was getting a smaller share of a submarket that was winning a larger share of the total market; therefore it recorded a larger share of the total market. In 1955, 1956, and 1957, the company captured a significantly larger share of two declining submarkets (regular and king-size cigarettes) and only a moderately increasing share of the expanding filter tip submarket; the net effect is a decrease in its share of the total market.

In general the 1951–1959 trend in the net changes in American Tobacco's share of the total cigarette market reflects the company's product development strategy more than its marketing (that is, advertising and sales promotion) strategies. The company was a leader in king-size cigarettes and benefited from the consumers' shift to king-size cigarettes which occurred from 1950 through 1954. The company failed to exploit the filter-tip cigarette markets which gained increased importance beginning in 1955 and the mentholated cigarette market which began to grow relatively rapidly in 1956.

My point in introducing this example is to illustrate in concrete terms the importance of developing a planning system at the proper level of aggregation. It is clear that the diagnostic value of analyzing the single share of the market statistic was limited if not completely misleading. The analysis of individual submarket market shares and of the changes in the structure (composition) of the total market, however, offers valuable insights useful in appraising the company's true market position. The use of computers and mechanized planning models makes it practical to consider the operations of a company at a relatively fine level of detail. Before high-speed electronic computers were widely available it was not practical to build a large-scale planning model incorporating the degree of detail (level of disaggregation) necessary to answer questions that must be answered to develop a corporate strategy. But this bottleneck has been broken. Using modern computers, it is both feasible and practical to consider the interactions and interrelationships among thousands of variables.

In addition to having the ability to analyze problems marginally or incrementally and at a realistic and meaningful level of aggregation, the strategic planning system must consider two other needs. It must provide a basis for understanding (and defining) the interrelationships between interrelated activities. The importance of this point is obvious. Consider the following example. A large West Coast air-conditioning sales and service company was about to discontinue its servicing operations. The company's accountants indicated that in 1964 the company made 163,822 service calls. On the average, each call cost the company 9.27 dollars. Because of the high degree of competition in the air-conditioning service business, the company's average service charge was only 7.85 dollars. Reviewing the service activity alone, it was clear that gross income was 1,286,600.27 dollars, and total costs and expenses were 1,518,629.94 dollars, yielding a net loss of 232,029.67 dollars.

But the service activity should not be considered in a vacuum. It should be reviewed as part of the company's total operations. An analysis of the company's sales records showed that on the average about 12.3 per cent of the service calls resulted in the sale of a new air-conditioning unit as a replacement for the existing unit. The company's salesmen were not paid full commissions on these service-referred sales. The average commission paid to salesmen was 38.45 dollars a unit on new business, and only 15.10 dollars on service-referred business. The service activity resulted in 20,150 (163,822 × 0.123) replacement air-conditioning unit sales. These sales were made at the reduced sales commission, saving the company 23.35 dollars a unit in sales expense. The replacement sales therefore contributed an additional 470,502.50 dollars to the company's profits (that is, 23.35 × 20,150). While the service activity yielded a *direct loss* of 232,029.67 dollars, it also yielded an *indirect profit* of 470,502.50 dollars. The true net contribution of the service activity to the company's profits was, therefore, 238,472.83 dollars. This activity should not be discontinued.

The planning system must recognize interrelationships between activities of the type discussed above. For purposes of analysis, any business can be regarded as a collection of activities each consuming inputs (from other activities) and producing outputs. The planning model will represent a mathematical formulation of these input-output relationships. One of the greatest values of the strategic planning system is that the development of the planning model itself requires careful analysis and consideration of the interconnections between the various factors that contribute to the company's profits. In building the planning model, we have an unusual opportunity to review and evaluate all aspects of the company's operations. Since the model is formulated mathematically, there is little room for vague or "fuzzy" thinking. As the model is being developed, many important questions that would otherwise be avoided must be answered. As these questions are answered, management will gain new insights regarding many of the more subtle factors that influence the company's profits.

The final basic need that must be recognized in developing a strategic planning system is the one to recognize and understand timing patterns— that is, the time-lags and lead-times that will determine the ultimate feasibility or success of a venture. Here we are concerned with developing a time-phased schedule of the actions that must take place, or the resources that must be committed, to achieve a desired objective. Time is one of the most important variables in the strategic planning equation. A strategy that does not consider lead-times and make proper allowances for time-lags will be doomed to failure. As indicated, every action a business takes must be specified in two dimensions. The action itself must be defined, and the timing of this action must be indicated. In addition to knowing what to do, management must know when to do it. The importance of timing is emphasized in management's current interest in PERT, Critical Path Scheduling, and other network analysis planning techniques. Only by understanding the dynamic (temporal) interrelationships between the factors that determine the ultimate outcome of each strategic decision can we be sure that the actions specified in the company's strategic plan are consistent, feasible, and optimal.

In the discussion above we were concerned with some of the specific technical or methodological needs that must be considered in developing a strategic planning system. We might call these needs "design specifications" or "requirements." Consider now the needs of the users of the strategic planning system. How will top management use the strategic planning system? The system will provide corporate management with a tool for testing and evaluating decisions involving the major strategic "trade-offs" that must be considered in setting the company's objectives and in developing corporate strategy. The system will assist management in determining the most profitable balance between conflicting objectives. With few exceptions, the major problems concerning top management fall into the following five broad categories: 1) short-term profits *vs.* long-term growth; 2) profit margin *vs.* competitive position; 3) direct sales effort *vs.* market development effort; 4) penetration of existing markets *vs.* the development of new markets; 5) related *vs.* unrelated new opportunities as a source of long-term growth.

The five strategic "trade-offs" are fundamental to the management of any business. The long-term success of any large enterprise is crucially dependent on top management's ability to establish corporate policies and objectives and develop growth strategies that reflect the most favorable combinations of these "trade-offs." An analysis of the growth and profit performance of leading American chemical companies since 1955 illustrates the importance of these "strategic trade-offs" to the chemical industry. Consider first the industry as a whole. The Federal Trade Commission-Securities and Exchange Commission *Quarterly Financial Report for Manufacturing Corporations* publishes timely data on net sales and net profits after taxes for the Chemicals and Allied Products Industry (SIC Code 28). In 1955, total industry sales were 20,099 million dollars. In the nine years between 1955 and 1964, total industry sales grew at an average rate of 6.8 per cent per annum. By 1964, total industry sales were 36,336 million dollars. Between 1955 and 1959, total industry net profits after taxes averaged 7.74 per cent of net sales. Between 1960 and 1964, the industry's average profit rate declined modestly (about 2.7 per cent) to 7.53 per cent. Against this background it is interesting to consider the growth and profit performance of specific leading chemical companies. Table 11 was computed from data contained in the company annual reports and the *Fortune* 500 List.

Table 11 compares the growth and profit performance of the five largest American chemical companies with that of the total industry. This table may be used to analyze the net results of the various growth and profit strategies each of these companies followed during the 1955–1964 period. The following major trends appear evident:

Table 11. Growth and profit performances of leading American chemical companies.

| Company | Nine-year (1955–1964) average annual growth rate per cent (1) | New profits after taxes as a percentage of net sales | | Percentage change in net profit rate (4) = (3)/(2) |
		1955–1959 Average (2)	1960–1964 Average (3)	
Du Pont	4.2	20.31	18.21	−10.34
Union Carbide	5.2	10.65	9.76	− 8.41
Monsanto	11.2	7.22	7.59	+ 5.55
Dow	8.4	8.62	7.99	− 6.98
Allied	5.8	6.81	7.38	+ 8.82
Total industry	6.8	7.74	7.53	− 2.71

1) In general there is an inverse relationship between the growth and the profit rate. For example, Du Pont and Union Carbide followed a strategy that maintained their profit margins at a level significantly above that of the industry as a whole. To maintain this position, however, the companies had to be highly selective in their choices of markets resulting in a significantly below-average nine-year average growth rate. Allied Chemical appears to have followed a strategy that would allow the company to improve its below-average profit rate. To do this the company also sacrificed growth.

2) Monsanto's performance in the chemical fiber market (through the acquisition of Chemstrand in January 1961) and in developing other new products and markets yielded both an improvement in the company's profit rate, against the total industry trend, and a significantly higher-than-average nine-year growth rate.

3) Dow Chemical appears to have been able to maintain both a higher-than-average growth rate and a higher-than-average profit rate.

4) In general, the higher above average a company's profit rate was during the 1955–1959 period, the more it declined during the 1960–1964 period. This trend reflects the high degree of competition within the industry. Conversely, the only improvement in profit rates was achieved by the two companies with below-average profit rates during the 1955–1959 period.

The five strategic "trade-offs" are particularly important to the chemical industry. The problem of determining the proper balance between short-term

Table 12. Comparing expenditures with current net profits after taxes in leading chemical companies.

Company	1964 research & development and related expenditures		1964 net profits after taxes (3)	Research & devel. expenditures in post-tax dollars as a percentage of net profits (4) = (2)/(3) — 100
	Pre-tax dollars (1)	Post-tax dollars (2) = 0.52(1)		
Du Pont	59[a]	30.7	471.4	6.51
Du Pont	110[b]	57.2	471.4	12.13
Union Carbide	80	41.6	189.1	22.00
Monsanto	67	34.8	114.9	30.29
Dow	64[c]	33.3	93.8	35.50
Allied	29	15.1	81.0	18.64

Source: Company Annual Reports except as noted.

[a] Pioneering research only as reported in Du Pont's 1964 *Annual Report*.

[b] Total research and development estimated by the author, based on the 1960 relationship between total research and development expenditures and pioneering research expenditures as discussed in the company's 1960 *Annual Report*.

[c] The author's estimate based on the statement that research and development expenditures are roughly 6.0 per cent of sales (Dow 1964 *Annual Report*).

profits and long-term growth is one of major importance to the management of any research- and development-based industry. Consider the impact of research and development and related activities on the short-term profits of the five companies discussed above. Company annual reports show current research and development expenditures, and for the purpose of analysis it is useful to compare these expenditures, not to company sales but to current net profits after taxes. That is, we can answer the question, "How much greater would the company's net profits after taxes be if the company *were not* investing current dollars for future markets?" Table 12 answers this question.

From Table 12 it will be noted that in 1964 the companies' net profits would have been from 12.1 per cent (Du Pont) to 35.5 (Dow) per cent greater if they were not required to maintain the research and development programs necessary to protect their competitive positions and assure future growth. Taking the 1960–1964 period as a whole, company total research and development and related expenditures measured in post-tax dollars expressed as a percentage of total 1960–1964 net profits after taxes were as follows (per cent):

Du Pont[1]	6.82
Du Pont[2]	12.84
Union Carbide	26.14
Monsanto	34.01
Dow	35.73
Allied	18.52

The percentages shown above correspond to the percentage shown in Column 4 of Table 12. The earlier table considered only 1964, a year in which the companies' profits were relatively high. The 1960–1965 percentages are more indicative of the long-term trend of management's decisions to "trade-off" short-term profits for long-term growth.

The most important and difficult strategic decisions that top management must make are those involving the "trade-offs" between protecting an existing profit rate (or attaining a desired profit rate) and maintaining the company's competitive position. This is particularly true for companies which enjoy a significantly higher- or lower-than-average (as compared to their competitors' or to the industry as a whole) profit rate. The former companies are faced with the problem of protecting a high profit rate in the face of competition. The latter companies are faced with the problem of improving their profit rate without seriously weakening their competitive positions. To be fully meaningful, any analysis of the "trade-off" between profit margin and competitive position should be carried out on an individual product, product group (to include competitive or substitute products), or market sector basis. It is possible, however, to use the company and industry data we have discussed above to develop some rough measures of the significance of this "trade-off." Table 13 shows each company's 1955–1964 ten-year average profit rate, 1955 and 1964 net sales as a percentage of the total sales of the five companies and of total industry sales (the FTC-SEC estimates), and the percentage change in each company's position relative to the five company and total industry sales between 1955 and 1964.

From Table 13 it is clear that a company with a higher-than-average profit rate (Du Pont and Union Carbide) faces a problem in protecting this position and maintaining its relative sales position. For all practical purposes in a mature or maturing industry, one of these two positions must give way to the other. A company that is willing to accept an average or even below-average profit rate will be able to find marketing opportunities

[1] Pioneering research only as reported in Du Pont's 1964 *Annual Report.*
[2] Total research and development estimated by the author, based on the 1960 relationship between total research and development expenditures and pioneering research expenditures as discussed in the company's 1960 *Annual Report.*

Table 13. Ten-year profit of leading chemical companies.

Company	Ten-year (1955–1964) average profit rate (1)	Company net sales as a percentage of five-company total sales		Company net sales as a percentage of total industry sales		Percentage change in the companies' net sales position relative to five-company and total industry net sales, 1964 vs. 1955	
		1955 (2)	1964 (3)	1955 (4)	1964 (5)	Five companies (6)	Total industry (7)
Du Pont	19.15	39.93	33.91	9.50	7.60	−15.08	−20.00
Union Carbide	10.16	24.83	23.07	5.91	5.17	− 7.09	−12.52
Monsanto	7.47	10.93	16.68	2.60	3.74	+52.61	+43.85
Dow	8.24	11.16	13.53	2.66	3.03	+21.24	+13.91
Allied	7.14	13.15	12.81	3.13	2.87	− 2.59	− 8.31
Five companies	12.38	100.00	100.00	23.79	22.41	—	− 5.80
Total industry	7.62	—	—	100.00	100.00	—	—

that will allow it to maintain or improve its relative market position. Monsanto's sharp improvement in relative market position illustrates this point. Dow was able (through new product and market development) to maintain an above-average (but declining) profit rate, and still improve its relative market position. Since the Allied Chemical Company acquired the Union Texas Natural Gas Company during the period, the Allied comparison is distorted.

Decisions involving the "trade-offs" between direct sales effort and market-development effort are particularly important to companies engaged in basic materials or new product industries. How can a company maximize its sales and profits? Is it more profitable to enlarge the sales force or increase promotional effort, or to engage in research programs designed to find new and additional uses for the company's products? This point will be discussed more fully below. In general, we are concerned with establishing the most profitable balance between those expenditures designed to convert a prospect for the company's products into a customer and those expenditures that are designed to increase the number of prospects by finding new uses for the product.

The last two strategic "trade-offs" are closely related. A company may achieve a desired growth objective by continuing to develop (penetrate) its existing markets or by developing new markets. If a company decides to develop new markets, the question of the relationship between the new product and the company's existing products becomes important. Top management must decide on a strategy regarding unrelated new market opportunities. For example, at what point will the company not consider a new opportunity because it is too unrelated to the company's existing products? The importance of a new product strategy to companies in the chemical industry is clear from any analysis of chemical company annual reports. For example, Monsanto's 1963 *Annual Report* (p. 12) highlighted the contribution of new products to the company's high growth rate with the following comment: "In 1963, following a 10-year period in which more than 500 products were introduced by Monsanto, these products contributed over 50 per cent of total sales and more than 60 per cent of gross profit."

Dow Chemical Company's 1964 *Annual Report* (p. 10) also highlighted the success of the company's new product development programs: "The long-term record shows that products introduced within the past five years accounted for about 10 per cent of 1964 sales. More significantly, products less than ten years on the market brought in just over 30 per cent of 1964 sales income."

Table 14. Product group distribution of Monsanto's annual sales (1955–1964).

Product group	Percentage of total sales, by product group		
	1955ᵃ	*1955ᵇ*	*1964*
Chemical fibers	—	16.5	29.1
Plastics, resins, & coatings	29.4	21.9	25.2
Phosphates and detergents	18.3	15.0	10.1
Intermediates and plasticizers	14.0	12.0	8.7
Agricultural chemicals	10.0	7.4	7.4
Rubber and oil chemicals	6.9	9.4	6.6
Petroleum—net of purchases	9.3	7.1	5.0
Pharmaceuticals, flavors & condiments	3.7	4.2	2.7
Textile and paper chemicals	2.7	2.1	2.5
Heavy chemicals	4.3	3.8	2.1
Other	1.4	0.6	0.6
Total	100.0	100.0	100.0

ᵃ Monsanto Chemical Company and Consolidated Subsidiaries as reported in the company's 1956 *Annual Report*.
ᵇ Parent Company and All Subsidiaries (*including Chemstrand*) as reported in the company's 1960 *Annual Report*.

The introduction of new products can alter the structure of company sales significantly.

From Table 14 it will be noted that Monsanto's success in achieving an 11.2 per cent per annum long-term growth rate (as compared to a total industry growth rate of 6.8 per cent per annum) reflected its management's ability to develop new product and acquisition strategies that lead to significant changes in the structure of the company's sales over the 1955–1964 period. We shall discuss some important aspects of new product strategies when we consider the nature of a corporate alternative evaluation and strategic planning model. Before we discuss this model, however, it is useful to consider the total corporate planning system.

A complete corporate planning system will consist of five basic functional elements: (1) the corporate alternative evaluation and strategic planning model; (2) a problem analysis, model selection, and activity level generator subsystem; (3) an activity level to transaction input converter subsystem; (4) a transaction subsystem; and (5) an output analysis and display subsystem.[3] Consider each of the functional elements and their interrelations with each other:

[3] In actual practice these elements may be combined, and the functions of one or more subsystems can be combined into a single subsystem.

1) The corporate alternative evaluation and strategic planning model is the heart of the corporate planning system. This corporate model will consist of a set of interrelated submodels. The number or types of submodels included (required) in any specific corporate model will depend on the nature of the company's business and its planning philosophy. In general these submodels will describe one or more of five basic types of relationships: a) the structure of the company's operating environments (market potential, market maturity nature and degree of competition, and so forth); b) input-output or resource expenditure productivity relationships (production functions, market and product development requirement functions, and so forth); c) competitive interactions (competitive exchange rate relationships, and so forth); d) timing response relationships (the relationship between the time-shape and intensity of an outcome and the level and rate of input resources expended); and 3) the implications of alternative timing decisions (the impact of different action—new product announcement dates, timing of advertising and marketing campaigns, and so forth—timing patterns on the company's ultimate revenues and profits).

2) The purpose of the corporate planning system is to solve planning problems of the type discussed above. When these problems arise, they will be formulated in the language of management and not in the language of the corporate planning model. Often these problems will be stated in a very loose and imprecise manner. *The problem analysis, model selection, and activity level generator subsystem* must be designed to analyze the problem, formulate it in terms of the variables included in the planning model, and select that combination of submodels that may be combined to generate a solution. In general the solution of a planning problem will involve finding the answer to three interrelated questions; a) should a given action be taken? b) if the action is to be taken, when should it be taken? and c) what resources should be committed to the action? These questions must be answered relative to the objective (or purpose) the company expects or desires to achieve by taking the proposed action.

3) The ultimate measure of the attractiveness of any action the company is considering must be expressed in financial or accounting terms. That is, how will the proposed action affect the company's profit rate or rate of return on investment? What impact will this action have on the company's profit and loss (income and expense) statement or balance sheet? The output of the problem analysis, model selection, and activity level generator subsystem may often be measured in terms of "physical" activity levels that are not comparable to the "standard" inputs required in the company's financial or accounting transaction recording system. If this is the case an *activity level to transaction input converter subsystem* must be developed. This is a translation subsystem designed to convert "physical activity" inputs into "standard financial" inputs for the transaction subsystem.

4) To be useful as a practical working tool, the corporate planning system must provide management with analyses, evaluations, and recommendations regarding possible action alternatives expressed in terms that are both familiar and acceptable as part of the company's normal decision-making apparatus. Any projections of the results that might be expected as a result of the action being considered must be expressed (measured) in terms of those income statement, balance sheet, and related analytical (ratios) data that management normally considers in evaluating any action recommendation. Ideally, the system should provide a basis for rapidly preparing a series of "before and after" income statement, balance sheet, and operating ratio projections that can be compared, thereby providing an objective, factual basis for decision. *The transaction subsystem,* therefore, must be designed to provide the capability for quickly projecting the impact of any contemplated action on the company's income statement, balance sheet, and operating ratios. The transaction subsystem will represent a mechanized miniature aggregate version of the company's accounting and financial measurement systems.

5) *The output analysis and display subsystem* becomes important when many different possible alternatives are being considered. In developing a corporate strategy it would not be unusual to consider several hundred or even several thousand different possibilities (indeed, in the analysis of many complicated problems involving national defense strategy and the selection of weapon systems, Department of Defense analysts have successfully employed computers to examine and evaluate tens of millions and more possibilities). In considering even a relatively few important strategic "trade-offs" it would not be difficult to generate enough raw computer output to swamp even the most enthusiastic management. The output analysis and display subsystem must be designed to perform an analysis and synthesis function by "digesting" the output of the transaction subsystem and displaying this output in a form that will provide management with the most useful and meaningful analytical basis for decision.

I have discussed some of the more common problems of strategic planning and have outlined the elements of a generalized corporate planning system. This corporate planning system was designed to provide management with an analytical basis for solving strategic planning problems. As discussed above, the heart of the planning system is a series of submodels which are combined to develop the corporate alternative evaluation and strategic planning model. I would like to conclude this paper with a brief discussion of the elements of this model, since the *preparation of its required building blocks represents the major contribution market research can make to the top management planning process.*

As indicated above, the strategic planning model can take many forms. A full discussion of the many different submodels that might be combined to develop a specific corporate model is beyond the scope of the present paper. I will discuss the strategic planning model in its most general form. The basic relationships described represent a system that can be adapted to almost any strategic planning problem. Consider first the kinds of data required to build the planning model. The construction of a strategic planning model will require the development of seven sets of basic building blocks. These building blocks are: 1) total market potential or economic environment planning factors; 2) market development (product coverage and scope) planning factors and resource expenditure productivity relationships; 3) market realization (or penetration) rate-planning factors and resource expenditure productivity relationships; 4) share of market and competitive impact-planning factors and resource expenditure productivity relationships; 5) price structure and pricing policy-planning factors and market response (price elasticity) relationships; 6) fixed or overhead cost-planning factors and resource (or investment) requirement relationships; 7) variable cost-planning factors, production functions, productivity relationships, and resource requirement relationships.

In developing a corporate (or divisional) growth and profit strategy, seven basic questions must be answered. These questions are: 1) What is the economic opportunity? 2) What is the saleable market potential? 3) What are the total industry sales? 4) What are the company unit or constant dollar sales? 5) What are company dollar sales? 6) What are company costs and expenses? 7) What are company profits? The first five questions, involving the factors which will determine the company's revenue or sales volume, are answered by combining the first five building blocks. Each of these building blocks requires data that must be supplied by the company's market research or market-planning activities. To answer the sixth question, cost and expense data from the company's financial departments are required. The last question can be answered by merely combining the answers to questions five and six.

Given the structure and organization of the economy and the level of economic activity, business opportunities exist independently of the company's ability (or awareness) to take advantage of these opportunities. The first question that must be answered in developing a corporate strategy or establishing long-term objectives is, "What are the economic opportunities for the company?" To answer this, an estimate of the total market potential for all products and services that might logically fit into the company's product scope must be developed. This estimate should include *all* products and services, even those that are not presently included in the company's existing or planned product line. It is important to recognize the distinction between market potential and total industry sales. A market potential estimate is a conditional, "if—then," statement. It should be constructed by answering the question, "What *would* total industry sales be *if* every possible prospect for the product were to become a user, and *if* all users of the product were to become 'maximum' or 'optimum' users?" The total market potential estimate can be regarded as an estimate of "potential-potential." It is important to consider an all-inclusive definition for total market potential to provide management with an estimate of the extent to which the company's saleable market potential can be increased through new product development or by adding new products through merger or acquisition. The total market potential estimate will also provide a basis for estimating the extent to which the company's product scope might have to be expanded to attain a desired long-term growth objective.

The second question that must be answered is, "What is the company's saleable market potential?" That is, given the company's *actual* products and services, what is its "real" market potential? While total market potential considers all products and services the company *could* market (consistent with the constraints imposed by its product scope), saleable market potential considers only those products actually *included* in the company's product lines. The market development rate is a measure of the extent to which the company has developed its market by including all acceptable products in its actual product line. If the company has included all possible products in its actual product line, its market development rate would be 1.0 (or 100 per cent), and saleable market potential would equal total market potential. By definition, saleable market potential is equal to the product of total market potential multiplied by the market development rate. The company can increase its market development rate by adding new products to its product line.

The third question to be answered is, "What will total industry sales be?" Once the company's saleable market potential has been estimated, a total industry sales estimate can be derived by multiplying saleable market potential by an appropriate market realization (or penetration) rate. The market realization rate may be considered as being an index of market maturity measuring the extent to which all prospects for the products have entered the market and all users of the products have attained a full usage rate. If the market is completely developed the market realization rate will be 1.0 (or 100 per cent), and total industry sales will be equal to saleable market potential. In the case of new products, there will be a low market realization rate indicating that only a small fraction of potential users have entered the market. Any action the company takes to convert nonusers into users or to increase the usage rate of existing users will increase the market realization rate.

The fourth question answered is, "What will the company's sales be?" Company sales will represent a fraction of total industry sales. The competitive impact factor will measure the company's share of the market. Company sales will represent the product of total industry sales multiplied by the competitive impact factor. Any action the company takes to increase its share of the market will improve its competitive impact factor. Any actions competition takes to increases its share of the market will weaken the company's competitive impact factor.

One of the most important instruments a company can employ in developing its corporate strategies is price competition. The company's prices relative to competitor prices for competing products or the prices of substitute products will determine the company's market share (competitive impact factor) and the rate of product acceptance (the market realization rate). The company's pricing strategy will also determine its actual dollar volume, given its unit (or constant dollar) sales. The fourth question is, "What will the company's actual dollar sales be?" I have included this relationship and expressed the first four relationships in physical or constant dollar terms to provide an explicit basis for considering the implications of pricing strategies.

The final questions to be answered are, "What will the company's total costs and expenses be?" and "What will the company's profits be?" To answer the first question, a set of cost and expense factors must be developed covering all phases of the company's operations. It is useful to consider both variable cost factors and fixed or overhead cost factors. The former factors consider those costs and expenses that are dependent on the company's sales volume, and the latter factors consider those costs and expenses that are independent of sales volume. For the purposes of developing a strategic planning model it is useful to consider costs and expenses classified according to *objective categories* rather than conventional income statement accounts. That is, all cost and expense-planning factors and relationships should be summarized and classified according to the objective the company expects to achieve as a result of the resource commitment rather than in some more conventional accounting record summary. Since the strategic plan is concerned with determining the most profitable set of strategic "trade-offs," all cost and expenditure data must be classified into objective categories that match the "trade-offs" being considered. For example, marketing expenses can be classified into those that are required to maintain (or attain) a given share of market position, expenses (customer development) designed to improve the company's market realization rate, or expenses intended to open new markets thereby improving the company's market development rate. Similarly, product development expenses might be classified into those expenditures required to keep the company's existing product lines competitive, to add new products to the product line (thereby improving the company's market development rate) or develop improved versions of existing products to attract nonusers (thereby improving the company's market realization rate). The success of the strategic planning system will critically depend on the ingenuity of the company's financial personnel in developing cost and expense objective category data. Once a projection of the total revenue and costs and expenses is developed, the final profit estimate may be derived by subtraction.

The ultimate success of any strategic planning program will depend on the ability of the company's market research and market-planning personnel to develop the various market structure data necessary to relate the company to the industry and the industry to the economy. Consider the fundamental choices available for management. Any corporate strategy must place first priority on protecting the company's existing market position or improving this position by capturing some of its competitors' market. The second priority must involve programs designed to improve the company's market realization rate by converting unsold market potential into sales. The third priority is to increase the company's saleable market potential by developing the new products necessary to convert undeveloped market potential into saleable market potential. The fourth priority involves changing the company's product or service scope to increase its total market potential. Management must determine the most profitable "trade-offs" in setting the company's competitive impact factor, market realization rate, and market development rate. These represent *all* the actions the company can take in the marketplace. Through new product development, merger, or acquisition, the company can change the markets in which it operates, but, once its markets are determined, only the choices outlined above exist. The other side of the profit coin is skillful control of costs and expenses. The importance of such control should not be minimized. Each of the company's discretionary expenditures should be carefully reviewed to determine its exact contribution to the company's ultimate profits. Every discretionary cost or expense should be analyzed to determine its impact on the three key ratios (market development rate, marker realization rate, and the competitive impact factor), its contribution to increasing total market potential (by broadening the company's product scope), or its attractiveness as a cost and expense reduction investment.

Rapid changes in the business environment, new technologies creating opportunities, new competition at home and abroad, the high cost of undertaking new ventures, the large investments and long lead-times necessary to enter new markets, increasing labor costs and severe price competition, and the increasing complexity of business operations—all these factors place a high premium on thinking ahead, planning ahead, and staying ahead. The development of a meaningful strategic planning program is one of the greatest challenges facing corporate management and its professional staffs in the next decade.

Chapter 8

PLANNING IN THE ITALIAN ENTERPRISE

GIORGIO RUFFOLO

Ministry of Finance

THE LARGE ENTERPRISE IN THE INDUSTRIAL SOCIETY

In the neoclassical theoretical model, a firm is little more than a meeting place for market forces. That model—although in a simplified and abstract way—mirrors the conditions prevailing in the economy a century ago: keen competition between comparatively small-sized enterprises, with very little market power.

This situation has thoroughly changed as a result of the development of large production units, which operate in the main under oligopolistic conditions. The extensive market power large companies possess enables them to develop a strategy of their own. The equilibrium between individual strategies does not necessarily represent an economic optimum.

Any attempt at determining the laws of behavior of the firm and of market equilibrium under oligopolistic conditions failed because of the interdependence of the oligopolists' decisions.

It may be asked nowadays whether—instead of attempting an analysis of the firm, through an analysis of its policy *vis-à-vis* other firms—it would not be more expedient to approach the problem *from inside,* by analyzing the features of the firm's social structure, and the bearing of such structure on the firm's management. This explains the growing interest of economists in a problem which used to be regarded as trivial not too long ago: enterprise organization.

According to this approach, the first task is to define the process through which enterprises have enlarged. On the basis of recent studies we can detect five stages in this process: 1) introduction of innovation by a small-sized enterprise, which thereby gets ahead of its competitors; 2) cut-throat competition in an unstable market, as other competitors catch up; 3) attempts, mostly unsuccessful, to reach an agreement; 4) concentration, first horizontal, then vertical (integration); 5) decentralization.

In the course of this process a small family business becomes a managerial unit—the enterprise switching from family to managerial shape, going through a series of intermediate changes where the moment of absolute leadership is particularly important: the heroic time of the Schumpeterian founder. It is at this stage that the managerial metamorphosis occurs. The capital passes from the owner (who for the last time combines the functions of the financing capitalist and the enterprise manager) to the enterprise. Ownership is integrated into the organization, and the entrepreneurial function becomes the very core of the new establishment.

The size and complexity of the enterprise calls for a delegation of duties to executives whose mission it is to insure their coordination. The financial size demands the splitting up of capital into a number of shares.

Management, however, once it has been established does not confine itself to acting as a simple instrument for interests placed outside the firm. In fact, it soon becomes an active and self-conscious force. It is an organ of the enterprise, but a member capable of coordinating the activities performed by all the other organs—its very central nervous system. It represents only one of the enterprise's resources, but it is the strategic resource and thence the factor that conditions the firm's development.

Management's objective interest lies in the protection and expansion of its sphere of authority and power. To the extent to which, through the differentiation process, it becomes aware of this, it becomes capable of working out a policy intended to further that interest. At a certain stage, the elaboration of this policy actually takes the shape of a plan.

The major long-term target of the plan is the achievement of a rate of growth set by the largest possible utilization of the enterprise's current and potential resources. Since the limiting resource is ultimately represented by the staff's organizing capabilities, the potential rate of growth of the enterprise is determined by the managerial resources—the number and quality of top executives, and the degree of cohesion of the group.

The drive for development, inherent in the nature and the interests of the managerial staff, unfolds in an environment conditioned by constraints to be complied with and resistances to be overcome. In this connection the problems of supply of finance, costs, sales and public relations become prominent.

As to finance, the problem the managerial staff has to face is reconciling the urge for expansion with the need to finance the expansion so as to maintain good relationships with shareholders (by keeping dividends at a level sufficient to avoid the risk of open rebellion and "take over") and with creditors (by keeping the ratio of loans to assets within safe limits).

As to costs, the basic problem concerns the ratio of wages to productivity. The management will strive to keep the increase of the former within the limits of the growth of output per man.

As to demand, the enterprise will tend to come to terms with the other large companies in the more or less settled markets by respecting the existing market shares and using its redundant productive capacity in new markets through a differentiation process which will involve on the one hand a systematic effort toward research and technological development and, on the other, a massive "persuasion" pressure on consumers.

Finally, the company, as it gets bigger, will tend to become an active subject in its noneconomic relationships with the other institutions of the national and international community, mainly through its public relations policy and its more or less open lobbying activity.

Therefore, in each of these fields, the technical problems the managing staff must tackle involve political problems, connected to the relative positions of strength between management itself and other managements and institutions in the community; and they will be solved by a dynamic balance insuring maximum growth along with maximum safety and autonomy.

IMPORTANCE OF THE LARGE ENTERPRISE IN ITALY

What is the Italian situation like, in the general context of the problems of managerial evolution?

Unfortunately, in Italy information concerning large companies is very scarce. Any appraisal of their importance and behavior is much more the result of empirical observation than of systematic surveys.

The importance of Italian large enterprises can be assessed from three different viewpoints: 1) size, compared with the major international companies; 2) size, against that of the sectors in which they operate (degree of concentration); 3) rate of growth compared with that of the national economy.

The list of the 246 leading world companies published by *Fortune* included in 1963 only six Italian companies; according to that list, Italy ranks seventh after the USA (127 companies), the United Kingdom (31 companies), Germany (25 companies), France (16 companies), Japan (16 companies), the Netherlands (three companies, whose aggregate turnover exceeds that of the six Italian companies by 40 per cent).

In the list of the 200 leading industrial concerns outside the USA, Italy ranks sixth with eight companies; the United Kingdom is first (with 56 companies), Japan second (with 34 companies), Germany third (with 32 companies), France fourth (with 24 companies) and Canada fifth (with 13 companies).

From the second viewpoint, only a few data are available concerning: 1) the importance of financial concentration; and 2) the importance of industrial concentration.

As to the first, available data show that in 1964, 0.19 per cent of Italian companies absorbed 49.55 per cent of the over-all capital of joint-stock companies.[1]

As to the second, an indication is provided by the data concerning the 200 leading enterprises in Italy:[2] this group of companies (0.03 per cent of the total number of business concerns) accounts for 6.8 per cent of employment and for 17 per cent of turnover.

Of course, the weight of major companies in total production varies greatly from one sector to another. In general, it can be said that the degree of concentration is very low in the industrial branches where technological progress is less advanced or widespread: the textile and food industries, the building trades and a large portion of the engineering industry.

Conversely, concentration appears to be very high in the sectors where a higher technological dynamism prevails and in the capital-intensive branches such as iron and steel, textile fibers, cement, chemical and power industries.

Here are a few instances: in iron and steel, the first five companies account for 82 per cent of total production; in the sector of oil refining and

---

[1] Estimate from data published by Associazione Italiana per le società per azioni, *Le società italiane per azioni nel 1964*, Rome 1965.
[2] Data published by *Mondo Economico* and *24 Ore*.

distribution, the three leading companies cover more than three fifths of the national market; in the chemical industry, the first three companies control (for the main items) 50 per cent to 90 per cent of the whole national production; in the field of artificial fibers, the three major companies supply 80 per cent of production; in the sector of typewriters one single company accounts for three fourths of national production; in the automobile industry, the leading company provides 84 per cent of national production; in the sector of cement, three fourths of the national production comes from the five main companies.

The most concentrated industries are those which recorded the highest rate of growth over the decade 1953–1963:

Industry	Average annual growth, per cent
Cement	9.9
Iron and steel	10.6
Oil refining	12.9
Chemical	12.5
Artificial and synthetic fibers	15.5
Typewriters	17.0

Over the same period, gross national product rose at an average rate of 6 per cent per year, as compared with an average annual growth of production and value-added of 9.1 per cent in the manufacturing industry.

The dynamism of these sectors in the 1950's came mainly from the impetus provided by a handful of large companies which, thanks to the challenge resulting from a change in environmental conditions (especially keen international competition and contact with the most advanced industrial structures in the West through the sudden opening of markets) and to the effective response of an energetic industrial management, introduced innovations in techniques, structures and policies.

The history of Italy's industrial development is to a large extent connected with a limited number of entrepreneurial episodes of great value, not only from the technical and economic, but also from the social and moral points of view. These episodes cannot be accounted for unless one understands the tension and the emotional and political elements which characterized Italy in the postwar period: the painful but beneficial process of becoming conscious of the past, and the impetus arising out of the very contrasts existing in its economic structure and in its political life.

It is against this background that the outstanding entrepreneurial achievements recorded have to be viewed, such as: FIAT's passing from a highly protected production of 110 thousand motor vehicles to a highly competitive production of one million cars over fifteen years; ENI's developing a solid and modern national natural gas and oil industry from a practically nonexistent base, and its simultaneously imparting a tremendous thrust on two advance sectors: petroleum chemistry and nuclear research; IRI-Finsider's enabling Italian steel industry to rank seventh among world producers (Italsider is the second steel company in Western Europe); Olivetti's reaching a production of one million three hundred thousand typewriters and computers; Montecatini's and Edison's setting up an expanding chemical industry (in conjunction with ANIC, of the ENI group) which is now the pace-setter and stimulates over-all industrial development.

In summation, even though extensive data and information are not available, it can be concluded that: 1) the size of large companies in Italy is not comparable with that of major companies in other countries; 2) the degree of financial and industrial concentration is rather high in some of the basic sectors of the national economy; and 3) large companies, owing to a rate of growth much above the average, are acquiring an ever-greater importance within the national economy.

Managerial development in Italian enterprises. To what extent is the impetus given by large enterprises to Italy's economic expansion also the result of a development of company structures toward managerial forms?

On this point, information is still scanty. Therefore one can only formulate assumptions based on scattered surveys, empirical observations and symptomatic data.

Among the latter, one meaningful element is the rapid increase in the number of managers in industrial concerns, a number which has more than doubled over the past ten years: 26,038 in 1964 as against 12,100 in 1954.[3] This phenomenon is particularly important in the economically and technologically advanced industrial sector (2.4 managers per one thousand workers in the textile industry, 7.1 in the engineering industry, 12 in the chemical industry, 17.5 in the electrical industry, as compared with an over-all average of 6.1 per one thousand).[4]

The proliferation of managers, however, is more a symptom of an improved organization of companies than of their swing from traditional and paternalistic to more objective and scientific forms of management.

[3] Data derived from the annual balance sheets of the Instituto Nazionale di Previdenza per i Dirigenti di aziende industriali.
[4] *Statistiche del Lavoro*, XV, Nos. 1, 2, 3, 1963.

From this standpoint, it cannot be said, at least as a rule, that large companies in Italy have completed the whole process conversion.

In this connection, one should not be misled by the companies' enthusiasm for management techniques typical of management at its most sophisticated or by the often impressive display of management techniques and organization charts. There are grounds for doubt if these are not the result of the all too ready and uncritical acceptance of models derived from foreign—mainly American—experience, by an environment hardly prepared to receive them. And whether the illuministic enthusiasm for public relations, for the "elegant little bunches"[5] of organization charts, does not conceal some ambiguity.

It is an established fact that a great many Italian companies are still considerably imbued with authoritative paternalism. Undoubtedly this is due in part to the fact that owner families still play an important part in the companies' management and policy-making; and even where the differentiation process between ownership and management has brought the company into the hands of nonowners, the latter still hold the same position as the owner and discharge their functions in an atmosphere of authority which leaves a limited scope for the free play of managerial forces.

Nevertheless, the prevailing tendency is definitely toward managerial development. The heirs of the founders of large industrial estates are now more and more often making a clear choice between the euthanasia of the *rentier* and the "animal spirits" of the executive. This process is already apparent in some of the major companies, where, regardless of ownership structure—spread or concentrated—management has assumed a marked professional character. This tendency is strengthened by the growing importance and the original role performed in Italy by public enterprise—a heterodox result of a specific experience, which cuts across current classifications and enhances the managers' autonomy and responsibility.

In general, it can be affirmed that Italy's large companies are now undergoing a transition from the concentration/integration stage to the decentralization/differentiation stage—with an increasingly marked tendency to assume the form of a differentiated industrial group.[6]

From a more contingent viewpoint one might assume that, in the large companies, this organizational development, already in progress, is lagging

[5] G. Martinoli, "Il Mulino," *Trasformazione nell'organizzazione aziendale in funzione del progresso tecnologico,* Società Editrice, 1961.
[6] P. Saraceno, "Imprese pubbliche e imprese private dinanzi al problema della dimensione ottima," *Il Mondo dell'Energia,* No. 2, 1962.

behind technological development; this assumption would help—along with other factors—to explain why, after the tremendous expansion recorded in the 1950's, Italian industrialists have seemed dispirited when confronted with recent economic difficulties.

Planning procedures and techniques. The conclusions set forth in the foregoing paragraphs are endorsed by an analysis of planning techniques and procedures adopted by some of the leading national public and private enterprises.

From such an analysis, one derives the general impression that planning procedures are marked by a high degree of operational concentration and a low degree of formalization.

However, during past years, considerable progress has been achieved toward reducing the former and increasing the latter.

Increased size, drive toward production diversification, establishment of multisectoral groups, are all elements which fostered decentralization processes in the organization as the need arose to entrust production units—departments or enterprises—not only with operational, but also with planning, activities, at least in the field of the group's ordinary productions. A case in point is Montecatini's reorganization which occurred in 1963 and resulted in the setting up of decentralized structures (departments) divided by organic production and sales cycles and given operational autonomy and specific planning responsibilities.

In other large companies the decentralization process was based on different criteria: companies which operate essentially in one production sector, such as FIAT in the field of motor vehicle production, have divided their base operational units according to functional criteria; those where the distribution activity is prominent, on the basis of territorial criteria.

Moreover, the complexity of operations, the expansion of markets, the length of the investment period, the exigency to keep competitive all induce management to base their essential decision-making on less empirical and more rational foundations.

A first step has been taken toward the adoption of more rational management techniques, thanks to the spread of two practices which are now quite extensively adopted (not only in large companies but also in medium- and small-sized enterprises), namely: 1) market research and sales planning; and 2) annual capital budget.

Market research and sales planning are carried out, according to a recent sample survey, by 73 per cent of Italian large- and medium-sized companies.[7]

---

[7] Survey carried out on behalf of the Italian Marketing Association, the results of which are published in *Studi di mercato* April 1965. The sample was represented by 700 companies, 512 of which have capital above 500 million lire.

The annual capital *budget* has become accepted procedure in large companies and is substituted for traditional control techniques; this has led to a yearly plan, with usually quarterly or four-month slices.

In some companies, the targets set by the budget are binding for the base units, whereas in others they are simply meant as a guide.

At any rate, the adoption of the budget provides an analysis of the gaps between the targets set and the results actually achieved in the year.

The first step, adoption of budget and market research, has been followed by actual planning activities. It deals, in the main, with attempts rather than with systematic experiences.

The formalization of planning procedures and the adoption of sophisticated global planning techniques are still limited for the time being to a few companies, and in these cases a clear distinction has to be drawn between organization charts and reality.

The setting up of a planning department or office is only an indication, and sometimes misleading, of management's actual inclination to allow the adopted planning criteria (even if flexible) to condition its decisions.

This is proved by the fact that some officers, in the planning bureaus of large companies, feel uneasy and awkwardly estranged from the often unfathomable will of top management and from the very cognizance of essential data about the company's activity.

The fact is that any management's attempt—often sincere—to carry out a planning activity is bound to fail because of the company's centralized structure.

This accounts for the unquestionably limited part the planning staff takes in top management decisions and for the fact that these decisions seldom stem from formal procedures but are normally the result of intuitive choices made by a small number of executives, on the basis of data and intelligence supplied by staff units.

The foregoing preliminary remarks enable us to better detect what planning techniques and procedures adopted in some of the major Italian companies, about which information could be gathered, actually consist of.

As to procedures, it seems that two essential specific functions can be distinguished, as far as base operational units, top management and staff units are concerned.

Planning at base unit level is confined to ordinary activities, and essentially consists of forecasting sales, profitability of individual production cycles, and investment requirements.

Central planning, besides screening the proposals put forward by base units and coordinating them as far as ordinary activities are concerned, covers new ventures (development planning) and financial problems involved by the whole of planned operations.

This stage of planning is normally one for which formal procedures are most seriously lacking. The relevant tasks are usually performed by top management which normally exercises its decision power in an informal way.

Staff units are chiefly entrusted with research tasks consisting of the elaboration of general economic and market forecasts, directed toward the outside rather than toward the inside of the enterprise. This does not mean that top management does not avail itself, in certain cases, of the cooperation of these units in the analysis of specific aspects of the company's plan; as a rule however this does not occur in the over-all framework of the enterprise's development planning, and it happens on the basis of a personal confidential report rather than of a formal report.

The stage reached by the planning procedure formalization process in Italy is reflected in the progress of planning techniques in various fields where planning is adopted—namely, sales, investment, and finance.

Of these three fields, which are independent of one another, sales planning can be regarded as the pace-setter in respect to method and technique development, and sometimes achieves original approaches and sufficiently sophisticated marketing techniques and statistical models. This mainly stems from the already mentioned fact that market and external intelligence are particularly important in this respect: and this is the very area which offers the widest scope for the research department's activity.

As to investment planning, the over-all approach to this phenomenon is still essentially reserved for top management and is still connected, to a large extent, with the business's financial plan, for which no formalization process in fact exists: this approach takes of course into account the general planning lines suggested by base operational units, and such aspects (technical-economic analysis concerning possible new ventures) as top management can refer for study by specialized staff services in order to have available technical data in their decisions.

From the foregoing, the conclusion can be drawn that as a rule in large Italian companies essential planning functions do exist, but they lack a functional liaison and a coordinating point other than top management, which exercises its decision-making functions in an informal way.

There have been very few instances of attempts to set up a staff unit to try and consolidate the miscellaneous aspects of planning into a single framework (into a *real company plan*).

However, these are examples rather than accomplished achievements—attempts by approximation.

However, even under the impetus of an economic development which is less and less liable to be controlled and directed by traditional management criteria, such attempts multiply and extend in a succession of partial successes and disappointing failures.

In this framework, whose outlines are still rather imprecise, a new development factor has recently been introduced, likely to give a more definite impetus to the modernization process of the Italian enterprise system: the national plan.

Chapter 9

PLAN AND MARKET IN AGRICULTURE

MAKSYMILIAN POHORILLE

Central School of Planning and Statistics, Poland

This report is not a description of the existing planning methods in agriculture of the Socialist countries but is an attempt to present a few selected problems based on the Polish experience.

The problem of plan and market is, of course, different for countries with collective farming and for those in which individual farms are still the dominating form of land ownership. The author has based his work, above all, on the experience of his country. The present report does not relate to the specific features of planning in Poland, but to problems of a more general nature.

The methodology of planning in agriculture has not been worked out in a satisfactory manner as yet. A number of the author's theses are, consequently, postulative.

ADAPTATION OF PRODUCTION TO THE NEEDS OF THE SOCIETY

Plan is not meant as a negation of the market, but as the negation of its spontaneity. The planned economy, aiming at the maximum satisfaction of the needs of the society, uses, to a certain measure, the mechanism of the market, but it does not confine itself to that.

The use of the mechanism of the market for the adaptation of the structure of production to needs means: 1) the observance of freedom of consumption as a general rule,[1] to be guided, when determining the structure of production, by consumer preferences as they appear in the effective demand, if they are not explicitly contradictory to social preferences.

The structure of consumer needs in a society finds its expression (though not fully) in the structure of effective demand. The deviations in the relationships between equilibrium prices and social costs reveal the deviations in the structure of production and the structure of needs.

In a longer period, investments are decisive factors in adapting production to needs. Long-term investment decisions cannot be made exclusively or mainly on the basis of market signals. Even the best knowledge of individual consumer preferences is of small importance when dynamics are involved. Tastes and likings undergo changes. Individuals have no clear view about future consumption.

Long-term investment decisions are guided by the interests of accelerated economic growth, structural social and economic changes in the country, and maximum satisfaction for the needs of the society in the future. *For this purpose a certain vision of a future society is required, and a final model of social consumption should be determined.*

Is it possible to determine future needs scientifically? To a certain extent —yes: there exist certain objective regularities in the development of social needs which can be scientifically investigated. Examples are the famous Engel's laws.

The trend toward a quick distribution of new products (of the type which make life more comfortable) is commonplace. In the development of towns and settlements, it is possible to use certain standards (more or less precise forecasts concerning practical needs—municipal transport, and so forth).

Research concerning the structure of consumption and its rationality, the scientifically justified consumption standards of certain products, the role of services associated with consumption (consequences which the shortening of the working day would entail, and so forth) will no doubt gain more and more importance.

---

[1] Freedom of "consumption" is meant here as a contradiction to the administrative rationing of consumption. It means a free choice of consumer goods. In a broader sense, consumer freedom assumes the existence of market equilibrium, as only then does the consumer have the real possibility to purchase the required commodities.

For the needs of long-term planning, the Polish physiologists have prepared consumption standards, in terms of products, on four different levels. The physiological standards make food diversification possible, insuring at the same time a balance of nutritive components. The shaping of the demand for food depends, however, not only on biological need but also on the intensity of other needs. Therefore, the planning of food consumption is only an element in planning the model of total social consumption. An important source of information on the shaping of social needs is the family budget as well as the experience of the more advanced societies. Data drawn from these sources require, of course, keen analysis (for instance, tastes change with time, and deformations appearing in the consumption model of richer countries should be avoided). Analysis of the trend in technical progress is also of essential importance. For example, rapid progress in the technology of plastics opens a wide prospect for the development of inexpensive items and the mass production of many articles made at present of natural raw materials.

I believe that a wide development and concentration of research along all the lines mentioned in connection with long-term planning should be our goal. Only on the basis of such research will it be possible to answer the questions regarding the *required* model of consumption in a more detailed way.

However, it would be, in my opinion, an illusion to believe that such research and even the use of the most modern computers can free us from the necessity of evaluating and determining social priorities. The final model of consumption is not unanimously determined. This signifies a certain degree of freedom of choice. The point is to know the alternatives and conditions of choice thoroughly, to ascertain the existing limitations and to insure internal consistence in the program. The range of occurrence in so-called preferences is considerably wider than is commonly presumed. These preferences cover not only individual products and services, the consumption of which the society wants to stimulate (books) or restrict (alcohol), but they also cover a very extensive and ever-widening domain of collective consumption.

The preferences also cover the external effects of the consumption of certain products. The mechanism peculiar to the market economy takes no account, as a rule, of this side of the problem. The market economy is also deprived of future vision; it is not able to forecast correctly the changes which result from the superimposing and the crisscrossing actions of an immense number of consumers and producers. In general, we can state that in the Socialist system it is necessary to associate the tasks concerning the best possible adaptation of the structure of production to the existing consumption habits, tastes and likings (due consideration is given to effective demand when constructing a consumption plan), with the tasks concerning the shaping of the final consumption model in a conscious, planned and rational way. This requires going outside the market and its mechanism.

This approach suggests the revision of views regarding two essential problems: 1) It is generally believed that individual consumer preferences cannot be evaluated. This is, no doubt, correct. What can be discussed is the method, or the shaping of the tastes and likings, and the existing model of consumption; 2) Social preferences are regarded, as a rule, from the viewpoint of possible correctives which social representation brings into individual acts of choice. Consequently, they are considered over a short period of time, while of fundamental importance are social preferences concerning long-term trends in the development of society.

SPECIFIC FEATURES OF THE PLANNING OF AGRICULTURAL PRODUCTION

Planning in agriculture has a number of specific features, the following of which in my opinion are the most important:

Character of demand for agricultural products. The overwhelming part of agricultural production is foodstuffs. As to consumer choice dictated by individual likings and habits, here it is much more limited than in other fields. Also the consumption habits of the population are much more stabilized. Thus, the structure of the demand for food is more easily defined and is subject to less violent changes than that for industrial products.

A fairly essential role in the shaping of demand for agricultural products is played by the phenomenon of self-consumption on farms, which is governed by regularities and therefore requires separate examination.

Planning in the conditions of uncertainty. Agricultural production undergoes fairly strong fluctuations depending on weather conditions and other haphazard factors. Therefore, in a short period of time the element of uncertainty in planning agricultural production is much more pronounced than in the planning of industrial production. In the long run, however, the situation is reversed. Uncertainty connected with unforeseeable changes in techniques, methods of production and the appearance of new products is much greater in industry than in agriculture.

Links between the central plan and the controlled market. Planning in agriculture involves the necessity of going beyond the state sector. This fact, as well as the immense diversity of conditions of production in individual forms, imposes the necessity of utilizing indirect rather than direct methods of planning. The market mechanism plays a much more important role in these conditions.

THE CONSTRUCTION OF THE PLAN

One of the most important stages in preparing the agricultural production plan is the confrontation of anticipated development trends for individual agricultural products in a given period (assuming a certain increase in income of population and a given birth rate) with standards corresponding to the final consumption model and with the set of natural, economic and demographic factors characterizing the production potential of agriculture.[2]

In the case of essential discrepancies between anticipated demand, planned production and the structure of consumption (recognized as the most required from the social viewpoint), the planner must think of actions to remove these discrepancies. Then the following has to be examined: 1) possibility of appropriate changes in production; 2) possibility of certain shifts in foreign trade; and 3) methods of exerting appropriate influence on consumer demand.

It should be stressed that the forecast concerning the possible development of the market situation plays a different role in the Socialist system from that in the capitalist system. The use of economic forecasts in planning does not mean that past trends like factors governing future development are simply extrapolated. The plan is shaping future development and introducing a number of new elements. The extrapolation of trends observed in the preceding period indicates only one of the possible alternatives of the development of certain economic processes.

The plan determines definite aims and the means by which the given aims have to be achieved.

The correct plan has to be balanced. In our previous practice the balances were the weakest points in agricultural planning. In spite of the apparently correct elaboration, the balances were not fully reliable. Their main deficiency was that they took no account of limitations in the mobility of the

[2] The previous method has taken the so-called "potential production possibilities of agricultural areas" as a starting point for planning. It is primitive and conducive to wrong results. Progress in the field of planning methodology involves a wider consideration of economics and the comparative analysis of a number of alternative versions.

factors of production in space, the possibility of "shifts" in time, nor the problem of substitution. This deficiency may be partly eliminated if the national balances are based on net regional balances.[3]

Linking the central plan with the regional and district plans of agricultural development as well as with the investment programs prepared on the basis of these plans has become at present more and more important. These programs are based on those of the so-called agricultural *gromada* (the smallest administrative unit in rural areas). This agricultural unit forms an agricultural and service development center which should, at the same time, perform organizational and administrative functions. The central plan sets up definite frames for the detailed plans covering a region and *gromada*. Development projects of a *gromada* include, besides productive investment, social and cultural facilities. In regions with a high level of agriculture and a high participation in the Socialist sector, investment programs contribute to a rapid increase of specialization in production.

PLANNING UNDER CONDITIONS OF UNCERTAINTY

Planning in agriculture contains, as has already been mentioned, many elements of uncertainty. Generally speaking, the basic reason for uncertainty is our incomplete knowledge of economic events. This problem has many aspects. I shall confine myself to two of them.

Data in a plan usually contain a smaller or larger margin of error. The danger of committing an error is, of course, much greater when these data refer to future events. Frequently, however, the planner must also use the estimates for data on the present and the past. In agriculture this problem is particularly complicated. Some French economists indicate, for example, that the impossibility to determine precisely the volume of goods sold at different periods of time (and consequently at different prices) causes inaccuracies of the order of 15 to 20 per cent when calculating the income in agriculture.[4]

The errors accumulate because the volume of crops itself is speculative, and the degree to which farms participate in processing and selling products is not known in detail. The evaluation of self-consumption on farms, calculation of production costs, estimate of reserves and increase in weight of farm animals, and so forth, present many complicated methodological

[3] See C. Bobrowski, "Limits and Conditions of Planning in Agriculture: Problems of Agricultural Economics," *Zagadnienia Ekonomiki Rolnej* no 2, 1965.
[4] See "Etude du revenu de l'agriculture et des agricultures," Raport presenté au nom de la Section de conjoncture par J. Milhau, *Revenue National*, 1961.

problems. These difficulties also appear, of course, in the Socialist economy. However, it should be made clear that data are more easily obtained here than under a capitalist system. For example, amounts spent by farms for fertilizer, machines, building materials, and so forth, are known very accurately. Also information on the income from agricultural products is available. In short, in the planned economy there exist objective possibilities to enrich the sources considerably and to improve the system of information —thus decreasing the degree of uncertainty in constructing the plan.[5]

However, the problem of forecasts remains unsolved. The fundamental conclusion which should be drawn from the fact that it is not possible in agriculture to guarantee a certain volume of production in a single productive process is the necessity to accept a wider time-horizon. Switching over to five-year planning is the proper way to determine the prospective data with a higher degree of reliability and, at the same time, a basis for more correct methods of analysis of previous events. Only the trend in the production of individual agricultural products which can be expressed by the chain-means, based on three- to five-year periods, may be the object of planning.

One of the important sources of uncertainty is the incomplete knowledge of functional interdependence between variables in the plan and of the effectiveness of economic measures. The determination of the production effects of an investment is much more difficult in agriculture than in industry. It is also difficult to foresee accurately, for instance, the effects of a price increase in agricultural products, a price reduction in fertilizers, and so forth.

It seems that here also the time-horizon of the plan is of essential importance. In a longer period it is possible to impart a more complementary character to the investments (this being extremely important in agriculture) to carry out the necessary organizational changes and to obtain better effects. In a several-year period it is also possible to test the effectiveness of certain measures of the economic policy (price change, for example), and amend, if needed, the system of stimulating agricultural production.

Of essential importance for the improvement of planning methods in agriculture is the problem of aggregating the data. Without breaking the extremely heterogenous statistical mass into more homogenous units (covering farms of a definite and homogenous type from the point of view of nature, soil and other conditions), it is difficult to foresee correctly the reaction of farms to economic stimuli and the effectiveness of individual

---

[5] This does not mean that the existing state of agricultural statistics is in my opinion satisfactory.

measures of the economic policy (and it is also difficult to determine the correct balances).

All these measures (and a number of others not mentioned in this paper) may, no doubt, help diminish the degree of plan uncertainty. Nevertheless, the degree of uncertainty always remains sufficiently essential. Therefore, the plan must be provided with appropriate shock absorbers.

The main shock absorber is the reserves.[6] The more tense the plan, the bigger the reserves have to be. This problem has been the subject of many discussions. Some express the opinion that constructing cautious plans for agricultural production development deprives them of one of their main values, that is of mobilizing social force. Other economists believe that the necessity to envisage deep reserves in a tense plan results in a decrease in the rate of growth, which in the last instance prevents the plan from being more ambitious. In other words, in a cautious plan reserves are envisaged in the planned volume of agricultural production itself.

This problem cannot, in my opinion, be solved by embracing this theory. Of course, the best plan is neither too low nor tense, but real. But this is an ordinary truism. Progress in solving this problem may be achieved only through a gradual improvement in planning methods and the generalization of practical experience. Reserves do not preclude the problem of shock absorbers for the plan. Experience shows, for example, that stabilization of prices plays a positive role in the development of agriculture. However, excessive stiffening of economic policy tools (invariable prices, charges, and so forth) does not favor the mitigation of phenomena disturbing the planned production processes in agriculture. These tools become, as a matter of fact, destabilizers of the economy.

Therefore, the problem of such a drawing-up of plans and establishing agricultural prices and methods of purchase to insure conditions for a steady increase in agricultural production and a stabilization in retail prices for foodstuffs, as well as retaining the necessary elasticity in the whole planning system, is becoming tremendously important.

Tools of plan implementation. The best way of fitting agriculture into the central plan is to use voluntary contracts with farm enterprises as a means of arriving at the desired composition and volume of agricultural output. These contracts stipulate the sale of produce of defined standard to the state trading organizations: they are concluded *ex ante*—that is, before production decisions are taken—and for this reason exercise a highly effective influence on the planning of agricultural production itself.

---

[6] Also the reserves in foreign trade are included here.

The essential point is that the contract system can reconcile general social interests with the individual economic interest of agricultural producers. Thus production plans are transmitted to agriculture not in the form of administrative orders, but in the form of economic incentives, and farmers are completely free to choose whatever pattern of production seems most advantageous.

In Socialist countries the contract system tends toward general application in agriculture—that is, toward encompassing all agricultural production and all farm enterprises. It is indeed only as a general system that it can gain its full usefulness as an instrument of planning agricultural production. However, it will need long preparation before the contract system can be generally applied. The logic governing the development of the contract system is as follows. Apart from industrial crops, the agricultural products to be drawn into the system first are: 1) exports, which must therefore meet certain quality standards and delivery dates; 2) those whose production particularly needs to be stimulated; 3) those which help the contract system itself to develop its function in agricultural production. (The organizations which award the contracts exercise certain rules which influence the very process by which the goods subject to these contracts are produced.)

In Poland (as in most other Socialist countries), besides the contracts there are other forms of commercialization for agricultural products. One of them is their sale in local market places. The consumers are generally people living in the country.

In the current system of agricultural purchasing, the contract occupies a front-rank position. This is evidenced not only by the growing share of contract-buying in total state purchasing of agricultural products, but also in the steadily increasing part the system plays in creating conditions of balanced growth in agricultural production.

In this last connection, four important points must be made: 1) The contract agencies are increasingly active in the planned supply of basic inputs (for example, fodder, fertilizers, and so forth) to farmers—a matter of decisive importance to an expanding agriculture; 2) The contract system relieves farmers of all risks of price fluctuations on the market; 3) The system is used as a means of adjusting the structure of output to the social and economic structure of agriculture. The contract plans are designed to develop labor-intensive crops on farms having unutilized manpower reserves and to adapt the geographical pattern of production to the quality of the soil in different parts of the country. Thus the system plays an important part both in resource utilization and in putting a given social policy into effect; 4) More and more frequently, the contract agencies undertake projects designed to base relations with farmers on contracts stretching over several years. This means that particular areas can be given over permanently to certain crops, but, in order to encourage farmers to conclude such contracts, the government must provide investment credit.

The contract system certainly is no panacea which will automatically resolve the problem of balancing demand and supply with respect to farm products. This depends upon the general condition of economic growth, and requires the most diverse means of influencing agriculture—first of all stimulation of investment in agriculture and its ancillary industries, intensive promotion of technical progress, higher expenditure for infrastructures, and so forth. The most important stimulation to the implementation of the investment and contract plan comes from the price and credit policy.

In price policy, the point of departure is the distinction between the problem of the general level of agricultural prices and the problem of price relations between separate agricultural products. Farmers have to make a choice among various possible ways of using the factors of production at their disposal, and they base their decisions not on absolute profit, but on the relative profit of the farming branch under consideration. At given production cost, the relations between the prices for different agricultural products are of decisive importance in arriving at a suitable structure in agricultural production.

The general level of agricultural prices (and its relation to the prices of services and of industrial goods bought by farmers) determines the level of real income and the volume of farm-household consumption and accumulation. In its turn, the rate of increase in agricultural production depends upon the level of accumulation. The general level of agricultural prices must therefore be determined in close connection with the planned increase in national income, its distribution and the actual methods of its distribution.

When I speak of the distribution of national income, I have in mind its allocation to the accumulation fund and the consumption fund just as much as distribution among social classes (workers and peasants). In mentioning the actual methods by which the national income is redistributed, I want to stress the close link which exists between the level of agricultural prices and the various forms of income-transfer as applied in any given period. Suppose, for example, that, in accordance with the general principles of economic policy, the greater part of investment in agriculture is made by the state (for instance, in the form of tractor stations), then prices paid to farmers should be lower than they would have to be if farms took care of their own investment. It follows that any changes in the system and the scope of agricultural finance must be accompanied by well-defined changes in the general level of agricultural prices.

The reasoning is as follows: The plan provides for a specified increase in agricultural production; the achievement of this increase needs a given amount of investment in agriculture and ancillary sectors. Part of this investment is financed by the state; part by the farmers. But this decomposition of investment expenditure according to sources does not depend alone upon the planned increase in production. It depends upon a whole series of economic, political and institutional factors, which also govern the rate of increase in farm-household consumption (included in the general economic plan).[7]

Increase in agricultural production, prices, incomes, consumption and accumulation are interconnected magnitudes. It is obvious that the level of agricultural income depends upon the volume of output and upon prices, and that, on the other hand, the achievement of a given volume of output requires a corresponding level of farm incomes (during the preceding period), of which a well-defined portion must be devoted to productive investment.

On collective farms, according to the statute law, a definite income rate is designed for expanded reproduction. In Poland, the government influences the distribution of farm income (between consumption and investment) by means of a system of tax relief on invested funds, low-interest credits, and assistance from the Agricultural Development Fund.

Once a feasible rate of increase in farm consumption and accumulation has been determined, and once practical arrangements have been put to work to assure that the accumulated funds will be used for investment (to raise agricultural production by a given percentage, for instance), the basic data for defining the general level of agricultural prices are at hand.

Given this general price level, the relations between the prices of different agricultural products must be so shaped that they discriminate in favor of certain crops and induce changes in the structure of production to match as far as possible the changes in the structure of society's consumption needs.

---

[7] In Poland, we usually adopt rather similar rates of increase for the household consumption of the farming and the urban population. But this rule is not obligatory in all circumstances. In the presence of major divergences between the standard of living in the towns and in the country, it may be necessary to raise rural consumption more quickly than working-class consumption. Throughout the ten years since the war, incomes have been growing much faster among the agricultural population than among the workers.

In this connection, the calculation of production costs plays an important part. Attempts at fixing prices directly on the basis of unit cost have been disappointing; what is needed is to follow the dynamics of price and cost changes in order to gain a picture of variations in the profitability of the different lines of production and of the farmers' reactions. Cost calculations are equally indispensable for fixing agricultural incomes. Thus the production/distribution formula does not exclude the calculation of unit costs in agriculture, but merely divests it of its absolute significance and avoids oversimplification of the cost/price relationship.

In the view of some economists, the complex study of correct price relations is completely redundant, since the market resolves this problem perfectly. It is true that information obtained from market analysis is very helpful in the consideration of the problem under discussion, but the question is not as simple as all that. First of all, it is not merely a matter of identifying the equilibrium conditions of the market at any given moment, but of forecasting future changes with accuracy. Secondly, prices which are subject to volatile and transitory factors can give no proper guidance to farmers in their choice of the right line of production.

Unexpected price changes generate uncertainty. In contrast, expected changes play a constructive part, in that they are an incentive to farmers to alter production in the desired sense. Price policy acts like a sieve: it lets through certain price changes and holds back others. This brings me to the fundamental question of how to link up the theoretical system of farm prices (as defined by the formula outlined above) with the actual price system for end-products of agricultural origin, which comes about under the influence of the factors which determine market equilibrium (supply and demand).

Then two price systems can be combined by manipulating five factors: 1) the margin between the retail price of the end-product and the producer price; 2) taxes levied from farmers; 3) subsidies and credits to agriculture; 4) the prices of agricultural inputs; 5) the prices of industrial consumer goods which farmers want.

By manipulating these factors, the plan can be made internally consistent —that is, its targets for an increase in agricultural production and incomes can be harmonized with an economically justified system of retail food prices.

Any effort at insuring general market equilibrium in the course of the process of economic development also depends decisively on the wage policy, in so far as effective demand for consumer goods should increase in proportion with the rate of increase in their supply.

The principles underlying the determination of agricultural prices, as discussed above, can aptly be called the production/distribution formula. These principles indeed rest on the premise that prices should be fixed in close relation with the planned proportions of income distribution and with the long-term development targets for agriculture.

This formula constitutes a sufficient foundation for a rational price policy in the purchase of agricultural products. In this field, much scope is left for ad hoc decisions. Such decisions indeed intervene in every price formula, as we know from experience. Contrary to appearances, no formula provides a hard-and-fast answer to the question of the desirable level of prices for different agricultural products. It is undoubtedly one of the virtues of the system described that it establishes a more flexible link between prices and production than other systems, such as, for instance, the system of parity prices or those based on the so-called cost-of-production formula.

An important role in the development of agricultural production is played by the policy of low prices for the means of production in agriculture.

It seems that the following thesis may be formulated: The question of what stimulates the intensification of agricultural production more—rise in prices for agricultural products or reduction in prices for means of production being purchased by farms (assuming that the rise of general income is in both cases the same)—is less significant for a country where the farmers are accustomed to using huge amounts of fertilizer, machinery, and so forth, than for countries where modern soil-cultivating methods still need to be more widespread. Consequently, the policy of low prices for means of production is playing a particular role in countries aiming at an accelerated rate of increase in agricultural production. It should be emphasized in this connection that such a policy may give positive results only if the danger of violent fluctuations in agricultural prices is eliminated. Therefore, the reduction of costs cannot replace the guarantee of agricultural prices.

Similarly, credit is an effective aid to farms only in conjunction with many other measures of economic policy.

Traditional credit policy aimed at providing low-interest credit for farmers to promote enterprises favoring the growth of agricultural production and productivity, as a rule, became especially active in periods when the agriculture was critical and was not able to overcome the accumulated obstacles by itself.[8] In a planned economy, credit operations in agriculture have assumed a new character. They have become fully subordinated to general targets of the agricultural program.

[8] W. Abel is of the opinion that aid to farms in critical situations is the characteristic feature of agricultural credit. See W. Abel, *Agrarpolitik*. Göttingen, 1958, p. 288.

FINAL REMARKS

In the Socialist system, four spheres of market and exchange relations may be distinguished: 1) market of consumer goods; 2) sphere of exchange between the state sector and cooperative sector (in Poland and Yugoslavia a small-scale production sector covering individual peasant farms); 3) sphere of exchange of means of production between state enterprises; and 4) foreign trade.

In each of these spheres different problems come to the fore. From the point of view of problems dealt with in the present report, the first two are of special interest to us.

In the market of consumer goods, the prices in conjunction with money income of the population present the main instrument for the implementation of the plan of consumption. When drawing up the plan, the historically shaped structure of consumption is accepted as the starting point. The plan is, however, also a means for the realization of the determined consumption model. This signifies the necessity for a conscious and planned action upon the tastes and likings of the consumers. The market plays a double role: 1) it permits the verification of the plan of consumption; and 2) it allows acting on individual preferences to the extent required by social preferences.

With reference to farms not included in the state sector, prices (broadly understood along with prices for the means of production) are the main means of information about the planned tasks and conditions for the plan's fulfillment. Precepts (directive indices and orders) are the means of open information, while parameters (prices) are the means of coded information.

Both the first and the second are instruments for controlling the economy. The aim of both is, above all, to make the enterprises fulfill the tasks set out in the plan. The differences between them involves the manner in which the end is pursued. First, parameters are organically connected with the stimulating system, as they act only through the link of the parameter with the definite stimulus. Thus, the parameters are instruments of control through action on the economic interest of the enterprise. Breaking this link with the stimuli renders the parameters immediately ineffective as control instruments. Second, control by means of parameters is effected through independent judgment of the enterprise management and not by its omission.[9]

Third, the parameters provide the enterprise with neccessary information

[9] See J Zielinski. *Metody zarzadzania przemyslem socjalistycznym.*

on feedbacks in economy, thus making it possible for the enterprise to take an active part in the very preparation of the plan by the central planning organ.

In agriculture, the information supplied only by prices is not entirely sufficient—hence, the immense importance of the system of contracts as a second fundamental instrument of transmitting the tasks resulting from the plan.

It should be emphasized also that under conditions of uncollectivized agriculture, state control over the inlet and outlet points (that is, the farm supplies aggregate and processing-distribution aggregate) allows for fairly effective control of processes taking place both in the agricultural market and in production itself, and also for the regulation of income distribution.

The market mechanism solves two problems: that of prices and production. Fluctuations in demand (at a given level of production) cause changes in prices, and, in turn, the latter exerts an influence on production. However, the adaptation of production to the new structure of consumer needs usually requires certain time during which prices can be ruinous or advantageous for agriculture. Therefore, it is necessary to create between the prices and agricultural production a less stiff and automatic link than is the case with the free play of economic forces, but, at the same time, serving better the general ends of the state economic policy. This is possible owing to the relaxation to some extent (if no need arises) of the link between the prices paid to the agricultural producers and the retail prices for final products (through an appropriate policy of trade margins, subsidies and charges for processing operations).

Of fundamental importance for the distribution of income between classes of society in the Socialist system is the relationship between agricultural and industrial prices. In the Socialist economy, the sense of the concept of equivalency in exchange between industry and agriculture is undergoing changes. An equivalent exchange is not an exchange according to value, production prices or a definite relation accepted as a reference point (as it was assumed in the concept of parity prices in the United States in 1938), but an exchange corresponding to the principles of distribution ruling in the Socialist economy. According to these principles, the agricultural population should participate in the consumption fund, according to the work performed, while the share of agriculture in the accumulation fund should depend on general proportions of economic growth assumed in the plan (on investment needs of agriculture).

Chapter 10

AGRICULTURAL ORGANIZATION AND PLANNING IN RUMANIA

DUMITRU DUMITRIU

Economic Institute of the Rumanian Academy

Agricultural planning is an essential component of total national economy planning. Actually, it is carried out on the same fundamental principle as in the other branches of the national economy. This is because of the necessarily unitary character of the plan as well as to the fact that agriculture is organized on the selfsame type of Socialist ownership of the means of production (91.3 per cent of the agricultural area and 95.4 per cent of the arable area belonging to the Socialist sector).

At the same time, there is a series of peculiarities in agricultural planning, determined by the characteristic features of the production processes in this branch and by the social and economic traits of the various types of agricultural establishments. The mechanism of agricultural planning is thus permanently linked to the organizational and managerial forms and methods in existence in the various types of agricultural units.

ORGANIZATIONAL AND MANAGERIAL SYSTEMS IN AGRICULTURE

There are two socio-economic sectors in Rumanian agriculture: the state sector and the cooperative sector, with different agricultural functions.[1]

The state sector includes state farms and machine and tractor stations. The farms are Socialist agricultural units organized on land belonging to the state; all means of production and the whole of farm output are state property. At the beginning of 1966, the 721 state farms covered 14 per cent of the country's agricultural area. The average arable area of such farms amounts to about 3000 hectares. Important expanses of pastureland and hayfields in the mountain areas (some 17 per cent of the country's agricultural area) where no agricultural units have been set up are also state-owned; the respective expanses have been given for use to agricultural production cooperatives.

The state farms are enterprises organized on the principle of Socialist administration; they enjoy economic and operational independence, and are endowed with the necessary production means (arable land, housing, installations, tractors and farm machinery, animals, and so forth). The state also allocates monetary means, especially through bank accounts.

A managing director is appointed, assisted by a board of the state farm, comprising expert employees. The board's contributions include drawing up draft plans, analysis of the operational plans—monthly, quarterly and annual—and the adoption of measures for the running of the farming unit.

The higher leading bodies of the state farms are the trusts grouping some five to ten farms, and the regional trust which supervises a given area. Their main task is to insure the drawing up and implementation of production and delivery plans established for the farms in a particular region. The director of the regional trust is backed by a board of directors, made up of the directors of all state farms in the area; this insures expeditious and competent production.

The executive managerial body of the farms on an all-country level is the State Farm Department under the Higher Council of Agriculture. This department is headed by a council of state farms comprising a group of experts.

The machine and tractor stations are state units furnished with tractors and farm machines which assist the cooperatives. The 260 machine and tractor stations, located in compliance with the requirements of the me-

---

[1] In the hilly and mountain areas, there are a number of individual peasant holdings which owing to natural conditions could not constitute agricultural production cooperatives.

chanization of farming operations, have over 55,000 tractors (about 68 per cent of the national fleet), more than 23,000 cereal combines, some 50,000 seeders, and so forth. The average number of tractors for a machine and tractor station is from 150 to 300.

In contrast to the state farms, the machine and tractor stations have neither land nor production of their own. They are units meant only to service the cooperatives. Their activity is financed by the state, and the income goes to the state budget. They are run by a director who is answerable for plan fulfillment at all junctures and makes decisions on all production and administrative problems in the unit. On a regional scale, the activity is controlled and guided by the Machine and Tractor Station Service under the regional agricultural council.

The central leading body of machine and tractor station activity is the Agricultural Mechanization Department under the Higher Council of Agriculture. The contributions of the Agricultural Mechanization Department and of the regional machine and tractor station services relate to the long-range planning, development of the units, and the teaching of new techniques, as well as any other problems connected with the activities of machine and tractor stations.

The agricultural production cooperatives are farming units organized on the basis of cooperative ownership by the respective collectivity of the land and other means of production (animals, farms, machines, implements, and so forth). The entire output is the common property of the members. The 4680 cooperatives in existence at the beginning of this year owned 60.8 per cent of the country's agricultural area. The average area of a cooperative is about 2000 hectares of arable land; this average expanse varies according to the production profile, location in relation to populated centers, and so on.

The agricultural production cooperatives are independent farming units organizing their entire activity in compliance with the development requirements of the respective cooperative, the interests of the members, and the needs of the national economy.

In conformity with the characteristic features of cooperative group ownership, the leading body of the cooperative is the general meeting, the only one having the power to decide on all economic, financial and organizational activities. According to rule provisions, the general meeting debates and endorses the long-range plan, annual production and financial plans, establishes the volume of investments to be made out of funds and credits, decides on the distribution of output and of incomes; elects the chairman, the vice-chairman, as well as the other members of the executive board, the members of the auditing commission, and so forth; approves the conclusion of contracts for work to be carried out by the stations and by other enterprises servicing the cooperatives, analyzes the possibilities of turning to account the marketable farm output and approves its sale to state and cooperative organizations under contracts concluded by common agreement; decides on association with other agricultural cooperatives for carrying out projects of common interest or other actions of mutual assistance; approves affiliation with the district union of agricultural production cooperatives, and so forth.

The executive leading body of the agricultural production cooperative is the executive board which controls activity in the interval between the general meetings and is elected for a two-year period.

The conduct and guidance of the agricultural cooperatives pose complex problems because of the diversity of natural and economic conditions, by relationships between the cooperatives, and by their share and place in the general progress of agriculture. The solving of these problems demands taking into account the characteristic features of the cooperatives' commonly owned property and the nature of the relationship established between the state and the peasantry. The Congress of Agricultural Cooperatives held in March 1966 decided on the setting up of the National Union of Agricultural Production Cooperatives, and of regional and district unions.

The cooperative unions facilitate the pooling of the efforts of the entire peasantry for the economic strengthening of the cooperatives, enabling intercooperative assistance, and insuring the consolidation of inner cooperative democracy.

The basic link in the system of public leadership of cooperative agriculture is the district union, set up by the free association of the cooperatives of the district. It coordinates and guides the activity of the agricultural cooperatives by detailed economic planning, a good organization of the production process, strict observance of the rules of democracy, insures the cooperatives' supply according to production needs, organizes the repair of farming equipment and the means of conveyance on cooperative property, mediates exchanges and mutual assistance between cooperatives in the matter of seeds, fodder and other necessities.

The district union initiates and organizes joint actions involving irrigation, draining and damming, combating soil erosion, and so forth.

The regional union of cooperatives coordinates and guides the activity of the district unions.

The National Union, the central coordinating and guiding body, collaborates with the Higher Council of Agriculture and the State Planning Committee in the elaboration of the plan, joins with the state bodies and organizations in working out the sales system for the produce of the agricultural cooperatives, makes general recommendations to guide the cooperatives in their orientation toward production, investment, labor organization, rate-setting and remuneration, the distribution and employment of material and monetary means, and keeps a watchful eye on the implementation of the investment plan in cooperative agriculture. Participating in the working out of all the norms, the National Union represents the economic, legal and social interests of the agricultural cooperatives.

In the framework of the managerial system of agriculture as a whole, a particular role is played by the Higher Council of Agriculture whose task it is to carry out state policy. The council conducts general guidance over the whole of agriculture, insuring its planned development, steady progress, the growth of plant and animal output, and the economic development of Socialist state and cooperative organizations. The council has, as territorial bodies, regional and district councils. In their capacity as state bodies, the councils concern themselves with problems related to production, means of production, the labor force, investment and the remuneration of agricultural branches; they insure expert technical guidance for the whole of agriculture and a correct distribution of crops per zone within each farming unit; the plans and land melioration work for irrigation systems and direction for the best possible use of irrigated areas; steady improvement in the activities of the machine and tractor stations; the expansion of scientific research in close connection with the practical needs of agriculture; the introduction and generalization of positive results in production; also, by cooperation with the Ministry of Education, the training of experts with secondary and higher education; the organization of mass zoo-technical schooling and the distribution of technical information.

THE AGRICULTURAL PLANNING SYSTEM

Agricultural development plans are worked out with lavish documentation and economic analysis, after research into resources and possibilities, of the most necessary and efficient channels to use during the period covered. Account is taken, on the one hand, of the farm produce requirements of the national economy (foodstuff for consumption, raw material for the food and light industries, state reserves, and export availabilities) and, on the other, of agricultural potentialities for insuring the output to meet these needs.

Substantiation of the calculations concerning the development of agriculture implies a deep examination of the possibilities for increasing marketable output at the main plant, and animal produce, based on the extensive and many-sided developments in agriculture.

A first group of factors taken into account when determining the possibilities of stepping up agricultural output and marketable farm produce is: growth of the stock of tractors and farm machines, the amounts of mineral fertilizer and insecticides, the inclusion of new land into the agricultural circuit, fighting soil erosion, and so forth.

A second group of factors covers the most rational use of the land stock, widespread use of the latest gains in technology, the supplying of choice seeds and planting material, and of pedigreed animals, and an increasingly large-scale application of the whole set of agro-zoo-technical operations. Surveying for the zoning of agricultural production is of great help in establishing the most profitable use of the land stock. Such surveying supplies the planning bodies and the Socialist farming units with information to insure a better orientation of agricultural plant and animal output. By making use of the elements furnished by zoning, the most adequate technico-organizational and economic measures are defined for every zone, as well as the most efficient use of the production reserves at hand, of investments and of labor force resources with a view to achieving a steady increase in agricultural output, higher labor productivity and lower costs.

Another group of factors taken into account in determining the agricultural development potentialities consists of economic conditions insuring material incentives to producers for stepping up plant and animal output.

Besides these factors, the improved qualification of agricultural workers, the development of mass agro-zoo-technical schooling, and the steadily increasing role of engineers and technicians in the Socialist agricultural units are analyzed.

In determining the development potentialities of agriculture, thought is given to the mutual correlation of its two chief branches: plant output and animal output.

Scrutiny of the possibilities for progress in agriculture includes—besides quantitative definitions of the rate of growth of output—the conditions under which growth is to be achieved: the necessary investments and their efficiency, the number of personnel and their training, the rate and standard of labor productivity, increased economic efficiency materialized in a (relative) reduction in costs, and so forth. Highly important, too, is the study of agriculture's links with the other branches and spheres of activity in the national economy.

The development plan of agriculture comprises the following main chapters: plant and animal output, volume of operations carried out by machine and tractor stations, investment construction and capital repairs, and import-export.

The draft plan is being worked out—on the basis of proposals which come from the production units—by the Higher Council of Agriculture in cooperation with the National Union of Agricultural Production Cooperatives and the ministries or other economic organizations concerned (the Ministry of Food Industry, the contracting organizations, and so on). This draft plan is circulated to those in charge of implementations for further improvement. The general plan and correlation with other branches of the national economy is examined by the other ministries concerned and by the State Planning Committee; the final draft plan is thus worked out.

The plan of agricultural development, incorporated in the single draft plan of development of the national economy, is submitted for endorsement to the Council of Ministers and the Grand National Assembly. Once endorsed, it becomes the state plan, binding for all those in charge of its implementation.

The plan tasks are made known officially to those in charge: the State Farm Department, the Agricultural Mechanization Department, and the regional and district people's councils as local bodies of state power.

Both when framing the plan and its implementation, emphasis is placed on the particularities of the types of Socialist ownership in agriculture. The state farms and the machine and tractor stations draw up their plans based on the information they receive.

Plan tasks are not transmitted to the agricultural production cooperatives. The plan is phased out only up to the level of the District Agricultural Council in charge of the plan for the respective district.

On the basis of the plan targets, the contracting bodies, together with the executive boards of the agricultural production cooperatives, examine the contract possibilities for the sale of farm produce.

The executive boards and the district unions of the agricultural production cooperatives assist the agricultural cooperatives in concentrating on the marketable output of every crop and animal.

On the basis of contracts concluded by common agreement with the contracting bodies, of the unit's own needs of farm produce for both production and individual consumption, the executive boards draw up a draft plan of production and finances and submit it for endorsement to the general meeting of the cooperative membership. The general meeting is the only authority to make decisions on the production plan and concluding contracts for the sale of produce.

Economic levers used in the orientation and implementation of the plan of agricultural development. The orientation of agriculture is buttressed by economic levers, among which the most important are the financing and credit systems and the system of contracts and purchases of farm produce.

The financial system is an important means by which the Socialist state orients, organizes and coordinates the whole process of economic development, including agriculture. In this context, there are two categories of financial relations: financial relations proper and credit relations. Whereas the credit relations reflect the formation and distribution of money funds to be repayed, the financial relations reflect the formation and distribution of nonrepayable money funds.

The system of financial relations contributes to the harmonious blending of centralized state direction of the development of the national economy with the creative initiative of the enterprises and of all participants in the production process. By finances, the state exercises control over the efficient use of investments, the observance of a strict savings policy, systematic increase in labor productivity, and cost cuts. The centralized system combines economic independence for each state enterprise through the application of the principles of Socialist administration for each unit.

The farms are state-financed for investments under nonrepayable financing.

For the needs of their production processes, the necessary circulating assets are insured to the farms through two channels: their own, normative circulating assets established according to minimal needs throughout the year, and bank loans. These loans are granted by the units of the National Bank, bearing interest at the rate of 4 per cent annually, and repayment proceeds in step with produce deliveries.

As already mentioned, the state farms are enterprises organized on Socialist principles, which insures their operational economic independence within the single plan, and offers material incentives to the units and to all employees. The economic independence of each unit is insured by its contribution to inner organization and production planning, the introduction of new technologies, technical and material supplies and the sale of output, recruitment and training of the labor force, contract relationship, and the employment of material incentives. In this context, the state farms aim at insuring from the outset not only recovery of production costs, but also profit. This profit, as a net income of the unit, depends directly on the manner in which the production costs plan is being implemented, and, thus, stimulates fulfillment of the tasks concerning the reduction of cost prices. The portion of profit left for the farm is meant to be used for meeting the unit's own needs: forming its fund, improvement of production technology, for improving employees' living conditions (especially housing), and for bonuses.

The agricultural cooperatives make important investments and finance their whole economic activity primarily out of their own incomes.

At the same time, the state grants to the cooperatives long-term loans for investments and short-term loans for production purposes.

In the 1961–1965 period, the cooperatives were granted long-term loans amounting to 3900 million lei (that is 2.9 times more than the volume of loans granted from 1956 to 1960). These loans are granted to the cooperatives by the National Bank of Rumania, for land melioration work, purchase of livestock, expansion of the material basis needed for zoo-technology, vineyard and orchard plantation, construction of storing spaces for farm produce, introduction and extension of small-scale mechanization, water supply, and so forth.

The loan terms are most advantageous. Loans bearing interest for cooperatives are at a rate of only 2 per cent annually. Moreover, repayment is phased out—in relation to the object of investment—for a period ranging from three to twelve years. Hence, loans for strawberry plantations are repayable in three years, while those for irrigation in twelve. Noteworthy also is the date when repayment starts. For instance, the repayment of loans for irrigation starts in the third year after the loan has been granted, those for the purchase of calves in the fourth year, and so forth. Start of repayment is based on the principle of payment to be carried out after the object of the investment has started production.

In order to spotlight the significance of long-term loans for the development of the cooperatives, suffice it to say that in the 1960–1965 period, these loans contributed upwards of 40 per cent to the growth of the basic means of the agricultural production cooperatives. With the help of loans, the cooperatives increased—especially their livestock—and insured most of the zoo-technical constructions needed.

Short-term loans, too, are granted by the state under advantageous conditions. As a rule, the cooperatives meet the cash expenditures out of income derived from the sale of farm produce. Since the sale of farm produce takes place generally in the second half of the year, whereas production expenditures occur mostly in the first half, a gap appears between spending and income, and this gap is covered by the short-term loans. These are of two types: loans for production purposes and advance loans for farm produce contracting.

Production loans are granted for a fixed time, not longer than a year, and are repayable under agreed terms. Such loans bear small interest (an annual rate of only 3 per cent).

Advance loans for contracting are granted by the state units which conclude contracts for the purchase of farm produce, and may be as high as a maximum of 50 per cent of the value of contracted produce.

Farm produce is correlated with the other branches of the national economy through the marketable output realized at the state central fund of agricultural produce. Marketable output is the fundamental element in establishing the profile of farm output, the principal premise in determining the level of production needed for meeting both home consumption and export requirements, and for defining the technical and material basis to insure the planned level.

The sources for the state central fund of agricultural produce include deliveries by state units (marketable output of state farms, remuneration in kinds of work carried out by the machine and tractor stations) and the contracts and purchases from agricultural cooperatives and from individual producers.

The state farms deliver marketable output at plan-set prices; these vary according to the quality of produce, the period of delivery, quantity, and so forth. The prices are set to insure (under normal production conditions) a remuneration from production.

The establishment of the most adequate forms of exchanges with the peasantry is highly important and a most intricate problem. The organization of commodity exchanges between town and country must be in compliance with the socio-economic objectives of state policy, being channelled toward a steady rise in farm output, improvement of the urban population's supply of farm products, of the peasantry with industrial products, and of industry with agricultural raw material.

The Socialist organization of exchanges between town and village insures the establishment of a harmonious relationship between the sale of farm produce to the state and the purchase of industrial goods needed by agriculture.

The basic sales system of marketable output for the chief produce of the agricultural cooperatives is achieved by contracts concluded with the state purchasing organizations or with the supply and retail sale cooperatives. Vegetables and fruit are even sold through the cooperatives' own system.

The contracts concluded between the cooperatives and the trade organizations are based on the principle of free agreement.

The contracting system blends in a single context the principle of granting material incentives to the cooperatives with the needs of creating the central fund of farm produce, under the conditions of exchanges carried out on the basis of trade relations. Both the state and the agricultural cooperatives and their members are interested in the firm establishment of such a relationship.

The state uses this economic lever in order to direct the cooperatives toward the development of those branches which are particularly important for the national economy, as an efficient instrument for solving problems related to a planned orientation of Socialist agriculture. With the help of this system, the attainment of the indicators of the agricultural production plan is buttressed by the economic stimuli furnished by the contracts.

The contracting system provides material incentive to the agricultural cooperatives as well. Under conditions when marketable produce is sold to the state at prices which take into account actual production expenses (thus insuring the remuneration of output), the contracts help the cooperatives to organize their production, to distribute the crops over their area correctly, and to develop a branch relying on sound sales conditions.

The manner in which the contract system has been conceived and is being applied insures material incentives to the peasantry for selling their produce to the state.

The contracts provide a guarantee of a certain sale of output. In instances when they are concluded for a period of several years, not only do the contracts provide an opportunity for a long-range orientation of production, but extra prices too are insured. With rice, for instance, contracts concluded for several years secure an extra 20 per cent over the basic price.

Contract prices insure a refund of production costs and profitableness of production. The average basic prices are differentiated according to production zones. In order to encourage the growth of output and conclusion of contracts, basic prices are supplemented with extra rises contingent upon the quantity and quality of output. Hence, the agricultural cooperatives selling cereals to the state in amounts upwards of 30 tons benefit by a 10 per cent higher price; for each additional kilogram in terms of hectolitre weight, 1 per cent more is paid. There is a similar differentiation of prices in relation to quantity and quality for all produce: fruit, vegetables, meat, milk, wool, and so forth.

An important advantage enjoyed by the contracting agricultural cooperatives is loans without interest, which granted at the conclusion of contracts, represent some 50 per cent of the contract value. These sums are spent partly for meeting some production needs, and partly for a regular, periodic advance payment in cash for workday units, which gives the farmers income all year round.

The contracts concluded for farm produce, as a main form of the realization of the agricultural cooperatives' marketable output, has proved an adequate relationship between the state and the peasantry. This is borne out by the steady growth of produce for which contracts are concluded by the cooperatives with the state. The positive results obtained in recent years in the formation of the central fund show that the contract system has greatly contributed to the growth of production and to a greater volume of farm produce and to an improved living standard for the peasantry.

The organizational and planning system of agriculture has proved its efficiency. The most telling fact is that agricultural output permanently increased throughout the period of Socialist agricultural transformation as well as thereafter.

The growth of agricultural output has brought an improved supply of farm foodstuff to the population, agricultural raw material to industry, and, moreover, an increase in export availabilities.

The methods of agricultural organization and planning are, however, not ideal. They are steadily improving with experience from the new phenomena emerging in economic development. Therefore, the questions related to the improvement of agricultural organization and planning are a main concern to economists in Rumania.

Table 15. Growth of gross agricultural output in Rumania (1950–1964).

Category	1950–1954	1955–1959	1960–1964
Gross agricultural output	100.0	124.9	144.2
Population (July)	100.0	106.9	112.1
Per capita agricultural output	100.0	116.8	128.6

Chapter 11

PLANNING AND MANAGEMENT OF ENTERPRISES AND FIRMS IN THE USSR

D. ALLACHVERDJAN
Academy of Sciences of the USSR

The Soviet Socialist economy is a planned economy. The state disposes of the basic means of production owned by the nation, manages the processes of production and distributes the gross national product and national income over the whole economy scale. Naturally, therefore, the economic interbranch and interplant relations are also planned.

The objective economic mechanism in the USSR is free of capitalist production features such as market competition and the fact that private profit is the basic source of private wealth accumulation and the main incentive for social production on the grounds of spontaneous economic relations. Under socialism, *planned* economic relations have been developed; the goal is fullest satisfaction for national, collective and personal needs instead of private enrichment.

The objective economic proportions are established by the conscious activity of the people—the blind forces of the market having been eliminated. This is the aim of central state planning. Economic planning generally springs from a necessity for providing stable proportionality consciously maintained. In practice, it sometimes happens that a certain plan, after its fulfillment, does not achieve the desired proportionality. Such cases represent the drawbacks in working out the plans.

The objective grounds of economic proportions are the development of productive forces, rates of material-production development and the accumulated skill level of manpower. The main point centers on certain social and technological economic conditions. When these are dynamic, the proportionality conditions considered in the methods of national planning are also consciously changed. Therefore it becomes possible to use various proportionality patterns.

Thus proportionality is achieved by planning based on the rates of development of the whole national economy and individual enterprises, as well—the proper utilization of all the material resources being considered. In outlining its concept of planning, the Socialist state aims at establishing the optimum proportions grounded on proper scientific methods, norms and calculations. It implies the most effective allocation of the resources available in compliance with the objective economic laws of socialism.

With conditions changing, the problem arises of permanently modernizing the methods of planning and management. To solve this, large-scale economic reform has been in operation since the beginning of 1966. The solution of any problem is reduced to revealing all the possible variations and choosing the best. In practice, we have the means to achieve this goal. Thus, planning should reveal the most efficient manufacturing variations to secure the best results under available possibilities. These variations are based on administratively set targets for output product-mix and location of production. The variations differ in the amount of capital outlay and current expenditures and their correlation.

The know-how of choosing the best variation related to the level of scientific elaboration of the planning methods depends on the knowledge and skill of the executives responsible for the working out of plans. The most effective decision-making can be considered the main function of management—the essence of the Socialist economy-planned management.

To facilitate this choice, the newest computers and economic methods are being used. Planning accounting is extremely complex and many-sided, and it is possible to analyze the many variations and find the best only with the help of computers and econometric methods.

The system of planning and management is being improved every year with advances in science and with experience. We use current plans (the yearly plans broken down quarterly and monthly, and long-range plans set for five and more years). Our current planning constitutes a part of the long-range plan, since otherwise it would lose its perspective and become inefficient.

To correlate the current and long-range plans effectively, the method of permanent planning is used, implying ever-delayed schedules in long-range plans. It means: when the calendar year scheduled for the fulfillment of the five-year plan is over, the plan for the sixth year is already under development, and so on. The idea of permanent planning has proved to be necessary to avoid disproportions in the national economy.

We have two types of planning in the USSR—centralized and decentralized. The first means government centralized planning for the whole economy—all composite parts and items considered. The second is used at the individual enterprise level and at various economic sectors. The effective management of the national economy under public ownership of the means of production can be achieved if the management of basic economic activities is centralized.

Under socialism, the objective economic laws cease to be spontaneous. They are realized through the conscious will of the collective represented by the state. Therefore, central planning appears to be the objective necessity for the functioning of the economic system based on Socialist ownership. Centralized planning coordinates all the stages and aspects of national income distribution and the determination of the national economy pattern —its rates of growth and major proportions. The plan enables the state to carry out a single fiscal and technological policy, to create price formation, and so on. Centralized planning serves to establish the most efficient social and technological economic proportions. Thus the state is meeting the requirements of the objective law of socialism—the law of planned proportional development of the national economy.

However, the above-mentioned factors do not justify direct administrative planning in all stages of expanded reproduction, determining all the mix-up, marketing, and so on. Administrative centralized planning has proved to be effective only when it refers to the most flexible and mobile factors of expanded production, vital for establishing proportionality—for instance, the proportionality between accumulation and consumption funds on the one hand, and the set rates of expanded production on the other.

As far as establishing proper economic relations is concerned, that should be the responsibility of individual enterprises and firms interested in the most effective fulfillment of the national plan targets. The relations between the plan targets set by the state and individual enterprises are naturally flexible.

The efficiency of national production and consequently the validity of the plans themselves depend mostly on the proper determination of economic criteria for the central and local bodies, ministries, firm and enterprise activities. Yet the proper criteria determination does not fully exhaust all the opportunities for successful plan fulfillment. The opportunities available could be carried out only through the conscious activities of the people. The possibility of planning itself does not guarantee the planning bodies with the issue of scientifically sound, detailed economic plans.

The working out of plans is assigned to the highly skilled professionals experienced in economy, technology and management. When planning and fulfilling the state plan, the fact should be considered that the Socialist economy has some nonantagonistic contradictions. For instance, central and local interests often vary. The same is true of the needs of the nation on the whole and those of individual enterprises. Consideration of these contradictions and of their solution is necessary while working out and fulfilling the single state plan. This points to the fact that planned development is not realized automatically. The optimum efficiency of real plan fulfillment depends on knowledge achieved and on the nation's mastering the objective economic laws, all practical factors considered.

Planned Socialist economy is confronted with the existence of the law of value and with market relations. Therefore, the utilization of related value categories—such as money, price, credit, and finances—appears to be an objective necessity. The value categories function at all the stages of economic turnover. The amount of fixed and circulating capital is determined by their value; capital depreciation is measured by the cost of its amortization; the surplus product is distributed and redistributed by means of money, finances and prices; manpower is paid wages according to labor, and so forth.

In the latter case, the value form is used for providing material incentives, while saving the social labor, for increasing labor productivity. At the same time, the value serves as the necessary measure of planned accounting of labor resources, as a means for the state to supervise labor expenditures and consumption.

Planning is based on balance-method accounting for resources and expenditures. The balance method allows for establishing detailed economic proportions and finding a means for their improvement. The balances are made up in material form (for ferrous and nonferrous metals, fuel, cereal, and so on) and in value form for financing, income and the expenditures of the population, national income, and so forth. The material- and value-balance forms account for all kinds of resources in the plan projects and the consequent evaluation of real possibilities for plan fulfillment. Planning balances are made up not only at the center level but also at the level of individual enterprises—for instance, income-expenditure balance.

Economic reform in the USSR contributes to flexible coordination of centralized planning and economic initiative of the enterprises. It promotes the expansion of commodity and money turnover among enterprises, while organizing and planning the development of material incentives aimed at production increase and cost-saving. The main point is to abolish the inefficient system of rigid, centralized decision-making for all the stages of expanded reproduction.

We consider as groundless the statements of some Western economists that the idea of centralized planning will have to be abandoned and replaced by a free market mechanism, that the plans are to become unnecessary check figures (so called "indicative" or "informative" planning).

Under the new reform, the enterprises and firms would be assigned only a minimum of the aggregate indices within which they would freely plan their activities and negotiate with their contractors and consumers.

The measures being undertaken could be summarized as follows: 1) limiting the administrative planning indices at the enterprise level; 2) rejecting the system of the petty tutelage of enterprise work; 3) evaluating enterprise activity on the basis of the sold product and profitability; 4) leaving the considerable share of profit received by enterprises as well as amortization at their disposal for expanded reproduction (a part of the profit being used for material incentives); 4) expanding to a greater extent the direct market relations between enterprises and consumers; 5) introducing interest payment for funds used; 6) substituting to a greater extent credit for budget outlays; and 7) strengthening economic sanctions.

As one can see, the planning system is aimed at promoting the effective development of the national economy. The achievement of this aim depends mostly on the advanced forms and methods of economic management.

Planned economy is characterized by the specific forms and methods of management. The solution of a particular management problem—that is, distributing its functions, establishing administrative managerial bodies, and choosing the methods and forms—is directly influenced by production and national conditions and by the economic tasks set.

Production management is complex, requiring various practical measures to achieve the set target and organization measures to reach this goal. This process implies the collection and analysis of data on running economic activities and proper decision-making.

The efficiency of management is ultimately characterized by 1) quality and quantity of the manufacturing data to be analyzed; 2) promptness in data collecting and analyzing; 3) the effectiveness of the data analysis, the profoundness and optimality of decision-making; and 4) the effectiveness of decision-making realization.

The availability of equipment and advanced manufacturing methods per worker contributing to a rise in productivity is of the utmost importance in effectively carrying out decision-making. As is well known, cybernetic, electronic and automatic devices help the manager find the most efficient solutions.

The development and usage of computer technique for national economy planning and production management is ever expanding in the USSR. An extensive technological development program has been included in the new five-year plan for the period of 1966–1970. Technological progress, however, does not make management practice wholly automatic, yet it changes the managers' work making it more effective. Social production management, besides the pure technological aspects, is and always will be connected with the organization activities of the masses. It means that any automatization of management would not be feasible without the active participation of the people.

The essential change in social and economic aspects of production management in the USSR is revealed first of all in the fact that the producers of material goods cease to be the object of management as the material objects of production are. They have become the subject executing management in all the spheres of the national economy. Production management in the USSR and in other Socialist countries is no longer a prerogative of individual competitors. It is a social function executed by the state and various collective organizations. Thus, management is carried out for the benefit of the whole nation in the frame of the single state plan with all members of society involved.

Industrial management consists of a broad system of economic, organizational and educational measures contributing to the effective functioning of all the industrial links. The enterprise as the free economic unit has specific interests that should be combined with the interests of the state. Because the state enterprises enjoy economic freedom, they are able to employ the best means for achieving national economic targets determined by the single centralized state plan.

Science of management deals with the problem of recommending sound economic measures for supervising the producers' activities as well as for the organization of the current administration. This points to the following two aspects in production management: a stable economic mechanism and a single economic plan on a countrywide scale are required for the enterprises to execute their production and financial activities, and management is assigned to the central administrative bodies promoting plan fulfillment and maintaining the given level of economic development. Management is responsible for coordinating enterprise activities, assisting when necessary, and for taking administrative measures to improve poor production factors.

Presently the usage of appropriate economic levers on the basis of the expanded self-accounting principle (*chozraschet*) has priority over administrative measures. Centralized planned management based on public ownership of means of production combines the single-person and collective leadership with the broad participation of the working masses.

The Socialist economy is a complex system where the unity of the whole does not exclude yet imply the relative freedom of the individual parts. The enterprise is the main economic unit of the Soviet economic system. Such a concept of management, when the freedom and initiative of individual economic units are combined with state centralized planning, is called "democratic centralism."

In October 1965, the new decree was issued characterizing the Socialist state production enterprise:

> The Socialist state production enterprise using the state property legalized for its administration and disposal and relying on hired manpower under the guidance of the above administrative body executes the economic activity (that is, producing output, fulfilling the planned and contracted tasks, rendering service) in accordance with the national plan target on the basis of the self-accounting principle. The enterprise carries out all the obligations and enjoys rights related to the mentioned activity, makes up its own balance and possesses legal rights.

The forms and methods of Soviet industry management are developed according to the objective factor of the enterprises functioning on a self-accounting basis. The objectively needed principle of self-accounting under planned management secures the proper balance of input-output. This principle requires that the enterprises be responsible for profitability and expand material and moral incentives to achieve it.

Production management on a self-accounting basis results in the following rights and obligations in the spheres of economy, organization and law: 1) The work of each enterprise is organized according to the state plan for production volume and for the main technological and economic indices; 2) To fulfill the state plan, the enterprise is provided by the state with the necessary fixed and circulating capital of which it may freely dispose within the framework of the plan and the law; 3) The enterprise possesses legal rights, and contracts for deliveries and selling; it is materially responsible for the fulfillment of contract obligations and funds; 4) Each enterprise has its accounts of loss and profit and makes up its own balance; 5) Enterprise work is financially supervised by the above credit organizations, influencing its economic activity through various economic levelers—the material sanctions included; 6) A special fund is created to provide material incentives for the effectively working enterprises, collective units, and individual workers.

Enterprise management is based on the principle of single-person responsibility combined with the broad participation of the workers collectively in the discussion and implementation of measures for state plan fulfillment. The enterprise manager is assigned to his post and dismissed by the above administration bodies. He is fully responsible to the state for enterprise work.

Within his rights, the manager issues orders in accordance with the labor law, employs and dismisses workers, gives incentives and penalizes when necessary. All these functions must be sanctioned by the enterprise trade-union committee.

Among a large number of mass organizations participating in the enterprise management, the trade-union committee plays an important role. The committees take part in working out production plans and investment projects and sponsor the building of houses and cultural programs. The enterprise administration must consult the trade committees when determining rates for different job categories, setting the skill categories, revising current norms, introducing an incentive system of wages and distributing bonuses. The trade committees undertake proper safety measures, care for improving labor conditions, and provide for cultural and social welfare. They are given the right to request the manager to report on production plan fulfillment. Thus, the trade committees act as worker representatives in bargaining agreements.

One of the most effective organizations involving the masses in production management is the permanently functioning production council established at enterprise and shop levels and numbering no less than a hundred workers and employees. The members of the production council are elected yearly at the general meetings summoned by the workers and employees, trade, party and council organizations and by scientific, technological and inventors' societies. The administration representatives also take part in the council. The production council enables the workers and employees to take an active part in managing enterprise production and financial activities. The enterprise council is summoned as often as one or two times a quarter. The production council meeting at the shop level takes place once a month. Council meetings deal with the most important production problems of advancing interplant and shop planning, mastering new techniques, modernizing manufacturing methods, improving the quality of goods, and many others. The manager orders that the measures recommended by production councils be fulfilled. It is headed by the enterprise trade-union committee.

The activities of public organizations contributing to the perfection and democratization of production management forms are ever expanding in the USSR. Economic management is executed by the state authoritative bodies exercising legal sanctions, yet the process is essentially based on the system of economic interest. The self-accounting principle is the most effective tool for coordinating the administrative and economic aspects of management.

This means that production management being essentially economic possesses the legal form embracing both aspects of management. As far as the problem of relating the economic and administrative sides is concerned, it is being solved in accordance with the concept of the priority of the economic basis over the legal superstructure in state management.

This peculiarity of state-management production was repeatedly pointed out by V. I. Lenin who especially stressed it in the first version of his article "The Urgent Tasks of the Soviet Power" first published in November 1962:

> The problem of state management is also distinguished by the specific feature consisting in the fact that we now should speak of such a management only when the prevailing significance is attributed to the economics and not to the policy . . . when the political tasks are submitted to the economic tasks. And presently it should be quite clear for us that the task of state management is to be reduced first and foremost to the purely economic. It is reduced to the task of economic reorganization.[1]

This means first that the pattern of managerial bodies and their divisions should be established not on an administrative but on a production basis, and second that the administrative and economic functions should not be divided (one managerial body should execute both functions).

[1] V. I. Lenin, *The Complete Works*, v. 36, p. 130.

The subordination of the economic aspects of management to the administrative results in bureaucracy, rigid administration and illegal actions. Recently in the USSR the administrative methods of production management have been given too much attention at the expense of the economic methods. Consequently, superfluous regulation of enterprise work occurred, restricting economic freedom and initiative and ultimately releasing the workers from responsibility for production development. The formal approach to the self-accounting principle rendered its usage inefficient.

The aim of the current economic reform is to find the enterprise work-evaluation factors that would enable us to set the closest correlation between state and individual enterprise interests. The proposed system of planning and management implies that the workers should receive material incentives not only for increasing the output but also for improving its quality as well and for revealing and using local reserves on the basis of the self-accounting principle. The greatest significance is attributed now to such factors as profit, profitability and the recently introduced index of the sold output.

The former practice of supplying the enterprises with fixed and circulating capital gratuitously from the state budget has not stimulated them enough for efficient allocation of funds. On the contrary, there were a large number of cases when the enterprises, disregarding their benefit, strove for spare assets, piled stocks, and reserved uninstalled equipment.

Under the new reform, the enterprises would not be supplied with the fixed and circulating capital free of charge. They must pay interest. Bank credit is to become the source of investing in the running of enterprises and of extending their circulating capital to create incentives to use all the material and financial resources available.

The success of the new reform will depend to a great extent on the methods of economic management which should be worked out to meet the real economic needs of enterprises. Under the new reform, the managerial and economic freedom of the enterprises should be expanded to a considerable extent.

The first successful results achieved at the enterprises working on new bases enable us to come to the most optimistic conclusions. The data for the first quarter of 1966 collected for the first 43 enterprises where new methods of planning and management have been introduced justify this. While adopting the new system, the enterprises put forward their own plans requiring that the yearly index of sold product should be increased to 25 million rubles. At the mining metallurgical trust in the town of

Norilsk, the increase in profit amounted to 63 per cent. At the first Moscow watch plant it amounted to 41 per cent, and at the Saprudnensky glass plant to 33 per cent. The 43 enterprises considered have contributed to the budget 4 million rubles above the plan. The material incentive funds established at the enterprises amounted to 18.2 million rubles; the house building, social welfare and cultural funds amounted to 3.2 million rubles; the production development fund to 5.6 million rubles. Presently the 200 enterprises have launched work on a new basis. In the future, all Soviet industry will be reorganized, and the new system will be expanded at the national economy scale.

Production management of the individual enterprises is not the single form of Socialist economic relations. The Socialist society is the society of associated producers closely related to the whole system of branch and regional management. In this connection, the establishment of branch self-accounting production firms has become of the utmost importance.

In the USSR, the branch (vertical) system of industrial management is being presently used, as distinguished from the former (horizontal) system of management, by the regional economic councils. The self-accounting production firms will be gradually developed within the framework of the various branch industries and the appropriate ministries.

The self-accounting firms have the following advantages: 1) the possibility of expanding specialization and cooperation within a firm to curtail the number of duplicate service departments and shops and consequently lowering production cost; 2) firm management is given legal and material responsibilities. It disposes of the single balance and accounts using the common incentive—resulting in the common interest on the part of the enterprises and in the direct responsibility on the part of the firm managers. Besides, opportunities are created for flexible allocation of material and financial resources.

The branch production firms are organized according to three main patterns. The establishing of the firm on the basis of an economically and technologically developed head enterprise is most widespread. In this case, the enterprise manager is simultaneously assigned management of the firm. The functions of the firm's managerial body are assigned to the administrative office of the head enterprise; the latter is also responsible for some additional centralized functions such as technological planning and financing. The managerial body is subordinated to the appropriate deputy managers of the firm.

Either all the enterprises and units amalgamated in the firm work on a full self-accounting basis, or only a number of them do. In the latter case, the remaining number work on the inner self-accounting basis. All the enterprises are headed by firm managers.

The second pattern refers to the firm where all the administrative and service functions are wholly centralized. The enterprises amalgamated into a firm have neither economic nor legal freedom. They become productive units working on the inner self-accounting basis and headed by the unit managers preserving their administrative office. Production shops and other divisions are reorganized on the basis of detailed manufacturing specialization for profiled output.

The third pattern is sort of intermediate. Similar to the first, it is characterized by the existence of the head enterprise, and, similar to the second pattern, it has centralized administrative and service departments.

The difference lies in the fact that under the third pattern all the enterprises amalgamated into a firm preserve their economic and legal freedom. Some enterprises have at their disposal no service departments—only small managerial groups—others, especially distantly located ones, preserve some service departments such as planning and production, labor and wage, accounting, and so on. Yet all these enterprises enjoy legal and economic freedom and have an account current at the state bank.

The legal status is one and the same for all three organization patterns.

The firm features can be summarized as follows: firms are free economic units functioning on the self-accounting basis; their activity is directed to the fulfillment of the planned targets set by the appropriate ministries; they dispose of fixed and circulating capital and of their own accounting balance keeping their account at the state bank.

The choice of pattern depends on the nature of production. All the organization patterns can be effective (as has been proved in practice).

Planning and management in the USSR is being constantly developed and modernized. By using the advantages of planned management, the country has achieved great success in the field of national economy, culture, and the people's welfare. Presently a new five-year plan has been worked out and executed in the USSR for the period of 1966–1970. The plan will greatly contribute to Communist construction and to economic competition with capitalism.

The report naturally does not deal with all the problems of planning and management of the Socialist economy and related forms and methods. Only some major problems have been discussed giving a general notion of the planning methods and organization patterns in the USSR.

Chapter 12

RECENT DEVELOPMELTS IN MANAGEMENT AND PLANNING IN YUGOSLAV ENTERPRISES

NENAD MILEUSNIĆ
Yugoslav Institute of Economic Research

In order to examine the recent developments in management and planning in Yugoslav enterprises, one should consider the problem throughout the period beginning in 1945 when industrialization started, and ending in 1965 when economic and social reform was introduced in the country. In the course of those twenty years, the systems of management and planning were developing from centrally planned (on the part of the state) to decentralized (open to competition and to the influence of all the forces acting on the market). The management system within the enterprises was evolving in accordance with this development. The economic and social reform introduced in 1965 has brought about further improvements in the methods of management and planning which should contribute to an increase in productive and economic efficiency within the individual enterprises.

DEVELOPMENT OF MANAGEMENT AND PLANNING IN THE YUGOSLAV ENTERPRISES FROM 1945-1965

In 1938, the national income in Yugoslavia, coming mainly from agriculture, amounted to $8.00 per capita. After the Second World War, the country was gradually industrialized so that within the period 1945–1965 national income increased to $50.00 per capita. This increase was largely due to the industrial development of the country.

The development of the Yugoslav economy started in 1945. First of all, the "basic" industries and power systems were developed, whereby we relied upon the natural resources of the country and partly on tradition. This primarily concerned coal and nonferrous metal mines, next the enterprises for further processing nonferrous metals, and then the power plants. Immediately after this, the metal trades began developing (the machine building industry and related enterprises).

From 1945 to 1952, Yugoslavia was building its industry on the basis of economic plans created by special institutions. These institutions were part of the state administration on the level of the federation, the republics and communities, and their participation in planning depending on the importance of the plants (the construction or operation of which was to be planned).

The investment plans determined plant size, allocation, manner of construction, personnel, and so on. The production plans of individual enterprises specified the variety and volume of production in physical and value terms. They also indicated the number of items to be produced by individual enterprises, keeping in mind the requirements of the country as a whole.

The Yugoslav experience at the beginning of the industrialization period might be of use to the developing countries; therefore we shall make a brief review of some of the troublesome problems and their solutions.

The first that were faced when planning the development of Yugoslav industry were whether one should give priority to investment in "basic" industries and power systems or to other industries. The former were given priority because of the supply of natural resources and because in this way a material basis for a faster development of the over-all economy could be created. However, such an approach to planning required large investments followed by a decrease in the standard of living.

The second group of problems was whether one should invest in new technology and equipment or buy up old equipment to be used by workers coming from the country. In some factories, old equipment, obtained through the war reparation scheme, was installed, and, in others, new machines were bought so it was possible to make comparisons. We found that old equipment and technology hampered development. New equipment, however, demanded special training for the workers.

The third group had to do with product development. Yugoslav industry at that time did not have enough engineers to design modern products. For that reason we made use of the technical documentation obtained through the war reparation scheme or through technical assistance organizations. Somewhat later, modern foreign licenses were bought, and that helped accelerate industrial development. Purchase of licenses was conditioned by importing product parts. As the assembly jobs were being replaced by complete production of the parts, this type of industrial development proved very useful.

In this first period of development, individual enterprises were managed by boards that belonged to the state. They took care of the execution of plans, kept records of plan tasks, and so forth. They coordinated individual enterprises, securing raw material and manpower, and distributed the final products. Also, the boards appointed managers.

At that time, the managers only carried out operative tasks. These tasks were within the framework of the economic policy of the enterprises, and the policy was determined by the boards. The share of the manufacturing departments in the organizational structure of the enterprises was great, production being of primary importance. The functions of the purchase and sales departments were insignificant. Apart from accounting and book-keeping, the departments also recorded the execution of the plans. Such an organizational structure created considerable reserves, the use of which increased productivity and contributed to lower costs.

The first five years of development in Yugoslav industry demanded centrally planned and managed investments and production. However, we were able to see the economic deficiencies of the systems, so that in the period 1950–1952 they were replaced by systems of self-management and individual planning.

The enterprises were gradually becoming independent; the functions of determining their economic policy was transferred from the planning boards to the workers' councils and managing boards of the enterprises themselves. The independent enterprises were now subject to competition in the market, which led to increased labor productivity and decreased cost of production.

The members of the workers' council of the enterprise are elected for a limited period (through general vote). The council determines the economic

policy of the enterprise, makes decisions about its organization and reconstruction, elects and appoints managers, approves of the plans and decides
on the use of funds and distribution of profit.

The members of the workers' councils elect managing boards which
have fewer members, meet more frequently and make operative decisions.
These boards are also the executive bodies of the workers' councils and, as
such, are responsible to the latter.

In addition to this self-management system, the classical system of management at the level of general manager down to foreman has been preserved. The general manager of the enterprise is a member of the managing
board and responsible for the execution of the decisions of the self-management bodies.

The introduction of the self-management system aims at engaging and
stimulating all employees to work better and waste less. The producers
themselves make decisions concerning planning and organization of work
and distribution of profit. In this way the state ownership of the means of
production is replaced by public ownership.

Any employed person can be a member of the workers' council or the
managing board; the number of members depends on the size of the enterprise. The general manager cannot be a member of the workers' council.
The members of the self-management bodies must excel morally and pro-
fessionally.

The enterprises are now faced with the problem of succeeding on their
own; they have to supply the necessary raw material and equipment and
sell their products on the market. The market becomes the regulator of the
economic justification of the production in a Socialist set-up.

However, there are still boards for planning at the level of the federation,
the republics, and the communities. They are now primarily concerned
with investment and exert their influence through the banks.

These institutions are functioning on the basis of plans of individual industries but are mostly concerned for the economic growth of the country
as a whole. Through various regulations (taxes, credit, loans, price limits,
customs, and so on), they influence the execution of the comprehensive
plans.

This has given birth to new problems.

The first has to do with further investment in "basic" or manufacturing
industries. Actually, the manufacturing industry in Yugoslavia has developed faster than the production of raw materials and has created the
need to import them. On the other hand, due to the shortage of raw ma-

terials, the capacities of the manufacturing industry have not been fully used. The conclusion is that, should there not be too great a disproportion, we must invest more equally in the two groups of industries.

The second was whether to establish small, middle-sized, or large enterprises. Practice has shown that it would be best to have a combination because small and middle-sized enterprises cooperate and produce standardized parts, subassemblies and assemblies of products. These problems concerning the best use of enterprise capacities are being given special attention in Yugoslavia. Today we have a shortage of small, well-organized cooperative enterprises that would contribute to better specialization in the industries.

The organizational structure of the enterprises has been changed considerably. The supply and sales departments developed services to analyze the market. In the manufacturing departments, greater attention is paid to designing, finishing and controlling the quality of the products, because consumer requirement has been gradually increasing. The accounting departments have started planning, recording, analyzing and controlling the economic results of production and business. In order to make the work of the managing bodies and the general manager more efficient, a group of experts has been organized to program production and business. All these changes have contributed to more rational and economical production, so that the enterprises are able to face world competition and take part in international labor division.

RECENT DEVELOPMENTS IN MANAGEMENT AND PLANNING IN YUGOSLAV ENTERPRISES

Yugoslavia's aspiration to speed up its economic growth has brought about the need to change and further improve the system of management and planning. These changes started in 1965, and their goal is to decentralize, as far as possible, the management and planning of the national economy.

The plans of the enterprises are based on optimization of production and business programs. In order to assess the optimal programs, the experts of the enterprises undertake the following analyses: market, prices and costs, capacities, and financial funds.

The well-organized enterprises avail themselves of mathematical, statistical and other analyses of the market, of the methods of linear and dynamic programming, and more. These analyses aim at making the possibilities of the enterprises and the needs of the markets compatible in order to attain maximum income. It is of vital importance to make the plans in accordance with the possibilities of both domestic and foreign markets. With some enterprises, the influence of the foreign market and international labor division is predominantly important. After the economic reform, about two-thirds of social accumulation is at the disposal of the enterprises and their banks. The enterprises and their associations are now programming and planning for themselves and investing out of their own funds with some loans from Yugoslav banks and possibly foreign loans. They endeavor to feed back investments as soon as possible and so attain the highest income.

The participation of the workers in decision-making, while programming and planning production and investment, is assured by their participation in the management of the enterprises and their associations. In the same way, we have made provision for the participation of the workers in the distribution of enterprise income into a part denoted for personal incomes and a part for investment and other uses. In this way the workers see the end results of their work.

In order to make the participation of the workers in decision-making as direct as possible, a further improvement in the system of self-management is envisaged. In addition to the central workers' councils and managing boards, which take care of the policy of the enterprise as a whole, a number of councils have been set up at the level of smaller business and production units which are technologically and economically self-contained. These units have their own alternative plans prepared by experts but adopted and controlled by the workers' councils of the units.

Because of the direct interest of the producers, the plans are made, followed and fulfilled much better, and this leads to increased output and trading.

Social planning is still carried out by the boards of social and economic planning at the levels of communities, republics, and the federation. Economic development on the social level is planned for groups of allied producers; the plans are medium-term, covering periods of four to seven years. Production is planned for groups of allied producers on the basis of the plans developed by enterprises and their associations. The same planning institutions create forms of investment in which communities, republics or the federation are to participate using their own funds.

If it proves necessary to make more extensive economic and social surveys of national development, long-term programming of the economy will also be developed; but this will not have the character of planning.

This means that the tendency of the new system of economic planning in Yugoslavia will be to delegate economic planning, as much as possible, to the actual producers, whereas the political territorial units (from communities and republics to the federation) will direct their planning institutions to combine the plans of the producers in the light of the growth of national economy, and to involve them as much as possible in regional planning.

Recent developments in the Yugoslav economy have pointed out new problems that must be solved in the future.

The first refer to the organizational structure of the enterprises. Lack of industrial tradition has made the organizational level of new established factories lower compared to the modern equipment which is being used. This leads to large, latent reserves for an increase in productivity and decrease in cost of production. To solve this problem, some specialized institutions dealing with problems of enterprise organization have been established. These institutions cooperate with foreign consulting firms.

The second group of problems refers to the research work necessary for further development of the economy. In Yugoslavia there are a number of institutes that are asked to help the enterprises. However, these institutes often do not have enough laboratory equipment, and a limited research staff.

The organizational structure of the enterprises is undergoing certain changes. Because of the stronger influence of the market, the commercial and financial departments of the enterprises are growing stronger. The manufacturing departments strive to use latent capacities and increase output. In all the departments of the enterprise, stimulative systems of income distribution and wage-incentive methods are being used. Some larger enterprises introduce departments for development, and some establish research institutes.

It has been anticipated that the new system of management and planning will provide conditions of economic activity to enable industrial production to grow at an annual rate of 10 per cent. A 15 per cent annual growth of exports and imports, with fuller inclusion into international division of labor, has also been forecast. The social plans forecast growth of national per capita income from the present 500 to some 800 by the end of 1970; whereby the share of industry is of vital importance.

PART THREE

PRICES
AND
INVESTMENT

Chapter 13

THE PRICE MECHANISM
IN A PLANNED ECONOMY

J. A. MIRRLEES
Trinity College, Cambridge

Prices are important in any economy. What part *should* they play in the organization of economic activity? That is my subject, and it is a large one for a small paper. I have two excuses. A quick survey allows the problems to be seen as a whole. And certain simple arguments, which I shall outline, do suggest conclusions that, if correct, are important. For the sake of concentrating on a few central issues, much that is of some importance is neglected. The guiding question is: to what extent can actual computations, carried out by government agencies, assist or supplement the operations of the price system?

The discussion is couched in terms of that abstraction, a completely planned economy. By this phrase, I mean an economy whose organization is completely subject to political decision: the government determines the form it will take. I shall assume that households purchase goods and services, and offer labor, freely at the ruling prices; but producers take their decisions according to rules laid down by government, and are answerable to government for their performance. It is unnecessary to insist that no government has perfect control over its servants. Fortunately, in the economic sphere, it may be possible to arrange that the interests of producers lead them to act as the government wishes. In any case, even the governments of Western countries pursue—with unequal vigor no doubt—the twin aims of influencing production decisions by fiscal arrangements and "central planning" on the one hand, and measures, such as antitrust legislation to restrict the pursuit of profits to approved channels, on the other. We must bear the imperfections in mind, but satisfactory control is probably not too far out of reach.

Let it be granted, then, that producers are prevented from exercising significant monopoly power: that is, they cannot allow, in their behavior, for any influence they might have on the prices they pay and receive. Then there are surely great advantages in a system where each producer seeks to maximize his "profits" by suitable choice of products to produce and means to produce them; provided that the prices at which profits are measured are such as to equate supply and demand.[1] Such prices can be determined by allowing producers and consumers freely to trade the goods and services for one another (through the medium of money). It is useful to remind ourselves of at least two of the advantages claimed for this system.

The first virtue is fundamental. The market prices for outputs and inputs give the producer all the information he requires about the rest of the economy (under certain circumstances). Thus the computation of the desired state of the economy is accomplished by means of a large number of relatively small-scale computations, carried out by the individual producers, each making special use of the information about production possibilities that he is in the best position to obtain. Even the individual producer cannot use *all* the available evidence about production possibilities in his own field; but it is generally thought that more centralized methods of computation are bound to neglect more of the relevant information than a thoroughly decentralized market-price system.

It is also true that a market-price system diffuses decision-taking among a great many individuals. Instead of a system of authority and instructions, we have, in the use of market prices, a system that requires and allows individual initiative, subject to universal, and binding, rules. In effect, the government says, not "do this," but "act according to these rules." Thus the price system can be made to some extent self-policing, avoiding the detailed checking of performance that would be necessary under a more authoritarian system. It may also, if individuals are allowed personal gain related to the

---

[1] In the case of goods or services that turn out to be free (such as obsolete machinery) it is only necessary that supply exceed demand.

results of their production decisions, encourage a more vigorous search for relevant information.

I do not wish to exaggerate these advantages, though I think that they are real enough to render *some* degree of decentralization, by means of a price system, desirable. It should be noticed that one might perhaps obtain some of the advantages of the second kind—that is, avoiding exact quantitative instructions—even when it is not desirable to attempt to decentralize computation. For economic incentives and disincentives might be so adjusted that a centrally computed plan is in fact realized. This sounds difficult; but if some class of producers does not in fact act according to the rules desired by the government, the use of such computations might be very valuable.

Now an extremely serious objection to market-price systems is that we apparently cannot perfectly correct the income distribution resulting from their free operation. If individuals were identical, we could perhaps largely prohibit inheritance, insure equal provision of education, and so on—thus achieving, in conjunction with a price system, an ideal distribution. But the actual problems of income distribution are more complex and largely unsolved. I think it likely that we should, if we fully understood the problems, want to use a market-price system, suitably modified by subsidies and taxes; so that the arguments which follow would still be relevant.

The faults of the free market system that I want to examine, because they are important, and because there is good reason to think that a judicious use of central computations, and possibly quantitative instructions to individual producers, would go some way to removing them, are the following:

1) Many production decisions, including the important strategic ones, have to be taken in the light of expectations about prices yet to be determined. While there obviously must be some uncertainty about the future, and there may, in a free market system, be some incentive to guess well, there is reason to think that mistakes in estimating future prices are greater than they need be.

2) Knowing the prices of all inputs and outputs may not in fact define the profit-maximizing decisions for the enterprise very closely. To take the extreme case: if an enterprise has no reason to think that the problems of operating ten identical plants are very different from the problems of operating one, then the prices that will make one plant just profitable, will also make ten plants just profitable. The enterprise has, apparently, no way of deciding how many plants to install. And even if we do not have constant returns to scale, as in this case, small changes in prices might imply quite considerable changes in decisions. It is not quite true that the price system is powerless to deal with this problem, but we must examine how well it can deal with it.[2]

3) An important class of decisions taken in an economy concern the appointment of the managers of enterprises—the decision-takers. A free enterprise system is *supposed* to insure that management is the best available because incompetent businessmen fail to gain or keep command over capital. But even if monopolistic behavior is impossible, the average size of profits may be a poor indicator of management efficiency. In a planned economy, other criteria of performance might be used as well, and duplication of management activity reduced.

Before going on to expand these points, and indicate how a planned economy might deal with them, it will be necessary to describe in some detail how a price system would have to operate in practice.

The price system in operation. At any particular time, prices for most goods and services must be taken as given: if it turns out that supplies and demands do not quite balance—and that is bound to be the usual situation—prices will have to be adjusted, but that will only affect demands and supplies in the next period. The satisfactory working of a price system depends ironically on the way in which prices are adjusted from period to period. We should like, if it were possible, to create a system in which, taking any substantial period of time as a whole, the production of any commodity is more or less equal to the amount that consumers and other producers want to purchase, plus a reasonable increase in the stocks of the commodity held awaiting purchase. But that is not all: we should want the average level of stocks of commodities to be approximately right, and the average amount of spare productive capacity, the average length of queues, and so on, to be right in the eyes of the producers. Similarly, the employment that producers wish to provide to the various kinds of labor, should on average be just equal to the amounts of the various kinds of labor that individuals are, in aggregate, willing to provide; and the extent to which producers find themselves waiting for labor, or hoarding it, should on average be what they would wish it to be.

It is clear, then, that (disregarding the case of economies of scale) prices should probably be adjusted upward when purchases (or orders) are greater

---

[2] If there are economies of scale internal to the enterprise, some of the outputs and inputs will probably have to be determined by central computation. The rest of the paper refers to parts of the economy where economies of scale are exhausted.

than desired production[3]—or, in the case of labor, for example, when the number offering themselves for a particular kind of employment are less than the number of jobs available. But prices should also be adjusted upward if inventories are too small, queues too long, or spare capacity insufficient. The actual price change will have to be related both to the difference between production and sales, and so forth, and to the difference between actual and desired levels of inventories, and the like.

The actual process of price adjustment in any economy is bound to be rather complex, since information on production, sales, inventories, queues, and so on can be hard to collect rapidly. But it will be convenient to suppose that these price adjustments are made by special public authorities. It cannot be assumed in advance that such an arrangement for determining prices as I have outlined will in fact achieve the ends it is designed to; one hopes that in general it could be readily modified so as to do so.

The producers in the economy are supposed to be taking their decisions in order to maximize their profits. For some few of these decisions, they need know only the current prices—the ones they actually pay for their inputs and receive for their outputs. But most actions they take affect future outputs and inputs as well as present ones. If profit-maximization is meaningful, they must be able to use prices to compute the significance of these future inputs and outputs too. If we think only of one particular future date, the relative prices, used in the enterprise's computations for goods and services at that date, ought to be (if we could know them) the relative prices for current transactions that will actually rule at that date. The enterprise must also compare profits accruing in one period with profits accruing in another: I shall suppose that the government tells enterprises what (social rate of discount) to use for this purpose, and say no more about it.

Meanwhile, let us decide how the enterprise should respond to its assumptions about prices now and in the future. I have so far supposed that it should do such calculations as it conveniently can, so that its production decisions can be expected to come close to maximizing profits. However, this rule must be modified, by saying that the enterprise ought to proceed *cautiously*. Calculations might seem to require one, as from period to period expectations about price changes, to revise production plans rapidly and radically: but, though it may this year seem right to plan for enormous expansion, and next year seem right to abandon all these plans, the enterprise should rather modify its plans by relatively small amounts from month

---

[3] Actual production might, when it comes to the point, fail to maximize profits; for it may often be best to fulfill orders if possible in the face of unexpected spurts in demand.

to month, or even year to year. For example, consider what might happen if enterprises did blindly follow the calculations of the moment. If, as is quite likely, the scale of production that would maximize profits is very sensitive to small changes in the relative prices expected, the adjustments in current prices that are made in the manner described above to improve the balance between supply and demand would probably fail to do so; instead, stimulating large excess supplies where there were moderate excess demands before, and vice versa. So our government must require of the enterprises under its control that they adjust the proposed scale of production by quite small amounts from period to period, but always moving in the direction suggested by prices, and by inventory levels, volume of orders, and the rest.

We can imagine, then, how an actual price system might be established. Under this regime, the economy would naturally never be in "equilibrium." Indeed economists have not, to my knowledge, ever provided convincing arguments that such a system as I have described would be closer to the desired state of the economy on average than would any feasible system based on centralized computation and a hierarchy of instructions. It might be rather far away. But it is a flexible system, which *looks* as though it should perform well in an economy whose circumstances do not change too violently. If systems of this kind tend to be inefficient, it is my belief that the reason is poor prediction of future prices; and we ought to be able to do something about that.

The prediction of prices. I suspect that in private enterprise economies (and not only there), producers assume, unless they have inescapable evidence to the contrary, that relative prices will remain unchanged. They hedge by assuming obsolescence, and keeping plants flexible; but they probably give altogether too much weight to present experience. This economic sin, if it exists, is partly to be explained by the lack of other information at the disposal of individual enterprises. Whatever the reasons, it is probably true that the *main* function of market prices in most economies is not to prevent short-run bottlenecks and surpluses but to influence investment decisions by providing information—such as it is—about the relative prices that are likely to hold in future. The fact, if it is a fact, that a freely operating price system insures on average a balance between supply and demand, is no guarantee that the economy is thereby being made to operate efficiently: for efficiency, we also require that future prices have been foreseen as well as is reasonably possible.

The productive system of the economy grows and develops in response to changes in productive potential and demand—both public and private. But there is more than one way of responding to these changes: the burden of adjustment may be thrown primarily upon production decisions taken not long before the actual trading of goods and services; or, if the changes are foreseen—at least in outline—long in advance, they will influence decisions taken many years, or even decades, before the actual point of sale and purchase. In the latter case, expensively rapid adjustments will be more often avoided, and the productive potential of the economy will be more efficiently used.

We cannot pretend that the future state of the economy, and in particular the prices ruling in it, can be predicted with close accuracy. What we can say with some confidence is that the individual enterprise does not have readily available to it all the relevant information for estimating the prices it will in future receive and pay. When it comes to the prediction of prices, decentralization appears to have no virtue. This is not quite true. If enterprises, being in pursuit of higher profits, were to do their best to find out about future prices, they would enter into contracts with one another for the forward delivery of goods wherever possible. If this could be done extensively, the resulting markets in future commodities might well convey the necessary information about the likely future balance between demands and supplies in precisely the form required by the enterprise. There are many reasons why this cannot be done: a sufficiently precise description of future commodities is difficult; the number of markets would be far too great to organize effectively; households will not enter into such contracts. Anyway, it does not happen, and it is quite hard to imagine how it could be done. The alternative is for a central authority to process the relevant information, and to use a suitable economic model to compute predictions of future prices.

Let me be a little more precise about the way in which price predictions could be generated, and the arrangement of computations that might be adopted. The number of distinct commodities for which enterprises might wish to know the future prices is very large, and, in many cases, prices would be required for a great many future years. No economic model could encompass the whole range of relevant prices in detail. Any economic model that can be used for practical purposes must operate in terms of index numbers, each of which represents a large number of different economic variables. So in this case, if the authorities are to compute predictions of future prices, they must in fact provide the economy with predictions of the changes in various price indexes; just as interindustry models used for predicting outputs and demands in fact predict aggregates made up of many distinguishable and different outputs and demands.

We might then suppose that the individual enterprise should use the predicted indexes in preparing its own estimates of the price movements of more detailed categories of goods and services. But our criterion for deciding what the individual enterprise should do, ideally, is that it should only do computations that are useful to itself. The estimations we are considering now will not usually be of this kind. Many enterprises have an interest in the accurate estimation of, say, prices of peak and off-peak electricity in a particular region, or the cost of some particular category of labor, on the basis of a price index for fuel and power, and a price index for skilled labor (and probably some more local information as well). It would be absurd to decentralize these computations to the level of the individual enterprise. We had better assign such estimations to local planning offices, responsible for the predictions required by enterprises in a particular industry, or region.

Even then, the enterprise, which has to concern itself with the quality and design of products, the characteristics of the local labor force, and other individual details, will not always be able to apply the predicted price indexes supplied by government offices directly and without further thought to the assessment of its own production alternatives. But it will not lack information about the effect of large changes in the economy on the relative demand for its products, or on the relative scarcity of the different inputs it uses. It will not neglect to prepare to economize in labor, if that is becoming more costly, or to expand its production if the predicted (and intended) development of the economy requires it. Errors are bound to remain, both in the central predictions, and in the application of them to the particular decisions of the enterprise; errors which can, of course, be compensated for by last-minute adjustments. Errors cannot be eliminated by any system.

Because the enterprise must apply the predicted price indexes in the way it thinks best, it is scarcely possible to require that the predictions be treated as instructions; for no precise check is possible on whether the enterprise has used the official predictions in making its investment decisions. A planned economy requires some system of inspection, of economic, as well as financial probity: no more can be required than that the enterprise be able to give reasons, if asked, for the way in which it has used official predictions—and no less should be required of it.

Governments and their agencies do not usually provide predictions of price movements: is it perhaps impossible, in the present state of econometric art, to predict price movements more reliably than enterprises can do for themselves? It is difficult to believe that no help could be given by economic models. At least it should be possible to provide predictions of the movements of real wage rates, of interest rates, of the relative prices of capital goods and consumer goods, of foreign-produced and domestically produced goods. Consider, however, more disaggregated models. Interindustry models are used to predict future outputs and inputs in quite a disaggregated form: must it be more difficult, or more treacherous, to predict prices in the same degree of disaggregation? Now most interindustry exercises assume constant relative prices (except, I suppose, for labor): it is this assumption that makes them computationally simple, and relatively undemanding in terms of data; and also, as it seems to me, relatively inaccurate in detail. There seems to be no comparable simplification available to the economist who wants to construct a model for predicting prices.

That is not to say the exercise could not be simply done: one could prepare quite serviceable estimates merely by extrapolating past movements of prices. But if one has available a computational system for predicting future outputs and inputs, or even for predicting future consumer demand, one can adopt a procedure that might be quite satisfactory. The government could require all enterprises to report (say, quarterly) not only current outputs and inputs, but also estimates, based on current and intended plans, of future outputs and inputs (including capital investment). If, for some particular year and some particular commodity, the intended supply were less than the demand predicted by the government's economic model, this would be a signal to increase the predicted price of that commodity or the period in question. Such a "feedback" method seems very natural; it has the disadvantage of placing considerable computational responsibility upon the individual enterprises, which are perhaps unlikely, even in a planned economy, to be able to provide very accurate estimates in detail of their future outputs and inputs. No doubt methods can be developed that give more weight to past evidence of the relation between market prices and the production activity of enterprises, and rely on less onerous reports by the enterprises themselves.

It is possible, however, that apart from a few major price indexes, such as those mentioned above, relative market prices would change on average only very slowly. Then, granted that the main price indexes were satisfactorily predicted, the problem for the planners would be to insure that the planned scale of production corresponded to the demands that can reasonably be expected. I have already remarked that the price system may be thought an unsatisfactory way of trying to achieve this balance; in which case it may be argued that in a planned economy, a particular level of production should be assigned to each enterprise, on the basis of centralized computations made by government agencies using, for example, interindustry methods.

The scale of enterprises. We have observed, to express the matter in a simple example, that relative prices may tell a regional electricity-generation authority what kind and combination of new plant to build, but not whether to build two new power stations in the next two years, or ten. Though in fact the particular characteristics of different locations affect the profitability of the different plant under consideration, slight changes in the expected product prices will nevertheless often imply very different scales of production if profits are to be maximized. If the price system is to provide for this situation, the managements of the enterprises will have to be instructed to revise their plans cautiously. Then if the planners foresee a shortage—say, of electricity production capacity in five years' time—they will predict electricity prices to encourage an expansion of capacity in that year, and beyond. Enterprises—or local authorities, or whoever the agents responsible for investment decisions—will plan additional investment accordingly, more in those places and in that design of plant whose profitability appears to be greatest, but not taking full advantage of the newly predicted profits, at any rate until they have been confirmed by the planners' failure to revise prices downwards again when they obtain evidence of the newly planned expansion.

The advantages of such an arrangement as this should not be underrated; but it by no means disposes of all problems. The adjustments in price predictions required might well give rise to fluctuations in predicted prices rather greater than fluctuations in actual market prices: if it is necessary to encourage some degree of justified confidence in the predictions of the planning authority, these fluctuations are a disadvantage. Much more serious, the adjustment process just described may be slowly operating and rather ineffectual. In many industries, the lag between beginning to install new capacity and the date when it comes into operation may be rather long. There is usually some opportunity for speeding up the process, so that the lag is reduced, but only at a cost. Suppose that in the electricity industry, the best technique requires that construction be begun five years before output is first produced. Information as to the number of plants it is deemed profitable to begin in some particular year may not become available to the planning authority until a date quite close to that when construction is to begin. If the planners then revise price predictions accordingly, they may—allowing for the necessary caution of the managers—be too late to encourage the necessary expansion or contraction of these particular production plans, and the price change may be too small to encourage the more expensive investment in a plant with a shorter construction lag that might be a desirable second-best in place of the plant it has become too late to build. This account may exaggerate the problems, but there must be at least some tendency to throw an increasing burden of adjustment on decisions close to the date when the production is required—a result that a satisfactory price system is supposed to avoid.

The alternative is to predict future demand for each enterprise. The predictions must refer to the enterprise, since it is otherwise unclear what action the enterprise should take in the light of, say, demand projections for a whole industry. But, as in the case of price predictions, central computations must be carried out in order to predict outputs and inputs only in a relatively aggregated form. It seems appropriate to give the task of disaggregating these aggregates—which would refer, presumably, to a whole industry or region—to local planning offices. These offices would be able to use local information to help them in deriving figures for the individual enterprises, just as they could do for price predictions. It will be recognized that in the system I am suggesting, the enterprise would not be given predictions or instructions about all its outputs and inputs, but only some index of the scale of its activities. The detailed choice of technique must still be a matter of decision in the light of forecast prices and knowledge of the markets.

If we give decisions about the planned scale of enterprises into the hands of special planning offices, we are giving them a considerable say in the relative scale of production to be commanded by the different managements in the industry. This is not unimportant. Left to itself, the management of an enterprise might, for the sake of growth, seek orders to an extent unjustified by the narrower economic calculations it is supposed to be allowed; and skill in obtaining orders need not be closely related to skill in reducing costs, introducing new products, or even skill in adjusting quality to the wishes of the customer. In the system I am discussing, management will presumably argue with the planning offices for a good share in the activities of the industry, but in the last resort will be required to base its plans on the demand forecast assigned to it by the planners.

The task of dividing the predicted scale of production in an industry between the different enterprises it comprises, in the light of the claims, and arguments of the managements of these enterprises, is bound to be complex. If the investment decisions of the industry can be satisfactorily centralized, so that a single enterprise controls the whole industry, these problems will be quite eliminated. It will not always be possible to make the relevant information available in accurate form to a single decision-taking unit; but if it can be done, are there any objections to it? It may be argued that the spur of competition is lost, and that the enterprise will make undesirable use of the monopoly power so created. As to the supposed spur of competition, that quickens the urge of management to experiment, innovate and improve, what reason have we for thinking that the gains from free availability of information about new methods will fail to compensate for any likely loss in local inventive vigor? The second argument about monopoly can be countered by pointing to the effect of regular inspection of the manner in which decisions are taken, and the fact that price-setting in the markets of our imagined economy is regulated by government.

Within the large decision-taking units that seem to be desirable, there can be little doubt that decentralization should be encouraged. The different subunits of the enterprise can, and should, act independently when trading for goods and services in actual markets. Not even in capitalist economies is it universally the case that the unit of organization responsible for investment decisions is also the smallest independent trading unit when the produced goods come to be sold. There is no reason why in a planned economy the two should ever be the same. The argument can be carried further. The largest decision-taking unit, which I have above conventionally identified with the industry, could concern itself with the strategic investment decisions; production decisions of less weight, even if they involve trading in several periods, if they require special, local information or expertise, being taken by smaller units of management, subordinate in other matters to the main enterprise, which would also be responsible for allocating the different responsibilities. But the scope for decentralization within the enterprise should not be exaggerated. Many allocations might be better performed by computation than by trading between the departments of the large organization, provided only that the relevant information could be collected in sufficient detail.

It should be noticed, finally, that the forecasts of output scale that are needed for the satisfactory operation of the economy cannot really be regarded as instructions. When the products of the enterprises are finally being produced, it will be desirable that some should produce more than their plant was designed ideally to do, and some should produce less. Prices for current trading should bring this result about in an approximately satisfactory way. If enterprises were committed to make available for sale the amount that five years previously they had been instructed to *assume* would be demanded of them, the admirable flexibility of the price system would have been lost, to no advantage.

The shape of the ideal. I have examined briefly, and—for that reason at least—inadequately, the way in which a government might hope to make the economy approximate to a desired state by getting the necessary calculations done in a partly decentralized way. We have seen how, for its proper operation, the economy must rely on various forecasts, which, because of their general relevance, and the widespread sources of information required for their construction, it is desirable to centralize to a considerable extent. The making of these forecasts—of prices and quantities—is, in a sense, decentralized, but in a way quite different from the decentralization of production decisions achieved by these forecasts and market prices in conjunction within one another.

One may wonder what the most important elements in such a system are. Is it the impressive equalization between supply and demand that is achieved by the movements of prices in the markets for actually traded goods? Is it the operation of plant at intended levels of output, which, hopefully, good demand predictions can make possible? Or is it the less dramatic, less verifiable, good investment decisions—the optimum use of resources—that good price predictions allied to present value investment rules provide? In "normal" times, when no hostile external forces threaten the economy, it does seem that both the demand pattern and the production potential of actual economies progress evenly and undramatically. Under these circumstances, I cannot see that *very* much in terms of human welfare is likely to be gained by an improved balance between supply and demand once the long-term investment decisions are rightly made; and I suspect too that in a smoothly developing economy, the prediction and allocation of prospective demands between enterprises would not greatly improve the scale decisions. Granted large-scale production units, for the reasons discussed above, it may be that good price predictions are the most important contribution that central computations can make to the workings of a free-market price system. Without them, I doubt whether, however smoothly the economy adjusts actual supplies to actual demands, we should have much reason to approve of the result.

Chapter 14

INVESTMENT-DECISION CRITERIA, CAPITAL-INTENSITY AND THE CHOICE OF TECHNIQUES*

G. C. HARCOURT
Cambridge University

Introduction

Some aspects of the current theory and practice of investment decisions at the enterprise level in both the United Kingdom and the European Socialist countries are discussed in this paper. In recent years in the United Kingdom, government departments, academic and business economists and businessmen themselves have been advocating the use of Discounted Cash Flow (DCF) procedures as aids to investment decisions.[1] At the same time, empirical research and official inquiries have increased the knowledge of actual business practice in the United Kingdom.[2]

* The writer is most grateful to Amit Bhaduri, Donald J. Harris, James A. Mirrlees, D. M. Nuti, Graham Pyatt, R. E. Rowthorn, E. A. Russell, Aubrey Silbertson, Ajit Singh, G. Whittington, K. J. Wigley, F. K. Wright and the members of the Conference at Nice for helpful discussions and comments.

[1] See, for example, National Economic Development Council, *Investment Appraisal* (London: H.M.S.O., 1965); A. M. Alfred, "Discounted Cash Flow and Corporate Planning," *Woolwich Economic Papers,* no. 3, July 1964; A. J. Merrett and Allen Sykes, *The Finance and Analysis of Capital Projects* (London: Longmans, Green and Co. Ltd., 2nd Impression, 1965).
[2] See, for example, Tibor Barna, *Investment and Growth Policies in British Industrial Firms* (N.I.E.S.R. *Occasional Paper,* no. 20) (Cambridge University Press, 1962); A. S. MacIntosh, *The Development of Firms* (Cambridge University Press, 1963); *Report of the Committee on*

While DCF procedures, especially the *internal rate of return* and *present value* of investment projects, are becoming more familiar, they are still used in only a small minority of cases. The most popular measure of the profitability of investment projects is some variant of the *accounting rate of profit,* often *before* tax, on the original investment. And replacement decisions, as well as the choice of investment projects, or of different methods of producing the same level of output, are still more likely to be decided by the application of a rough rule of thumb such as the *pay-off period criterion,* or by a comparison of accounting rates of profit, than by the use of DCF procedures. The latter, especially the internal rate of return, are, of course, not without their critics.[3]

This paper is confined to one aspect of the theoretical and practical issues which have been thrown up by the advocates of these various criteria. Suppose that there are a number of known ways of producing a given stream of output per year, and that certain expectations are held concerning the rates of increase of the price of the product, the prices of its raw material inputs, and money wages. What is the *relative* capital-intensity of the techniques which would be chosen by following some of the criteria either in use or recommended in the United Kingdom? Four criteria are considered: 1) the *present value criterion;* 2) the *internal rate of return criterion;* 3) the *pay-off period criterion;* and 4) the *accounting rate of profit criterion.* In addition, the capital-intensity of the techniques which would be chosen, given the same basic technology and expectations, by the application of 5) the *recoupment-period criterion,* the criterion that is commonly applied by investment decision-makers in the European Socialist countries, is compared with the capital-intensities which result from the use of the four "capitalist" criteria.[4] The paper is not concerned as such with the "rightness" or "wrongness" of particular criteria but with some of the economic implications of putting them into effect.

The paper is in four sections. In section 1 the description of the profitability of investment projects in terms of the internal rate of return and

Turnover Taxation, Cmnd. 2300, 1964; R. R. Neild, "Replacement Policy," *National Institute Economic Review,* November 1964, pp. 30–43; D. C. Corner and Alan Williams, "The Sensitivity of Businesses to Initial and Investment Allowances," *Economica,* February 1965, pp. 32–47.

[3] See, for example, M. S. Feldstein and J. S. Flemming, "The Problem of Time-Stream Evaluation: Present Value *versus* Internal Rate of Return Rules," *Bulletin* of the Oxford University Institute of Economics and Statistics, February 1964, pp. 79–85.

[4] The paper is essentially an extension of the analyses of Meek and Nuti respectively, to take account of expected inflation and variations in the *economic* life of equipment. See Ronald L. Meek, "Ideal and Reality in the Choice between Alternative Techniques," *Oxford Economic Papers,* October 1964, pp. 333–354; Domenico Mario Nuti, "Recoupment Period and Investment Criteria in the Socialist Economies," unpub., King's College, Cambridge, December 1965.

present value is discussed, together with some general comments on the current state of the theory of the firm in capitalist economies and its relevance for investment-decision rules. In section 2, the two rules most used in practice in the United Kingdom for investment decisions—the pay-off period and the accounting rate of profit—are briefly discussed, together with an outline of two possible variants of the recoupment period. The main part of the paper is in section 3, where the capital-intensities resulting from the application of the various rules are compared. The main conclusions of the paper are gathered together in section 4.

1. DESCRIPTIONS OF THE PROFITABILITY OF INVESTMENT PROJECTS

The profitability of an investment project can be described in a number of ways, two of which are discussed here—the *internal rate of return* of a project and the *present value* of a project. These are two examples of what have come to be known as Discounted Cash Flow (or DCF) methods.

Internal rate of return. Suppose that the *initial outlay* on an investment project is £I, and that the project is expected to add to the *net receipts* of the business over the next n years (the expected lifetime of the project) the stream: £$q_1, q_2, \ldots, q_n$. The q_i's are the *expected* increases in annual sales receipts *less* the accompanying expected increases in wages, raw material and maintenance costs. The project is expected to have a scrap value, £K, at the end of the nth year. Then, the internal rate of return (or *expected rate of profit*) of the project, ϱ, is defined as that rate of discount which makes the present value of the expected net receipts, including any scrap value, equal to the initial outlay on the machine. That is, ϱ is the rate of discount which satisfies the following equation:

$$I = \left\{ \sum_{i=1}^{n} \frac{q_i}{(1 + \varrho)^i} \right\} + \frac{K}{(1 + \varrho)^n} \tag{1.1}$$

Another interpretation of ϱ, perhaps more illuminating, is: if the expected rate of profit of an investment project with an initial outlay of £I and a series of net receipts (including any scrap value) of £$q_1, q_2, \ldots q_n$ is ϱ, it will be possible to provide a series of annual payments at a rate of ϱ per year on the initial outlay *and* to accumulate a sum of money which at the end of the life of the project will be equal to the initial outlay; always provided that the *cash surplus* resulting from the difference between the annual net receipts and the annual payments $[£(q_i - \varrho I)]$ can be reinvested at a rate of return of ϱ per year.

Present value of an investment project. The present value of an investment project is calculated by discounting the expected net receipts (including any scrap value) of a project by the *marginal cost of finance* to the business considering the investment[5] and subtracting from this the initial outlay.

Let V' = present value of a project with an expected life of n years;
  q_i = expected net receipts of year i $(i = 1, \ldots, n)$;
  K = expected scrap value at end of year n;
  I = initial outlay;
  R = marginal cost of finance to the firm.

Then,

$$V' = \left\{ \sum_{i=1}^{n} \frac{q_i}{(1 + R)^i} \right\} + \frac{K}{(1 + R)^n} - I \tag{1.2}$$

If $V' = 0$, then $R = \varrho$ (see [1.1] above), that is to say, the project's expected rate of profit, or internal rate of return, equals the marginal cost of finance.

It will be noticed that, in the descriptions of the profitability of investment projects, while I and (in the second description) R may be known, the expected net receipts are estimates derived from expectations about the future courses of revenues and costs.[6] Perhaps the most simple, plausible expectation is that the physical productivity of the plant or equipment involved in the

[5] The marginal cost of finance is either the rate which must be paid for additional funds, or the interest foregone when firms use their own funds. It may include elements of imputed psychological cost, for example, those associated with high fixed interest claims on uncertain, fluctuating future profits, or those which take account of the impact of new share issues on the returns to the old shareholders.

[6] The initial outlay may also be an estimated value, for example, when a businessman who is considering constructing a new plant within his business estimates its cost. Or, an investment project may contain several stages and take several years to complete, so that the outlays associated with the later stages of necessity must be estimates. An example of a multi-stage project would be the development of a housing estate over a number of years by a speculative builder. The expected rate of profit of a multi-stage project can be found by solving the following equation for ϱ:

$$0 = \left\{ \sum_{i=1}^{n} \frac{q_i - I_i}{(1 + \varrho)^i} \right\} + \frac{K}{(1 + \varrho)^n} \tag{1.1a}$$

The present value of the same project is:

$$V' = \left\{ \sum_{i=1}^{n} \frac{q_i - I_i}{(1 + R)^i} \right\} + \frac{K}{(1 + R)^n} \tag{1.2a}$$

where I_i = capital outlay in year i
and q_i, K, ϱ, V' and R are as defined in the text.

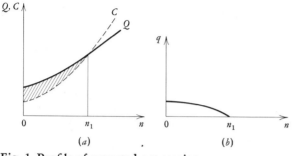

Fig. 1. Profile of expected net receipts.

project will be maintained, that the price of the product will rise (for simplicity, at a constant rate) and that costs will rise at a faster rate than price. Thus the expected sales receipts will change at the expected rate of change of the price of the product. Costs will rise at a faster rate than the price of the product, partly because maintenance costs may be expected to rise as the equipment gets older, but mainly because money wages, on average, can be expected to increase at a rate which reflects both the rise in the general level of prices *and* the rise in national productivity. These considerations give the profile of expected net receipts shown in Fig. 1*b,* and the rest of this paper proceeds on the assumption that such a profile is typical. If it is assumed that a machine will be scrapped when the net receipts associated with it first become zero, n_1 years is the expected *economic* life of the project shown in Fig. 1.

In principle, three main decisions with regard to investment expenditure may be distinguished: the *amount* of investment to be done per period, including any replacement expenditure; the *sort* of investment to be done, that is, the choice between alternative ways of producing the same product and, sometimes, level of output; and the method and cost of finance. Though in principle these are three separate aspects of the investment-decision, it is clear that the criteria which have to be satisfied for each have to be met *simultaneously.* Attention in this paper will, however, be concentrated on the second aspect (the choice of technique).[7]

In deciding the criteria to be used and met, the aims of the decision-makers of the business concerned need to be specified. In the theoretical

---

[7] If factor and product prices are assumed to be independent of the scale of operation of the individual firm, and if the inputs per unit of output of each technique are also independent of scale, the choice of technique can be discussed independently of the other two aspects of the investment decision. The arguments of this paper may be viewed in this way, in which case the problem discussed is the choice of the capital-intensity to be used to produce a *unit* of output.

literature, the most common aim is taken to be the maximization of the value of the firm to its shareholders, which is one variant of the traditional view that those in charge of firms wish to maximize profits. This basic assumption, however, has been challenged by another school of thought, which argues that managers aim to maximize the rate of growth of the firm, or, sometimes, the rate of growth of its sales, subject to the constraint that the rate of profit does not fall below a minimum or "satisfactory" level.[8] These conflicting aims obviously *may* imply different levels of investment expenditure per unit of time and, perhaps, different financial structures. It is not clear, however, that they affect the choice of techniques. A cost-minimization principle, at least with regard to production, seems to be consistent with all three views. In discussions of the choice of technique, the cost-minimization principle has been said to be satisfied by choosing either the technique with the *highest* internal rate of return, or that with the *highest* present value, though the two criteria do not necessarily result in the same technique being chosen (see section 3). This appears to be the implication of the arguments of the authors of *Investment Appraisal*. Meek makes cost-minimization the correct social criteria for the choice of technique and shows that maximizing the present value achieves it. Additional provisos, are, in the case of the internal rate of return criterion, that it exceed a required minimum rate, and, in the case of the present value criterion, that it at least be positive.[9]

2. PAY-OFF PERIOD, ACCOUNTING RATE OF PROFIT, AND RECOUPMENT PERIOD

There are two variants of the *pay-off* or *pay-back* criterion, one of which is relevant to the choice of technique, and the other to replacement decisions. The first variant argues that an investment project should be undertaken if it can be expected to "pay for itself" within an arbitrary period of time, usually between two to five years. By "pay for itself" is meant that the sum of the expected net receipts should at least equal the initial outlay on the project by the end of the pay-off period. In the context of choosing between investing in different methods of producing the same stream of

---

[8] The leading names associated with these alternative views are W. J. Baumol, Robin Marris, Edith Penrose and Herbert A. Simon. For a very useful discussion of the differences in behavior which result from these differing aims, see John Williamson, "Profit, Growth and Sales Maximization," *Economica,* February 1966, pp. 1–16.

[9] Feldstein and Flemming, "The Problem of Time-Stream Evaluation," sections I and II, have an excellent discussion of these matters, both with and without the assumption of a budget constraint.

output per year, the pay-off period criterion requires the choice of the technique which maximizes the sum of the expected net receipts over the pay-off period, subject to the constraint that the sum of the expected net receipts at least equal the investment outlay. This is discussed in further detail in section 3.

The variant of the pay-off period which is applied to replacement decisions is that the total savings in operating costs consequent upon replacing an existing machine by a new one should at least equal the initial outlay on the new machine by the end of the pay-off period. Neild found, in his study of a sample of firms in the engineering industry, that three, five and ten years were the most common values of the replacement pay-off period.[10]

There are many versions of the accounting rate of profit. Perhaps the simplest is average annual net profit as a proportion of the initial outlay, where average annual net profit is the average annual expected net receipts for the lifetime of the project *less* an arbitrarily determined, annual allowance for depreciation. It may also be defined as the first year's net profit as a proportion of the initial outlay; or net profit may be related to the average amount of capital employed, itself arbitrarily determined as, say, one half. Whichever variant is used—the first variant is used below—the choice of technique is decided by the instruction to choose the technique with the highest rate of profit, subject to it exceeding some required minimum rate of return.

It should be mentioned in passing that the United Kingdom company tax system contains very complicated methods of capital allowances, cash investment grants (these have recently replaced investment and initial allowances) and "wear and tear" allowances, which are sometimes (though not universally)[11] taken into account in the calculations of these various measures. Their *pre-tax* and *post-tax* versions should be distinguished in practice; however, they will be ignored for the remainder of this paper, as will the question of the cost and availability of finance and their relevance to investment decisions.[12]

Essentially, the criterion for the recoupment period requires that the total

---

[10] "Replacement Policy," p. 35.

[11] Corner and Williams point out that "The Richardson Committee . . . came to the surprising conclusion that firms are not likely to be affected by tax changes because they 'look principally at the return before payment of tax' (para. 282) . . . ," "The Sensitivity of Businesses to Initial and Investment Allowances," p. 34.

[12] The writer has discussed some of the implications of the change from initial and investment allowances to cash investment grants, and of the introduction of the corporation tax in place of the old profits tax and standard rate of income tax, for the present values of given investment projects in "Cash Investment Grants, Corporation Tax and Pay-Out Ratios," *Bulletin* of the Oxford University Institute of Economics and Statistics, August 1966, pp. 163–179 and February 1967, pp. 87–93.

reduction in operating costs consequent upon choosing a more capital-intensive rather than a less capital-intensive technique should *at least* equal, by the end of the period, the increase in investment expenditure entailed. While this criterion has features in common with the replacement version of the pay-off period criterion, they are *not* the same criteria. It is understood that in Hungary and Poland, a unique recoupment period is used for the economy as a whole; in Czechoslovakia and the Soviet Union, the length of the period varies from sector to sector.[13] The actual periods are said to be: five years in Hungary, six years in Poland, and between three years (for light industry) and ten years (for heavy industry) in the other two countries; the values most commonly fall between three and six years.

There are two variants of the recoupment period, one which includes only the costs of labor and raw materials in the operating costs (Hungary and Poland), the other which includes an allowance for depreciation (on a straight-line basis) as well (Czechoslovakia and the Soviet Union).

3. THE FIVE RULES

In this section, the choice of techniques at the enterprise level is analyzed, presuming the existence of a number of ways of producing a given stream of output per year. The five common rules mentioned in the preceding sections are considered. The decision-makers in the enterprises have to decide which technique to invest in, and they are assumed to take into account the expected rises in the price of the product and in money wages. For the moment, raw material costs are ignored.

"Capitalist" rules. (1) Choose the technique with the *highest* present value; (the *present value criterion*); (2) Choose the technique with the *highest* internal rate of return; (the *internal rate of return criterion*); (3) Choose the technique with the *highest* expected net receipts over the pay-off period, subject to the constraint that these net receipts at least equal the initial investment outlay; (the *pay-off period criterion*); (4) Choose the technique with the *highest* average accounting rate of profit; (the *rate of profit criterion*).

It is assumed that there is at least one technique (not necessarily the same one in each case) which has a positive present value, or an internal rate of return, or a rate of profit above the required minimum rates.

"Socialist" rule. (5) Choose the technique for which the *sum* of average

[13] For details of the lengths of the period for various sectors in the two countries, see D. M. Nuti, " 'Recoupment Period,' " p. 16.

operating costs per year *and* investment outlay averaged over the standard recoupment period (and, in the second variant, per year as well) is *least*; (the *recoupment period criterion*).

Suppose that there are a number of ways of producing a given stream of output per year, characterized by decreasing labor requirements per year as current investment expenditures (initial outlays) increase. The saving in labor requirements is, however, subject to diminishing returns; that is, as the techniques become more capital-intensive, the saving in labor becomes less. The labor requirements per year of each technique are assumed to remain the same for the entire *engineering* life of the equipment associated with each technique. Maintenance costs are ignored; engineering lives are assumed to be *considerably* greater than economic lives (on this, see section 4). If investment expenditure (I) is plotted on the horizontal axis and labor requirements per year (l) on the vertical axis, the following curve, ll, is obtained. I_1, I_2, and I_3 are the investment expenditures associated with three of a number of different ways of producing a given level of output (x), and l_1, l_2, and l_3 are their respective annual labor requirements (see Fig. 2).

The price per unit of the product is expected to rise at a constant rate (g) per year; this rate of increase is expected to be less than the expected rate of increase (G) of money wages. These expectations have been discussed in section 1 where it is argued that they are likely to be very widely held. The expected economic life of the equipment associated with a given technique is assumed to be given by the point where the expected net receipts first become zero. The expected annual receipts and the labor costs

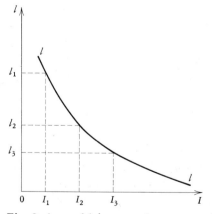

Fig. 2. Annual labor requirements and investment expenditures of the different techniques.

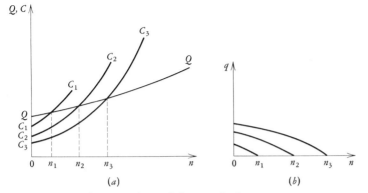

Fig. 3. Expected net receipts of three techniques.

of the three techniques marked on Fig. 2, are shown in Fig. 3*a,* together with their expected *economic* lives, n_1, n_2 and n_3 (all of which are assumed to be considerably shorter than their engineering lives). It can be seen that, with the present assumptions, capital-intensity and *economic* durability are positively associated. Length of life in years (n) is measured on the horizontal axis, annual sales receipts (Q) and labor costs (C) on the vertical axis. The curve QQ shows annual sales receipts, the curves C_1C_1, C_2C_2 and C_3C_3 show the annual costs of techniques 1, 2 and 3 respectively. Sales receipts at the end of year i $(i = 1, \ldots, n)$ are $Q_i = p_0 x \, (1 + g)^i$, where $p_0 = $ price at the beginning of year 1, and $x = $ output per year. Labor costs of technique j $(j = 1, \ldots, m)$ at the end of year i are: $C_i{}^j = w_0 l_j \, (1 + G)^i$, where $w_0 = $ wage at the beginning of year 1, and $l_j = $ annual labor requirement of technique j. The totals of the expected net receipts (q) are the areas between QQ and the respective CC curves; they are shown separately in Fig. 3*b*.[14]

Investment-decision rule 1 states:

Choose I_j such that

$$\sum_{i=1}^{n} \frac{(Q_i - C_i{}^i)}{(1 + R)^i} - I_j = max,$$

where R is the marginal cost of finance to the firm.

Investment-decision rule 2 states:

Choose I_j such that ρ in the expression,

[14] If it is assumed that factor and product prices, and the inputs per unit of output of each technique are independent of scale (see footnote 7), then $x = 1$ in the expressions which follow and *l* and *I* should be interpreted as labor requirements and investment expenditures *per unit of output,* respectively.

$$\sum_{i=1}^{n} \frac{(Q_i - C_i{}^j)}{(1 + \varrho)^i} - I_j = 0,$$

is a *maximum*, where ϱ is the internal rate of return.

Investment-decision rule 3 states:

Choose I_j such that

$$\sum_{i=1}^{b} (Q_i - C_i{}^j) = max,$$

subject to

$$\sum_{i=1}^{b} (Q_i - C_i{}^j) \geqq I_j,$$

where b is the pay-off period, measured in years.

Investment-decision rule 4 states:

Choose I_j such that

$$\frac{\sum_{i=1}^{n} (Q_i - C_i{}^j) - I_j}{nI_j} = max$$

Investment-decision rule 5 states:

There are two versions of the recoupment period, one excluding depreciation, the other including it on a straight-line basis.

Variant 1 is to choose I_j such that

$$\frac{I_j}{z} + \frac{\sum_{i=1}^{n} C_i{}^j}{n} = min,$$

where z is the standard recoupment period, measured in years.[15]

---

[15] Let $I_2 > I_1$ and

$$\frac{\sum_{i=1}^{n} C_i{}^j}{n} < \frac{\sum_{i=1}^{n} C_i{}^2}{n}.$$

Then the recoupment period criterion requires that, for the technique associated with I_2 to be chosen,

$$\frac{I_2 - I_1}{\dfrac{\sum_{i=1}^{n} C_i{}^1}{n} - \dfrac{\sum_{i=1}^{n} C_i{}^2}{n}} < z.$$

This is equivalent to the instruction to minimize:

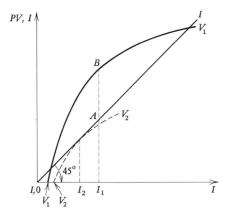

Fig. 4. Choice of technique by rule 1.

Variant 2 is to choose I_j such that

$$\left(\frac{1}{z} + \frac{1}{n}\right) I_j + \frac{\sum\limits_{i=1}^{n} C_i{}^j}{n} = min.$$

Now suppose that a decision-maker at the enterprise level decides, on the basis of *one* of these rules, the technique in which to invest. The question with which this section is concerned is: can the resulting six techniques be ordered according to their *relative* capital-intensities?

Consider, first, investment-decision rules 1 and 2. In Fig. 4, the present value of the expected net receipts (PV), discounted at the marginal cost of finance, and the investment expenditure on each project are shown on the vertical axis; investment expenditure is also shown on the horizontal axis. II, the investment expenditure line, is clearly a 45° line. V_1V_1, the PV curve, is shown as increasing at a *decreasing* rate. Undiscounted expected net receipts increase as I increases, because labor requirements fall, and the lives of the projects lengthen. But, because the saving in labor requirements gets smaller and smaller, and because money wages grow faster than the product price, the *discounted* value of the expected net receipts increases at a decreasing rate.

If the PV curve is V_1V_1, the technique associated with an investment ex-

---

$$\frac{I_j}{z} + \frac{\sum\limits_{i=1}^{n} C_i{}^j}{n}$$

(see D. M. Nuti, " 'Recoupment Period,' " p. 6).

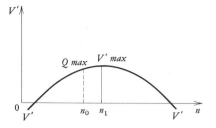

Fig. 5. Choice of technique by rules 1 and 2.

penditure of I_1 will be chosen, because at this point V_1V_1 is parallel to II and AB, its present value, is a maximum.[16] (If V_2V_2 were the PV curve, there would be a tangency solution and the technique associated with an expenditure of I_2 would be chosen.)

If now the present values of the projects $(V' = PV - I)$ are plotted against their lengths of life, the curve $V'V'$ in Fig. 5 is obtained (it will be remembered that there is a positive association between I and n): n_1 is the length of life of the technique associated with an expenditure of I_1 in Fig. 4. Any techniques with positive present values must have internal rates of return which are greater than R. ($V' > I$ implies $\varrho > R$.) However, because the lives of the projects also vary, it is clear that the rate of interest which would reduce the present value of the technique with a life of n_1 to zero is *not* the greatest rate of interest required to reduce the respective present values to zero. The present value at n_1 exceeds those of its neighbors to the immediate left, not only because its undiscounted annual net receipts are greater than theirs, *but* also because it has a longer economic life. A given increase in the length of life has a less than proportional effect on the discounted value of a stream of payments. Somewhere to the left of n_1, therefore, a greater rate of interest will be needed to reduce the present value to zero, say, at n_0. The maximum internal rate of return equals this rate of interest. It follows that investment-decision rule 2 will, with the present technology and price and cost expectations, result in the choice of a *less* capital-intensive technique than investment-decision rule 1. (There is one exception to this statement; if there is a tangency solution [see Fig. 4], the same technique will be chosen by the two rules. A tangency solution implies, of course, that $V' = 0$ and that $\varrho = R$.)[17] Because maxi-

---

[16] I_1 in Fig. 4 is not necessarily the same investment expenditure as I_1 in previous figures. It is assumed that the curvature of ll is such that V_1V_1 is a concave continuous curve so that there is only one maximum value of $(PV - I)$.

[17] An alternative explanation of why rule 2 results in the choice of a *less* capital-intensive technique than rule 1 is given in footnote 30.

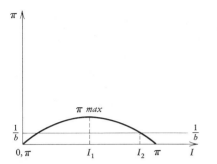

Fig. 6. First choice of technique by rule 3.

mizing the present value of a project also implies cost-minimization, it is clear that maximizing the internal rate of return does not.

None of the three remaining rules uses a rate of discount or a rate of interest; it is obvious, therefore, that they will lead to different techniques being chosen than those chosen by rules 1 and 2. Consider, first, the pay-off period criterion (rule 3). In Fig. 6,

$$\pi_j \left(= \frac{\sum\limits_{i=1}^{b} (Q_j - C_i{}^j)}{bI_j} \right)$$

is plotted on the vertical axis and n on the horizontal axis. The values of π_j on the vertical axis are the values of the expected average gross rates of profit for the pay-off period of each technique and are the *inverses* of the number of years that it takes to "repay" the respective investment outlays. Because the discounted net receipts of the techniques are bounded by the pay-off period and because labor requirements decline at a decreasing rate as I increases, π will rise to a maximum and then decline as I increases, giving the curve $\pi\pi$ shown in Fig. 6.

If the decision rule were an instruction to choose the technique with the *lowest* pay-off period, the technique associated with an expenditure of I_1 would be chosen and π would be maximized. However, it would be possible both to increase expected net receipts *and* to satisfy the pay-off period criterion by choosing the technique associated with an expenditure of I_2; at which value, $\pi = \dfrac{1}{b}$, the inverse of the pay-off period.[18] With this technique,

$$\sum_{i=1}^{b} (Q_i - C_i{}^j) = I_j,$$

and is also maximized.

[18] See D. M. Nuti, " 'Recoupment Period,' " pp. 11–13.

It is not clear whether this technique is more or less capital-intensive than those chosen under rules 1 and 2. The ordering depends upon the length of the pay-off period, the rate of decline in labor requirements, the rates of increase of the product price and money wages, the lengths of life of each technique, and the value of R. If, however, the expected net receipts for the years outside the pay-off period are ignored, it is clear that the pay-off period criterion results in the choice of a technique which is *more* capital-intensive than that chosen by the present value criterion. Therefore, the greater is b and, thus, the closer is it to the values of n, the economic lengths of life of the techniques chosen under rules 1 and 2, the more likely is it that the pay-off period criterion will result in the choice of a more capital-intensive technique than either rule 1 or 2.

In order to facilitate the remaining comparisons, and to establish rigorously the results of the preceding paragraph, it is necessary to obtain expressions for the rates of substitution of annual labor input for investment expenditure of the techniques which are chosen by rules 1 and 3. (The rate of substitution is $\dfrac{\partial l}{\partial I}$, the slope of the curve, ll, in Fig. 2.)

Rule 1 (the present value criterion) may be written as:

$$V'_j = p_0 x B - w_0 l_j A - I_j = max \tag{3.1}$$

where

$$A = \frac{(1 + G)\left\{\left(\dfrac{1 + G}{1 + R}\right)^n - 1\right\}}{G - R},$$

$$B = \frac{(1 + g)\left\{\left(\dfrac{1 + g}{1 + R}\right)^n - 1\right\}}{g - R} \quad \text{and} \quad R > G > g,$$

by assumption. (For moderate rates of increase of prices and money wages, this seems a reasonable assumption.)

To find the first-order condition for (3.1) to be a maximum, partially differentiate (3.1) with respect to I and put the resulting expression equal to zero.

$$-\frac{\partial l}{\partial I} = \frac{1}{w_0 A - \dfrac{\partial n}{\partial l}\left(p_0 x \dfrac{\partial B}{\partial n} - w_0 l \dfrac{\partial A}{\partial n}\right)} \tag{3.2}$$

is obtained.[19]

---

[19] $-\dfrac{\partial l}{\partial I}$ is shown, in order to have positive values.

Rule 3 (the pay-off period criterion) requires that:

$p_0xB' - w_0l_jA' = max$, subject to $p_0xB' - w_0l_jA' \geqq I_j$,

where

$$A' = \frac{(1 + G)\{(1 + G)^b - 1\}}{G} \quad \text{and} \quad B' = \frac{(1 + g)\{(1 + g)^b - 1\}}{g}$$

Write:

$$l = \frac{p_0xB'}{w_0A'} - \frac{I}{w_0A'} \tag{3.3}$$

(3.3) is a straight line (*LL* in Fig. 7) with a slope of $\left(-\dfrac{1}{w_0A'}\right)$ and

an intercept on the vertical axis of $\dfrac{p_0xB'}{w_0A'}$. The curve, *ll*, of Fig. 2—the annual labor requirement, investment expenditure relationship—is also shown
in Fig. 7. Provided some labor and investment are needed to produce a given
level of output, it is clear that *LL* will either intersect *ll* at points such as
P_1 and P_2, or will be tangential to *ll* at a point such as P_3 (or not cut *ll*
at all, in which case no technique will satisfy the criterion). At P_2, the
pay-off period criterion is satisfied and the technique associated with an

investment expenditure of I_2 is chosen (see Fig. 6). At P_2, $-\dfrac{\partial l}{\partial I} < \dfrac{1}{w_0A'}$,

because *ll* cuts *LL* from below. (The other possibility is the tangency solution at P_3, and, there,

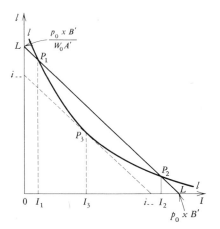

Fig. 7. Second choice of technique by rule 3.

$$-\frac{\partial l}{\partial I} = \frac{1}{w_0 A'}.\text{)} \quad \text{Therefore,} \quad -\frac{\partial l}{\partial I} \leqq \frac{1}{w_0 A'}.^{[20]} \tag{3.4}$$

Now compare (3.2) with (3.4) and suppose, initially, that $n = b$ for all techniques. (3.2) therefore becomes:

$$-\frac{\partial l}{\partial I} = \frac{1}{w_0 A''} \tag{3.5}$$

where

$$A'' = \frac{(1 + G)\left\{\left(\frac{1 + G}{1 + R}\right)^b - 1\right\}}{G - R}$$

Because $A'' < A'$, it is obvious that $(3.5) > (3.4)$.

In (3.2), $\left(p_0 x \dfrac{\partial B}{\partial n} - w_0 l \dfrac{\partial A}{\partial n}\right)$ may be $\overset{\geqq}{\underset{<}{=}} 0$. If it $\leqq 0$, $(3.2) > (3.4)$, for a wide range of values of n;[21] that is to say, the present value criterion results in a *less* capital-intensive technique being chosen. If $\left(p_0 x \dfrac{\partial B}{\partial n} - w_0 l \dfrac{\partial A}{\partial n}\right) > 0$, it does not necessarily follow that $(3.2) < (3.4)$ especially as $w_0 A < w_0 A'$, for given n, and $\dfrac{1}{w_0 A'}$ is the *upper* value of the inequality, $-\dfrac{\partial l}{\partial I}\dfrac{1}{w_0 A'}$. Thus, it seems reasonable to conclude that, given the present assumptions, in many circumstances, the pay-off period criterion results in the choice of a *more* capital-intensive technique than does the present value criterion (and, *a fortiori*, the internal rate of return criterion).

Another investment-decision rule which is often used in practice in the United Kingdom is the accounting rate of profit criterion (rule 4). This may be written as:

$$P_j = \frac{1}{nl} \{p_0 x B''' - w_0 l_j A''' - I_j\} = max \tag{3.6}$$

[20] The writer is indebted to R. E. Rowthorn for this proof.

[21] If

$$\left(p_0 x \frac{\partial B}{\partial n} - w_0 l \frac{\partial A}{\partial n}\right) \leqq 0,$$

and because

$$\frac{\partial n}{\partial I} < 0, \quad -\frac{\partial n}{\partial I}\left(p_0 x \frac{\partial B}{\partial n} - w_0 l \frac{\partial A}{\partial n}\right) \leqq 0.$$

It therefore is an offset (or, at least, not an addition), to $w_0 A$, which, however, becomes greater as n increases, so *that the value of* $-\dfrac{\partial l}{\partial I}$ which satisfies (3.2) decreases with n.

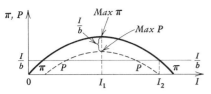

Fig. 8. Choice of technique by rules 3 and 4.

where

$$A''' = \frac{(1+G)\{(1+G)^n - 1\}}{G}$$

and

$$B''' = \frac{(1+g)\{(1+g)^n - 1\}}{g}.$$

A rough idea of the relative capital-intensity which results from this rule, as compared, first, with the pay-off period criterion, can be obtained as follows. Suppose that annual *net* profits are averaged for a period equal to the pay-off period, and that depreciation is reckoned on the straight-line basis as $\frac{I}{b}$ per year, so that $\frac{I}{b}$ increases as I increases. Then, it is clear that if p_j is plotted against I as the curve PP (see Fig. 8) and compared with π_j (see Fig. 6), it will reach a maximum at the *same* investment expenditure (I_1) as π (see Fig. 8). Therefore, with these assumptions, rule 4 results in a *less* capital-intensive technique being chosen than that resulting from rule 3.[22]

If, now, the assumption that $n = b$ is dropped, the maximum of the accounting rate of profit curve may well occur at a value of I which is closer to I_2; but it does seem that there will be a considerable number of cases where this rule results in *less* capital-intensive techniques being chosen.

What can be said of the ordering of rule 4 (accounting rate of profit)

---

[22] If $n = b$, rule 4 becomes:

$$P_i = \frac{1}{bI_i} \{p_0 x B' - w_0 l_i A' - I_i\} = max. \qquad (3.6a)$$

The first-order condition for a maximum is:

$$-\frac{\partial l}{\partial I} = \left(\frac{p_0 x B' - w_0 l_i A'}{I}\right) \left(\frac{1}{w_0 A'}\right) \qquad (3.7a)$$

For $P \geqq 0$ (an obvious condition), $p_0 x B' - w_0 l A' \geqq I$, and $\dfrac{p_0 x B' - w_0 l A'}{I} \geqq 1$. It follows that

$$(3.7a) > -\frac{\partial l}{\partial I} \left(\leqq \frac{1}{w_0 A'}\right).$$

in relation to rule 1 (present value)? To answer this, consider the first-order condition for a maximum P. It is:

$$-\frac{\partial l}{\partial I} = \left\{ \frac{p_0 x B''' - w_0 l A'''}{I} \right\}$$

$$\left[\frac{1}{w_0 A''' - \frac{I}{n} \frac{\partial n}{\partial l} - \frac{\partial n}{\partial l} \left\{ p_0 x \left(\frac{\partial B'''}{\partial n} - \frac{B'''}{n} \right) - w_0 l \left(\frac{\partial A'''}{\partial n} - \frac{A'''}{n} \right) \right\}} \right] \tag{3.7}$$

Comparing (3.7) with (3.2)

$$\left(-\frac{\partial l}{\partial I} = \frac{1}{w_0 A - \frac{\partial n}{\partial l} \left(p_0 x \frac{\partial B}{\partial n} - w_0 l \frac{\partial A}{\partial n} \right)} \right),$$

and ignoring the last two terms of the denominator of (3.7), and the last term of the denominator of (3.2), the ordering is seen to turn on whether the effect of $\dfrac{p_0 x B''' - w_0 l A'''}{I} > 1$, which tends to make (3.7) > (3.2), outweighs, or is outweighed by the effect of $w_0 A''' > w_0 A$, which tends to make (3.7) < (3.2). It appears, therefore, that while both rule 1 and rule 4 result in less capital-intensive techniques being chosen than does rule 3, it is not possible to order the techniques corresponding to rules 1 and 4 themselves.

Comparison of the recoupment period criterion (rule 5) with the pay-off period criterion (rule 3). As the pay-off period criterion (rule 3) often results in the choice of the most capital-intensive technique of the four "capitalist" rules, it seems sensible to make it the first "capitalist" rule to be compared with the recoupment period criterion (rule 5). As defined above, the recoupment period criterion requires that the savings in costs which result from choosing a more capital-intensive technique cover the increase in investment expenditure within the period of time defined as the recoupment period. This can be shown to be equivalent to minimizing one of the expressions given in the fifth paragraph of Section 3, depending upon which variant of the criterion is used. In order to simplify the comparison with the pay-off period criterion, variant 1 with a recoupment period equal to the pay-off period and with all techniques given the same arbitrarily determined life, $\bar{n}$, is examined (a special case is: $\bar{n} = b = z$). The assumption concerning n is dropped later (see below). The values of the recoupment periods for different industries are mostly within the two- to five-year range associated with the pay-off period.

The recoupment period criterion (variant 1) then is:

$$\frac{I}{\gtrless} + \frac{1}{\bar{n}} w_0 l_j A'''' = min \tag{3.8}$$

where

$$A'''' = \frac{(1 + G)\{(1 + G)^{\bar{n}} - 1\}}{G}$$

and $\gtrless = b(= \bar{n})$.

The first-order condition for this to be a minimum is:

$$-\frac{\partial l}{\partial I} = \frac{1}{\gtrless}\left(\frac{\bar{n}}{w_0 A''''}\right) \tag{3.9}$$

For

$$\bar{n} = \gtrless (= b), \quad \frac{1}{\gtrless}\left(\frac{\bar{n}}{w_0 A''''}\right) = \frac{1}{w_0 A'},$$

the upper value of the pay-off period criterion. However, except in the special case of a tangency solution, $-\dfrac{\partial l}{\partial I} < \dfrac{1}{w_0 A'}$ for rule 3, so that for $\bar{n} = \gtrless = b,$ the recoupment period criterion results in the choice of a *less* capital-intensive technique.

As $\bar{n}$ increases, $\dfrac{1}{\gtrless}\left(\dfrac{\bar{n}}{w_0 A''''}\right)$ will fall because, though the numerator increases arithmetically, the denominator increases geometrically. There is, therefore, a value of $\bar{n}$ at which the same technique will be chosen by the two rules. But it seems clear that there may be a considerable range over which the recoupment period criterion results in a *less* capital-intensive technique being chosen.

If the second variant of the recoupment period is considered, that is, depreciation is taken into account, the relevant condition for the recoupment period criterion is that:

$$-\frac{\partial l}{\partial I} = \left(\frac{1}{\gtrless} + \frac{1}{\bar{n}}\right)\left(\frac{\bar{n}}{w_0 A''''}\right) \tag{3.10}$$

This results in the choice of a less capital-intensive technique than the first variant, that is,

$$\left(\frac{1}{\gtrless} + \frac{1}{\bar{n}}\right)\left(\frac{\bar{n}}{w_0 A''''}\right) > \left(\frac{1}{\gtrless}\right)\left(\frac{\bar{n}}{w_0 A''''}\right),$$

which, of course, is to be expected. The range within which the recoupment period criterion results in a *less* capital-intensive technique being chosen is widened.

The comparisons are now repeated, supposing n to be determined by the criterion that the expected net receipts be either positive or zero (see Fig. 3). With variant 1, the condition for the recoupment period criterion becomes:

$$-\frac{\partial l}{\partial I} = \left(\frac{1}{z}\right)\left\{\frac{n}{w_0\left[A''' + l\frac{\partial n}{\partial l}\left(\frac{\partial A'''}{\partial n} - \frac{A'''}{n}\right)\right]}\right\} \tag{3.11}$$

This expression is very similar to (3.9), but now has an additional product in the denominator which is negative.[23] If, therefore, $n \leqq \bar{n}$, a less capital-intensive technique will be chosen if this version is used; and there is a range of values of $n > \bar{n}$, where this still holds. It seems possible, therefore, to accept the previous findings, provided n is relatively close to $\bar{n}$.

With the second variant of rule 5, the first-order condition for the recoupment period criterion becomes:

$$-\frac{\partial l}{\partial I} = \left(\frac{1}{z} + \frac{1}{n}\right)\left\{\frac{n}{w_0\left\{A''' + l\frac{\partial n}{\partial l}\left(\frac{\partial A'''}{\partial n} - \frac{A'''}{n}\right)\right\} - \frac{I}{n}\frac{\partial n}{\partial l}}\right\} \tag{3.12}$$

If it is assumed that the last two terms approximately cancel one another $\left[-\frac{I}{n}\frac{\partial n}{\partial l} > 0\right]$, for $n = \bar{n}$, the criterion is the same as before. It may be concluded, then, that the assumption of a variable n is unlikely to alter the results significantly.

Comparisons of rule 5 with rules 1 and 4. If variant 1 of rule 5 is considered, and if $\bar{n} = z = b$, then the present value criterion condition is:

$$-\frac{\partial l}{\partial I} = \frac{1}{w_0 A''} \tag{3.5};$$

the accounting rate of profit condition is:

$$-\frac{\partial l}{\partial I} = \left(\frac{p_0 x B' - w_0 l A'}{I}\right)\left(\frac{1}{w_0 A'}\right) \tag{3.7a};$$

and the rule 5, variant 1, condition is:

$$-\frac{\partial l}{\partial I} = \frac{1}{w_0 A'} \tag{3.13}$$

Both (3.5) and (3.7a) $>$ (3.13), that is to say, the recoupment period criterion, variant 1, results in the choice of a *more* capital-intensive technique than either rule 1 or 4.

However, if rule 5, variant 2 is considered, even under the present re-

[23] $w_0 > 0, l > 0, \frac{\partial n}{\partial l} < 0, \left(\frac{\partial A'''}{\partial n} - \frac{A'''}{n}\right) > 0.$

stricted assumptions, this ordering no longer holds.[24] And when a variable n is considered, nothing definite can be said about the ordering of rule 5, variant 1 in relation to either rule 1 or 4, though the results above suggest that rule 5, variant 1 will result in *more* capital-intensive techniques being chosen in a number of cases, as, perhaps, is to be expected.

Raw material inputs. For completeness, something should be added about the influence of raw material costs on the choices of technique resulting from the five rules. It is assumed that the raw material input per year (k) is the *same* for *all* techniques, and that the rate of increase of the price of the raw material input is the same as that of the product price (g). With these assumptions it can be shown, first, that the present value criterion results in a *less* capital-intensive technique being chosen than when labor alone is considered.[25]

Second, by reasoning similar to that used in the eighth paragraph of this section, it is clear that the internal rate of return criterion will still result in a *less* capital-intensive technique being chosen, relative to rule 1, and that it will be *less* capital-intensive than with labor alone. Third, the choice of technique resulting from the pay-off period criterion is now *less* capital-intensive than that associated with labor alone.[26]

Fourth, if the accounting rate of profit criterion is considered, then, within the bounds of a given period, say b, a *more* capital-intensive technique than previously will be chosen, though it still will be *less* capital-intensive than that chosen by the pay-off period criterion.[27] However, if

[24] The rule 5, variant 2, condition, with $\bar{n} = z = b$, is:

$$-\frac{\partial l}{\partial I} = \frac{2}{w_0 A'}$$ (3.14a)

[25] $V'_i = p_0 x B - w_0 l_i A - r_0 k B - I_i = max.$ (3.15a)

where $r_0 =$ price of raw material input at the beginning of year 1. The first-order condition for a maximum is:

$$-\frac{\partial l}{\partial I} = \frac{1}{w_0 A - \dfrac{\partial n}{\partial I}\left[(p_0 x - r_0 k)\dfrac{\partial B}{\partial n} - w_0 l\dfrac{\partial A}{\partial n}\right]}$$ (3.16a)

$$> -\frac{\partial l}{\partial I} = \frac{1}{w_0 A - \dfrac{\partial n}{\partial I}\left(p_0 x\dfrac{\partial B}{\partial n} - w_0 l\dfrac{\partial A}{\partial n}\right)}$$ (3.2),

the analogous condition for labor only.

[26] The slope of the line analogous to LL in Fig. 7 is the same, but the intercept on the vertical axis

$$\left\{\frac{(p_0 x - r_0 k)B'}{w_0 A'}\right\}$$ is less.

[27] In this case, the rule 4, first-order condition for a maximum is:

$$-\frac{\partial l}{\partial I} = \left[\frac{(p_0 x - r_0 k)B' - w_0 l A'}{I}\right]\left[\frac{1}{w_0 A'}\right]$$ (3.17a)

$$(3.17a) -\frac{\partial l}{\partial I} = \left[\frac{p_0 x B' - w_0 l A'}{I}\right]\left(\frac{1}{w_0 A'}\right) \text{ but } > -\frac{\partial l}{\partial I}\frac{1}{w_0 A'}$$

n is variable, the technique chosen may be either more or less capital-intensive than before.[28]

Both versions of the recoupment period criteria result in the choice of a *less* capital-intensive technique than before,[29] except, of course in the special case of $n = \bar{n}$ (see above), when the choice is not affected. These results therefore confirm the ordering of rules 1, 2, 4 and 5 in relation to rule 3, leave unchanged the ordering of rules 1 and 2, and still leave indeterminate the relative capital-intensities resulting from rules 5 and 4, in relation to rules 1 and 2.

The main results of this section are summarized conveniently in Fig. 9. $-\dfrac{\partial l}{\partial I}$, the slope of the annual labor requirement, investment expenditure relationship, is plotted on the vertical axis of the top half of the figure. n, the *economic* length of life, is plotted on the horizontal axis. As n increases, and $-\dfrac{\partial l}{\partial I}$ decreases, as I increases, a downward-sloping curve such as AA (drawn, for simplicity, as a straight line), is obtained. Now $-\dfrac{\partial l}{\partial I}$ is also a function of n in the expressions for the first-order condition for a maximum associated with investment-decision rules 1 and 4, and in the expressions for the first-order condition for a minimum associated with the

---

[28] The rule 4, first-order condition is:

$$-\frac{\partial l}{\partial I} = \left\{ \frac{(p_0 x - r_0 k)B''' - w_0 l A'''}{I} \right\}$$

$$\left\{ \frac{1}{w_0 A''' - \dfrac{I}{n}\dfrac{\partial n}{\partial I} - \dfrac{\partial n}{\partial I}\left\{ (p_0 x - r_0 k)\left(\dfrac{\partial B'''}{\partial n} - \dfrac{B'''}{n}\right) - w_0 l\left(\dfrac{\partial A'''}{\partial n} - \dfrac{A'''}{n}\right)\right\}} \right\} \qquad (3.18a)$$

This compares with

$$-\frac{\partial l}{\partial I} = \left\{ \frac{p_0 x B''' - w_0 l A'''}{I} \right\}$$

$$\left\{ \frac{1}{w_0 A''' - \dfrac{I}{n}\dfrac{\partial n}{\partial I} - \dfrac{\partial n}{\partial I}\left\{ p_0 x\left(\dfrac{\partial B'''}{\partial n} - \dfrac{B'''}{n}\right) - w_0 l\left(\dfrac{\partial A'''}{\partial n} - \dfrac{A'''}{n}\right)\right\}} \right\} \qquad (3.7)$$

The expression in the first bracket of (3.18a) is less than that of (3.7), but the expression in the second bracket is greater.

[29] The rule 5, variant 1, first-order condition for a minimum is:

$$-\frac{\partial l}{\partial I} = \frac{1}{z}\left(\frac{n}{w_0\left[A''' + l\dfrac{\partial n}{\partial I}\left(\dfrac{\partial A'''}{\partial n} - \dfrac{A'''}{n}\right)\right] + r_0 k\dfrac{\partial n}{\partial I}\left(\dfrac{\partial B'''}{\partial n} - \dfrac{B'''}{n}\right)} \right) \qquad (3.19a)$$

$$(3.19a) > -\frac{\partial l}{\partial I} = \left(\frac{1}{z}\right)\left(\frac{n}{w_0\left[A''' + l\dfrac{\partial \bar{n}}{\partial I}\left(\dfrac{\partial A'''}{\partial n} - \dfrac{A'''}{n}\right)\right]} \right)$$

The rule 5, variant 2, first-order condition for a minimum is similar to (3.19a), except that the first bracket becomes: $\left(\dfrac{1}{z} + \dfrac{1}{n}\right)$, and the denominator of the second bracket contains an additional term: $-\dfrac{I}{n}\dfrac{\partial n}{\partial I}$. It, therefore, is also greater than its "labor alone" counterpart, equation (3.12).

two variants of investment-decision rule 5. These relationships are shown by the curves BB (rule 1), EE (rule 4), FF (rule 5, the variant *excluding* depreciation) and GG (rule 5, the variant *including* depreciation). $-\dfrac{\partial l}{\partial I}$ is a function of b, w_0 and G in the inequality condition associated with investment-decision rule 3; it is shown in the figure as the horizontal straight line, DD. Investment expenditure, I, is measured on the vertical axis of the bottom half of the figure. The relationship between I and n is shown by the curve, HH.

The economic lengths of life associated with the techniques chosen by each rule are those corresponding to the intersections of the various lines—BB, EE, and so forth—with AA (for example, n_1 is the life associated with the technique chosen by rule 1). The investment expenditures associated with each is found from the investment expenditure, economic length of life relationship, HH (for example, I_1 is the expenditure associated with the technique chosen by rule 1). In Fig. 9, rule 1 results in the choice of a *more* capital-intensive technique than rule 4 and rule 5 (the variant which includes depreciation); but this is for illustrative purposes only. The length of life and investment expenditure associated with investment-decision rule 2

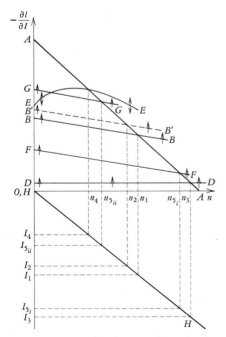

Fig. 9. Choice of technique by rules 1 to 5.

are also shown (n_2, I_2 in Fig. 9).[30] The arrows attached to the lines, *BB*, *EE*, and so forth, show the influence of the introduction of raw material costs on the techniques chosen by each rule.

4. CONCLUSIONS

Before setting out the main conclusions of this paper, some of the limitations of the analysis are discussed. First, the analysis consists, essentially, of comparisons between different situations where only the investment-decision rules used are allowed to change. It may well be, though, that changes in factor and product prices as between the "otherwise situations" are such, that the results of the comparisons cannot be applied to situations of *actual change*. Second, *higher* investment expenditures in fact may not be associated with *lower* labor inputs over the entire life of the equipment involved. The greater the investment expenditure, the more complex the equipment is likely to be, and, therefore, the greater may be its maintenance costs (and, thus, indirect labor inputs) in its later years of operation. This point has been guarded against to some extent by supposing that *economic* lives are considerably shorter than *engineering* lives. Third, the expected economic life may be *less* than that determined by the point where q_i first becomes zero, if the expected rate of technical progress is taken into account by businessmen (in a more sophisticated way than is assumed in this paper), or if they operate in an imperfectly competitive situation. However, these considerations probably do not affect the *ordering* of techniques by length of life, which is the relevant factor for the present analysis.

The fourth limitation is that the relative capital-intensities which result from the use of the various rules have been discussed in the context of a situation in which the *level of output* is assumed to be given. However, if, instead, the *level of investment expenditure* is assumed to be given and constant, it can be shown that the pay-off period criterion and, perhaps, the

[30] The line, *BB*, shows the relationship between the expression for the first-order condition for a maximum associated with the present value rule (expression [3.2]) and *n*, *given* the values of R, w_0, G and g. The greater is the value of R, the smaller is the value of A, for *given* values of *n*, and, therefore, the *greater* is the value of (3.2) (ignoring the other terms in the denominator of [3.2]). Therefore, *BB* will be higher at each value of *n*, the greater is R, and the intercept of *BB* with *AA* will move to the *left*, implying that a *less* capital-intensive technique will be chosen. Suppose that R is so great that only one technique has a present value of zero, that is, $R = \rho$ for this technique, and all the others have *negative* present values. If the *BB* line corresponding to this R is drawn (it is the line, *B'B'*, in Fig. 9), it will intercept *AA* to the left of any of the other *BB* lines associated with lower R's and, therefore, with more than one technique having a positive present value. This is the alternative explanation of why the internal rate of return rule results in the choice of a *less* capital-intensive technique than the present value rule (see footnote 17).

present value rule, will result in the choice of *less* capital-intensive techniques than those indicated by the analysis of this paper. Therefore, if businessmen are in the latter situation, or if they see the problem of the choice of techniques as one of allocating a given amount of investment funds rather than as one of deciding the capital-intensity to be used to produce a given level of output, the orderings of the capital-intensities associated with each rule *may* differ from those suggested by the analysis of this paper.[31]

Bearing in mind the above limitations of the analysis, the analysis of this paper suggests that, with the technology and price and money wage expectations assumed, the *pay-off period* criterion often results in the choice of a technique which is *more* capital-intensive than those resulting from the other four criteria examined: that is, the three other "capitalist" rules, and the "Socialist" rule, the *recoupment period* criterion, which has two variants. The technology and expectations assumed, though simple, seem plausible. Therefore, as the *pay-off period* criterion is used widely in prac-

---

[31] The writer is indebted to Graham Pyatt for this point. These results can be shown as follows: Let $\bar{I}$ be the fixed amount of investment expenditure and suppose that factor and product prices, and the inputs per unit of output of each technique, are independent of the scale of operations (see footnote 7). The pay-off period criterion now requires the investment of $\bar{I}$ in the technique with the greatest expected net receipts for the pay-off period, subject to the constraint that they at least equal $\bar{I}$. This may be written as: choose the technique for which

$$U \{ = (p_0 B' - w_0 l A') x' \} = max, \qquad (4.1a)$$

subject to $U \geqq \bar{I}$ where $x' = \dfrac{\bar{I}}{I}$.

The first-order condition for (4.1a) to be a maximum is:

$$-\frac{\partial l}{\partial I} = \left(\frac{p_0 B' - w_0 l A'}{I} \right) \left(\frac{1}{w_0 A'} \right) \qquad (4.2a)$$

As $(p_0 B' - w_0 l A') \geqq I$ (otherwise no technique will be chosen),

$$\frac{p_0 B' - w_0 l A'}{I} \geqq 1,$$

and

$$(4.2a) \geqq (3.4) \left(-\frac{\partial l}{\partial I} \leqq \frac{1}{w_0 A'} \right),$$

the corresponding condition for satisfying the pay-off period criterion with a given level of output. It follows that a *less* capital-intensive technique will be chosen when investment expenditure rather than output is fixed. Similarly, *if* the present value rule is interpreted as an instruction to choose that technique, the *present value* of the expected net receipts of which exceeds $\bar{I}$ by the greatest amount, then, again, a *less* capital-intensive technique than that indicated by the analysis of this paper will be chosen. The first-order condition for a maximum in this case is:

$$-\frac{\partial l}{\partial I} = \left(\frac{p_0 B - w_0 l A}{I} \right) \left(\cfrac{1}{w_0 A - \dfrac{\partial n}{\partial l} \left(p_0 \dfrac{\partial B}{\partial n} - w_0 l \dfrac{\partial A}{\partial n} \right)} \right) \qquad (4.3a)$$

Because $p_0 B - w_0 l A \geqq I$ (otherwise no technique will be chosen), $\dfrac{P_0 B - W_0 l A}{I} \geqq 1$ and (4.3a) $\geqq$ (3.2) (for the case of $x = 1$ and remembering that l and I are inputs per unit of output).

tice, it may be tentatively concluded that, in many instances, businessmen in the United Kingdom would install *more* capital-intensive techniques than would managers in the Socialist countries faced with the same expectations and the same technology. (This conclusion abstracts from the impact of tax provisions on investment decisions.)[32]

The second conclusion (which follows from the first) is that if the use of DCF (Discounted Cash Flow) procedures becomes more widespread in the United Kingdom, as appears to be the aim of both the government and leading business firms, there may well be a switch to investment in *less* capital-intensive techniques than otherwise would have occurred. The adoption of the *internal rate of return* criterion would cause a greater switch than would occur if the *present value* rule were adopted.

The variant of the *recoupment period* criterion which takes no account of depreciation results in a *more* capital-intensive technique being chosen than does the variant which includes depreciation.

In general, the relative capital-intensities of the techniques chosen by the *present value, internal rate of return, accounting rate of profit* and *recoupment period* criteria, cannot be ordered. With very restrictive assumptions, it can be shown that the variant of the *recoupment period* which takes no account of depreciation results in the choice of a *more* capital-intensive technique than would result from either the *present value* (and, *a fortiori,* the *internal rate of return*) or *accounting rate of profit* criterion. But, even with the same restrictive assumptions, this degree of generalization is not possible in the case of the variant of the *recoupment period* criterion which includes depreciation.

If raw material costs, as well as labor costs, are considered, the preceding conclusions are not affected. When compared with the results of the "labor costs only" comparisons, it is found that *less* capital-intensive techniques are chosen by all the rules examined except the *accounting rate of profit* rule, where the outcome is indeterminate.

[32] The writer has analyzed the impact on the ordering of the capital-intensities associated with rules 1, 3 and 4 of taxation and investment incentives in "Investment-Decision Criteria, Investment Incentives and the Choice of Techniques" to be published in the *Economic Journal.* While the capital-intensities associated with each rule change as between the *pre-tax* and *post-tax* situations, the *orderings* of the rules do not seem to be affected.

Chapter 15

PRICES IN THE NEW ECONOMIC SYSTEM OF MANAGEMENT IN A SOCIALIST ECONOMY

OTA ŠIK

Czechoslovak Academy of Sciences

In a commodity-money (market) economy, prices are an economic relationship, by means of which the exchange of use-values between economic subjects is carried out in quantitative relations, regulated by the law of value. In this sense, price is a way of expressing value, and its basic economic function is to assure the equivalent exchange of the amount of socially necessary labor expended on the production of commodities (expenditure of living and material labor). The value can appear directly as the basis for constructing prices or in modified form, that is, as the production price. Price usually deviates quantitatively from value (or the production price) when the use-value of the exchanged commodity causes an unbalanced relation between supply and demand in the market. This, at the same time, stimulates the changing of use-values in production. Under certain economic conditions, these deviations in price from their basis cause changes in the relations between production and demand for goods and help to harmonize supply and demand on an equivalent cost basis. In this way, value (or the production price) works within price trends as a long-range tendency to form the basis for prices.

In the system of management of a Socialist economy, which makes a synthesis between planning for society as a whole and market relationships, price becomes strategic. The general functioning of the system is conditioned by the rehabilitation of the economic function of prices—something which had been severely suppressed in the centrally administered, directive-based model of management. In this connection, the necessity for making a theoretical analysis of these problems comes again to the fore: a) basic constructing of prices in production; b) specific wholesale prices; and c) construction of retail prices.

In the Socialist stage of development of the economy, price is fundamental in importance from the point of view of developing the economic interests of the enterprises and their workers, on the one hand, and from the standpoint of a planned orientation of production and distribution on a macroeconomic scale, on the other. Here price always is a relevant instrument, even when it functions indirectly under the conditions of a Socialist economy within the general, directly planned framework, and is constantly supplemented and corrected by a number of other direct distribution processes.

A very important question is what construction or type should be chosen for the wholesale prices—that is, the prices for which a producing enterprise sells its products to a purchasing economic unit (which might be a production unit, a trade organization, and so forth) to create an optimum basis for the effective economic functioning of price. In discussions on this subject, two alternative proposals have been presented: "value-based prices" and "production prices." A value-based price assumes a dependence of s (value of surplus product) on v (value of employees), in accord with the labor theory of value, which states that only labor power is the creator of new value $(v + s)$. Production price, on the contrary, is derived from the value of the production funds (total capital used) by the enterprise.

In the discussions, the argument was brought up from time to time that the method of interesting Socialist enterprises in production decides the price type: An interest in gross income (return from sale of commodities minus the material costs and depreciation), it was argued, corresponds to the construction of prices based on value, while an interest in net income (profit—returns minus all costs of production) corresponds to the production price. But in Socialist enterprises there should not be personal material interest alone (the employees' interest in personal remuneration). When there is a tax on production funds, and the investments are financed by the enterprise's own means, the enterprise has an interest in maximizing gross income which can be used to cover both wages and investments as well as all types of payments to the state. In this situation there can be no value-based price which would lead the enterprises to give preference to producing goods with a relatively high content of $v + s$.

If we are to judge the advantages of constructing prices by the criteria of the most economical use of all production factors—their optimum combination with the fullest satisfaction of society's needs—then the most favorable is the production price. It has a healthy economic effect which presupposes that wages are not linked by directive to plan targets, but that the interest of the enterprise, in being able to pay as high wages as possible, is linked with an interest in maximizing gross income. The short-range interest in maximizing wages should not lead to neglect of long-range interests in developing the enterprise. That is, investment funds must be safeguarded.

Under socialism, as distinct from capitalism, it is not a question of appreciating capitalist ownership, and the rate of profit cannot be formed within the competitive struggle as a magnitude expressing the appreciation of capital. A planned society assures harmony between the interest of society in an effective development of the economy with the interests of the enterprise and its employees in maximizing incomes. This goal can be reached when production prices of the different types of goods are formed by deriving the profit/share of the price from the value of fixed assets and circulating capital, as well as from the value of the wage funds (production funds used).

The formula for the production price can be expressed as follows:

$$P_j = \frac{C_j}{Q_j} + z_j,$$

when

$$z_j = \frac{F_j^{(z)}\rho_1 + F_j^{(0)}\rho_2 + v_j\mu}{Q_j},$$

where:

$P_j =$ the production price of the "j"*th* type of product

$C_j =$ cost $(c + v)$ of producing amount Q_j of the "j"*th* type of product

$C_j = i\,A_{ij} + V_j$

$A_{ij} =$ the material cost of the "i"*th* type necessary to produce the Q_j amount of the "j"*th* type of goods (including amortization)

$V_j =$ the wage cost for producing Q_j amount of the "j"*th* type of goods

Q_j = the amount of the "j"th type of goods (in material units) produced in a given unit of time

Z_j = the profit rate in the price for a unit of the "j"th commodity

$F_j^{(z)}$ = the value of fixed assets after amortization necessary to produce Q_j of the "j"th type of goods in a given unit of time

$F_j^{(0)}$ = the value of circulating assets necessary for producing Q_j of the "j"th type of goods in a given unit of time

V_j = the wage payment needed for production of Q_j

ρ_1 = the coefficient (percentage) established by society expressing the dependence of part of the profit rate in the price on the value of fixed assets

ρ_2 = the coefficient established by society which expresses the dependence of another part of the profit item on the value of circulating assets

μ = the coefficient established by society expressing the dependence of a third part of the profit item on the value of wage costs

The above construction of production price presupposes a system of distribution of gross income where the enterprises pay the state a certain per cent of the gross income, calculated in relation to the value of production funds, plus a certain share of the gross income (after deducting the payments from production funds) and perhaps also a percentage calculated on the value of wage payments. The production price must be understood only as the base construction that should eliminate the greater differences in return on the different products; it should furthermore be considered a fundamental tendency of development of wholesale prices that should assert itself over a longer period within the range of more flexible price movements and deviations. The practical application of these two principles assumes a general price reform carried out according to the formulae above by means of coefficients in certain aggregated price groups.

Furthermore, in long-term decisions on the development of the basic proportions of production and allocation of material inputs, the use of this construction of production prices makes possible a comparison of the effect of different variants of development more easily than with the value-based price. To judge the optimum variant, it is necessary to study the assumed long-term development of production costs (the costs of investment, material and wages in different combinations). Calculations of the optimum solution made in comparable prices, using the production price, show which of the possible variants makes it possible to minimize the costs of reproduction at the enterprise or branch level, or for the entire national economy.

Comparison with capitalist production price shows that Socialist production price differs in the following ways: 1) it does not come about spontaneously through competition (of the conflicting interests of capitalists), but through a socially planned process; 2) it is not formed only as the result of past development of production costs and the class distribution of created value, but also in accordance with the future planned development of production and the socially necessary distribution of created value; 3) it is not formed as an expression of the necessity to appreciate privately owned capital and to attain the general rate of profit on capital used, but as an expression of the calculation of the general social need for gross profit in relation to the individual shares in the socially necessary reproduction costs.

Specific wholesale prices will deviate more or less from production prices understood as the basic price construction. At the same time we should bear in mind that the price level acts on the enterprises which are suppliers whose interest is oriented toward maximum gross income (and therefore on the highest price for products sold) and on the enterprises which are purchasers whose interest lies in minimum costs (and therefore as low a price as possible for goods purchased). This conflict is solved by Socialist market relations.

In addition to the relation between value (social costs) and price, we must take into account the relationship between use-value and price, manifested chiefly in the trends of demand for certain goods. Differing use-values and interchangeability of products affect the extent and structure of demand. Adapting supply to change in demand requires flexible deviations of wholesale prices from their base, that is, from production prices. Only this way can price equilibrium be assured.

Divergences of wholesale prices from production prices should be only temporary. From the standpoint of the effect of price on the purchasers, raising the sale price above the production price actually should occur only if, for objective reasons, a higher demand cannot, over a relatively long period of time, be satisfied (lack of raw materials, or production capacity, and so forth), or if the demand for the new product cannot be adequately forecast, and production or stocks of the old similar product cannot be reduced or cut off. In the latter case, it is always easier later to lower the price set for the new product than to raise it. Each raising of the wholesale price over the production price, made from the standpoint of effect on the purchasers (restricting their demand for goods in relatively short supply), will call forth the corresponding interest of the producer-supplier—an interest in speeding up as rapidly as possible the production of goods in question. Thus the effect of this movement in sales price is seen in a gradual expansion of production, and a balancing of supply and demand creates conditions for a gradual narrowing of differences or a balancing of wholesale prices and production prices. A continual practice of relatively higher prices for new products with higher use-value arouses in the producers a material interest in constantly replacing or improving use-values to satisfy the customers.

One of the most important problems is that of returning wholesale prices to the level of production prices, so that there is a long-range tendency to assure equivalent exchange. In the broader context this is a problem of the relation of the market mechanism and the socially planned procedure in assuring the proportional development of a Socialist economy.

It is found that, even though socialism has better objective conditions for long-range, planned economic decisions, it is not always possible to assure an absolutely correct prognosis in the social plan. Therefore, there must constantly be additional corrections to previous basic decisions. The less need there is for such correction of past decisions in production—and particularly in investment—the less is the conflict between supply and demand and the less need for sales prices to deviate from production prices. The market relationships do not exclude a planned priority for social reasons, but this can be only temporary and limited.

The argument is sometimes raised against combining the market mechanism with Socialist economic relations—that there is considerable monopoly of supply as compared with demand. Oscar Lange had already pointed out this problem in the 1930's, when he proposed measures against the abuse of the monopolistic position of Socialist production units in regard to prices. He suggested that the setting of "parametric" prices, or the working out of appropriate yardsticks, be transferred to the central bodies.

Experience today shows that, neither from the standpoint of a possible recognition by the center of the price equilibrium of each individual product, nor from the standpoint of the conflict of interest in cases of setting the rules by central institutions for the enterprise, can Lange's idea be carried out.

The equilibrium function of prices can obviously be achieved only by a direct clash of interests of producers and consumers in the market.

In order to cut down on the one-sided advantage of the producers, there should be a restriction, under socialism, on unjustified monopoly. Forms of competition should be developed among Socialist enterprises, a use should be made of pressure from foreign markets, and all measures against speculation should be introduced by the central bodies, without preventing the economic, relatively free formation of prices.

The most important instruments, next to competition in the market, for restricting monopoly and speculative increases in price, are the state financial instruments—such as credit, interest, taxes, foreign-trade measures, and so forth. A Socialist state cannot relinquish certain administrative measures; it will draw off the obviously speculative profit and lower prices if a check made on these unhealthy phenomena signals the need.

It is useful to determine centrally the economic level and trend of prices of the products that have decisive influence on the production process and the living standards. This would mainly concern staple foods, durable consumer goods, raw materials, fuels, power, and so forth. But here, also, prices must be based on the development of production costs and the effect of the relation between supply and demand.

Today, a significant role is being played in planning and forming prices, by mathematical methods. They are used to calculate the purposeful price deviations from the production price, in connection with the envisaged development of supply and demand brought about by a mutual relationship and a substitution of use-values. But we cannot agree with an approach that proceeds from the pure theory of equilibrium prices and ignores the long-range determinant connection between value (or production price) and the specific sales price. Each calculation of price, if it means a deviation from the price that assures cost equivalence, must sooner or later compel an expansion or restriction of production of the goods in question, if the basic principle of commodity-money exchange is not to be violated.

In the case of some means of production or aggregates of means of production, we can gradually proceed not only to a central direction of prices according to an *a posteriori* study of the development of costs production, but we can also on the basis of scientific predictions of all the essential economic relationships that determine the movement of sales price (trends in production costs, use-values, interchangeability of use-values, and so on), plan the necessary development of sales prices of these means of production.

Planning of this nature is not easy, for it requires very intricate comparisons. One must know not only the future possible development of costs of production, but also the different use-values of the mutually interchangeable products, calculate the different effects on the customers and predict the possible changes in the production proportions. The most realistic appear to be the calculations of those basic means of production where the use-value is generally simpler, and one can approach it more easily by means of a limited number of technical parameters.

Of decisive influence on consumption are the retail prices of consumer goods sold in Socialist trade to individual consumers. The construction of trade prices, forming the base for calculating specific retail prices, cannot diverge for long from the level of production prices, if a serious violation of the proportionality of development of the national economy and of the equivalence of exchange is not to occur.

Retail prices in selling consumer goods serve to realize the same total value of surplus product, designed to assure all final individual and collective consumption, which exceeds the consumption of employees for production. Wages and prices are therefore the basic instrument for distributing the national income and for covering certain social needs.

If the total average profit contained in the production prices represents the money form of part of the surplus product, then the rest of the surplus product takes the form of turnover tax and trade differential—the difference between the total production price of consumer goods and its total trade price.

The producers, therefore, do not receive directly in return for their disposal the entire value from the sale of the enterprise's commodities. Part of the surplus product, by means of the system of trade prices, with certain planned distribution processes, is realized in favor of society without being first appropriated by the producers.

The greater part of the value of the surplus product has in previous practice been drawn off through retail prices and at that level was redistributed through the state budget. The marked difference in level between retail and wholesale prices made a flexible manipulation of prices and calculations for purposes of comparison or of seeking optimum solutions very difficult. At the same time, the fact that decisions on using part of the national income was separated from the production sphere where it was created and where it was to be used again (especially in investment in production) violated the principle utilizing the enterprises' material interest and responsibility.

The elimination of these negative phenomena will be made possible by a reduction in the turnover tax and increase in net returns to the production enterprises (realized in the wholesale prices). At the same time, the relation of trade prices commensurate with the level of production prices will be assured by means of a uniform rate of the turnover tax. This will eradicate the previous economically unjustified differences in rates of the turnover tax.

This will be the precondition for retail prices that will not deform the pattern of consumption and will notify the producers of the undistorted trend of demand. Of course, the new tax must be introduced gradually and cautiously.

The amount of markup in trade prices will be treated in a way similar to the measures concerning turnover tax; its amount covers trade costs and must assure the necessary return to trade organizations.

The general markup in trade prices is determined by the given trade costs for a certain planning period (changing according to the extent of trade activity) and will be included in the trade price by a basically uniform percentage. This percentage must not be a directive indicator, but an orientational figure, with deviations for some types of goods. It would be useful, for example, to set a relatively greater markup for cheaper goods. Since the remuneration of the workers in trade will also depend on the level of gross income achieved by the trading enterprises, and that income, in turn, will depend on the amount of over-all markup prices, the trade employees will be interested not only in increasing the total turnover in trade, but also will have greater interest in selling cheaper goods.

This markup will be used not only as income of the trading organizations, but also to set up an insurance fund that will change, especially according to changes in market prices.

From the foregoing it follows that the relation between the specific retail price of consumer goods, which we also call the market price, and the trade price as the basis for constructing the market price, is similar to the relation between the production price and the wholesale price. The trade prices embody the value relationships in a way that assures essentially the equivalence and proportions of the fundamental distribution processes in society. The specific market prices, on the contrary, cannot be formed merely on a value basis, but must express the relation between value and use-value, and must therefore temporarily deviate from the value base, under the influence of demand and supply.

It is extremely difficult to discover the effect of use-value on demand, because the use-value of consumer goods is itself immensely complex, because here function is in addition to the technical parameters also the esthetic aspect, the rapid changes in taste, the greater interchangeability than in the case of means of production, and consumer preferences according to different social strata.

The use of mathematical methods in calculating the elasticity of demand for different incomes and prices does not yet make possible a reliable forecasting of detailed changes in the structure of demand. It would seem that even in the future these methods will be more suitable for making prognoses of consumption in certain aggregate groups of consumer goods, and not specifically for the currently produced or new products.

Nor will larger inventories of trade commodities solve contradictions between the structure of supply and the structure of demand, if the old system of rigid prices without any economic function and the old method of planning by volume indicators is still in effect. In such a case the conflicts of interest will only deepen between the trade enterprise and the individual consumers.

Only a relatively free movement of market prices around the trade prices can solve the contradiction between value and use-value in a suitable way. Market prices should react flexibly to changes in the relation between supply and demand.

To a limited extent the official price organizations can also determine the limits of movement of market prices, differentiated for the industrial branches or groups of commodities. These limits can prevent too great deviations in the price movements of some groups of products, caused by large disproportions in going over from the old directive system of management to the new economic system.

The fundamental solution to disequilibrium in the market is to decide on a production program. However, this cannot be assured by detailed orders based on expert knowledge from central bodies. Detailed changes in the production programs must be flexibly decided by the enterprises themselves. The changes must also be stimulated by a flexible price movement that will help solve minor conflicts more rapidly.

If price movement is really to function as a market signal and a stimulus for a needed change of production, there must be a direct relationship between the movement of market (retail) and wholesale prices. Raising or lowering market prices of consumer goods in accordance with trends of supply and demand should call forth the corresponding increase or reduction in wholesale prices and also a corresponding change in production. This movement should not be understood mechanically—it must be the result of negotiations between trade and producer organizations. The trade organizations must, however, be under pressure of competition and their material interest to reduce market prices rather than raise them.

In case the trade markup for certain types of goods is increased, as a result of market prices being forced up by the market, the income of the trade organization does not increase, only its insurance fund which is at other times used to cover losses arising when market prices were cut on other types of goods. If trade increases market prices by reducing the turnover of the goods in question, and their stocks rise, the trade organization will be forced to pay more interest to the bank, because it buys goods from the producers on credit. It is therefore interested in having its stock at the optimum level.

A rise in market prices of currently produced products (unlike the newly introduced products) can occur under socialism only in exceptional cases (and within set limits). This is when producers for one or another objective reason cannot increase their production. In such cases, also, where the growth in demand for a given product was not foreseen in time, trade organizations should, rather than permit a rise in market price of this product, demand expansion of production and deliveries, by making special additional payments to the wholesale price from the insurance fund (if the unforeseen change in production involves extraordinary costs). Only when this is not possible or if producers cannot assure larger deliveries of this particular commodity, must there be a temporary rise in the market price.

Together with a partial freeing of price movement within the framework of certain limits controlled by society, all possible antimonopoly measures, including competition in the market, should be taken, to prevent the high concentration of production, and the greater weight of the supplier on the market, from causing profiteering and taking advantage of the free prices.

The principle of market competition must have the same weight with the central directive bodies as the principle of concentration and specialization of production, and they must be constantly observed in their interrelationship. Concentration and specialization of production make it possible to extend mass production and to reduce production costs. But if this integration is brought about more by administrative, organizational and institutional forms and does not correspond to the physical concentration of production—as is sometimes done in our country, especially in the consumer-goods industry—then it becomes necessary to do away with the administrative barriers and clear the way for full action of market competition between the enterprises.

In every case, especially when products cannot compete on world markets without considerable monopoly (as, for instance, in some branches of engineering, metallurgy, and so forth), this market competition must be exerted through foreign trade. The competitive pressure of world production must be considerably increased on our producing enterprises through imports and exports of products of manufacturing, especially capital goods, but also consumer goods. While the prices attained for our products on world markets must put pressure on production costs and on development of quality goods in our producing enterprises, imports will have a decided effect on the consumer and thus will indirectly exert competitive pressure on producers.

Foreign trade must have a decisive influence in bringing the level and relation of domestic prices closer to world markets. The reason for exerting this pressure is not simply to conform domestic prices with foreign prices, but primarily to effect a reduction in production costs and raise the quality and modernity of home products in a way that will overcome the negative features of the monopolistic position of Socialist producer enterprises.

Chapter 16

INVESTMENT AND ECONOMIC GROWTH IN CZECHOSLOVAKIA

KAREL KOUBA
Czechoslovak Academy of Sciences

Present economic reform in Czechoslovakia is concerned with replacing the existing directive system of planning and management with a new one based on nationwide economic planning in connection with a controlled market mechanism. The need for applying a more efficient system of Socialist planning and management emerged from theoretical analyses and a verification of statistical data, leading to the conclusion that the main hindrance to further progressive economic development and the strengthening of Socialist production relations is the discrepancy between the present conditions, the needs for economic growth, and the functioning of the outdated system of directive management.

The aim of the present paper is an attempt to elucidate some aspects of economic reform in Czechoslovakia, based on an investigation of the following problems: 1) changes in the rate of economic growth and the reasons (short-term changes and long-term changes); 2) choice of the rate of economic growth, industrial structure of the national product and investments.

THE CHANGES

An analysis of industrial production and investment activities in the Czechoslovak economy offers some remarkable results concerning short-term changes and long-term trends in the rate of economic growth.

Statistics show that Czechoslovak industry is characterized by a high rate of growth. Growth in industrial production and investments shows regular fluctuations. Maximum annual increments in the years 1950 to 1952, and again in the years 1958 to 1960, were followed by minimum increments in the years 1953 to 1954 and again in the years 1962 to 1964. In 1963, a decrease in industrial production was in fact recorded. For investment activities, we find even more marked fluctuations, generally synchronous with those in industrial activity.

For the period of time investigated as a whole, we observe a slight decrease in the rate of economic growth.

Short-term changes. Rapid development at the beginning of the fifties enabled the socialization of the production means, and a conversion to planning in the whole economy. Thus, it became possible to utilize the capacity reserves and concentrate material and labor resources on the rapid growth of labor productivity. Concern was mainly with noninvestment growth factors, whose effect was unpredictable.

Verification of the statistical data of the Czechoslovak economy (and of

Table 16. The rate of growth of industrial production and investments in Czechoslovakia (annual increments in per cent).

Area	Years					
	1950	1951	1952	1953	1954	1955
Industrial production	14.5	14.7	16.7	8.7	4.0	11.5
Investments	18.9	15.9	18.2	3.6	−1.9	7.6
	1956	1957	1958	1959	1960	1961
Industrial production	9.5	9.4	10.3	10.8	11.9	8.9
Investments	13.6	9.3	13.5	19.5	12.4	7.2
	1962	1963	1964	1965		
Industrial production	6.2	−0.4	3.6	7.9		
Investments	−2 6	−11.0	11.9	5 8		

Source: Statistical yearbooks.

countries, like Poland and Hungary) and theoretical analyses present the following description of the mechanism of fluctuation in the rate of growth.

In a relatively small, industrially developed Socialist economy with a limited raw material base, there is a tendency, when traditional methods of planned management are in operation, for the production of fuels, energy, raw materials, and so forth, to lag behind the growth of manufacturing industries whenever the rate of growth exceeds a certain optimum level corresponding to the conditions of equilibrium growth. (Equilibrium growth is understood here in the sense that it insures full utilization of productive forces, while maintaining proportionality—that is, dynamic equilibrium). As soon as the rate of economic growth exceeds a certain limit—this generally takes place at the peak phase of the fluctuations—a "material barrier" is formed, which makes it impossible for rapid growth to continue. While the capacity of the manufacturing industries (engineering and some branches of consumer goods) may be enlarged relatively rapidly, a period of some eight to ten years is needed from the start of large investment projects in the basic industries until they are in full-scale operation. Limitations of the country's own sources of fuel, ore, energy, and the like, make it necessary to increase imports, which again generally cause discrepancies in the balance of payment, and further growth is hindered by the "foreign trade barrier."

The disproportions, ensuing from an above-optimum rate of growth, are generally increased by a tendency to plan overly large investments. The excessive rate of growth and above-optimum investments are not identical processes, but it may be assumed that in the development of the Czechoslovak economy they are interrelated. The excessive rate of growth is stopped by the "material barrier." Now, in an attempt to avoid a lack of fuel, energy and metals, the period of excessive rate of growth is accompanied by intensive investment activities in fuel, electrical power, metallurgic and other material industries. Especially under the conditions of the Czechoslovak raw material base, these sectors demand very great investments. The choice of an excessive rate of growth is accompanied by a propensity to overinvest. In such a case, the disproportions ensuing from the excessive rate of growth are enlarged.

The resulting disproportions and economic difficulties can only be overcome immediately by slowing down the pace of economic development. Acceleration thus alternates with deceleration. The decreased rates are maintained until the slow-building investment projects (mainly in the fuel, power, and materials industries), started predominantly during the peak phase of the fluctuations, are finished and put into operation. Due to the slow-down in growth and the contribution of new output facilities in the basic industries, stabilization of supply of power and materials sets in, and the rate of growth starts to improve. In preceding years this improvement always became the basis for a new cycle. Theoretical analyses as carried out up to now in Socialist countries justify the point of view that these fluctuations are not inherent in a Socialist economy, but are due to an insufficient understanding of the laws of economic development and voluntarism in relation to the directive system of planned managements.

The choice, and after a certain time the realization of an excessive rate of growth—as well as overinvestment—may take place in any system of management. However, the directive system of planned management has a special tendency to overestimate the possible rate of growth and investment. This system allows a large concentration of means for speedy industrial development. On the other hand, it does not possess an effective series of instruments by means of which it could avoid—at the time that proportions are being set in the preparation of the statewide plan—a one-sided stressing of the rate of growth and of accumulation. The traditional system of planned management lacks an economic mechanism—represented mainly by a market mechanism controlled in a planned manner—which would allow an early response to disturbances at a time when they are still growing under the surface of the current economic life and are not yet fully visible.

The tendency toward above-optimum growth and overdimensioned investment is a danger, accompanying the essential orientation to rapid industrialization in Socialist countries. Without an historical approach (which, however, is not the subject of the present paper), it is impossible fully to elucidate the positive and negative aspects of the directive system of management. Let us at least mention the fact that the economic underdevelopment of the majority of countries which have set out upon the path to Socialist development, and frequently also the unfavorable situation in international politics, have required an orientation to a speedy industrialization process.

The tendency to an above-optimum rate of economic growth and investment in practical planning has been supported, for a certain period, by a dogmatic theoretical conception of some processes in Socialist economics (the mutual relation of the output of means of production and of the output of consumer goods). A number of conflicting factors influence the mutual relations and relative rate of growth of these two groups of production. Greater increments in the output of means of production continue to be the prevalent tendency in Socialist countries including Czechoslovakia. The Marxist economic theory has explained this circumstance for a certain period of time in a simplified and nonhistoric manner. In practical planning, this has supported orientation toward a rapid advance in output of means of production before the output of consumption goods, and an underestimation of the basic criteria of the growth of a Socialist economy, consisting mainly in the field of personal and social consumption (as the material base of a complex, harmonious development of man). Deeper theoretical analyses based on the creative evolution of economic thought have revealed that an increasing rate of accumulation (and, thus, a preferential growth of the output of means of production) will be encountered in principle in cases where there is acceleration in the rate of economic growth with unchanged capital/output ratio, or of maintenance of a given rate of growth with rising capital/output ratio. In economic theory and practice we are mainly interested in production accumulation from the point of view of its function in the process of reproduction (as a means of a lasting increase in the sources of consumption). Under normal, peaceful conditions of development in a Socialist economy, the problems of the volume and structure of accumulation are subordinate to the aim which the Socialist society endeavors to achieve. The optimum rate of growth and an economically justified rate of accumulation are only the means by which a society can achieve this goal.

The new system of economic planning and control, consisting of unity in the state plan, economic tools and the application of a controlled market mechanism (which Czechoslovakia is now starting to implement) may help in choosing the optimum rate of growth, in overcoming the disproportions and insuring a relatively rapid and stable rate of growth.

Long-term changes. The dynamics of growth in industrial production in Czechoslovakia exhibits a slightly decreasing trend beside the short-term fluctuations. Economic theory is faced with the difficult task of explaining why the rate of growth is slowing down in this manner notwithstanding a relatively large and growing proportion of accumulation in the national income.

Detailed research has shown that this circumstance is influenced only to a slight extent by the gradual exhaustion of the initial reserves, by the distorting influence of the gross production index, and by the fact that Socialist countries are approaching a "stage of maturity." It may be said, that the contradiction between the conditions of economic growth on the one hand and the directive system of management on the other is the basic cause for the decreasing rate of growth in Czechoslovakia. This contradiction has been a source of some negative tendencies for some time already. Analyses have shown that economic growth is retarded mainly by: excessive amounts of incomplete construction projects and stocks, excessive material consumption per unit of production, and a decreasing efficiency of foreign trade. In relation to our topic, let us examine the decelerating effects of excessive, incomplete constructions and of excessive stocks.

Table 17 shows that a substantial part of accumulation, nearly one third as an average for the period of time in question, has been bound by the rise in stocks and amount of incomplete construction. The rise in stocks and incomplete construction bind the major part of the increment of the national income, thus decreasing the part of the increment which is available for accumulation into basic funds put into operation. This may be understood as the retarding effects on the over-all rate of growth of consumption as well as of national income.

These two are part of the over-all decelerating effects of the directive system, distinctly affecting the economic situation at the present stage of development in the Czechoslovak economy.

Notwithstanding the difference of opinion still existing, and the varying stress laid on one or another aspect of the given problem by various authors, it is still possible to find throughout the Marxist economic literature an analysis of the following decelerating effects of the traditional system of management: inflexibility of production from the point of view of adjusting the range and quality of products to the structure of consumer requirements; excessive costs per production unit; insufficient stimuli for technical advance and innovations of all kinds; drawbacks and inner discrepancies in the system of economic stimuli, weakening the correlation between the interests of the individual, of groups, and of society as a whole (a correlation characteristic of socialism), and a tendency to bureaucracy.

Under certain historic conditions of its origin, the directive system of man-

Table 17. Evolution of the rise of stocks, incomplete construction, accumulation and national income in Czechoslovakia (billion Kčs).

Category	1956	1957	1958	1959	1960	1961	1962	1963	1964
Rise in stocks	3	1	4	1	5	9	9	6	—
Increase in incomplete construction	3	4	7	4	1	10	9	−1	−4
Accumulation, total	16	21	26	27	28	35	32	22	17
National income formed	133	141	149	152	163	172	175	173	170

Source: Statistical yearbooks and other sources.

agement has allowed a concentration of material and personal factors in the interest of a very rapid economic growth by means of industrialization. In a period when there were free reserves of manpower and other productive factors, this system has demonstrated significant success and the advantages of Socialist planning. However, this traditional system maximizes output and does not minimize input sufficiently. It allows extra-economic preferences to play a great role, but it does not sufficiently respect the principle of economic calculation (minimization of input by substitution of production factors and maximization of output) as a means of insuring rational economic processes.

At the present stage of development in the Czechoslovak economy there are some circumstances which cause an extraordinarily strong demand for a relatively rapid and radical economic reform, and for the transition to a more efficient system of Socialist planning and management. The relatively high degree of economic development and the saturation of needs require such a system of management, which would flexibly adjust the structure of production to changing demand. Free manpower sources being exhausted, further economic growth can only be achieved by means of a system of management which stimulates technical advance in many ways. The relatively great extent of participation of the Czechoslovak economy in the worldwide division of labor requires such a system of management, which increases the efficiency of production and of foreign trade.

The conversion to a Socialist system of management based on an organic interrelation of statewide planning with a controlled market mechanism (a Socialist market) makes it possible to increase the efficiency of investment factors of growth and to utilize fully noninvestment factors of growth, for which Socialist production relations offer specially favorable conditions.

It may be expected that a system of statewide planning together with the utilization of the market mechanism will allow a more consequent application of the principle of rational economy on the macro- as well as microeconomic scale.

CHOICE OF THE RATE OF ECONOMIC GROWTH, INDUSTRIAL STRUCTURE OF THE NATIONAL PRODUCT, AND INVESTMENTS

The central question in the long-term plan is the choice of the rate of economic growth. In the "Outline of a method for constructing the long-term plan," M. Kalecki states: "We can consider the average annual rate of increase of the national income as the most important parameter in long-term planning. Therefore, selecting the best variant for the plan means de facto choosing the requisite rate of growth of the national income." [1]

The approach to the choice of the rate of economic growth is predetermined, to a large extent, by the functioning model of the Socialist economy. Every system of management solves the problems of growth and development of the sector and branch structure of the national income in a specific manner. A characteristic trait of each system of management is the pattern of solving individual growth problems—that is, a pattern of growth.

The character of the directive plan, and its position in a centralistic management model, predetermines in many ways the approach to the choice of the rate of economic growth by setting the rate of growth of individual branches. This "pattern of growth" is derived from the possibilities of the capacity of the engineering and construction industries, and their rate of growth is expressed in the proposed level of investment. The demands on the rate of growth of metal production, fuel mining and electric power and the demands on foreign trade are then decided on this basis. As a consequence, the limits are set for the rate of growth in the production of the other branches of manufacturing industry and of final consumption.

This "pattern of growth," which is more or less specific to the directive model of management, deduces the required rate of growth of national income particularly from the projected rates of growth of the different branches, and thus of the branch structure of the national income. In this way, the fundamental objective relations of the Socialist reproduction process are set by incorrect relations of interdependence, and the planning procedures influence the resulting rate of growth of national income in a direction opposite that required by the objective course of balanced economic growth. A condition for a balanced, economically sound rate of economic growth is the initial determination of the rate of growth of national income, which through the structure of final consumption influences in a decisive manner the choice of the branch structure of the national income.

In contrast, the reverse procedure—deriving the rate of growth of the national income from a proposed branch structure of the national income—is a voluntaristic approach.

However paradoxical this may sound, voluntarism is that the central planning institution should not determine the branch structure at all. As Kalecki has shown, the central planning institution has practically no scope

[1] M. Kalecki, *Outline of the theory of growth of socialist economy* (Prague: NPL, 1965), p. 137.

for decision-making as far as the branch structure of the national income is concerned. The reason is that the required structure of the national income necessarily ensues from the required level of the national income itself. The required consumption structure is achieved from the planned over-all growth of national income in a planning period by means of coefficients of income elasticity in demand. Moreover, the required structure of production is achieved from the required structure of consumption by means of technical coefficients and input-output relations.

As one can see, the required branch structure of national income necessarily follows from the planned rate of growth and structure of consumption, and not from any subjective decisions. As far as the branch structure of the national income is concerned, the central planning institution is not obliged to select or optimate this structure. It must, however, insert the branch structure, ensuing from the over-all level of the national income, correctly into the plan by means of realizing and understanding it scientifically.

We believe that there exist unequivocal optimation criteria for the choice between variants within one branch. Within one branch or field, there is generally a great variability as to the choice of the best technological processes and equipment. This offers a wide field for optimizing the plan, since one and the same product can generally be made with different demands on investments and manpower.

On the other hand, there are no optimization criteria and no variants at all in a closed economy, as far as distribution of means for investments to individual branches of the economy is concerned. This follows from the required structure of consumption, which is obtained by means of Engel coefficients and projected through technical coefficients and input-output tables into the required structure of production.

There are two exceptions to this principle. First, the central planning institution has some relative freedom of decision-making as far as public consumption, investments into the infrastructure, and so forth, are concerned (nonproductive investments). Within certain limits the proportions may be chosen freely in this field, or, more precisely stated, they may be chosen from the viewpoints of different social preferences.

The second exception has to do with the fact that the principle mentioned holds fully only in a closed model. When speaking of an open model (that is, respecting external economic relations), the central planning institution has some freedom of decision-making in another field. It is able to decide, according to calculations of economic effectiveness, whether anti-import or pro-export investments are more advantageous. In other cases, calculations of the efficiency of investments can only be applied to the choice of different variants within a given sector.

"On the whole it may be stated, that the branch structure of the national income is determined by: a) its rate of growth; b) the final structure of consumption and its relation to nonproduction investments; and c) the assessment of the efficiency of alternative methods of production and the orientation of foreign trade." [2]

Our explanation, however, is somewhat schematical. In reality, matters are not as simple as this. The central planning institution actually has no freedom for decisions in the given field (with the exceptions mentioned), but it is faced with a difficult and highly responsible task in choosing (the Engel coefficients for long-term planning, for example). More exactly stated, it is when carrying out a statistical estimate of such coefficients valid for a long time ahead and in choosing technical coefficients for the input-output table. There is also the question of whether coefficients empirically determined are valid throughout the whole planning period and whether their linearity may be assumed at all.

Conventional, traditional planning practice, which does not recognize the principle of predetermination of the required branch structure of the national income, leads to grave consequences. Such planning processes open the doors wide for disrespect of the principle of rational management. One of the consequences of these planning methods is the fact that there are deficiencies in one sector, while there may be excesses in others, and the situation is mainly judged from a viewpoint of material balancing. Existing deficiencies are corrected by making the rate of growth of the respective branch more realistic, while excesses in adjoining sectors are included in reserves, frequently without regard to the degree to which such reserves of the given use-values are actually needed. M. Kalecki correctly states, in relation to similar planning procedures:

> This is a wrong approach, because in the plan it leads to the fact that the need of certain products is overrated, or that the excess of other products is denoted as reserves. Of course reserves are very useful in a plan, but they must be formed where there is a danger and not in a random manner, not just to maintain a high indicator as a symbol of progress. In actual fact such tolerance to "excess" indicators leads to extravagance, either by overrating the demand in the plan, or by assuming unnecessary reserves which "whet

[2] M. Kalecki, *Outline of the theory of growth of socialist economy* (Prague: NPL, 1965), p. 1950.

the appetite" and may become the cause of increasing demand in the course of fulfilling the plan.[3]

The traditional choice of the rate of economic growth form considerations of the proposed branch structure of the national income generally allows greater production increments to be planned, but at the same time it supports the reproduction of bottlenecks accompanied by the excess of other products. Under conditions where there is insufficient saturation of the demand, the market will eventually absorb these excesses. But with the increasing industrial level and a higher degree of saturation of the market, this one-sided approach to choice of the rate of growth of the national income and the effects of the directive model of management will lead to a greater waste of social labor.

In the conditions of the directive system, the plan determines branch and sector proportions mainly from the point of view of material balance relations, without sufficient regard to natural long-term development trends of the market. This then leads to discrepancies between the structure of production, predetermined by preceding allocation of investments, and the structure of final demand, developing under the influence of market forces in the conditions of commodity money relations.

Balanced economic growth demands such an economically justified allocation of investments into sectors and production branches so that price relations will tend to equal value, cost-type relations. The state plan can insure a balanced economic growth if it respects the allocation function of the law of value. That means such a distribution of social labor, where the relation of profit to socially necessary costs is basically equalized between individual production branches.

Respecting the law of value and the price mechanism does not mean that the market mechanism is to determine the allocation of investments. It is generally known that it does not give a reliable image of the efficiency of investments. Market signals, in the form of rather long-run deviations of price and cost relations—as long as those are not being kept up by the authorities for extra-economic reasons—are a signal of certain defects in the reproduction process. However, the differences in relations between costs and equilibrium prices of the initial period are not decisive in determining the degree of efficiency of investments allocated to one or another branch.

[3] M. Kalecki, *Outline of the theory of growth of socialist economy* (Prague: NPL, 1965), p. 151.

To achieve this, the proposed price development must be taken into account, which again will depend on the development of supply and demand. The rational allocation of investments can be effectuated by means of a plan which is a model of the future market and considers not only equilibrium prices of the initial period, but also the future price dynamics based on a study of the elasticity of demand and supply.

The system of planned management with utilization of the law of value and of the market mechanism represents, compared to the directive distribution of production factors, a higher type of planning, since it offers better possibilities of insuring a stable and balanced economic growth and rational criteria for determining the structure of social production.

Chapter 17

THE PROBLEM
OF OPTIMIZATION
IN PLANNING

BRONISLAW MINC

Polish Academy of Sciences

A SYSTEM OF INDICATORS

The definition of optimization criteria at various levels (the enterprise, an industrial trust, branches of industrial enterprises, and the national economy) is of paramount importance in optimal planning. Contradiction between the enterprise and society finds its expression in the difference between the general objective of Socialist production and the objectives set by the enterprises on the basis of their conditions of action (directive plan targets and systems of success indicators for wages, bonuses, and prices). The general objective of Socialist production is the maximization of a broadly defined consumption fund based on the development of productive resources, that is, an optimal magnitude of the national income has not—until now—found its proper counterpart in objectives set by the Socialist enterprises. By means of mathematical concepts, it is possible to analyze more precisely the problem of indicators for appraising the economic activity of enterprises and the extent to which they can contribute to the attainment of the general objective of Socialist production (the criterion of optimization for the national economy). The indicators should be distinguished from the criteria of optimization. An indicator is a sort of measuring rod characterizing some aspect of economic activity. In the practice of Socialist economy, the concept of an indicator has been developed as a measure connected with the appraisal of the economic activity of enterprises and serving as basis of bonuses paid to the managing and specialist personnel of the firm. The setting up of such indicators influences the conduct of the Socialist enterprise, steering it toward economic decisions and definite economic objectives.

The indicators of economic activity should be considered from the point of view of time. The synthetic or main indicators (those that link the appraisal of the work of the enterprise and the bonuses of the managing personnel with a single measuring indicator), if they are yearly, unavoidably lead to the neglect of inputs which will yield economic effects after the lapse of one year. This applies to total gross production as well as profit. The use of synthetic or main indicators induces the enterprise to concentrate on one aspect of activity. It is clear that if the enterprises are appraised according to yearly gross output, and if their managing personnel is paid premiums accordingly, they will strive to maximize this output during the current year. The outcome will be a preference for production with a high material content, deficiencies in the assortment structure and neglect of quality in economic activity. (It will in turn result in a low utilization of productive resources and in a slowing down of technical progress.) The appraisal of the enterprise's economic activity based on the indicator of normative labor content of processing will again result in deviations in the assortment structure. Labor intensive processes will be preferred in some circumstances and will have adverse effects on technical progress.

Maximization of profit and more precision. First of all the period in which profit is to be maximized will have to be specified. Without this, the maximization of profit cannot be quantitatively defined. Theoretically speaking, this can either be the short period of a year or less, or a long period of several years. Usually what is meant by maximization of profit is annual profit (profit as shown in annual statements, and balance sheet bonuses for management and workers linked with annual profits). But maximization of profits in a year will result in the neglect of outlays not connected with profits in this period and will result in a cutback of expenses which will diminish profits. Therefore, maximization of profits for a year will lead to a discontinuation of inputs whose effects appear after that time. It would tempt the managing personnel of the enterprises not to engage voluntarily in the production of new goods or improvements of goods already produced which would diminish profits for the current year, even when in the longer periods such decisions could considerably increase profits. Since present-day technical progress requires inputs which always, or almost always, bear fruit in the long run, the principle of maximization of annual profits would tend unavoidably to slow down technical progress or to stop it altogether. While analyzing the importance of profit as a motive of enterprise behavior and as an instrument of distribution of national income, we can define external profit as the part of annual profit which originates independent of any improvements in the work of the enterprise. To put it another way, by external profit we mean the part of total profit which does not come from the effort of the enterprise to increase production or lower costs, but comes from the exploitation of a monopolistic position to a choice of the convenient assortment which does not correspond to needs or to the neglect of inputs for the development of the enterprise (outlays for new products, fixed investments or capital repairs). A part of the external profit originates as a rule from the price system (from the existence of prices which secure a profit higher than normal).

Improvements in the price system can diminish unfair advantages enjoyed by the enterprises, but it seems Utopian to try to construct an ideal price system that would neutralize enterprises in their choice of products, if the appraisal of the enterprises depends on profit earned. There will always be some products more or less convenient as far as profit or any other indicator is concerned. Prices are an instrument of short-run regulation of the economy. Any long-term regulation requires the use of other instruments in addition to prices.

While the target of maximization of general profit can be, with additional assumptions, expressed quantitatively, the target of maximization of profit in a longer period requires a decision as to the length of this period, but even if we choose a fairly long period of maximization (five years, for example), new difficulties would arise in solving the problem of investment and capital repairs where the effects stretch beyond this period: how to link the maximization in the chosen period with bonus payments which, to be effective, will have to made in short periods, and so forth.

Total and partial optima. Total and partial optima have to be distinguished. Total optimum is for the national economy as a whole. Partial optimum is only for a sector or branch of the national economy or for institutional units—enterprises, branch organizations or ministries. An optimum can be wider or narrower. An optimum is generally speaking the highest relation between economic effects and inputs. Optima have to be considered in a definite period (timeless optimum has no economic meaning). So we have to consider long- and short-term optima. Long-term optimum relates to a period long enough to obtain full economic effects of investment decisions taken. Short-term optimum relates to a period where productive capacities are fixed and cannot as a rule be increased. The concept of long-term optimum is connected with perspective planning (for a number of years) and the concept of short-term optimum with planning for a year or shorter periods.

Total optimum for a period is unique. Definite partial optima correspond to such an optimum, because they are obtained in relation to resources allocated among sectors, branches and enterprises in such a way that total optimum be obtained. So we come to distinguish between partial absolute and partial relative optima. Partial relative optimum signifies the highest possible relation between economic effects and inputs obtained in a sector of the economy—where the resources are allocated in order to secure total optimum. Absolute partial optimum means also the highest possible relation between economic effects and inputs, but in a situation where no account is taken of the allocation necessary for a total optimum. A complete correspondence exists between total optimum and relative partial optimum because the attainment of partial relative optima is a necessary condition of total optimum. But there is a contradiction between total optima and partial absolute optimum as some parts of the economy attain higher economic effects, while other parts with not enough resources achieve lower economic effects, and thus the whole national economy has effects below optimum.

Total optimum regarded from the long-term point of view cannot as a rule coincide with the sum of partial absolute optima and, if regarded in the short-term, can coincide with the sum of absolute partial optima only in certain circumstances. Total long-term optimum cannot coincide with the sum of long-term partial absolute optima because investment possibilities are restrained, and, in order to get total optimum, a proper allocation between sectors, branches and enterprises forming the economy is necessary. But all sectors, branches and enterprises can individually attain better results if better endowed with investment funds, particularly if these are destined to lower production costs. There is thus a natural contradiction between total long-term optimum and partial long-term absolute optimum.

The lack of contradiction between total short-term optimum and partial absolute short-term optima can occur only in special circumstances—namely, if there are no free resources. We shall explain with a simple example. Let us picture two enterprises with annual production capacities of

100 and 80 units of the same product. The costs of production are 1.0 and 1.2 in the two enterprises. The supply of raw materials can be enough only for 150 units of product. Each enterprise taken separately could achieve better results if granted a supply of raw materials corresponding to its productive capacity. To insure an optimum for the two enterprises considered jointly, the first enterprise should be allocated a supply of raw materials for a production of 100 units of the product and the second enterprise a supply for the production of only 50 units of the product. With such an allocation, there are no free resources in the first enterprise, and the partial absolute optimum coincides with the partial relative optimum. But in the second enterprise there are free resources in the form of unutilized capacity. Allowing 30 more units, relative partial optimum does not coincide with the absolute partial optimum.

Short-term optimum for a branch of production, and to an even higher degree total optimum for the whole economy, is not equal to the sum of partial absolute optima because the condition that all kinds of resources be mutually complementary, so that there be no free resources, is only fulfilled in exceptional cases.

To describe more fully the optimum for a given period, one should take it to mean the maximum of final product with definite product-mix in relation to resources. Final product should be considered as that part of production which is disposed of outside the organization unit. Final product of the national economy is production for consumption (individual and collective) and for accumulation (net investment and increase in stocks).

Important in the concept of optimum is the fact that not every production should be maximized, but only production with a definite structure.

Considering the structure of production one should distinguish: the share of production of investment goods and its structure and the share of production for current use and its structure. To determine the share of production for investment and its inner structure we have to know the dynamic model with the future consumption fund as the objective function to be maximized within an accepted time horizon, while the requirements of further growth should be insured. The inner structure of the consumption fund in the target period should determine the present directions of investments.

The magnitude and structure of production for current use is determined by the possibilities during the given period and particularly by existing productive capacities and by the demand (or planned requirements) for the products.

Generally speaking, if we assume that the conditions as to structure are met, the problem of optimization can be the maximization of final production with given resources. Thus if the volume and inner structure of investments can be taken from long-term plans, the problem of annual planning can be solved by maximizing production for current purposes corresponding to requirements (demand) and within the limitations of resources.

The correspondence between total optimum and partial optima and particularly between the optimum for the national economy and optima for the enterprises cannot be insured by direct imposition of tasks for enterprises, industrial trusts and ministries by the central authority. Such ordering would be against the objectively necessary regularities of present-day Socialist economy which are: national ownership of means of production with indirect appropriation. So it would contravene against the principle of democratic centralism, and it would limit the initiative of the enterprises and other units. Therefore the correspondence between total optimum and partial optima should be brought about by a system of steering lower organization units by higher units which will limit the independence of lower units only to the extent required for the attainment of total optimum.

Optimization criteria and the programming system. The objectives of the enterprises as laid down in their plans cannot directly enter as parts into the national plan of Socialist production, but it seems possible to create conditions insuring correspondence between the objectives of national economy and those of the enterprises.

The objective functions and restraints for the economy as a whole, for sectors and branches of production and for enterprises have to be different. Their general character has to be similar, and the objective functions and restraints for the enterprises have to be subordinate to the objective function for the national economy as a whole (while restraints will have to be taken into account). So the objective functions and restraints in the enterprises can only give sub-optimal solutions. However, the general intention should be to make objectives of the enterprises and trusts approximately those contained in the national objective of Socialist production. The maximization of gross production as well as the maximization of profits as targets set for the enterprises and trusts do not insure the correspondence and can even be directly opposed to the national objective of Socialist production as outlined above. Insuring a dynamic development of Socialist enterprises is necessary, however, for the enterprises to have an objective function which they could maximize subject to definite restraining conditions. The activity of the Socialist enterprise should be based on scientific programming, and the enterprise and its executives should be appraised on the basis of over-all achievement, the chief criteria being the delivery of orders to the satisfaction of customers and provision for the future development of the enterprise.

Programming should replace the traditional system of commands and indicators, which was established at times when scientific programming methods were not known. Programming is superior to the traditional methods, because it makes it possible to establish an interrelated and ordered system of objectives (one objective being maximized, the other serving as a restraint). The maximization of the objective function within the restraints is not equivalent to the maximization of one definite indicator within the existing system of planning.

One-year planning in the enterprises should be based on linear programming, and for longer periods on dynamic programming. Of course one-year planning should be more detailed than planning for longer periods.

It is possible to apply linear programming to one-year planning because the productive capacities of the enterprise during the year are virtually given (productive capacities existing at the beginning of the year and those to be installed during the year in result of previous investment are known). Therefore, basing one-year planning on linear programming is feasible and makes possible the maximization of the ratio of economic achievements of the enterprise to its productive resources.

Assuming that the objective function is the maximization of the final product and that existing resources act as restraints, we assume further that the relationship between output and input of labor and materials is linear in character (for instance, output increases in the same proportion as input). However, in reality this relationship to some extent may be nonlinear. If this is the case, the appropriate correctives should be introduced into the calculus.

In view of the variability of the techno-economic coefficients in longer periods, long-term planning should be based on dynamic programming. Only this method can take into account the economic consequences of investment.

From the long-term plans of an enterprise, some definite conclusions should follow in regard to yearly plans and to investment and outlays which start production of new products. These conclusions should be considered within the restraints of the yearly plans of the enterprise. It should be noted that the long-term plan of the enterprises should be to a large extent determined by the general conception of development and in consequence by the directives of the central plan.

The maximization of the final product in relation to resources allocated should be the objective function of the yearly plans of the enterprises. Only sales should be considered as final product. In this way the production of unsaleable products would not pay. To counteract the excessive use of materials, the final product should be calculated as the difference between the output sold and the value of materials used.

In terms of programming, restraints should be taken in particular productive capacities of the enterprises and demand for produced goods, supply limits of scarce materials and possibly the manpower limits, the wage-bill limits, targets concerning the more important assortments of goods, the directives consequent upon the central plan concerning the production of new products, investment targets and limits, magnitude of profit and of financial accumulation in general.

The restraints expressing the targets in the sphere of new products are particularly important, since the problem of determination of proportion of goods being already produced and of the new products boils down to the problem of choice between the satisfaction of present needs and future needs. It is therefore the same problem which is present in such economic decisions as the choice of investment rate and the choice of technique.

In other words, the enterprise should tend to maximize its part of the national income within objective restraints such as some targets set by the enterprise itself in its long-term plan and directives of the central plan.

The restraints may take full account of the financial targets and in particular the minimum magnitude of profits which should be realized by the enterprise.

After all, the number of restraints should be suited to circumstances. In some conditions the wage-bill limit may be left out, because its magnitude is determined by the regulations in force and collective agreements, which the enterprise must adhere to. In any case the proportions of division of the net product of the enterprise between wages and profit, and of the profit between that part which is transferred to the state and the part left in the enterprise to serve its developmental aims, should be determined by the higher authorities of the enterprise on the basis of central directives.

The subtraction of the value of materials used from the final product, the difference being the objective function to be maximized, should not be a neutral act toward the use of materials in the enterprise. The objective function achieves maximum only when, given the stocks of materials at the disposal of the enterprise, the final product reaches a maximum. Therefore the economies on materials, possible to achieve in the given period, condition the maximization of the final product, and every waste of materials reduces final product.

The objective function of the enterprise expresses the aim of achieving final product as an aggregate of use-values. Therefore the final product should be calculated at the prices of the preceding year. The same is valid for the means of production. If, however, in the planned year-period some price changes essential for the choice of the assortment by the enterprise are to take place, they should be taken into account. In any case it would have been contrary to the aims of Socialist production if an enterprise could raise prices and profits taking advantage of its monopolistic position.

When the definite resources are given, the problem of optimization of the economic activity of the enterprise reduces to the problem known in linear programming as the best utilization of resources.

Such a problem may be demonstrated by a most simple example. The enterprise has at its disposal a definite quantum of resources—namely, equipment, manpower and two kinds of materials. Therefore, there are four kinds of resources R_1, R_2, R_3, R_4, in quantities amounting respectively to b_1, b_2, b_3, b_4 units. Definite norms determine the number of units of a resource going into the production of a unit of product. The number of units of resource R_i $(i = 1, 2, 3, 4)$ necessary to produce a unit of product P_j $(j = 1, 2, 3, 4)$ is a_{ij}.

The magnitude to be maximized is the value of sales. The price of unit of the first product is c_1, of the second c_2, of the third c_3, and of the fourth c_4. Let us denote by x_1, x_2, x_3, x_4 the respective quantities of products P_1, P_2, P_3, P_4, which within the restraints as presented below, maximize the objective function (S):

$$S = c_1 x_1 + c_2 x_2 + c_3 x_3 + c_4 x_4$$

The restraints concerning resources are as follows:

$$a_{11} x_1 + a_{12} x_2 + a_{13} x_3 + a_{14} x_4 \leq b_1$$

$$a_{21} x_1 + a_{22} x_2 + a_{23} x_3 + a_{24} x_4 \leq b_2$$

$$a_{31} x_1 + a_{32} x_2 + a_{33} x_3 + a_{34} x_4 \leq b_3$$

$$a_{41} x_1 + a_{42} x_2 + a_{43} x_3 + a_{44} x_4 \leq b_4$$

Besides, the conditions of non-negative quantities of products should also be included into the restraints:

$$x_1 \geq 0$$

$$x_2 \geq 0$$

$x_3 \geq 0$

$x_4 \geq 0$

We shall now introduce demand into restraints. The introduction of the new restraint means that in choosing the pattern of production, account must be taken not only of resources necessary to produce goods, but also of the possibilities of selling these goods. There are two possibilities. If demand (that is, the possibilities of selling products) is greater than the possibilities of their production, demand has no influence on the magnitude of maximized objective function. If, however, even for one product, market capacity is less than productive capacity, this will influence the results of the maximization of the objective function. The demand restraints are as follows:

$x_1 \leq t_1$

$x_2 \leq t_2$

$x_3 \leq t_3$

$x_4 \leq t_4$

For a planned economy it is essential that enterprises fulfill the targets of the central plan. These targets may be obligatory for the enterprises, and then they take on the character of commands. Let us assume that the target for the enterprise following from the central plan is the production of quantity m of product P_1. Then to the system of inequalities should be added the new restraint:

$x_1 \geq m$

The enterprise may also have the target of a definite amount of accumulation (profits), different products bringing different profits. Let us assume that the sum of profits is z, and profits realized on a unit of particular products are respectively z_1, z_2, z_3, z_4. Then the restraint to be included takes on the form:

$$Z_1 x_1 + Z_2 x_2 + Z_3 x_3 + Z_4 x_4 \geq z$$

Of course z, the profit target, should be less or equal to the sum of profits which would have been realized were the maximization of profits the objective function.

The list of restraints should also include targets concerning new products, if outlays on starting this production bring some economic effects in later periods than the year planned for, and targets of repairs.

So far we have considered the problem of optimization of the activity of enterprises in a short period assuming that resources at the disposal of the enterprise are given. In reality, however, resources may vary. It is possible to apply programming even to such a case, though it would be much more complicated.

The optimization of the activity of industrial trusts. The trust constitutes an intermediate level in the organizational sructure of the national economy—namely, the level between enterprises belonging to the trust and the ministry to which the trust is subordinated and the national economy as a whole. The task of the enterprise should be the achievement of partial optimum, in a short period as well as in a long period, of a relative character (consistent with the optimum of the ministry and optimum of the whole national economy). For this purpose the activity of the trust should consist in receiving information and directives from the ministry and transmitting information and setting directives for individual enterprises.

Let us consider first the problem of optimum planning in the trust for a short period. The trust receives from the ministry sets of targets, the fulfillment of which conditions the achievement of the ministry's optimum and total optimum. These targets enter the list of restraints, and the objective function of the trust is the maximization of the sum of the final products of all the constituent enterprises on the basis of allocated resources.

If in the enterprises there were no free resources, the short-term optimum for the trust would be equal to the sum of their short-term absolute optima. However, as a rule the situation is different, productive capacities are greater than the supply of materials. Therefore the allocation of resources to enterprises should assure the highest ratio of the sum of production to the costs for the trust as a whole. Such allocation requires a precise knowledge of costs of production and use of materials in the individual enterprises. The socio-economic factors should also be taken into account. Because of them, it is futile or impossible to decrease the production of an enterprise below a certain level. For it may happen that (surpluses of productive capacities and oversupply of materials being large) economic reasons may require such a reduction of output in certain high-cost enterprises which would practically mean closing them down or stopping work for longer periods.

The trust may consider itself as a single enterprise owning the resources of its constituent enterprises. The objective function may be set accordingly as a single function from which the targets for individual enterprises follow.

Such a procedure would, however, contradict the fact of the existence of enterprises and would restrict if not destroy their initiative. For this reason the trust should only see to it that the plans of constituent enterprises be optimal and that their relative optimum be consistent with the optimum of the trust. Three elements are of essential importance: demand on the same products produced by different enterprises, allocation of materials to enterprises, manpower and in particular skilled labor.

If demand on the same products produced by different enterprises is less than their productive capacities, the trust should assure that the production be in line with demand, using only the capacities of low-cost enterprises. In other words the trust should assure the proper adaptation of production to demand in such a way that the costs of production are minimized.

The trust should also distribute the targets of the central plan, concerning the assortment of goods, between the constituent enterprises. Here also the trust should insure that given production targets be achieved at lowest possible cost.

In case productive capacities are greater than supplied materials, the trust should allocate materials to the enterprises which can achieve production targets at lowest costs or maximize production on the basis of allocated materials.

When the labor force, and in particular the skilled labor force, is scarce, the trust should allocate it to the enterprises where it can be best employed and thus contribute to the achievement of optimum by the trust.

The extent of the increase of productive capacities of the constituent enterprises of the trust may be determined only on the basis of the long-term optimum of the national economy as a whole. After having determined what this increase is going to be, the trust must determine how to implement it (construction of new plants, extension of existing plants or their reconstruction and modernization, if this involves increase in productive capacity) and in which enterprises productive capacities are to be increased.

The entire investment resources, to be devoted to increase in the productive capacity, should be allocated by the trust. Allocating investment among constituent enterprises should be done in such a way that given the targets of increased productive capacity and the planned level of costs of production in the plants to be constructed, the cost of investment should be at its minimum, taking into account the time factor.

The other should be the case with outlays on the maintenance of efficiency of equipment in the existing enterprises. By efficiency we mean not only technical but economic (that is, ability to produce at social profit). Outlays on maintaining efficiency of equipment contain an outlay on replacement and reconstruction which need not involve increase in productive capacity. (Small outlays on investment should be treated in a similar way.) Outlays on maintaining the efficiency of existing equipment should be divided into two kinds depending on their magnitude: larger outlays should be decided on by the trust (on the basis of trust optimum and enterprise optimum).

The activity of trusts should also be based on scientific programming. In annual plans the objective function of the trust should be the maximization of final product, as defined above, in relation to productive resources. All these magnitudes should be considered jointly for all the constituent enterprises. Restraints should be treated in a similar way. Of course, to maximize the final product, trusts should allocate scarce materials, machines, and so on, to those enterprises with the greatest potential. To establish directions for the development of the line of production represented by the trust and long-term plans of enterprises, the long-term plans of trusts based on dynamic programming are essentially important. Those plans in turn should take into account the directive targets of central plans in relation to trusts as a whole.

Chapter 18

CHANGES IN THE PRICE SYSTEM AND IN THE PRICE MECHANISM IN HUNGARY

BÉLA SZIKSZAI

Hungarian Economic Association

The price system is an integrated system of industrial-producer prices, of foreign-trade prices, of agricultural procurement prices and of free-market prices, as well as consumer prices. Individual schemes may exist in certain spheres of the price system, but this does not mean that the particular spheres are insulated from one another; the connection is very close among the separate fields. It is necessary to emphasize this, because solving the existing problems in the several fields of the price system can be realized only by improving the system as a whole.

Nowadays reform in the system of economic management is under preparation in Hungary. If we want to sum up its main features, we can do so by saying that it comprises connecting the direction of the centrally planned economy with the active role of market conditions. In the new economic mechanism there will be changes in the means of the planned direction of the national economy; the means (of the planned direction of economic life) will appear as price policy, credit policy, and so on. It cannot be considered mere chance that the basic element of debate on economic reform in Hungary was the improvement of the price system and the improvement of the price mechanism.

Price policy is an organic part of the system of economic management. In case there are essential changes in the economic direction system, these, too, will have an effect on the price system. The changes in the price system are changing the principle of price formation (of the price type), and the modification of the price-forming methods (of the price mechanism).

SOME OF THE MAIN FEATURES OF THE SYSTEM

The system is characterized first of all by being official. The prices for 80 to 85 per cent of the commodity funds of the population are determined by the state. The remaining 15 to 20 per cent is bought and sold on the agricultural markets, where prices are not subject to restrictions. But, strictly speaking, this is not a free-price formation, because in this section the price movement is held between close frames through several means (directed prices) by the state. This influencing activity can be observed in the area of home crafts as well as in trade (market produce for example).

The prices of products bought and sold within industry are regulated by the state. The regularly produced means of production (in series and in bulk) have a fixed official price. The prices of single products manufactured occasionally are determined by the enterprises by applying compulsory computational directives. On the one hand, this price can be enforced over a certain value limit only with the consent of the price authority, and, on the other, the price formation of these products is limited by the official prices of certain component parts.

The over-all result is that in the present system of price formation the official prices extend over more than 10,000 products. This is such a great volume, that under these conditions it is almost impossible to solve the problems presented by a change in prices and the socially necessary labor. This problem is made even more difficult by the fact that in trade within the state sector, the official fixing of prices is decisive—flexible forms of prices seldom being used (maximum prices, free-price formation, and so on). As a consequence, the present price mechanism is characterized by a considerable inflexibility; prices are in force over a long period (six to eight years), and therefore they become separated from their own base, the labor input. In such circumstances the prices cannot properly serve for orientation in economic decisions.

A national system. The prices are connected with the national conditions of production. The endowments and objectives, under which the Hungarian people's economy thrives and develops, establish the starting base for the price formation. The state price regulation starts from the view that the price category can neither be opposed to nor separated from the state's economic policy. Taking into consideration the close connection between the state price regulation and the economic mechanism, of which the state price regulation is a very important part, this theory is obvious.

A state price regulation and the system of fixed prices conforming to the national conditions of production leads to a situation where domestic prices are separated from prices prevailing in foreign trade. This separation is realized through the mechanism of foreign-trade price-leveling. The essence of it is that the state equalizes (completes or subtracts) the difference between the two kinds of prices. The foreign-trade price-leveling system—in its present form—is functioning in a broad circle as a technical means of bridging the two kinds of prices. Only with a few groups of products is a so-called "foreign exchange proportionate" price formation period, where the connection between the two prices is closer and more organic.

In recent years, out of the economic debate which took place in Hungary, the majority of economists have come to the conclusion that the separation of domestic and foreign-trade prices, as one of the main features of the price system, must be eliminated.

This separation was justified when economic isolation was forced on the Socialist countries, but this is not the case today. The separation of the two price categories undoubtedly reflects the economic conception of autocracy—in an essentially changed internal and international situation.

The close connection between domestic and foreign-trade prices is decisively important for a country which is so widely dependent on international division of labor. Such a situation, characteristic also of Hungary, demands that the national and international value conditions be brought into synthesis. But essentially this point of view is supported by a more energetic development of the Socialist division of labor and by the promotion of internal structural changes which take into consideration profit requirements.

There is still much discussion in Hungary about the means to a solution. But it is clear that the close connection of the two prices can be realized only through a realistic rate of exchange (a foreign-exchange multiplier) which expresses the real domestic inputs of obtaining foreign exchange. This will be certainly an average (uniform) rate of exchange—though several people argued in favor of a marginal rate of exchange, a higher one than the average foreign-exchange multiplier. It is also clear that in the course of the reform of economic management, the system of price-leveling must be changed, and the effects of price equalization must be connected with the system of material incentives of the producing enterprises.

The close connection between home and foreign-trade prices does not mean—in my opinion—that the center of domestic prices should be world-market prices. Not only because the world-market price is not an exact category, which can only be accepted as the measure of the international-value situation with strong reservations, but, first of all, because a country developing according to plan cannot renounce the orientating role of the prices (which are built on the national conditions of production). In course of the reform of economic management, in the price formation of the bigger part of the Socialist countries, elements are deliberately stressed which create material interest in developing planned connections. This is unattainable by taking over external price conditions. It can only be done by a method of price formation which would start from production conditions serving as a basis for a goal with the objectives of the long-range plan. The price must orientate in economic activities in accordance with the plan. Particularly so, if we consider that with many products, exporting or importing is not a realistic alternative.

A nonuniform system. This particular aspect of the price system is based on whether the products belong to the state sector or are outside the circle of state property.

With products belonging to the state sector, the main purpose is that state direction based on the compulsory plan indices should also prevail effectively through price formation in the enterprises.

With products not belonging to the state sector, the function is used by the state to exercise a planned influence over the economical processes. Thus, agricultural price policy plays an important role in forming the planned income conditions and the desired production structure. Consumer-price policy plays an important role in assuring the balance of supply and demand.

These circumstances explain the fact that in the price system of the Hungarian people's economy, industrial-producer prices, agricultural state procurement prices, as well as consumer prices, are separated from one another and in a certain sense from independent systems.

Besides, the price system is characterized by the features of a price system based on costs of production. This means: 1) prices must contain all the costs qualified as socially necessary; 2) the social net income appears in the prices in proportion to the cost of production. This distinguishes the cost-type price system from other systems. Meanwhile some changes have occurred in the type of price system. In 1964, there was a partial industrial price reform whose intention was—among others—that the volume of fixed and circulating assets used in production (the capital intensity of production) should be taken into consideration in industrial price formation. In other words, the Hungarian price system is developing along the line of the production-price system.

The change carried out in price type is closely connected with the question of price center.

The center of prices. Marxist economists studying the price problem start from Marx's labor theory of value and consider socially necessary labor as the basis of Socialist price formation. Price formation thus requires first of all the establishment of the volume of the socially necessary labor inputs (the value). To express the value in money, we use two accepted fundamental price forms: value price and production price.

According to the labor theory of value, the value of commodities can be measured with the volume of work performed (labor input). The formula of the value is $c + v + m$. The c is partly the value of the equipment used in producing the commodities (this is reflected by the depreciation allowance), and partly the value of the materials consumed. The $v + m$ is the new value, which is brought about by live labor. The new value is divided into two parts: one being the wages of the workers (v), the other the net income of the Socialist society (m). In case of value prices we express the value directly in the form of money. Therefore, we get the value prices by adding the social net income to the costs of production of all products in proportion to the wage costs, according to a uniform normative.

Production price is a modified form of the value. In such a case, the net income realized does not conform to the wage input but to the value of the assets used in production. Therefore we get the production price by supplementing the prime cost of every product with a social net income in proportion to the production funds (according to a uniform normative).

What should the center of prices in a Socialist economy be—the value price or the production price? Namely, the type of price is definitely connected with the system of material interest. Furthermore, the system of taxation which serves the value price differs from that used in case of production price. The establishment of the price center cannot be considered as a characteristic price problem; actually, the price center has an effect on the whole financial mechanism. The effect of the price center on prices appears as follows: the various price centers contain the net income according to different formulae, and, therefore, the relative prices are different in every price type. Relative prices always inform us more or less what the society pays in cost. The prices are adequate if the relative prices orientate well in the most important question: which of our decisions most conserves social labor.

The followers of the price center of production price types declare that, under the conditions of mechanical large-scale industry, if we want to see the relative costs of products clearly, it is not enough to express in the price center the proportion of the (current) inputs used in the course of production. We also have to prove that we produce products of the same value with different amounts of fixed and circulating assets (fixed and working capital).

The more developed the forces of production, the more differentiated the capital intensity of production by kinds of products. The more developed the economy of a country, the greater the damage (if we do not take into consideration the capital intensity of production).

As we mentioned earlier, we made the first step toward production price at the beginning of 1964 (having initiated the 5 per cent contribution on assets used). As an effect of this measure, about one third of the social income conforms to the value of assets. According to some conceptions, it would be better to distribute the greater part, about two thirds of the social net income (that is, 10 per cent of the value of assets), among the products in proportion to the value of assets. Essentially, our task is to put the profit regulation on new bases and to bring it in accordance with the requirements of a price system in which approximately two thirds of the net income conforms to the value of assets and one third to the wage costs.

The initiation of the production price means that the development advances toward a uniform price system. Accordingly, the distinctive marks of price formation in agriculture and industry as well as those of producer and consumer prices will gradually disappear (with some exceptions).

At the same time, price type can be determined only in the realization of net income in the individual product prices. Price type does not determine the price itself, only the price center of the products—the average calculated price—which can be equivalent to the concrete prices but may also differ from them. The distinction between price type (price center) and concrete price is based upon the fact that the concrete price need not be unconditionally equivalent to the socially necessary input. The deviation of these two is not only possible, but in certain cases even necessary. The aim of price deviation is appropriate orientation and stimulation: for example, to keep the balance of demand and supply, and to form such relative prices which express the utility of substitute products, and so on.

Flexibility of the system. To achieve reform in the system of economic management in Hungary, it is necessary to carry out a price reform which covers the further development of both price system and price mechanism.

The further development of price mechanism is going on together with the perfection of the whole system of economic management as an integral part. In accordance with this system, price forms must be used which enable the value judgment of the market to have an adequate effect on the formation of relative prices. That is how the interests of the producers and consumers can be made optimally consistent; such a price system can be a suitable connecting link between producers and buyers. But it must be seen, too, that the value judgment of the different consumers often varies. The price category can fulfill its role as an equilibrium price among the consumers with different value judgments only if it can be formed more or less free on the market.

At the same time, it is of utmost importance for the Socialist planned economy to preserve the stability of prices, to prevent the establishment of tendencies which push them up. As a consequence, a sign of equality cannot exist in the new system of directing the economy between the use of flexible price forms and free-price formation without more study. Though we want to introduce a flexible price mechanism, we also want to maintain the price regulation by the state, though in a changed form. We are changing the forms of the state price regulation to offer a larger scope for the price automation. We keep certain forms of the state price regulation to allow minimum room for price automatism, in order not to endanger the stability of prices.

To assure the stability of the price level a great variety of methods of price formation can be used. These vary by influencing the enterprises in different ways and to a different extent. According to debates up to the present, we shall use three main price forms in the flexible price mechanism.

1) The fixed (official) price (with its different versions). Several variants of this price form will be applied. The more important are: a) statutory fixing of prices by items; b) fixing of the basic official price from which deviations are possible in the form of price reductions or extra charges (on the basis of the qualitative characteristics of the commodities or on the basis of the volume ordered, and so on); c) fixing the price of a compound product (in most cases an individual product) by establishing a standard price for the various elements of the product, thus determining the price of the finished products according to the standard prices of the elements and according to the supplements chargeable by the regulations; d) building price formation on normatives and technical price rows, that is, when the price of a product is determined according to certain rules (for instance, it is fixed according to the technical characteristics of a product group with the aid of a parameter).

2) *Contracted prices with official price stipulations.* Within this, we want to use the following main price forms: a) determination of maximum price by items, when the prices can move within the upper limit; b) fixing the maximum price of a certain product within a product group (a representative product). We use this form with the consideration, that within a product group the fixed price of the leading type also stabilizes the price level of the product group with those products, where otherwise the price is not directly limited; c) fixing the price level of a product group—allowing the price to deviate from the price level from time to time, but for the period as a whole letting the guiding price prevail as an average price; d) authorizing contracted prices where the measure of deviation from the guiding price is limited—from above and below; e) determining compulsory guiding principles for price formation, by fixing the normatives of the cost and/or profit. It is permissible to deviate from the normatives upward or downward—to a certain extent. A looser imaginable version of this form is when there are only general instructions given to the enterprises, the prices are formed among the conditions of sale and purchase, but it is necessary to enter these settled prices in the price list of the enterprise, and deviation from them is possible only between fixed limits.

3) *Free prices.* Within this, the possible forms are: a) contracted prices, when the price forms according to the market price relations between the producer and consumer; and b) prices fixed unilaterally by trading organizations which makes it possible to use a consumer price moving independently from the producer price.

When using the various forms of price formation it is important to take into consideration that in each production branch the most suitable form for the peculiarities of the different product groups must be used. But at the same time, the essential requirement must be kept in mind that the direct official price regulation by the state should be limited only to the required minimum. Otherwise, the correct principle of the stability of the price level would cause the restoration or preservation of the inflexible forms of the official price system.

In summation, we set a double requirement against the new price mechanism: in the price formation we use or let prevail only such forms as make possible a flexible adaptation to the changing conditions of the market; and the flexible price forms should not result in endangering the stability of the price level.

To solve this double problem is very difficult economically. It is not possible to follow a uniform method in the field of industry, in the different industrial branches or in the different product groups. Because of the many-fold tasks of industry, the different characteristics of the individual branches and enterprises and the different purposes of the products, the differences in the market conditions and because of divergent methods of direction, the required price formation can only evolve through a differentiated price mechanism. This can be realized only when in the integral process lasting from the beginning of production till consumption, at the end points (that is, with the production of the main basic materials and with the consumption of the essential consumer goods) in the first period of the new mechanism certain official price forms play a larger role (these will be more flexible price forms than the present ones), but with the other part of the production process freer price forms will prevail.

Explaining this axiom more in detail, we get the following picture about the price mechanism which is going to come into play in industry.

With the prices of raw and basic materials, and the prices of important products, it seems to be most suitable to use the centrally fixed maximum prices. Thus, the direct official price regulation would remain in force. The direct official price regulation of these products is justified by the fact that the material costs of the enterprises in the processing industry (and through this, to a great extent also the costs of production) are fundamentally determined by the producer prices of these products, and that is why the elements of stability are felt in the price formation of the finished products. When suggesting this method, Hungarian economists took into consideration the fact that assuring stability with price prescriptions regarding the basic materials is an internationally adopted method—in spite of the fact that this means an essential official interference with the price formation. Besides, we have to take into account the fact that there is a certain shortage of raw and basic materials, and this shortage cannot be eliminated in the near future (but can be decreased to a considerable extent). However, using more flexible price forms, the prices of these products might rise.

Nevertheless, it must be realized, that it is not practicable to use the officially fixed maximum prices for these product groups in every production phase. It is necessary to differentiate even within that area. The operation with a maximum price is right in a field where raw and basic materials reach several enterprises of different industrial branches and thereby stabilize the price level. In other fields, more flexible forms must be used. It is of essential economic importance to resort to such methods if the enterprises processing the products of the extracting industries should feel, through the formation of their own costs, the changes in inputs of the raw material production or the changes in the costs of imports. This leads in the field of product-consumption in the direction of optimum decisions. The basic-material producing enterprises have the greatest opportunity to choose the product-mix. This possibility for choice is less at the later production phase, or it does not exist at all. So, if in the field of extracting industries, we used strong official price-fixing forms, this would limit those decisions for choosing the most profitable sources of supply or for using the most suitable technology in the production of basic materials.

Because of her natural endowments, Hungary has to procure a considerable part of the raw and basic materials through imports. The home producers get these commodities at a price converted to the home price with the aid of a foreign-exchange multiplier. It would be desirable if this price prevailed in every phase of production and consumption. The enforcement of this principle is prevented by the fact that we obtain raw and basic materials from different countries and at different prices. Sometimes we produce them at home. That is why the import price computed with the foreign-exchange multiplier must be adapted to the domestic price system.

The unification of the products purchased from several places is done by a body (price authority, the enterprise) which fixes the price. As an axiom, a foreign-exchange price must make its way to the production phase where there is still a real possibility to choose the most profitable source: for example, the domestic purchase price of iron ore or of nonferrous metals will be formed with the aid of the foreign-exchange multiplier, while the prices of metallurgical products (ingots or rolled steel) which are produced from imported materials will be officially limited by a maximum price. In such fields, the profit of the enterprises will change from time to time according to the movement of foreign-exchange prices, and this can be surmounted by using the reserve fund of the enterprises, while the steady tendencies of the world-market prices can be enforced by changing the official maximum prices.

According to the above methods (a price formed by using the foreign-exchange multiplier, unification of prices of imported and domestically produced goods), the price level of a product group will be formed. Within the price level, the prices of the single products can be established according to foreign relative prices, in conformity with the international conventions, or according to the domestic inputs and the relative domestic prices conforming to the conditions of supply and demand.

With the price formation of products consumed within the state industry (semi-finished products, component parts, and so forth), in the first period of the new mechanism the fixing of maximum prices by items should be used only rarely. In this area, more flexible price forms may be used in a wider circle. It must be assured that enterprises settle the prices in the contracts—taking into consideration some essential principles of pricing—and the price authority should rule only on the measure of deviation (price limits). In rare cases, with products of particularly great importance, whose prices widely influence the calculation of further processing units, the method of fixing the maximum price officially may be used for the most important variety.

In this field, imports are of less determinative character than in that of basic materials. The prices of imported component parts, semi-finished products, and the like, need not be regulated officially. These products come to the users at a price calculated with the foreign-exchange multiplier, and they charge them to buyers at prices of products according to an agreement or within the official price limits. Capital goods, as machines, are items of "final consumption," and their prices influence the price formation in all areas where they are used; therefore, it was debated for a long time which kind of price form would be best in the price formation of capital goods—the official price regulation or the use of free prices. The free-price form shows to good advantage because the combined effect of the different mechanisms may influence prices in the desired direction. It seems that financing and accounting methods and incentives for investment, as well as the economic policy in respect to investments, have a more decisive role in influencing the desirable price formation than the price mechanism (all the more so because a considerable part of the machines invested are individual products, and the price-stabilizing effect of the official price prescriptions was rather rigid in this field even in the past).

Besides the advantageous side, there is a problem—the production of machinery takes place in Hungary chiefly in monopolistic organizations.

It is important to create a situation where the "defenselessness" of the investing organs and their "passivity" in connection with prices should cease even if only one enterprise is able to produce the product at home. The prevention of price-raising tendencies, as well as the preconditions of suitable price formation, can be assured only in this way. The objective conditions of a suitable price formation can be brought into being if: 1) the price influencing effect of the "competition" of the imported and domestically produced machines prevails (that is, imported or home-produced machines are bought only after having weighed the price differences between the import price formed with the foreign-exchange multiplier and the home price); 2) the system of income withdrawal and the system of material incentives create a close contact between the enterprises' profit and the "management" of means.

Until the above requirements of direction are realized to some extent, it is desirable to keep the price formation of the most important machines within certain limits through different methods of (partial) official price regulations. Only rarely can a maximum price be set. When fixing the maximum price, we want to take into consideration, besides the costs of the machine factories, the relative prices of the export and import markets.

In the production of individually designed machines we also have to leave for future consideration a free scope for agreements between enterprises.

Price formation of consumer goods is one of the central questions of the economic policy which influences the whole price and wage level. A considerable part of consumer goods consists of basic products which cannot be replaced, and these are relatively narrow in assortment. It is advisable to fix the consumer prices of these products in the form of maximum prices, conforming to the present consumer-price level. The fixed maximum consumer price fixes or maximizes in most cases the industrial selling price of the volume destined for consumption by the population. The tensions arising from fixed prices will be solved by regulating the turnover taxes, by additional imports, and so forth.

In industries which are important in supplying the population but which produce a wide assortment of goods, various forms of partial price regulation must be used. Free prices (only influenced by economic measures) are proposed only for such articles which are of minor importance and whose supply and demand sharply reacts to the price changes.

Thus, in the first period of the new mechanism, in the field of consumer goods it will be characteristic that fixed (respectively maximum) and partially regulated consumer prices will function and, accordingly, limit industrial selling prices.

In industries, where supply and demand rates satisfactorily support the maintenance of the present level of consumer prices, less strict forms of partial price regulation can be used. In such cases, the industrial prices are freer. As the consumer price determines the industrial price, it is not necessary to issue separate industrial price prescriptions in these industries.

Chapter 19

ECONOMICS AND MANAGEMENT OF THE NATIONAL ECONOMY

YU. M. PAVLOV

Academy of Sciences of the USSR

The elaboration of scientific recommendations for improving economic management is one of the most urgent tasks of the economist. Soviet economists are faced with the problems of developing methods of industrial management much further and training managerial personnel in these methods. Management is an essential component of the social production process. Elaboration of these problems becomes a socially essential prerequisite for really full and rational utilization of the advantages of the Socialist economic system.

Scientific industrial management should be based on a knowledge of objective economic laws and the concrete forms and singularities of their operation in given conditions. It cannot be practiced at the discretion of more or less experienced production managers but must definitely be objective and substantiated and soberly take into account available resources and the actual possibilities of their maximum utilization.

Scientific management is also based on modern methods of quantitative measurement, mathematical simulation and statistical-mathematical analysis of economic activities and industrial complexes. Instead of vague opinions, it strives to establish exact quantitative indicators and criteria of the effectiveness of planned actions. It strives for quantitative measurement of the attained level of economic development and of the expected results.

Scientific management involves complete technical reequipment and, in particular, complete mechanization and automation of the methods of obtaining, coding, processing and utilizing diverse information, which is a key element in the system of control at all its stages. Scientific management has been made a possibility by the achievements of present-day electronics and cybernetics. Only high-speed electronic computers, which make it possible to process huge flows of information, provide the material and technical basis for a really scientific approach to the problem of management.

Management of the national economy as a whole is based on the all-round utilization of the intrinsic incentives of Socialist production. These incentives stem from the essence of the basic economic law of socialism, according to which the domination of social property inevitably subordinates production to the welfare of all members of society and all-round development of the personality of each. In the process, production gives rise to new requirements which predetermine its own further development. Here we see a development stimulant which is inherent in the Socialist economy and which society should take into account. In this sense, management of the national economy must be built up as a self-stimulating process owing to the properties of the social mechanism.

Management of the Socialist economy is faced with the task of insuring the interrelation of all parts of the national economy and of scientifically foreseeing both the immediate and relatively remote results of the country's economic activity (that is, of subordinating social production to the systematic, conscious control of society). As opposed to capitalist competition, Socialist production offers the coordination of economic activities on a nationwide scale and stimulation of industrial personnel on the basis of cost-accounting and widescale utilization of the mechanism of commodity-money relations. The system of Socialist management involves planning the national economy.

The theory of economic planning and management, the foundations of which were laid by Lenin, is an acknowledged achievement of Soviet economics. This theory and the methods of planning evolved on its basis have been used in drafting our long-term and current plans in the whole system of economic planning and cost-accounting. Now life faces economics with the task of further developing and improving centralized planning by combining it with full utilization of commodity-money relations, greater economic independence and initiative of individual units, and wider use of profits, cost-accounting and material incentive. The successful solution to this problem should insure complete community of the interests of society as a whole, each economic unit, and individual employee.

In solving this problem, economics must indicate the ways to utilize modern methods of mathematical economy and to improve the system of economic information and its processing on high-speed computers with the aim of selecting the optimum solutions of economic problems from all available variants and of best implementing the chosen lines of development.

This would make it possible to draft optimum economic plans that would insure achievement of the maximum effect for society with the resources it has available, plans that would be well substantiated and would permit choosing the best method for attaining the goals of Communist development indicated by the Party.

Such plans should be long-term in order that the main lines of development of the Socialist economy can be laid down, the quantitative ratios, rates and proportions of economic development can be scientifically established; and the prospects for development of individual economic sectors and regions can be correctly determined for shorter terms, in order to set about designing new units in good time.

The present achievements of economics in elaborating the theory of optimum planning should be of great help in practice. This pertains first of all to the solution of problems of improving price formation, material incentive, efficiency of capital investments, and so forth.

A category of Socialist planned production is the optimum of the national economy. The maximum economic effect can be established in the plan and achieved in practice in the process of plan fulfillment only by complete and all-round analysis of the objective conditions of the given stage of economic development, taking into account, of course, that these conditions themselves change in keeping with the laws of Socialist development. Hence, the optimum of the national economy will always be determined by the attained level of development of the social productive forces.

Among the economic problems requiring research is a determination of methods of optimum expansion of the country's fixed assets and an improvement of the efficiency of their utilization. This problem must be solved because of the need to boost labor productivity and the rates of economic development.

It is common knowledge that capital investments make up the decisive factor in the development of social production. The task facing economists is to find methods for correctly determining the volume of capital investments, their distribution among the sectors and regions of the country, and the optimum construction project for each unit. Improving the efficiency of social production is inseparable from the acceleration of scientific and technological progress, with the introduction of new machines. Methods must be worked out for determining the economic efficiency of the new machinery with a view to choosing and substantiating the best ways of designing it.

The general scheme for the location of productive forces, including a technical-economic assessment of available raw material, power, water and labor resources, should become the basic document substantiating the rational distribution of construction projects throughout the country. The planning of labor resources at present embraces three problems: 1) the planned employment of workers released as a result of technological progress; 2) the optimum distribution of labor power between productive and nonproductive spheres; and 3) the drawing into social production of new labor resources. One of the tasks facing the science of management is to plan these three processes as a whole.

Stimulation of production on the basis of cost-accounting is an inseparable side of management, a powerful lever for raising the efficiency of social production. The commodity nature of the relations between Socialist enterprises determines the form of the economic independence of the enterprises and the system of incentives and indicators of their activity. Collective and individual stimulation (both material and moral) makes it possible to take into account the interests of the personnel as a whole and each individual employee and, at the same time, insure the harmony of their interests with those of the entire nation. In a Socialist society, national, group, and individual interests, by their very nature, are not and cannot be antagonistic. Group interests reflect the need for the most rational organization of production at each Socialist enterprise—organization that provides the employees material interest in the success of the enterprise as a whole. Through individual interest, each member grasps the interest of his group as a whole. And through group interest, the employees of an enterprise come to understand the interests of the country.

But the science of management of the national economy is broader and more many-sided than scientific planning inasmuch as it includes, in addition, the entire complex of control of the social process of production.

Management of a Socialist economy is in a number of stages consecutively linked with a single system, consisting in the main of: a) management of the whole Socialist planned economy; b) management of the intersectoral and multisectoral complexes of the national economy; c) management of the economic sectors and, in particular, the industrial sector; d) management of enterprises and their subunits.

Research in this field is aimed at elaborating the optimum system of management in a Socialist society, at determining the principles and methods of industrial management, and also designing control technology.

At present, attention in economic management is being focused in the main on the enterprises: they are being given more business independence. But this does not to any extent decrease the role of national planning. On the contrary, freed from regulation of the activity of all enterprises in every detail, central planning agencies are able to concentrate their efforts on planning the main lines of economic development and scientific and technological progress.

Scientific elaboration of the problems of industrial management in the new conditions of the economic reform is especially urgent. Forty-three industrial enterprises were switched over to the new system in the first quarter of this year, and 200 more at the beginning of the second quarter. The results of the operation of the first group of enterprises prove the efficiency of the new system of planning and economic stimulation.

The new system of economic management is based on the utilization of potent factors and provides the necessary prerequisites for the steady improvement of the entire economic activity of enterprises. It provides the management and the entire personnel of each enterprise permanent incentives systematically to improve the organization of labor and production and to achieve optimum outlay of material, labor and financial resources.

It follows from this that, as the new business methods are mastered, enterprises will be more and more interested in employing scientific methods of management. Even now, each enterprise, in implementing economic reform, is compelled to organize cost-accounting actively in its shops and production sectors and refine bookkeeping and inventory control (that is, to reorganize and improve the entire system of business planning). These measures will invariably be followed by more profound and all-round application of the most improved management forms, methods and techniques.

A distinctive feature of the science of industrial management is its complex character. This sphere of knowledge includes the following range of problems: organization and methodology of planning and stimulation; accounting, control and analysis of social production; organization of the managerial apparatus (designing of structures, managerial functions), methods and style of economic management; forms of drawing the workers into management; technique and technology of the processes of control; and the gathering, the processing, the research, and storage of economic information.

Solution of problems of economic management should be based on a complex of fields of knowledge both of a general methodological nature (philosophy, political economy, theory of the state and law, cybernetics) and of a more particular nature, studying the laws governing the different aspects of social production (the economics and finances of the various sectors of the national economy, jurisprudence, labor psychology and physiology, and others). Industrial management has a scientific basis first and foremost in the system of laws that determine the development of the national economy and, in particular, industrial production. The system of industrial management draws on the results of research in sociology, and, in particular, concrete sociology, because industrial management is, first and foremost, the management of people in definite production relations and with their own social individualities. Managements are faced with the task of taking these singularities into account and influencing them; this task can be solved only with the help of electronic computers.

PART FOUR

WAGES
AND
MANPOWER

Chapter 20

WAGES AND MANPOWER PROBLEMS IN THE NEW SYSTEM OF MANAGEMENT IN CZECHOSLOVAKIA

BEDŘICH LEVČÍK
Czechoslovak Academy of Sciences

The measures, taken this year to introduce some elements in the new system of management, also touch on the field of wages and employment. Up to now, time has been too short to allow for an over-all evaluation of the efficiency of the tools and incentives which have come into operation. Also in this field the new impulses caused by some of the changes already introduced have not had the time to be fully effective. This is because the old tools of directive management have not yet ceased to operate and often assert themselves more strongly than the partial elements of the new system—characterized by compromises. Therefore, the further development of the new system is very pressing from the point of view of fuller application of material incentives.

The problems of wages and employment are among the most troublesome. According to the degree to which these problems will be solved, the people will judge the success or failure of the new system of management. Other fields (measures related to capital investment or foreign trade) are no less important: they however have only an indirect bearing on the citizen (in the process of distribution and utilization of the national income). The problems of material interest have a direct bearing on the working people, and thus their effect influences the results of activity.

Measures being proposed in this field for a more rapid implementation of the new system of management must overcome the effect of incorrect material incentives of the old system.

The full application of the new principles of personal material interest will be lengthy and difficult—a struggle between the old and the new. The assertion of new principles will be the more difficult, since certain old views and habits have to be overcome by management as well as by employees. These opinions and behavior are determined by certain aspects of perception and of interest. It is difficult to say, which of these aspects, whether misunderstanding the actual relations, or conflicting interests, acts as the stronger barrier.

The main traits of development in the sixties, in the field of wages and employment, are roughly: overemployment, a decline in social labor productivity, slow movement of nominal wages, near stagnation of average real wages in the 1961–1964 period, an over-all drop of wages in the nonproductive sphere, and, at the same time, a more rapid growth of the total wage bill compared to the practically stagnant national income. (See Table 18.)

These manifestations are closely connected. The increase in employment, especially in the productive sphere, during several years of stagnation in the national income has led to an uneconomic use of labor, to ineffectual overemployment (which has only negative effects). Employment was increased, while the unemployed proportion of the population of productive age decreased to such a degree that practically all unused sources of manpower were exhausted, and for the future only the demographic increment of the population capable of work will be available.

Table 18. Development of national income and total wage bill in Czechoslovakia (1960–1964).

Category	1960	1961	1962	1963	1964
National income	100.0%	106.8%	108.3%	105.9%	106.6%
Total wage bill	100.0	106.1	110.0	111.7	117.5
Average nominal wages in service industries as percentage of wages in production industries	91.2	90.1	89.9	90.6	89.5

Source: Czechoslovak Statistical Yearbook, 1965, pp. 67, 124, 139.

Table 19. Employment trends in Czechoslovakia (1960–1964).

Category	1960	1961	1962	1963	1964
Employed total	100.0%	101.6%	103.2%	104.2%	105.1%
Population of productive age	100.0	101.0	101.8	102.7	103.5
Employed as per cent of population of productive age	79.4	79.9	80.6	80.5	80.7

Source: Czechoslovak Statistical Yearbook, 1965, pp. 23, 121.

The ineffectual use of labor is the immediate reason for the decrease in labor productivity, and at the same time for the fact that the total wage bill rose in relation to the stagnant national income. However, in the years 1962–1964 the individual employee had almost no participation in the increased volume of wages, since his nominal wages moved upward only very slowly, and the real wages were practically stagnant.

There is also a causal relation between the insufficient growth of nominal wages (and stagnation of the real wages) and the excessive growth of employment. Administrative pressure to keep the planned index of average wages in line caused spontaneous pressure for an increase in employment, surpassing the actual needs of the national economy. This pressure originated at the level of factories and enterprises, whence it was transferred to the central authorities, as well as by individual employees and their families. Here personal and group interests joined together—unfortunately not in harmony with the interest of the whole society.

Excessive demands on manpower are also related to the efforts of the

Table 20. Productivity of labor, nominal and real wages in Czechoslovakia (1960–1964).

Category	1960	1961	1962	1963	1964
Percentage annual change of productivity of labor[a]	8.9%	6.4%	0.6%	−1.4%	1.7%
Percentage annual change of nominal wages	3.1	2.5	0.6	−0.1	2.8
Percentage annual change of real wages	5.2	3.1	−0.6	−0.6	2.3

Source: Czechoslovak Statistical Yearbook, 1964, pp. 44, 67, 141.

[a] National income per employee.

planning staff in enterprises not to exceed the pre-set index of mean wages. Diffusion of employment, especially the inclusion of non-qualified, low-paid labor, makes it easier to maintain the prescribed wage average. This tendency acts against rationalization measures, consisting of the introduction of labor-saving devices with simultaneous higher demands on the employee's training. Rationalization would thus lead to over-all savings in labor costs but at the same time to an increase in average wages over the "permitted" level.

The administrative form of wage control, mainly the policy of anxious "guarding and braking" the average wages has led to a situation in which wages have lost their incentive role. The reason is that the movement of wages was in no direct relation to the over-all economic results of the enterprise, and frequently it could not even sufficiently express differences in the amount and quality of work. On the contrary, labor output and, to a certain degree, the quality of work were leveled down, so that a certain "appropriate" wage level—agreeing with the generally assumed or permitted level of average wages—was not surpassed. This voluntary application of a "wage ceiling" was suffered without protest—not to say that it was openly supported by some levels of management in plants and enterprises, since it was a "necessary" price for the maintenance of "wage order" decreed by administrative means.[1]

An effect, accompanying all these processes, is the general narrowing of wage differentials. In 1964, a full 60 per cent of the total number of employees in the national economy were paid wages ranging from 1000.— to 1800.— Kčs monthly, that is within a range of ±28 per cent around the mean value. More than 25 per cent of the employees had monthly wages from 1800.— to 3.000.—, and only 1.5 per cent more than 3.000.— Kčs. While this leveling tendency is mainly the consequence of the administrative-directive management system, it must also be kept in mind that the equalitarian tendency has deep roots in the social consciousness of the general population. These persistent factors of social psychology sometimes are a stronger hindrance to increasing wage differentials than wage regulations.

Of course, it must be considered that the irrational behavior of individuals and enterprises under the traditional planning system cannot only be explained by conflicting interests, but also by insufficient perception of the real relationships.

[1] More general causes of all the effects described are related to the contradictions inherent in Socialist commodity production. These contradictions may be overcome only by use of market relations within the framework of over-all planned development. See O. Šik, *On the problems of socialist commodity relations* (Prague: Publishing House for Political Literature, 1964).

What I have in mind here is the widespread theory held in Socialist countries that labor productivity must grow faster than average wages. This theory was applied in an arbitrary manner during the fifties—and it is still in existence. The traditional viewpoint was that approximately one third of the means obtained by the preferential growth of productivity should safeguard an increased rate of accumulation, possibly an increase in social consumption and increase of means available for paying wages in the nonproductive sphere; the second third should permit the lowering of prices on consumer goods. Only the last third would then be left for the growth of average wages in production.

The initial argument of this theory was the view that a growth of labor productivity can only be achieved by increasing the proportion of net investment in the national income.[2] In this case, only one of the possible types of technical development is considered—the investment-intensive type. However, this is typical only for the extensive phase of economic development. Moreover, the role of noninvestment factors of growth has so far not been valued sufficiently in planning. Further, the view (now abandoned) was held for a long time that an improvement in the standard of living must be achieved mainly through lowering retail prices. And, finally, the theory is based on the idea that all the needs of the nonproductive sphere have to be paid for from the surplus product from the production sphere.

These arguments do not adequately explain the problem.[3] If, in the preceding year, a certain rate of accumulation has already been achieved, and if a certain volume of wages has been paid in the nonproductive sphere along with a certain volume of social benefits, then with a given initial level of labor productivity and a given level of average wages in the productive sphere a sufficient surplus product has already been formed to pay for these other components. If a certain increase of production is then achieved, with a simultaneous rise in labor productivity, then the average wages in the productive sphere can climb along with labor productivity, and the surplus product will rise at the same rate as the volume of wages. This increase in the surplus product allows maintenance of the same proportions, the same rate of growth of accumulation and income of the employees in the nonproductive sphere and of social benefits as the growth of the national income. The Polish economist K. Laski arrived at a similar con-

[2] See the *Textbook of Economical Planning in Czechoslovakia* (School of Economics, Publishing House for Political Literature, 1963), p. 518. This is only one of many examples.

[3] Beside theoretical arguments, the practical experience of the planning staff evidently also exerted its influence as far as productivity measurement of labor by means of the gross production index is concerned. This index generally overvalues the growth of productivity, which causes the planners to set a far lower rate of wage increases.

clusion; from an analysis of the relation between the rate of investment and the ratio between labor productivity and real wages, he offered mathematical proof that with a stable rate of investment the relation between real wages and labor productivity will be constant. "In this case, not only consumption, but also the productivity of labor and real wages increase at the same rate. If, for example, the productivity of labor rises at a certain rate, then wages rise at the same rate."[4]

Of course, labor productivity must grow faster than average wages[5] in the following cases (considering always only the change of one relation, without a change in the others): 1) if the rate of production accumulation is to be increased, either in order to accelerate the growth of the national income with unvaried capital coefficients, or if the present rate of growth of the national income is to be maintained, assuming a growing capital coefficient; 2) if net investment in nonproductive services is to grow more rapidly than the national income; 3) if the volume of wages of employees in the nonproductive sphere[6] rises more rapidly than the volume of wages of employees in the productive sphere; 4) if social benefits grow more rapidly than the income of employees in the productive sphere; 5) if the material costs of institutions in the nonproductive sphere grow more rapidly than the national income, and thus more rapidly than the personal consumption of the population; 6) if social reserves are to be enlarged more rapidly than the growth of the national income; 7) if the level of retail prices of consumer goods is to be lowered (that is, real wages are to grow more quickly than the nominal ones).

Only if some of these prerequisites are given, or if they are combined in some way, is it necessary to consider the need of a larger growth of labor productivity before a rise in wage averages. Of course, it holds similarly that the reverse relation (a slower growth of social benefits compared to income from work, for instance) will act theoretically in the direction of a possibly more rapid growth of average wages than the rate of growth of productivity.

This, therefore, means that the more rapid growth of labor productivity compared with the growth of average wages has no relation of absolute validity, but that it only holds under certain conditions which can be exactly determined.

[4] K. Laski, *Wachstumstheorie der sozialistischen Wirtschaft* (Vienna: Vorlesungen im Institut für höheres Studium und wissenschaftliche Forschung, 1964), p. 35.

[5] Here we are abstracting from the income of members of agricultural cooperatives and of self-employed persons.

[6] Only employees of budget-dependent organizations are concerned here, as will be shown later.

The notion that labor productivity must grow faster than average wages, assumed *a priori* without a study of the actual conditions, has become a hindrance from the theoretical point of view, contributing, especially in the sixties, to negative effects on our economy. In the years 1959–1961, a very strong wave of new investment projects got under way significantly increasing the rate of accumulation. For that reason, the plan objectively had to assume a far more rapid growth in labor productivity than in average wages. The slowing down of economic growth, which actually took place in this period, nothwithstanding the high rate of investment, caused the planners on all management levels to try to slow down the rise of average wages even more. This reaction was undoubtedly strongly affected by theoretical views of the necessary and significant advance of labor productivity. As a feedback, the slowing down of the movement of average wages has caused an ineffectual increase in employment, as already stated. At the same time, wages ceased to act as incentives, thus causing a loss of initiative on the part of employees. These circumstances alone contributed to the decline in labor productivity.

It seems that even today we have not fully succeeded in completely ridding ourselves of this arbitrary theory. This is also indicated by the discussion concerning the fourth five-year plan, where it is being said, in connection with the demand of a more rapid rise in average wages, that the growth of average wages ought not to exceed more than one third of the income obtained by increased labor productivity.

Looking, however, at the intentions of the fourth five-year plan, in the light of relations which demand that trends in labor productivity should outdistance trends in wages, the situation does not appear to be quite so unequivocal.

Some of the factors mentioned—like the planned rise of wages of employees in the nonproductive sphere, and cost of social benefits—point in the direction of the necessity of keeping wage gains in production under the rate of productivity trends. One of the most important factors, on the other hand—namely, the rate of accumulation, which is supposed to be kept constant till 1970—does not warrant an advance movement of productivity trends. Anticipated price movements connected with a price reform to be introduced next year, on the contrary, would in themselves allow an outstripping of nominal wages in production compared to planned gains in productivity.

Taking into account all the factors affecting the relation between trends in productivity and wages, there seems to be no justification for a very distinct advance in labor productivity over the growth of wage averages.

How should one now explain the fact that the proposal of the five-year plan still maintains the distinct advance of the growth of labor productivity over the growth of mean wages? The situation is the more risky, since in the new system of management, material incentives, allowing higher income depending on results achieved (and this to be verified by market relations) play a very significant role, and disregarding this circumstance might endanger the over-all effect of the tools of the new system.

It seems to me that the old ideas hamper the search for the real causes, which according to the construction of the plan make a more rapid growth of mean wages in the production sphere impossible.

It is outside the scope of this study to elucidate the actual, deeper causes. I have only intended to show that the development of the relations mentioned, in itself, obviously does not demand such a great advance in labor productivity over the mean wages as would follow from the actual proposal of the five-year plan. Therefore some degree of hope is justified that the further evolution of the new system of management and its fuller effectivity will gradually open up room for a mutual approach to the rate of growth of average wages and the rate of growth of productivity.

An analysis of the problems has shown that the common denominator of an insufficiently intensive effect of wages on the individual worker and of the rational utilization of manpower is, on the one hand, a tendency to an administrative slowing down of the rise of wages even at the price of lower labor productivity, and, on the other, deep equalitarianism in wages in all structural and social groups.

A rapid development of the new system of management in the field of labor and manpower policy therefore requires an opening up of the process of wage differentiation. Leveling of wages is generally understood only as insufficient wage differentials for work demanding various qualifications and skills. This, however, is only one aspect of the leveling process, as we have witnessed in the past. Another manifestation of the leveling process is also insufficient differentiation of wages according to the actual economic results of an enterprise. In a certain way, this is again a simplified comprehension of the principle "equal wage for equal work." This principle, applied to basic wage scales and to a certain degree to the whole wage system, necessarily leads to the conclusion that an employee having a given skill or degree of training, categorized in a certain wage class, should obtain equal wages for equal amounts of work whether this output has a greater or lesser economic effect, whether the products thus made are of technically outstanding quality, or whether they are outdated, whether they be popular items or obsolete.[7]

Further measures are now being planned, especially a price reform, unified rules for taxation of the gross returns of the enterprise, and a more elastic adaptation of price trends, which will hopefully gradually overcome the leveling of income between enterprises. This will make possible differences in wages paid by individual enterprises, depending on the results of their activity.

If this is a desirable process from the viewpoint of satisfying the needs of society, then it also follows that it would be incorrect first to concentrate means for the differentiation of wages to the central budget and then to redistribute them; on the contrary, the enterprises themselves, according to the effect of their economic activities, ought to begin such differentiation. This, of course, demands that the enterprises keep part of the income achieved by economic results surpassing the general average, in order to use them for their own immediate and future needs. This path would lead to a great change compared to the present state, where incomes obtained by favorable economic results are drawn off for the most part to the state budget by means of differentiated taxation and other economic tools.

Of course, it cannot be expected that income for wages which will be available to the enterprise, will be automatically used for increasing wage spreads. This is even improbable because of the fact that the present consumer-type approach to wages and equalitarian tendencies is deeply rooted. Clearly, it will be necessary to create the proper social and political atmosphere, allowing the formation of correct social attitudes on the merits of individual categories and groups of employees. Economic results in the first quarter of 1966 indicated that, even though the new system has only had a limited effect so far, the process of differentiation in income structure in enterprises has already produced higher salaries for professional and technical personnel.

If, therefore, the means for the deleveling process in the production sphere are to be found directly in the economic results of the enterprises, then this rule cannot be applied to the nonproductive sphere, mainly to

[7] The principle "equal wages for equal work" is being applied, correctly, by trade unions in capitalist countries. Under conditions where production and sales are being decided upon by the entrepreneurs, who follow their own profit motives, there is no need for employees to take upon themselves the risk of enterprise and therefore also the responsibility for the results of the economic decision of the entrepreneurs. Under Socialist relations, however, overcoming the wage character of labor demands a closer connection of employees with their enterprises, by means of material incentives, and to a certain degree, by means of material responsibility for the economic results.

budget-dependent organizations. The problem is the more difficult because the trends of average wages assumed in the plan up to 1970 would prevent removal of the retardation of wage levels compared to the productive sphere (which has occurred in the past). There is the unique situation that in some parts of the service industries (health services and education for instance),[8] there was practically no rise in wage and salary rates for more than ten years, while the level of wages in the production sphere increased from 1955 to 1965 by 24 per cent and real wages by 31 per cent. Of course, with the considered annual increase of average wages of around 2 per cent in the nonproductive sphere, it would be impossible to remove a disparity of longer standing.

This prolonged wage disparity of the nonproductive sphere already showed very unfavorable consequences in the form of decreased efficiency of the services concerned. For example, in the health services, stagnation of wages led to decreased interest and initiative on the part of employees.

If the process of wage adjustment is to have the desired effect in this field, then evidently it is not enough to remove the wage disparity in the nonproductive sphere by a single act: instead, it will become necessary to institute some economic regulation, which will avoid a repetition of this disparity compared to the productive sphere. Evidently quite a number of resources is needed for this. This leads to considering the possibility of allowing some organizations to demand partial or full payment from the population for additional nonessential services, while maintaining the principle of offering services on the present scale free of charge. By this means, the load on the central sources of finances, caused by wage claims in the nonproductive sphere, would be alleviated.

A contribution to the differentiation process in the nonproductive sphere would be to control wage trends with the help of budgeted total payrolls instead of controlling average wages. This would also lead to a more economic utilization of manpower in this field. This would have to be done carefully in order to avoid a situation in which wage changes within the frame of budgeted payrolls might take place at the expense of the quality of services offered. However, some experiments already in progress—health services, for example—show that they may even be offered to the population in better quality, without having the full number of planned doctors. The prerequisite condition is, of course, that the funds thus saved are used to raise the salaries of doctors and other medical personnel without increasing their number.

---

[8] At the end of the year 1965 the wages of university-level teaching staff were adjusted. From July 1966, salaries of some employees in the health services were adjusted.

In every case, funds from central sources will be needed to achieve a harmonious development of incomes in the productive and the nonproductive spheres. The dilemma is that sources which are available to improve the material interest are limited, and the objective need of funds to improve material incentives in the service industries is great.

We exclude the possibility of achieving a greater differentiation in wages in a way that the wages of some groups of workers would be lowered in order to improve wages in other categories. We can choose only a system which will slow down the further development of wages for some groups, while allowing a more rapid increase for others whose social function is especially significant at the present stage. At the same time, however, the increase of real wages should be safeguarded at least on a minimum level for all wage and salary earners.

Different considerations and calculations have led to the conclusion that for a correct effect of the incentive role of wages, for a removal of the disparity of the nonproductive sphere and to secure harmonious wage trends in the whole national economy, the rate of growth of average wages should be increased to about 3 to 4 per cent annually. The present construction of the five-year plan, however, gives no assurance of such a development. Improved wage trends could evidently be assured only by a substantially lower growth of employment compared to the planned figures, by increased production and formation of the gross income of enterprises compared to the plan, or by a somewhat slower rise in real wages compared to nominal wages. It is probable that the effect of the tools inherent in the new system of management in their more developed form will lead to a combination of the three methods.

Other measures in preparation are concerned with the regulation of employment trends. It follows from the preceding analysis that the unwanted development of real wages and the continuing leveling process in the past years were closely related to the rise in employment. In the sixties, at a time when the national income was stagnant, employment—especially in the production sphere—increased unnecessarily. The number of employees in industry and construction increased (but insufficiently) in one year even with a decrease in social labor productivity. Therefore we ought to select measures which would reverse this development and assure a gradual liquidation of overemployment by means of a purposeful use and distribution of existing manpower.

It seems that the change in the new system has not yet created incentives strong enough to stimulate enterprises to achieve their gross income with the least possible number of employees, which would permit the means necessary for wage increases. The results of the first quarter of 1966 show that employment in the production sphere continues to rise at quite a high rate, while average wages have changed only little compared to the first quarter of 1965. It appears that the scope allowed by the present system for independent decisions by the enterprises is insufficient, and that it will be necessary to remove hindrances of an institutional and psychological character.

First of all, the so-called wage ceiling will have to be removed. It is true that for years average wages have stopped being a binding indicator of the state plan, and that in 1966 enterprises were allowed to deviate to a certain extent from this standard. Actually, however, the tendency of the wage ceiling asserts itself through the instructions of central authorities and trust managements alike, as well as on various levels of management inside the enterprises. One solution would be to stop following average wages as a measure of desired or undesired wage trends in enterprises. Evidently, on the macro-economic scale, the development of average wages in relation to the development of the national income, consumption and accumulation has to be studied and analyzed. In the micro-economic sphere, however, the decisive economic criterion is unit wage costs, as a part of total costs per unit. In this context, the average wage of an employee of the enterprise will no more be in the center of interest. It is not by chance that in the most advanced capitalist countries the tendency is asserting itself in the largest companies to pay high wages for high productivity and high intensity of work. This logical consideration follows from the effort of maximizing profits, not from any interest of the entrepreneurs to pay wages any higher than absolutely necessary.

In conflict with this logic, regulations valid today require progressively rising additional taxation, if the growth of average wages exceeds a given percentage. The enterprise may not pay wages at all on a scale exceeding by more than 12 per cent the level of average wages of the past year. This actually determines a wage ceiling for the enterprise, which because of the high limit (a possible rise of 12 per cent) cannot gravely affect the majority of enterprises. Still it can become the brake on the efficient development in individual, but very important, cases. Even more detrimental are psychological elements which keep enterprises in the well-worn groove of guarding average wages instead of finding ways and means of improving labor productivity through wage incentives.

Added to this is the voluntary restriction on wages (and output) by the workers themselves. The limiting of work output according to an assumed and generally permitted wage level acts as an anti-stimulus to increasing labor productivity. A simple change of regulations cannot remove these psychological hindrances, which demand a change in the over-all attitude of employees toward their enterprises—overcoming the formality of participation in management and the creation of a climate which would connect employees with the material conditions of their production activity in a closer and more immediate manner.

With respect to limiting overemployment, the possibility is being considered of prescribing a special payment to the state budget for every employee, or a payment according to the increase in number of employees, especially in regions with an acute manpower shortage.

Among measures which act as impulses to a greater increase in labor productivity and removing ineffectual overemployment, an increased mobility of manpower should not be overlooked. According to the actual requirements of enterprises and of the entire national economy, certain changes in employment are necessary. This will have to harmonize with the interests of the individual workers. Today's regulations do not take sufficient cognizance of material and other prerequisites needed to facilitate a change in employment. This circumstance contributes to false solidarity in work collectives which refuse to accept a limitation of employment, even if the present degree of employment is unsupportable from the economic point of view.

In wider relations, every change of employment, even within an enterprise, is felt as an injustice, against which the "injured" and the wider work collectives try to defend themselves. This leads not only to insufficient mobility of manpower but also to its insufficient adaptability to new conditions and production needs. The resistance of employees to necessary changes probably cannot be removed by linking individual earnings with economic results of the enterprise alone—a fact which in itself should be an impulse to the enterprise to use manpower more economically. There will be the need of various measures of a social character to take care of employees who are discharged or transferred to a different job. What is meant here is compensation in cases when a plant is closed down, assurance of the present level of earnings for a certain time in the new job, economic provision for the employee during periods of retraining, financial aid in moving to a new place and finding a new home, and so forth.

A very difficult problem is the concept of control of the wage ratio inside an enterprise. The principle of economic management requires that enterprises have the possibility, after deduction of taxation by means of which the surplus product is divided between the enterprise and society (and after fulfilling all other obligations) of freely deciding, combining and substituting production factors to attain the most efficient development of production and maximization of their income. This means that according to the actual situation they should decide whether it is better for them to increase the proportion of wage costs, or the proportion of material or investment costs. In the next few years, however, it will be impossible to give enterprises this liberty to the full extent, and a certain degree of control of unit wages and wage ratios will be necessary. Under consideration is a payroll tax, which would have a slight progression and thus act as a brake on unwarranted wage increases.

The distribution of the enterprise's own assets into an employees' fund and other funds will have to be regulated within the next few years by binding rules, which would assure that investment and development funds and other funds will rise faster, or at least in proportion to the growth of the employees' fund. An extreme limit would be the principle that the ratio between the employee's fund and other funds may not decrease to the disadvantage of these funds. The planned rise of the volume of wages, based on the planned rise of gross income, will be possible only if at the same time funds reserved for the future development of the enterprise will grow, and if possible with preference. The same principle should be maintained also in the distribution of income from economic results higher than the original goals. In such a case, however, the proportion of means for the further development of the enterprise should generally be greater than in the initial state. The distribution according to these rules should become a part of the collective contracts, whose significance will increase substantially, compared to the present state, together with a broader participation of workers in management.

Doubtless the new system of management will also be reflected in the wage systems. The present arrangement already considers not only wages for individual work results, but also participation in the results of the economic activity of the enterprise. At present, however, these two components of earnings are not differentiated sufficiently. The difference in the two forms is connected with the character of work under Socialist commodity production. In the application of wages policies, as far as wages for individual work results are concerned, the immediate social character of work prevails, allowing nationwide proportions in wages to be maintained, mainly by means of centrally set wage scales. In this form, however, wages and salaries are actually predetermined and controlled, independent of the economic results of the individual enterprises.

However, we have shown that this form of wages is contradictory to the character of Socialist commodity relations, which require that the income of the employees depend on the results of their activity, which is tested and verified on the market. This shows that work is of direct social character only in a highly conditioned way, and only on the most general level.

Therefore a part of the earnings must be bound as closely as possible with the economic results of the enterprise. This can be achieved best by sharing in the economic results of the enterprise. The attempt to regulate wage proportions between industrial branches, trusts and enterprises by regulating the total earnings including the shares would necessarily conflict with the principle that the market must verify the efficiency of operation of individual enterprises.

Of course it must be understood that, in this way, in individual cases, prosperous enterprises, classified according to central wage scale-setting machinery on a lower level in the external wage structure, may come up to the level of other branches on a higher preference level, if the total earnings are considered. Assuming that such an enterprise actually satisfies the needs of society and of the population to an extraordinarily large degree (and for this reason it achieves the possibility of paying better wages), there can be no objections to such a situation. We do not believe that this would disrupt the whole nationwide wage-scale control, since such cases will necessarily be exceptional, indicating an extraordinary contribution by the enterprise and its employees. On the other hand, a repetition of such cases within one branch or field of activities might serve the central wages board as a signal to reassess the situation, especially from the point of view of centrally set wage-scale policy.

At present it will be necessary to strengthen the proportion of earnings from the economic results of the enterprise within the total earnings. At present such shares form a very small part of the total earnings (about 4 per cent) and cannot therefore be a sufficient incentive to employees to orient their activity toward the wider results of the enterprise economy. The increase of the proportion of shares for economic results will also have to be brought into connection with the entire process of deleveling wages. This means that such shares should not be paid in proportion to earnings based on individual work, but instead there should be a substantial degree of differentiation according to the contribution and responsibility for the economic results of the enterprise, plant, workshop or unit.

Payment of these shares might serve gradually to form a more long-term material interest on the part of the employees. A situation should be arrived at, in which the employees would feel themselves bound more to the fate of their plant or enterprise, not only seeing the present-day needs, but also the needs of future development. Especially in the case of managers, it will be useful to apply the idea of personal accounts, combined with extraordinary long-term bonuses. The increase of the proportion of the shares in the total earnings makes it necessary that the present wage-scale system shall not be changed in principle for the present without excluding some partial adjustments. The need for greater occupational wage differentials inside the individual categories, which of course must also relate to wages and salaries for individual results of work, will have to be solved in the near future by means of premiums, bonuses and other variable components of individual wages, rather than by changes in the wage rates. It will be possible to remove the drawbacks of today's wage-scale system only at a time when the shares for the economic results of the enterprise will have reached the required level, perhaps some 10 to 15 per cent.

The future reform of the wage-scale system should also solve the problem of "social" preferences, which ought to be separated from the wage-scale system proper. Especially will it be necessary to remove preferences related to whole industrial branches. It would also be possible at a later period to announce the centrally set wage scales as minimum ones, leaving it to the branches, trusts, or even enterprises to set definite scales according to the economic situation also above this minimum limit.

The envisaged changes in the field of wages and manpower policy are being worked out in greater detail at present in the respective state institutions and trade union organs. It must be considered, of course, that only practical application will test the complex effects of the individual measures and propositions, and will discover at the same time new possibilities and expressions. Doubtless the system of earnings and employment will have more diversified forms than was either possible or necessary under central directive planning.

Chapter 21

MATERIAL INCENTIVES AND RAISING EFFICIENCY IN THE UTILIZATION OF LABOR RESOURCES IN THE USSR

E. I. KAPUSTIN

Research Labor Institute, Moscow

In order to achieve maximum efficiency in the utilization of the main productive force of a Socialist society, labor resources play an important role.

Raising the efficiency of utilization of labor resources[1] means growth in the employment of the work-capable population and a more rational use of the labor force already engaged in production—that is, the growth of labor productivity on the basis of technical and technological development, improved labor organization, training opportunities for workers, and so on. In all these cases, the Socialist society devotes great attention to material incentives.

In the Soviet Union, conditions under the planned economy provide for

---

[1] In Soviet statistical and planning practice, labor resources are considered potentials—that is, that part of the population which possesses the complex of physical and mental abilities required for participation in the labor process.

The main group consists of people of work-capable age. In international statistics, persons from fifteen to sixty-four as a rule are considered work-capable. In the USSR, we include all men from sixteen to fifty-nine and all women from sixteen to fifty-four. The lower limit is chosen because youths under this age are legally obliged to study in eight-year schools; and the upper limit corresponds to the pension age established by the social security law. Also, there are groups beyond these limits who are still capable of performing and are included as part of the labor resources.

full employment of the whole work-capable population.[2] Practically everyone in this category is employed. The excluded are students or those engaged in caring for children, invalids, or the elderly within a family situation.

According to the 1959 census, out of 127.8 million people making up the work force, 100 million were employed in the social economy—in state and cooperative enterprises, in different organizations and offices; 5.8 million were in school; and only 2.2 million or 17 per cent were engaged in the cultivation of individual farming lots and in households. This is the highest level of employment among the industrially developed countries.

The main factors contributing to the solution of the problem of relative overpopulation (that is, of unemployment in our country) were industrialization and collectivization in agriculture.

The establishment of a great number of industrial plants naturally increased the number of manual and nonmanual workers; the annual increase of the labor force in industry and construction was at the average level of 1.45 million or 23 per cent, which made it possible to eliminate not only existing unemployment among the urban population but also latent unemployment—so-called agrarian overpopulation in villages. At the same time, the labor force liberated from agriculture in the process of the mechanization of the collective farms was absorbed into industry.

The high rate of industrialization in 1928–1940 recruited (along with the simultaneous growth of labor productivity) 20 million of the people liberated from farms—constituting approximately one fourth of the workers previously engaged in agriculture. This process continued, and today manual and nonmanual workers together with their dependents constitute 75.4 per cent of the whole population, and the collective farmers constitute 24.6 per cent.

The important factor in the increase of employment was and continues to be the high rate of development in the nonproductive spheres—education, public health services, science, and culture. Of great importance was the steep increase in the number of scholars (including those studying at higher levels of vocational training) outrunning the increase in the population. Thus during the period 1950–1954, the population increased approximately by 28 per cent, and the number of scholars by 41 per cent. Among the scholars we include students in technical high schools (a 150 per cent increase) and in colleges (190 per cent).

[2] In our country distinction is made between employment in the social economy, studies involving job discontinuation, work on individual lots of collective farmers, or in housholds. Under employment in the national economy, we include only employment in the social economy and on individual lots.

Naturally the number of teachers in schools of all grades increased accordingly. Thus the number of teachers in primary and secondary schools during the educational yearly period of 1950–1951 to 1964–1965 increased from 1475 to 2435, and a 65 per cent increase evolved in the spheres of health services, culture, and science.

Along with full employment, the efficiency in the utilization of labor also rose. This came about first of all through the complex mechanization and automation of industry and the application of progressive technological processes. Of great importance is the intensive introduction into industry of scientific organization in the working processes, which makes it possible to utilize production time with utmost efficiency without an overburdening work-load and also allows for improvement in the qualification of manual and nonmanual workers, cutting down the labor turnover, waste of time, material, and so on. The combination of these factors results in increase in labor productivity, higher quality of products, and better service for the customers.

Increase in labor productivity is the main criterion for efficiency in labor utilization. As compared with 1913, labor productivity in 1963 increased 13.2 times. During the postwar period, the rate of productivity growth was extremely high.

By 1964, the productivity level compared with 1945 increased in industry by 211 per cent; in construction by 265 per cent; in railway transport by 313 per cent; and on collective and state farms by 303 per cent. This was a result first of all of technical progress. For instance, labor in electrical equipment (as expressed in terms of capacity of electrical units per worker) during the last seven years rose by 60 per cent.

Growth in productivity was greatly aided by the growth in the cultural and professional levels of the workers.

Suffice it to say that in 1926, prior to the first five-year plan, the number of nonmanual workers ran to 2.6 million, including 0.5 million graduated specialists. By the end of 1965, the number of nonmanual workers had already reached 25.3 million, among them 12.1 million graduated specialists.

Some radical changes also took place in the educational level of manual workers. During the last seven years the number of persons in this group with secondary school education increased from 45 per cent to 58 per cent; and among collective farmers from 23 per cent to 31 per cent. Tremendous gains were also made in professional and vocational training. Nowadays the scientific organization of labor processes (or industrial engineering) is more widely applied in plants and factories. The aim is to utilize capital funds, working time, the skill and knowledge of workers and simultaneously to improve and ease working conditions.

At the same time, there still remain big reserves for more efficient utilization of the main production force of our society. The measures aimed at maximum labor force utilization were reflected in the directives of the twenty-third CPSU congress on the new five-year plan.

The new five-year plan, like the preceding ones, envisages full employment for the entire work-capable population on the basis of the high rate of capital construction in all branches of the national economy. Industrial production facilities, including those to be constructed in the next five years, can be fully utilized only if the number of manual and nonmanual workers in the national economy rises up to 91 to 92 million (taking into account the planning aspect of growth in labor productivity). So during the five years it should increase approximately by 20 per cent, while the whole population, in order to extrapolate its rate of growth in the last seven years for the new five-year period, will increase only by 8 per cent.

The new five-year plan envisages a high rate of development not only in material production but also in the nonproduction sphere, especially in such branches as education, medicine, repair services, trade, public catering, and cultural establishments. Especially high will be the rate of the development of these branches in rural areas where it will contribute to the gradual elimination of basic differences in urban and rural ways of life.

Of much importance will be the increase in pupils and students studying on leaves of absence from work—that is, persons of work-capable age. The five-year plan provides for the completion of the introduction of a universal secondary education for young people.

The plan is to increase admissions into special technical secondary schools (or junior colleges) up to 1,600,000 annually; into higher schools up to 940,000; and into professional schools between 1,700,000 and 1,800,000.

Students of higher schools alone by the end of the five-year period will number nearly 5 million. All this of course will play an important role in the provision of maximum employment for the population.

Since the natural growth of population cannot completely cover the labor-force requirements of the developing national economy during the five-year period, special measures are being drawn up to recruit more of the population into socialized production from households and from agriculture.

For this purpose, it is necessary to raise labor productivity in agriculture through wider mechanization—increased use of fertilizers, chemical weed and pest killers, by intensive soil irrigation, and the practical application of scientific achievements. To do this, the sum of state-centralized capital investments in agriculture for the construction of production facilities and the purchase of new technical equipment will be greatly increased. These investments, in the 1966–1970 period, will reach 41 billion rubles. Electricity consumption in agriculture will increase, in comparison with the beginning period, three times; the fertilizer supply will increase up to 55 million tons. All these and other measures will, according to calculations, permit a raising of the level of labor productivity in state and collective farms during the period by 40 to 45 per cent.

An important reservoir of additional workers for different branches of the national economy is in the household, where women are primarily engaged. The main precondition for making use of this reserve is further improvement and development of nurseries, kindergartens, schools, and situations where pupils can remain on a prolonged day regime. The solution of the problem is thus interwoven with the measures aimed at improving the living standard of the working people.

Another pressing problem is a more equal distribution and utilization of the labor force by area in our vast country.

The solution of this problem has two aspects: elimination of tension in the labor-force balance in the eastern and northern regions; and more efficient utilization of labor resources in central and western regions.

To solve the first part, the plan envisages a higher rate of labor productivity growth in the eastern and northern regions on the basis of certain advantages in technical equipment, especially in mining. It also intends attracting workers from central and western parts of the country to the eastern and northern parts. To do this, the plan prescribes concentrated housing construction, service, and cultural facilities for these regions for the five-year period. Together with this, a more complex development of the economy is planned for these areas; all this will directly influence the efficiency of the utilization of the local labor force.

The second part of the problem of a more even distribution and utilization of labor resources by areas cannot be settled by their interregional redistribution alone. Of great importance will be the construction in the central and western towns, especially small and middle-sized ones, of modern enterprises mainly for the production of labor-consuming products and also of small enterprises for food and light manufacturing industries processing raw materials. In such small enterprises the lower level of labor productivity (compared with big plants) will be compensated by the reduction in waste of raw material during transportation, by the reduction in transport expenses, and by better utilization of local labor resources.

A certain contribution to the raising of efficiency in labor-resource utilization in central and western districts will also be made by highly intensive work in agriculture; by the development of a means of transportation, which will insure comfortable and quick communication between these towns and regions with big industrial centers experiencing labor shortages; and by the establishment of branch enterprises affiliated to those situated in the industrial centers.

One can speculate that in the future the acceleration of technical progress will complicate the problem of the placement of workers released in this process. These workers are usually those less qualified, and thus economic expansion alone is not enough for their full employment. This puts special emphasis on the problem of raising qualifications and of retraining. Since the released workers as a rule are older with family responsibilities who often cannot afford studying without working, the plan envisages extension and improvement of the system of vocational training and retraining of workers directly within enterprises. This system will be organized mainly for retraining workers released by the particular enterprise and will supplement the system of professional training for young people in technical schools.

In the process of retraining and redistribution of the released workers, we take into account the possibilities not only of their requalification and their learning new trades, but also of promoting them into the category of engineering and technical personnel—mainly foremen. This would be first of all workers who have secondary or professional education or have passed courses in foreman training.

Another complicated problem which cannot evidently be solved in a short time in our country is that of raising the efficiency of the utilization of the rural labor force during the winter season. Conditions for the solution of this problem are provided by the high rate of cattle breeding, where workers are more evenly engaged throughout the whole year. Of great importance also is the development of hothouse horticulture, especially in those suburban collective and state farms which can utilize the surplus heat-energy of industrial plants. Considerable importance is attached to the development in rural areas of enterprises processing agricultural produce: canning milk, cleaning cotton, and so forth, the construction of which will be financed both through state capital investment and collective farm funds. It will also be very significant to increase construction activities on farms, especially in the interseasonal periods (building of production facilities including those destined for soil irrigation and draining, housing, service enterprises, and so on).

Together with this, another problem is presently being discussed. It concerns the widening and in some cases even the reestablishment and rebirth of traditional domestic craft industries.

In the new five-year period, the rate of productivity growth compared with the previous five years will increase. During the next five years, the productivity level in industry will rise by 33 to 35 per cent (that is, the annual increase will be some 6.1 per cent—1.3 times as high as in the previous five years). In agriculture the rate of increase will be even greater.

The main factors of productivity growth in industry are the application of scientific achievement and of more modern techniques and production technology, specialization and cooperation of enterprises, hastened development of the progressive branches of industry and improved industrial engineering. Unfortunately, in such a brief report it is impossible to discuss in detail all the factors influencing productivity growth. We simply have to stress that, because of productivity growth alone, we plan to gain 78 per cent for the whole industrial production increase in the five-year period.

Material as well as moral incentives play an important part in raising the efficiency of labor utilization resources in a Socialist society. It is necessary to emphasize that if, earlier, these material incentives were not adequately correlated with such important criteria as profit and efficacy and had not always provided for proper interest of the workers in the financial results of their work, they are now, under the conditions of economic reform, beginning to play a very important role.

According to new rules, enterprises form a special fund for material encouragement. This fund is allocated from profit in compliance with standard rates fixed for a long time period. Value of this fund depends on 1) the increase in sales or profit in comparison with the previous year and 2) the increase in efficacy of the production calculated as a ratio of the profit excluding the fixed payments and payments for the production facilities to the sum of the cost of production facilities and the capital stock and the individual (not borrowed) working capital of the enterprise.

This fund is used 1) for encouraging engineering, technical and clerical workers of enterprises according to the established premium rates which are differentiated by the sections of the enterprise according to their specific tasks; 2) for paying lump-sum premiums to individual workers for their high achievements; 3) for material incentives for manual workers in addition to their payroll; and 4) for awarding lump-sum premiums to workers according to the results of the yearly activity of the enterprise.

At present, about 250 enterprises have been converted to the new conditions, including 43 converted in the first quarter of this year, and the rest, since April 1. The conversion of all of industry carried out according to branches of production with the simultaneous introduction of new wholesale prices will start in the second half of the year and end in 1967.

The new system (as the experience of the enterprises already converted shows) guarantees the financial interest of both enterprise-collectives and individual workers in the most effective utilization of not only fixed productive and working capital, but also of living labor and working time. Thus, for example, in the first quarter of this year, growth in labor productivity at 43 enterprises was 7 per cent, which is approximately 1.5 times higher than in industry as a whole, while for the group at machine-building enterprises it was even higher—14 per cent. Enterprises converting to new conditions put forward counterplans, undertake increased profit obligations, as compared to the original approved plan, and not only successfully fulfill, but overfulfill, these plans. Thus, the above-mentioned enterprises pledged themselves to increase the volume at output by 25 million rubles and profits by 11.4 million rubles against the original plan, and in this new increased plan they fulfilled by 103.6 per cent in output and by 107.2 per cent in profits. In connection with this, for example, the share of premiums in the wages of engineering and technical personnel increased at these enterprises on the average by approximately 100 per cent.

In connection with the topic of this paper, it should be noted that the material incentive fund is also used at the enterprises to solve problems such as reduction in groundless labor turnover. As is known, in our country administration measures are not used to tie workers to one or another enterprise. Therefore, it is very important to stimulate the tying of stable personnel to the enterprise financially. Now it will be achieved additionally by the fact that the part of the incentive fund which is paid to the workers of an enterprise according to the yearly results will be distributed on the basis of two factors: 1) labor results of each worker which are reflected in the size of his wages, and 2) uninterrupted service of a given worker at the enterprise. This will undoubtedly exert an important positive influence upon reduction in labor turnover, along with measures to improve living conditions and cultural services for which, in addition to government centralized investments, the enterprise's resources will be widely used in the form of new socio-cultural funds also created out of enterprise profits according to established norms. In the new five-year plan, there are provisions for an increase in wages of workers and employees by 20 per cent. Only part of this increase will be provided for by creating new funds of material incentives. At the same time, there will be a further increase in minimum wages by 50 per cent, and also an increase in wages of workers receiving an average wage. In practice, this will be provided for by increasing basic wage rates and salaries which are determined in our country in a centralized manner. This will permit us to carry out a further improvement in the organization of wages simultaneously, which will solve some other problems including that of raising the efficiency of labor-resource utilization.

Specifically the twenty-third CPSU congress decisions envisage wider use of material incentives for attracting and settling workers in the eastern and northern areas, which will help to equalize labor force balance among the economic regions of the country.

Regional regulation of wages and salaries in the Soviet Union pursues two objects: 1) to provide equal pay for equal work and 2) to create additional incentives for workers engaged in eastern and northern regions of the country.

The first aspect of this problem is solved by taking into account zonal differences in prices when establishing regional wage coefficients for main food products and in standard family budgets which in their turn depend on the natural and economic conditions in a region and which manifest themselves in different expenditures for food, clothing, public services, and vocational accommodations. The second aspect of the problem is solved by increasing the regional wage coefficients with the object of materially stimulating workers to move to the eastern and northern regions, where natural conditions are more rigid, and conveniences scarcer.

In the process of improving the wage-payment system as a whole, many problems of regional regulations have been solved.

Nevertheless a set of problems still awaits solution. In particular, the regional wage coefficients did not affect workers in all branches of the economy. Besides, if, according to our calculations, these wage coefficients adequately reflect the differences in the regional cost-of-living indices, they sometimes are not sufficient for the attraction and settling of workers in these regions. We plan to solve these problems during the five-year period.

During the new five-year period, it is also planned to increase the wage of the workers in light and food industries and on state farms. This is very important for accelerating the development of these branches.

For the first time in our country, guaranteed wages equal to those paid on state farms are introduced on collective farms. Every farmer executing a certain job will be absolutely sure of his pay. Any additional income from the collective farm is to be distributed among farmers at the end of the year in addition to, but taking into account, the preliminary guaranteed payments. Special incentives encourage the farmers' interest in the raising of crops and animal produce.

There is no doubt that this will be a decisive factor in raising the efficiency of collective labor on farms.

Thus, material incentives play an increasingly important role in raising the efficiency of the utilization of labor resources in the Soviet Union.

Chapter 22

SWEDISH MANPOWER PLANNING

TORD EKSTROM
Wood and Paper Workers' Union, Stockholm

THE CURRENT MANPOWER POLICY

After the Second World War, manpower policy has played an increasingly important role in Sweden's economic policy. Though emphasis is still placed on traditional measures, such as emergency works and cash payments to the unemployed, modern manpower policy has been and will go on experimenting with new methods of providing employment for those seeking work.

It is no exaggeration to say that this new element in manpower policies has been inspired largely by statements and representations from LO (the Swedish Confederation of Trade Unions). Thus, as early as 1951, an LO inquiry[1] was outlining the framework for modern manpower policy, and ten years later an investigation was published on structural changes and policies.[2] The view on manpower policy included in these reports has to a great extent become the view of today's government.

[1] An abbreviated English translation was published by LO in 1953 under the title *Trade Unions and Full Employment*.
[2] *Economic expansion and structural change, A Trade Union manifesto* (London: G. Allen and Unwin, 1963).

International influence has also affected Swedish manpower policy. This is particularly true of the Common Nordic Labor Market, which entitles citizens of Nordic countries to work in another Nordic country without passport and work permit. Sweden has received stimulus for the development of her manpower policy both from this common market and from wider international cooperation within the framework of the ILO and the OECD. Particularly important is the ILO recommendation concerning employment policy and the recommendation on manpower policy as a means of promoting economic growth adopted by the OECD Council on May 21, 1964.

Current manpower policy can be divided roughly into the following groups: 1) forecasting, and planning measures against unemployment (the collection and working up of statistics and planning suitable work projects); 2) unemployment insurance and relief; 3) measures to create employment (emergency works, the placing of orders with firms experiencing employment difficulties to enable them to maintain production during a difficult period, and the provision of special work for the handicapped); location policy and other measures to promote regional development, and arrangements with investment funds; 4) measures to increase the labor force by helping categories now underemployed or entirely unemployed to enter the labor market or to become more closely tied to it (this refers particularly to women, the handicapped and older workers); 5) measures to stimulate geographical mobility through labor exchanges, including the granting of removal and family allowances, starting allowances, and various financial inducements to increased geographical mobility; and occupational mobility, through vocational training, further training and retraining.

Despite increased interest in recent years for action to stimulate mobility, this still accounts for a minor part of the total cost of manpower policy. However, the emphasis in this paper is on mobility problems since their importance will be growing in the future.

Plans to facilitate manpower policy. The 1965 Government Long-Term Planning Committee has recently presented a detailed analysis of development trends primarily for the period 1966–1970 and with a view toward 1980. According to this long-term survey, the working population (aged fifteen to sixty-four) will increase by 160,000 persons or less than 5 per cent up to 1980. Since the age groups under fifteen and over sixty-four grow at a more rapid pace than the groups between fifteen and sixty-four, the working population's share of the total population is expected to decline from 65 per cent in 1965 to 59 per cent in 1980. A prominent feature in the population trend is rapid urbanization. In 1960, 73 per cent of the population lived in urban areas (with more than 200 inhabitants) compared with 49 per cent in 1930. It is estimated that 85 per cent will live in urban areas in 1980.

If the reduction in working hours, agreed upon by the Employers' Confederation and the LO during the central negotiations in the spring of 1966, is included in the calculation of the labor input, this may be estimated to decline by as much as 0.5 per cent a year during the next five-year period. Information on the estimated demand for manpower provided by different economic sectors, indicates that the supply of labor would have to increase by 165,000 persons during the period 1966 to 1970 instead of by the expected 110,000. If compensation for the reduction in working hours is included, the demand may rise from 165,000 to 265,000.

These estimates are regarded as optimistic in the long-term survey. In the government's proposals for manpower policy, it says that the realization of the calculations will require more public measures than ever and a radical change in individual attitudes toward "male" and "female" occupations.

Thus, there is every indication that the 1960's and the 1970's will be characterized by a manpower shortage in Sweden. One might ask, however, whether there will be anything like labor shortage in a full-employment economy outside the Communist world by the end of the 1970's. The answer of LO economists to this question is yes. In the developed "capitalist" countries, governments understand the economic means to create and retain full employment. The question is whether they will use these means. If governments do not wish to for social reasons, they will be forced to for political reasons, because of economic and political competition with the Soviet Union and other Socialist countries. There is no reason to believe that this competition will be reduced in the economic field, and the full-employment situation in the industrialized market economies will accordingly continue.

Besides the government long-term survey, the National Labor Market Board makes short- and long-term investigations of its own. Also in these cases there is close cooperation among local government and private groups and firms. The bigger firms are of course interested in making estimates on their future manpower demand irrespective of their participation in official statistics. For firms with growing demand, it is often necessary to cooperate with the Labor Market Administration in order to obtain manpower. For firms with decreasing demand, such cooperation is at least as necessary.

There are agreements between the National Labor Market Board and certain central employers' organizations about advance warnings which should be given by a firm at least two months before a planned reduction in employment is to take place. It is evidently important that such a period be sufficiently long to give the authorities time for the necessary arrangements. In other cases, firms with decreasing long-term demand for manpower are apparently anxious to spread the employment reduction over a longer period, waiting for facultative retirements of part of their personnel.

Bigger firms with diversified production are in an especially favorable planning situation. For example, the Swedish Match Company recently announced a structural rationalization of its production of matches, which will substantially reduce the number of factories. As this company is successively increasing its production in other fields, especially in packaging, it will be able to transfer the employed to the new activities even without the assistance of the authorities, which may be advantageous to all sides. A special form for cooperation between the bigger firms and the labor market authorities (and the National bank) are the provisions for so-called investment funds,[3] the tax-free use of which is guided by the National Labor Market Board.

The new deal in manpower policy: the 1966 bill. The government has recently made clear its view on the future ends and means of manpower policy in the 1966 bill[4] which has been approved by parliament. According to this bill, one of the main objectives of economic policy is to promote growth. However, all sectors of the economy cannot expand, and a prerequisite of favorable economic development is therefore that uncompetitive sectors be allowed to decline in order to make it possible for more competitive sectors to expand. Manpower policy can make an essential contribution toward economic progress by measures facilitating and accelerating the structural changes in the economy. The anticipated development of the supply of and the demand for labor now more than ever calls for vigorous measures to help the unemployed and underemployed to enter the labor market.

The aim of manpower policy is to create and maintain full, productive and freely chosen employment. Of course, this cannot be achieved all at once. Full employment can only be secured by measures continuously adjusted to the prevailing situation. Productive employment is in itself a mobile target, which is moved as conditions of production change. Free choice of employment primarily means that the individuals' possibilities of

[3] For the empirical study see G. Eliasson, *Investment Funds in Operation* (Stockholm: National Institute of Economic Research, 1965); for a critical study see Lars G. Sandberg, "A New Look at the Investment Reserves," *Ekonomisk Tidskrift,* 1964:1.

[4] An English summary has been made by the National Labor Market Board under the title "The Framing of the Labor Market Policy: Decisions at the 1966 Spring Session of the Riksdag" (mimeographed).

obtaining jobs corresponding to their preferences and qualifications must be widened.

Out of the means at the disposal of manpower policy, many can generally be used only in case of unemployment. If manpower policy is to become a still more effective instrument of a dynamic economic policy, unemployment cannot be the only criterion determining the sphere of its application. This primarily applies to the training offered for labor market reasons and the means used to facilitate geographical mobility.

In Sweden, the attitude of the workers and salaried employees toward structural changes has been positive. Changes in the pattern of production and in the labor market are not regarded as a threat to employment but as a chance for better working conditions. This is an invaluable asset in an expanding economy. The positive attitude of the employed, even to rapid and radical changes in the labor market, is based on a certainty that the commitments of society offer them security in the face of any immediate difficulties or economic hardships which may result. And, of course, it cannot be regarded as equitable that those who are directly affected by changes which benefit everybody should bear the costs alone. A further motive for public effort in this field is that adjustment can take place more rapidly and without friction. This becomes increasingly important as the capital behind each employee grows from year to year.

As a rule, structural changes imply that workers can be transferred to more remunerative jobs. Structural changes are thus in themselves an effective means of improving the earnings of the workers. In Sweden, the general opinion is that wage-fixing and wage relations between different categories of the employed are matters that should be decided by negotiations between the parties concerned. These questions are therefore looked upon as being beyond the scope of government intervention. On the other hand, it is the duty of society to contribute to the development of conditions influencing wages so that an increase in earnings and a higher standard of living will be achieved. A manpower policy for facilitating structural changes will therefore also contribute to the solution of problems for low-income groups.

As long as it is possible to maintain an economic balance by promoting an increase in labor supply, this method is preferable to measures aimed at checking the demand for goods and services. However, a quantitative increase in the supply of labor is not enough. What is lacking in quantity must in many cases be made up in improved quality. The most important means for achieving this end is training. The basic training provided is of course of primary importance, but, in view of the rapid changes in the economy and in the labor market, adult training will become increasingly important.

By combating labor shortages which create bottlenecks, manpower policy may make an essential contribution toward achieving economic balance. In this respect, even marginal contributions may bring about the desired effect. Training may also be required as a remedy in situations of acute crisis (to satisfy the demand for certain personnel in hospitals, for instance). Retraining can also be framed in such a way that it accelerates structural changes and thus contributes to a more rapid economic growth. It is, for instance, possible to direct training toward widening the occupational choice of labor in the low-wage groups.

Training may already to a certain extent be offered to persons who are not unemployed but in danger of becoming unemployed. The government now supports a more generous interpretation of the concept of "risk of unemployment," on which the labor market authorities base their decisions on training. In practice, this more generous interpretation implies that training may also be offered in cases when long-term employment prospects suggest a change to another occupation. In other words, reallocation on the labor market need not be confined to times of crisis. This new interpretation is supposed to be based on the initiative of the labor market administration and to take effect when shortage threatens in sectors of particular importance for economic or other reasons.

Just as retraining may often be necessary to obtain a suitable job, moving to another area may also be necessary. In the future, the conditions on which transfer allowances are granted should be the same as those applying to training. This means that the field of application will be widened. Thus, persons in possession of auxiliary farms and small holdings who need a supplementary job to eke out their livelihood will be eligible for allowances, if they change to another occupation. As in the case of training for labor market reasons, transfer allowances will in certain cases also be granted to employed persons. This will increase the importance of the transfer allowances in areas with high and persisting unemployment. In such areas, the granting of transfer allowances will thus not necessarily have to be based on individual unemployment risk. Many people living in such sectors who are not unemployed may, for various reasons, find it easier to move than those who are unemployed or threatened by unemployment. In this way the prospects of the latter category to find employment in their place of residence will be improved.

However, the bill stresses that it is necessary to apply the rule with caution in order to avoid unfavorable effects for enterprises in places of emigration. With the restrictions involved in the proposal, that danger should be small.

ENDS AND MEANS OF MANPOWER POLICY: TWO DIFFERENT VIEWS

Traditionally, employers and industry in general, together with many liberal economists, have to some extent combated modern manpower policy and argued against checking market trends by government intervention. The government's position has been somewhere between these forces and the LO. Even if there is vast support for the current manpower policy, this situation in principle is also valid today.

The "classical" view. In a discussion at a meeting of the Economic Society in Stockholm in 1961 on the subject Wages and Prices, Professor Brent Hansen outlined the "classical" view on manpower policy. Hansen referred to the well-known theory that allocation of production factors is optimal in a situation where market prices determine their distribution among different industries. If the demand for a particular product increases, the price will rise which will give the firms an incentive to increase production. The firms will be willing to pay more for their production factors in order to lure them from other industries, and the result should be the optimal allocation of production resources.

Hansen doubts that this model could be used as a guide for action—partly because one assumption behind the model is that there are no monopolistic obstacles affecting prices, while the opposite is certainly the case in market economies. In the competition among enterprises, too often means other than price are used which usually increase costs. But, according to Hansen, the most important monopolistic elements are to be found in the labor market.

If trade unions maintain a policy of diminishing wage differentials through a wage policy of solidarity in times of decreasing demand for the products of a particular industry, the result will be reduction in production and employment. If the wages and salaries in that industry could be reduced (or at least if substantial increases could be avoided), and the monopolistic elements in the firms' pricing could be eliminated, then prices could be cut, and unemployment avoided.

Professor Hansen does not reject the use of manpower policy, but he stresses that the labor market authorities lack knowledge of whether decreasing employment in certain industries caused by wage and manpower policies is the result of a temporary or a long-term change in the industry. This ignorance can lead to a lot of mistakes. It can result in a large part of the labor force being transferred to other industries and regions, when the wage policy of solidarity and an active manpower policy are used to meet changes in the industries' conditions. Excessive transferring will increase costs and decrease productivity.

Professor Hansen also objects to the manpower policy approach on the ground that it is inhuman. The measures used are not successful enough to give new and more productive employment to everybody who loses his job. Most workers, he believes, would prefer an increase in wages by only 1 to 6 per cent plus a certain risk of unemployment. However, the result would be growing wage differentials, and against this he recommends a more advanced social security policy.

The LO view. The LO economists, on the other hand, claim that this "classical" view is far too shortsighted. In the short run, it is difficult to foresee the manpower needs of various industries, but it is often far more easy to do so in the longer run. It is a general experience in almost every developed country that there is a declining trend in agriculture and other primary producing sectors, whereas the shares in the economy of the building industry and services are growing. Within manufacturing, there is a similar development with shrinking shares of light industries such as textiles and food-processing but growing shares in industries producing the most processed goods, especially engineering. These market trends are generally accepted; the question is how to adjust to them in the most beneficial way.

LO economists claim that if the manpower policy promotes and creates favorable conditions for such a structural change in the economy, it will become an important means for promoting economic growth. An active manpower policy will result in a more rapid adaptation to changes in the demand for labor than a greater flexibility of wages and salaries—at least with the degree of flexibility that seems possible to imagine in practice. As to the use of a social security policy to aid the low-wage groups, the objection is that such a policy would also mean subsidies to weak industries in the long run.

The new LO report, concerned primarily with manpower problems, will be released to the congress early in 1967. As in the case of the 1951 and 1961 programs, much of what is said in this report may be included in the government's future proposals and realized later on. However, this time the points are more detailed and too lengthy to reproduce here.

Generally speaking, the authors have found much individual hardship in the reduction of personnel and the closing down of enterprises; in spite of the manpower policy, many women and older and handicapped employees have not found new jobs, or their earnings have been reduced. This finding has sharpened the claims against the manpower policy beyond those included in the 1961 LO report and the measures proposed in the government bill for 1966. The LO demands more accurate statistics and more research in manpower problems (cost-benefit studies of the effects of various manpower policy measures, for instance).

As we have already mentioned, the reallocation of manpower need not take place only in times of crisis. On the contrary, people should be encouraged to continue training and start retraining more normally in order to facilitate economic adjustment. According to one proposal, every citizen should have equal right to a certain minimum payment for training to be used at optional age and, as far as possible, in optional ways. It will be in the interest of society that this right be used by as many persons as possible so that they may rapidly become employed in trades and areas with acute manpower shortages, and suitable stimuli should be used to this end. Such arrangements would mean more people being trained in periods of reduced economic activity but less people depending on unemployment insurance and costly emergency works. It has also been proposed that the people should be economically stimulated to reserve part of their vacations for periods of slump in their respective industries.

This proposal, as well as many others, presupposes an employment service beyond that presently planned by the government. The argument is that manpower—as well as capital—is nearly always inadequate in a full-employment society, and, accordingly, every employer cannot be guaranteed the use of production factors in optimal amounts. Should the employment service in this situation direct the scarce labor to the low-wage paying as well as to the high-wage paying employers? The LO economists usually prefer the high-wage paying firms, which would force the low-wage paying employers either to close down or to move to countries with a lower wage level, where they will be better able to stand the competition. There are already examples of such developments.

One important prerequisite of such a policy is better information for the job-seekers on the conditions of work offered by various firms, which would increase the possibilities of the employed going to firms offering the best conditions. The trade unions should also take more active interest in the amassing of such information. The trade union movement is involved in the problem of having unjust wage differentials reduced or eliminated; what has been won to this end by contracts has in the last decade been lost by the unregulated increase of actual earnings (by the wage drift).

An open question is what the unions can do themselves—besides supporting manpower policies by the government—to effect a marginal transfer of members from trades and areas with low wages to others with higher wages and salaries in order to reduce existing wage differentials. Direct action by trade unions to this end could be looked on as a blockade measure conflicting with the Act on Collective Contracts. If this is the case, the legislation or at least the interpretation of it will first have to be changed. But some things can be and have already been done by the unions. Besides information on the existing conditions of work, collective insurance for members to cover part of future costs for retraining and resettling could be discussed and arranged with private companies.

What can the enterprises do to ease adjustment in the labor market? According to the LO, firms should not only rationalize existing production but should also take more interest in changing their range of production, when experiencing difficulties to cover rising costs. As mentioned, this can be done more easily by bigger, diversified firms. Such firms are also less hit by periods of slack than firms with only one activity: when demand is decreasing in one field, it increases in another. From these points of view, it would be advantageous for society to stimulate diversification of production, which is possible, in one way, by applying a gross turnover tax. Arguments in favor of at least a partial "gross taxation of enterprises" have accordingly been put forward by the LO on various occasions.[5]

In the process of adaptation, the smaller firms especially should be assisted by society more than they are now. This is especially important because entrepreneurs are likely to be more negative than their employees toward such adaptation, since there is the risk of losing capital invested in existing production. While adjustment of production will almost inevitably involve some disadvantages for employees as well as employers, the employers would bear a special risk. Any efforts to rationalize the structure of the economy would undoubtedly give rise to pressures in support of "conservation." The main task of the labor market authorities in a full-employment economy is, however, to act as intermediaries in transferring labor from surplus areas, sectors, and trades to those with shortages, and the authorities are therefore much less likely than others to lend their support to subsidizing

[5] LO, *Economic expansion and structural change,* ch. VII; and Lars G. Sandberg, "Net Profits Versus Gross Business Taxation: The Swedish Debate," *Quarterly Journal of Economics,* Harvard University, November 1963.

industries with excess capacity if this involves retention of labor and other resources.

From the trade union point of view, the essential thing is to insure that employees are given due consideration and that those firms and sectors which are in a position to offer the best working conditions are not denied the opportunity to expand. However, it is an essential requirement of more rapid structural change that both businessmen and employees should be able to feel secure about their livelihood, even if it means abandoning a former activity. A strong manpower policy would mean that structural rationalization could correspondingly be pursued at a more rapid rate in branches where excess capacity existed.

If one wishes to go beyond the fairly "traditional" type of manpower policy, it becomes necessary to think in terms of official loans or direct contributions. In the last resort, it is only through direct financial contributions to business firms that guarantees can be given against layoffs or the closing down of enterprises at a time which is unfavorable from the point of view of manpower policy. Such contributions ought of course to be used only temporarily, as a way of gaining time so that the employees can be given alternative jobs at a later date, and they should not be used to provide permanent support for weak firms. Direct contributions should be discontinued when the economic situation improves, and if firms are then unable to maintain their activity they would close down, while the labor force would be redistributed.

Even if this could be done without creating unemployment, it would of course be better if preventive measures could be taken in good time. For example, temporary direct contributions to help production could be linked with the condition that a firm discontinue part of its range of products and concentrate on a smaller selection. In such cases it is important for the labor market authorities to be able to act as an intermediary, or make available technical assistance so that firms can take up new and more profitable lines of production. The investment required could where necessary be financed in whole or part through official credit guarantees on the authorization of the National Labor Market Board or the Ministry of the Interior. Cooperation with various credit institutions should be developed with this in view, and it may be necessary to think of some government fund, coming directly under the board, for this purpose. The LO economists have also been arguing in favor of special "branch funds" to be created through agreements between organizations of employers and employees.

Given an active and more "aggressive" manpower policy, it will be possible and appropriate to use international trade, tax, and credit policies to provide greater compulsion and greater stimulus to adaptability within the economy. Proposals in this direction were accordingly made in the LO report "Economic Expansion and Structural Change."

A COMPARISON WITH CURRENT DEVELOPMENTS IN THE USSR

The possible realization of the proposals above, and, more generally, the further development of a modern manpower policy would mean that the element of planning in the Swedish market economy would be enlarged. From this point of view it is interesting to compare it with current developments in centrally planned economies.

To use the USSR as an example, manpower policy in our sense has been lacking there, mainly because the number of employed in enterprises has been decided by central planning along with other indicators. The current economic reform will now in principle give the enterprises themselves the right to decide their numbers of employed. Against the background of the rapid structural change of the economy, this has given rise to a debate (in *Izvestia*) where the creation of at least local manpower authorities has been proposed, mainly for employment-service purposes. This seems to be an indicator of the necessity of a modern manpower policy in our developed industrialized economies irrespective of political system.

PART FIVE

MODERN MATHEMATICAL TECHNIQUES

Chapter 23

MATHEMATICAL METHODS OF PLANNING IN THE UNITED KINGDOM

GRAHAM PYATT

University of Warwick, England

This paper is concerned solely with recent attempts to build medium-term planning models of the United Kingdom economy. As such, it includes some discussion of the work undertaken by the National Economic Development Office (NEDO), and by the Department of Economic Affairs (DEA), in constructing national plans. However, the larger part of the paper is a discussion of the private research of the Cambridge Growth Project under the leadership of Professor Richard Stone. Two reasons can be given for this emphasis. First, since I was until recently a member of the Cambridge Project team, it is this research about which I know most. Second, in so far as this paper is concerned with mathematical, as opposed to other techniques of planning, the selection of material is natural. Government activity in the field of planning is not distinguished by its mathematical content. Indeed, government economists tend to rely on the work of the Cambridge Project to the extent that they feel the need for a mathematical tool with which to fashion the official plans at some stage in their development.

While mathematical methods are the subject of this paper, the exposition adopted here is entirely literary. Thus the spirit of the present exercises is to explain something of the philosophy underlying the planning models and the problems encountered. Obviously I shall need to refer to mathematical techniques and concepts, but explicit formulation of relationships is not necessary to the present purpose.

The reader who wishes to know the precise detail of the techniques used in the Cambridge Growth Project is well served by a long list of publications which include a series entitled *A Programme for Growth*, published by Chapman and Hall. Six volumes have been published to date in this series, and more are forthcoming. Less detail is available on the government planning methods. The main references are, first, to a short series of publications by NEDO of which the first and most important is *Growth of the United Kingdom Economy to 1966*. Since 1964, the prime responsibility for medium-term plans has rested with the DEA. The latter produced a quite lengthy volume, *The National Plan*, in 1965. It is reasonable to hope and expect that more publications will be forthcoming. Meanwhile this Department puts out a monthly bulletin entitled *D.E.A. Progress Report*.

I trust that it will be appreciated that what follows is a personal view of mathematical methods of planning in the United Kingdom. To some extent the paper draws on an earlier paper of mine entitled "Some Aspects of the Cambridge Growth Model" which is published in *Programmazione Economica: confronti italo-inglesi* edited by G. Fua and published by the University of Urbino.

THE CAMBRIDGE GROWTH MODEL

Some general comments. The Cambridge Growth Project began in late 1959 with a team of six people including Professor Richard Stone and Professor Alan Brown, the latter now being at the University of Bristol. Since that time the team has doubled in size. With slender resources at its disposal, the team was, and remains, primarily concerned with demonstrating the feasibility of model-building in its various facets. Thus primary data has been collected in specific instances, but the extent to which this has been possible is strictly limited, and such exercises have only been undertaken when the expected payoff in terms of increased accuracy was large, or when it was important to demonstrate that a particular possibility existed. Similarly, while the object of building a complete model has obliged the team to consider all aspects of the economic system, the intensity of effort which has gone into the formulation and estimation of quantitative relationships varies considerably among different parts of the model. Thus very little effort has gone into the analysis of exports by comparison with research into interindustry relationships. However, piece by piece, the initial crude assumptions are being replaced by more sophisticated formulations, and hence improvement is a continuing process, dependent on the availability of personnel to tackle some facet of the model which is considered to be more in need of improvement than some others.

SAM (social accounting matrix). This is the framework within which the project gathers together the data describing the past behavior of the economy and expresses the configurations which it might have in the future. As such, it is incomparable as a data format for planning, and supersedes all previous systems of social and national accounts.

As the word "matrix" implies, SAM employs a particular framework for presenting social accounts. This framework distinguishes 253 accounts; 250 facets of the domestic economy, and three facets of the rest of the world. SAM is, therefore, a square array of 253 rows and columns. The receipts of a particular facet of the economy are shown as the elements of the relevant row of the matrix: the location of the elements in the row is determined by the specification of the facet from which the receipt originated. By implication, the elements in any column of the matrix are the expenditures of the facet to which that column refers. Thus the full account of each of the facets is given by its row and column of SAM. And, of course, rows and columns balance each other.

While there is no logical novelty in a social accounting matrix, there is much psychological novelty to be gleaned from looking at an economy in its SAM context. Such novelties arise from its twofold virtues: the flexibility it permits in defining facets, and the stringency of the consistency restraint which it imposes on the numbers recorded in it.

Exhaustive discussion of the concepts and detail of SAM is to be found in volume 2 of the *Programme for Growth* series. Some general points can usefully be mentioned here.

First, only current transactions are recorded in SAM: the compilation of a SAM showing the tenure of assets, being a composite statement of the balance sheets of each facet of the economy, is a further project which is currently in hand. Further, so far only two SAMs have been produced; a fairly crude one for 1959, and a more refined one for 1960, the latter having already been through several stages of revision. Currently a consistent series of SAMs for 1954, 1960 and 1963 are being produced. In the process of making these estimates, much has been learned about how to overcome *lacunae* in the data, and at what point it becomes critical to have information beyond that which can be extracted from official statistics.

Second, the freedom which SAM permits, within accounting restraints, for the determination of facets of the economy makes possible the use of published information involving a wide variety of classifications. For example, in official statistics, establishments are classified by industries on the basis of their principal products, but it is by no means uncommon for establishments in one industry to produce some of the principal products of another. Thus data on wages and profits refer to industries, while other industry expenditures, especially on raw materials, are available as expenditures on commodities and not as expenditures on the products of other industries. This distinction is recognized in SAM by including accounts both for industries and commodities: the intersection of these two sets of accounts is a statement of the extent to which industries produce their own principal products of other industries.

By including commodity accounts in SAM, the way is cleared for the use of a variety of commodity classifications. For example, government current expenditure is recorded in official publications according to purpose categories. Each of these purposes has its own accounts in SAM, implying that facts about government activity can be recorded in the form used in official publications. At the intersection of the current accounts for commodities and for government purposes, there is a "classification converter" —that is, a statement of the mixture of commodities involved in current expenditure on commodities for each government purpose. From this breakdown of total commodity expenditures for each government purpose, one can trace back through the intersection of the industry and commodity accounts to a statement of the demands on each industry by a given aggregate level of expenditure on commodities for each government purpose.

An analogous treatment of household expenditures is used in SAM. Here again the great virtue is that household expenditures can be analyzed in terms of the categories which make most sense—food, durable goods, entertainment, and so on—without involving at the outset the relationship among these categories and the 31 productive industries which are separately distinguished.

Net indirect taxes are, of course, an element in the translation between final expenditures and demands on industries. These have separate accounts in SAM. As a result, transactions can appear in SAM at the relevant prices: consumer expenditure at market prices is broken down via the classification converter into expenditures on commodities (and, hence, as demands on industries), at factor cost, and a transfer of income to the indirect taxes and subsidies accounts. Since one of the commodities distinguished in SAM is "distribution," the classification converter gives a picture of the extent to which market prices depend on indirect taxes and distributive margins.

Only one group of current accounts in SAM has not been mentioned so far. These are the accounts of the institutional sectors; the private sector, the public sector, and a third "dummy" sector which is in fact a part of each of the other two. Each institutional sector has several accounts in SAM. For example, within the private sector, separate accounts are distinguished for companies and persons. The dummy sector receives property income from domestic industry and abroad and distributes it in total to the institutional sectors. This device was adopted to bypass the problems of estimating the distribution of property income over its various sources. One development that is underway is to remove this circuit and to replace it by a proper income distribution analysis.

Half of the accounts in SAM are capital accounts analogous to the current accounts already discussed. Again there is a dummy institutional account, this time with the role of transferring assets and claims. The account receives net savings from all current accounts and distributes them as the necessary finance for net investment. One looks to current work on flow-on-funds to replace this dummy account.

Two further points concerning the capital accounts merit mention here. First, households' net expenditure on durable goods is recorded in the household capital accounts, where it properly belongs. Second, two capital accounts are distinguished for fixed assets; a replacement account, in which expenditures necessary to maintaining productive capacity are recorded, and an extensions account in which further fixed capital formation is entered. The replacements are financed by transfers of depreciation allowances from the current accounts: the extensions are financed by the residual depreciation allowances and funds for net investment from the capital accounts for institutions. Thus the two-dimensional nature of capital goods is recognized in the system.

Rocket. "Rocket" is the code name of the computer programme used by the Cambridge Project to explore what the economy might look like at some future date. As such it is the essence of the econometric work which has reached a final stage at any given moment in time. The name was chosen to invoke the analogy with George Stevenson's locomotive; in its day a significant step forward in engineering accomplishment, viable, but ripe for development.

It is important to see Rocket in the context of SAM for two reasons; first, because SAM describes the detail with which Rocket is concerned, both in its input and its output, and second, because SAM contains all the data needed for the simplest complete model of an economy, and it is with this simplest model that thinking on the development of Rocket began.

This simplest model is analogous to the model produced by Leontief, in which appropriate elements of SAM are assumed to be a constant proportion of the sum of the column in which those elements appear. Thus one can derive a table of input-output coefficients from SAM and, assuming a vector of final demands (the planning targets), work out the levels of activity implied for each productive sector. Assuming now that factor productivities are constant, factor requirements can be derived from the levels of productive activity.

To a very limited extent, the above is a crude description of how Rocket works. It is useful to have it in mind, however, as a framework within which the sophistications of the model can be put into place.

Final demands in Rocket are derived from a variety of sources. Current expenditure by households and government in the target year can either be assumed to be exogenous, or it can be derived from some more fundamental variables. Typically Rocket has been used so far to explore the year 1970, and final demands by government on both current and capital account have been taken exogenously from published forecasts of these variables. But there is no intrinsic reason why the model should not be used to examine the implications of a change in policy (for example, a run down in defence expenditure or an acceleration of slum clearance). Indeed some such experiments have been conducted. The contribution of household current consumption to final demand is most often derived within the model from assumptions about the aggregate level of consumption and its rate of growth. The derivation is via a set of demand functions generated from a dynamic linear expenditure system. This system is well known from many publications by Stone. Reference to it may be made through volume 5 of *A Programme for Growth*: its two great virtues in the present context are that, being linear, aggregation can be preserved within the system, and, being dynamic, it is not necessary to assume that tastes remain constant through the periods of past observation and future prediction.

If the economy were a closed one, then the only other element of final demand to be considered would be private investment. In the familiar Leontief model it is usual to include investment in final demand as an exogenous element. In Rocket, however, private investment is endogenous, and this is achieved in the following way. For household investment (which includes all domestic durables), demand analysis produces an estimate of the flow of services required from durables, given the over-all level of consumption. This flow in turn provides an estimate of the required stocks of household durables (including private housing). Similarly, an assumption about the rate of growth of aggregate consumption implies time series of the required stocks of domestic durables from which the levels of investment for replacement and extension of these stocks can be derived. Thus private investment in durable consumer goods is derived via demand analysis from assumptions about the aggregate level of consumer expenditure and its rate of growth. A similar procedure applies to the investment of production activities in plant and machinery, building and works, vehicles, and stocks of raw materials, work in progress, and stocks of finished products. To see how this works, assume that an estimate is made of final demand, excluding these investment components, both for the target year, and subsequently. Given the necessary input-output coefficients, this time series of final demand vectors can be translated into a time series of vectors showing the level of activity in each sector. Accordingly, the required increments to output year by year and industry by industry are known. Thus the investments required by each industry in each type of asset can be derived from incremental capital-output coefficients. Of course, these investments must now be allowed for in final demand. Accordingly, a further set of calculations is required, and an iterative process is enjoined which will eventually converge under quite general conditions. The mathematics of all this is set out in volume 5 of *A Programme for Growth*.

While this is by no means the end of the story, enough has been said so far to point out one of the major features of Rocket. It takes as datum an aggregate level of consumption and its rate of growth, and derives from these data estimates of what investment must be in the target year assuming that aggregate consumption is to grow at some specified rate from then onward. Thus the target is a level of consumption and a subsequent growth rate of consumption. It is not a level and growth rate of income. Furthermore, Rocket is not concerned with whether the target for, say, 1970 consumption can be achieved. It is only concerned with conditional statements about what the economy would look like in 1970 if it were producing the desired bill of consumption goods in 1970 and at the same time setting aside sufficient resources to insure that the desired growth in consumption as from 1970 could be realized. Thus nothing is said about the implications of reaching the target for the transitional period. It might well be that these implications are quite unpalatable. The philosophy is that we should find out where it is we want to go to before deciding whether the hardships of the journey are worthwhile.

So far nothing has been said about a major complication, namely balance of payments or, since exports are assumed to be given exogenously, the level of imports and the surplus or deficit of the current account. If the extent to which final demand was to be met by imports was specified and also the extent to which intermediate inputs into industry had to be imported, then the above analysis would yield a figure for total imports and, therefore, the balance of the current account with the rest of the world. This can be done. It is preferable, however, to distinguish two sorts of imports—complementary imports and competitive imports. Complementary imports have no substitutes in domestic production and are, therefore, obligatory. They are given, either as datum as a part of final demand, or as proportional to levels of domestic activity via coefficients in the input-output table. Competitive imports are discretionary, since they have perfect substitutes in domestic production. There is, therefore, indeterminancy between the level of competitive imports and the level of domestic activity. This is removed in part by including in the data of the analysis a figure for the balance-of-payments surplus of deficit: by this means, the aggregate level of competitive imports is fixed but not its commodity composition. This indeterminancy is removed by an essentially mechanistic procedure by which each type of competitive import is related to the over-all aggregate level, which is now known, and such that aggregation of the components to the total is guaranteed. Thus the desired balance-of-payments surplus is achieved.

Various alternative mechanisms for balancing current international transactions have been programmed and can be inserted into Rocket. None of them, however, has a strong behavioristic connotation. This and the assumption that exports are wholly exogenous is a serious limitation on some aspects of the work, but for the present there appears to be little prospect of doing the research on international trading functions necessary for its removal. Meanwhile some progress is beginning to be made on the explanation of import levels which should enhance the model considerably.

Reference has already been made to the use of interindustry input-output coefficients in the model. Considerable research has gone into the forecasting of these coefficients, and a technique known as RAS has been developed and is described in volume 3 of *A Programme for Growth*. The name RAS derives from R, a diagonal matrix, and S, which is a second diagonal matrix of column operators on A. Thus the elements of R describe substitutions of one intermediate input for another (for example, oil for coal, across all industries, while the elements of S describe changes in the scale of all inputs within particular industries). The basic proposition of RAS is that an input-output coefficient matrix at a moment in time is a RAS transform of a similar matrix, namely A, for an earlier moment. It has two great virtues. First, given a coefficient matrix for 1954 (the latest available in the U.K.), and the row and column sums of the matrix for 1960, a complete matrix for 1960 can be estimated. Second, in so far as direct observation of some of the coefficients of the 1960 matrix may be possible, RAS can be applied to the rest of the matrix in order to complete the picture. Experience recorded in the relevant volume of *A Programme for Growth* has shown that judicious selection of a few coefficients for direct observation, combined with RAS, yields a most powerful technique. There are some complications associated with the extrapolation of R and S, and these are dealt with in the literature.

Considerable research has also gone into the problem of forecasting incremental capital-output ratios. These are seen as being a facet of a general production model explaining the generation of value added in each sector of the economy. But this research has yet to yield the expected fruits, and meanwhile capital-output ratios are exogenous estimates derived by more or less conventional methods.

The deployment of labor which is indicated by a given set of industrial outputs in the target year is derived partly by reference to a relationship between changes in output and employment and the level of investment in each industry, and partly by reference to the aggregate labor supply. In effect, the relationship used implies that the distribution of income between wages and profits stays constant in each industry over time and that the restraint of a given labor supply is met through changes in relative factor prices. The technique is described in volume 5 of *A Programme for Growth* and elsewhere. It is at this point in the model that the lack of a supplementary model covering the transitional period is most seriously felt.

A further stage in the procedure for analyzing the deployment of labor is being developed and is sketched in volume 5 of *A Programme for Growth*. Just as we can have a matrix of input-output coefficients for raw materials, so we can have a similar matrix for labor of different skills. Thus given a level of output for each industry, the required inputs of each labor skill can be computed. These may or may not add up to the available supply. Assuming that they do not, but that the output plan will be realized, it follows that some different labor input-output coefficient matrix must maintain. If this new matrix is regarded as an RAS-type transform of the original, then it follows that the row multipliers can be regarded as changes in the relative efficiency of labor of particular skills, while the column multipliers represent changes in the general efficiency with which labor is used in particular industries. The earlier exercise concerning the relationship among output, employment and investment fixes the amount of labor required by each industry. This, together with the vector of supplies of labor of different skills, provides the marginal totals from which an RAS-type exercise on the deployment of labor by industry and skill can be undertaken.

Other developments. In the previous section I have indicated some of the developments taking place in the model. These are required to replace existing formulations by something better. There is, however, a further set of developments designed toward the extension of the model. This latter group is considered here.

Perhaps the most important extension of the model from the economist's point of view is to allow for changes in relative prices. The mechanisms required for this have been evolved. Taking the wage rate as numeraire, the rate of profit implied by the allocation of labor and investment to industries can be worked out. Together these make possible the calculation of net output prices—that is, of value added per unit of output. It is then a simple matter to translate these prices into final prices through the input-output table. It will be recalled that the target of the model is a level and growth rate of consumption. Accordingly, when prices change, the target must also be changed in money terms, in order to keep the target constant in real terms. This is not a difficult matter, since the utility index underlying the linear expenditure system is known. However, changing prices not only affect the money level of total consumption but also the demand equations via which this money expenditure is distributed. Accordingly, the parameters of the model change as prices change, and it is therefore necessary to iterate the model until convergence at a particular set of prices is obtained.

A further important development of the model is to incorporate within it a submodel of the educational system, viewed as a means of transforming the labor force from one type of skill composition to another. Work on this development has not been completed, and there are many difficulties. But a start has been made, both in the collection and tabulation of data and in producing a format for demographic statistics analogous to SAM. This work is described by Stone in *Minerva*, vol. IV, no. 3, 1966.

Flow of funds analysis is not as yet a part of the model, although two major pieces of work have been undertaken. The first is a study of the ownership of assets which will soon be published as volume 7 of *A Programme for Growth*. The second is the work of Stone on the savings behavior of the private sector. Both studies will be important ingredients of the flow of funds model when it is finally formulated. Since it is guaranteed by the model that there will be sufficient funds to finance the capital projects which are specified, the role of flow of funds analysis will simply be to insure that channels for routing funds from their source to their destination are open. If it is found that the private sectors of the economy are incapable of providing funds and of allocating them as the model requires, then this of course implies that some form of government intervention would be necessary for the realization of the plan.

Finally, and perhaps most significantly, work is well underway on a satellite model of the fuel and power industries. This model is a much more detailed description of the behavior of these industries than is possible within Rocket. Basically, the satellite is to operate by receiving information from Rocket about the other sectors of the model. This provides its environment. The satellite model then follows its own set of relationships and reactions, which need have no analogy with those assumed by Rocket. Once having worked out its reaction to the environment, the satellite must feed back to Rocket the outcomes of its reactions in the degree of detail which Rocket requires. That these reactions will differ from those which Rocket would have assumed if left to its own devices implies that there must be a process of iteration between Rocket and the satellites which is formulated to converge.

Some concluding comments. I hope that the description will give some impression of how the Cambridge Growth Model works and is evolving. Some concluding comments are perhaps useful here by way of giving emphasis to certain points.

First, we have already noted that the model is concerned with the implications for the future of the realization of certain targets set for future moments in time. It is not directly concerned in any way with the actions which must be taken now to reach targets in the future.

Second, the model is not an optimization model in the sense that it tries to maximize something. The targets of the model are levels and growth rates of consumption, and the model is a vehicle for deriving the long-run implications of these targets and for ascertaining how these implications vary as the targets vary. It is a political matter to decide what our targets should be. The model only acts as an aid to this decision by spelling out the long-run implications of each target. If it were to operate in conjunction with a transitional model which explained the short-run implications of reaching the targets, then the political decision process could be conducted in an atmosphere of awareness of all the implications. Obviously one would hope and expect that the political decision would be better as a result of this information.

Third and finally, the model is not necessarily a prediction model, but it can be used as such. If the targets set are the ones which it is expected to realize, then the SAM produced by Rocket is the SAM that it is expected will maintain. The only qualification of this is that Rocket does assume steady growth beyond the target date. At best, therefore, it can only be used to predict the trend in variables: it cannot tell us anything about deviations from trend in the target year.

GOVERNMENT PLANNING TECHNIQUES

It has already been indicated that the techniques of planning used first by NEDO and developed subsequently by DEA are not particularly mathematical.

As explained in *The National Plan* the main method of forecasting is based on iteration between estimates obtained directly from both industry and government departments in response to a questionnaire, and estimates made by government economists of the likely implications of 25 per cent growth in national product on particular industries. These estimates were reconciled to some extent by consultation and discussion. They were also further modified by an analysis of their mutual compatibility which made some limited use of the Cambridge Model. Each of these modifications is, of course, based on subjective evaluation of points raised in discussion and deliberation over the estimates.

There is no doubt that steps are being made to computerize much of the data-processing necessary to informed discussion between economists and the Economic Development Committees of industries. But there is no suggestion that computerization should be taken to the point where the need to specify a particular target for planning becomes redundant. Thus the government does not see planning as involving an initial exploration of what the capabilities of the economy are, but rather as an exercise in exhortation to achieve targets which are acceptable politically *ex ante* to the planning exercise. The point is illustrated by the following quotation from *The Plan*:

Just as the projections of output per head resulting from the Industrial Inquiry are below the 3.4 per cent annual rate of increase likely to be required, the sum of the projected demands for labor in 1970 is above the supply likely to be available. The demands for extra manpower total about 800,000 over the plan period. This compares with an expected increase in the labour force of about 400,000, which might be raised to about 600,000 as a result of successful policies designed to use more fully the labour reserves in the less prosperous regions. There would still however remain a "manpower gap" of some 200,000.

This gap is not large in relation to a total labour force of over 25 million. However, the estimates of manpower requirements were made in the knowledge that the increase in labour supply to the economy as a whole would be small and that a considerable labour-saving and productivity-raising effort would be required; and some of the estimates were later revised downwards. It must therefore be assumed that success in achieving the 25 per cent growth objective will depend on still greater efforts than have yet been envisaged to use manpower more effectively and speed up the rise in output per head.

However, while mathematical methods are only occasionally in evidence so far, there is some suggestion that the situation is evolving, and that a model of the price and cost implications of the plan is under consideration.

CONCLUSIONS

The general impression which I hope might be gained from this paper is that the use of mathematical methods in formulating medium-term plans has not as yet progressed very far in the United Kingdom. The pace is set by the Cambridge Growth Project, but it is not at all clear whether or not there are other runners in the field. Government planning appears to be more closely following the lines of the French, but as yet does not appear to have laid down such effective institutional machinery for discussions and consultation. In particular, deliberations between industries with common interests are not as yet a marked feature of the committee stage of plan development. Of course economists are well aware of the programming possibilities of two-stage planning models and would like to see an evolution in this direction. However, the basic difficulty of defining an objective function is one which few if any economists or politicians in the United Kingdom would care to hazard.

In this situation it is most regrettable to my mind that the government should choose to set the planning targets before building up a model of the long-term capabilities of the economy. I suspect that we pay a price for this in the degree of identification by management and unions with the objectives and prescriptions of the plan. Further, but less important, one can argue that consumption and not income should be the objective of a plan.

If there is no objective function which a plan is to maximize, and if setting planning targets before exploring what is possible is thought to be objectionable, what way might we choose to articulate our planning exercise? Perhaps not surprisingly, I see the answer to this problem in the Cambridge Growth Project approach. This model allows one to investigate just about any planning targets, and, in particular, to explore the implications of those targets. As it stands at present, there is a deficiency in the lack of information about the implications of given targets in the short run. But all the long-run implications are worked out. Particularly as satellite models are developed, these implications can be made consistent with the existence of behavior criteria, such as profit maximization, in subsections of the model. Thus in theory, at least, the model is potentially capable of informing the body politic of all the implications of adopting different targets and of the the policy measures which might raise or lower the potential of the economy. This most desirable objective is still not within reach, but it is clear that we shall never approach it until both economists and industry put more effort into analyzing the relationships between variables, and are less inclined to guess at the conclusions that such relationships might generate.

Chapter 24

LINEAR INQUIRIES INTO FOREIGN TRADE

M. AUGUSTINOVICS

Institute of Economic Planning, Hungary

A GENERALIZATION OF THE TREATMENT OF FOREIGN TRADE IN OPEN STATIC INPUT-OUTPUT SYSTEMS

The problems to be solved in this field are not raised for purely theoretical interest. They are connected with an actual computation being carried out, on the one hand, with the input-output tables of some Western European countries, and, on the other, with a certain time series of Hungarian-planned and statistical input-output tables.

The purpose of the computations is to disclose the effects of foreign trade on the structural relationships of gross output, final product and primary inputs as well as on their volume. The analysis is restricted to the data contained in the input-output tables; other information—statistics and surveys on foreign trade—is used only to check conclusions. From this point of view, the study is intended to answer the methodological questions: What relationships can be disclosed with the aid of input-output tables of a given type and containing a given quantity of information? Do the conclusions to be drawn from them correspond to or differ from the general knowledge based on other information?

Special interest in foreign trade justifies that a general examination of structural relationships not be dealt with in this paper (for instance, the analysis of the direct and inverse coefficients characterizing interindustrial relationships is omitted). On the other hand, special interest in the structural pattern of production forces me to omit a general examination of foreign trade as well (that is, the world-market aspects of foreign trade will be disregarded).

With this in mind, two particular assumptions are valid throughout the paper which should be called to the attention of the reader: 1) Since we are not interested in the actual state of the foreign trade balance of the country examined, we always assume that the balance is in a state of equilibrium (that is, the sum total of exports equals that of imports on each market);[1] 2) We do not make the usual distinction between competitive and noncompetitive imports. Imported goods will be treated as imports, no matter what the reasons are for having them imported.

The investigation is thus definitely aimed at the mutual relationships between the sectoral pattern of the economy and foreign trade. From among the matrix-equations describing the entire system, the ones to be emphasized will be those relevant for these interrelations (though, the various linear models describing the system might be discussed in fully general terms and might be used for the analysis of other interrelations as well).

NOTATIONS

1) Capital letters will always stand for matrices.

2) Small letters corresponding to a capital letter applied for a matrix represent: as a row vector—vector of sums of the columns of the matrix; as a column vector—vector of sums of the rows of the matrix.

3) Small letters other than those corresponding to a matrix also stand for vectors to be defined separately in each case.

4) Row vectors will be marked by asterisks but only if they stand alone. If multiplied by a matrix, the position of the vector indicates whether it is a row vector or a column vector.

---

[1] In practical computations, this assumption can be realized by having in the initial table as "exports" a volume of goods whose composition corresponds to the actual pattern of exports but whose volume equals the sum total of imports. The difference will increase accumulation (in case of an export surplus) or reduce it (in case of an import surplus).

5) E indicates a unit matrix, always of the order required in the given relation.

6) 0 is a zero-matrix, equally of the order required at the place where it is applied.

7) $1^* = (1,1, \ldots \ldots 1)$ sum of unity vectors, always of the order required.

8) $1 = \begin{bmatrix} 1 \\ 1 \\ \cdot \\ \cdot \\ \cdot \\ 1 \end{bmatrix}$ the same as column vector, always of the order required.

9) $<>$ denotes a diagonal-matrix consisting of the elements of the vector within the brackets.

THE ABSTRACT SCHEME [2]

An open static input-output system of n productive sectors, m sectors of final use and r factors of value added (primary inputs) are represented in Figure 10.[3]

Also:

$A'' = A <x>^{-1}$ (coefficients of intermediary inputs)

$H'' = H <x>^{-1}$ (coefficients of value added)

$Z = (E - A'')^{-1}$ (Leontief-inverse)

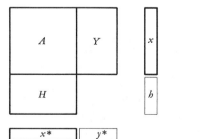

$A_{(n, n)}$ = flow–matrix of intermediary inputs

$Y_{(n, m)}$ = matrix of final use

$H_{(r, n)}$ = matrix of value added

$x_{(n)}$ = vector of gross outputs

Fig. 10. Open static input-output system of n productive sectors, m sectors of final use, and r factors of value added.

[2] Disregarding foreign trade.

[3] Introduction into the terms, assumptions and the entire logical structure of the input-output model is omitted. For the original exposition see W. Leontief, *The Structure of the American Economy, 1919–1939* (New York: Oxford University Press, 1953).

Then the basic relations of the system may be represented by the following equations:

(1) $(E - A'')\ x = y$

(2) $Zy = x$

(3) $b''Z = 1^*$

Equation (1) describes the direct allocation of gross output, stating that gross output minus direct intermediary inputs equals final output.

Equation (2) describes the final allocation of gross output, stating that final output multiplied by the total material inputs required to produce one unit of them equals gross output.

Equation (3) describes the final allocation of value added to final output, stating that the total amount of value added absorbed in one unit of each type of final output equals unity.

The above system still leaves open the question of the relationships between the different factors of value added (for example, wages, profits, turnover taxes) and the different sectors of final use (personal or government consumption, and investments). Therefore, it is usually called the "open" system.

A matrix, which would describe these missing relationships directly—that is, which would define, for example, the wages paid by nonproductive sectors, or taxes paid directly by investors—is often mentioned as the missing "fourth square"; though it need not necessarily be a square, it could be a rectangle as well.

Should the sectors of final use correspond to the sectors of primary inputs so that their "columns" could be regarded as input for producing the outputs of the latter, they would no more be considered as "final" and the latter as "primary"; they would be dealt with like ordinary productive sectors and the entire system would be called a "closed" system.

In this paper a different operation will be carried out with the aim of revealing the indirect, final relations between primary inputs and final uses within the open system. These relations are hidden by the mutual intersectoral exchange of goods in the process of production. Following this series of exchange up to its ultimate effects—that is, the computation of the "Leontief-type inverse" of the matrix of direct coefficients—affords an opportunity to eliminate this series itself and the double-counting of values in measuring production with gross outputs as well.

Thus the "ultimate balance" of the system can be established: the amount of each factor of value added finally employed in each sector of final use, can be defined. In other words, the total value of the bill of goods used up in each type of final use—and thus the total value of the system's entire final output—will be reduced to the original, primary factors of value added.

The keys to this operation are obviously given in equations (2) and (3). If we multiply not only by vectors, but matrices, we obtain an "allocation matrix" consisting of bilinear forms, which may be regarded as the "ultimate balance" of the system:

(4) $H''ZY_{(r,m)}$

$\{HZY\}_{g,j}$ = the amount of the gth value added factor absorbed in the goods consumed in the jth final use;

(5) $1^*H''ZY = y^*$ and

(6) $H''ZY1 = h$

The identities described in equations (5) and (6) are logically the basic requirements for $H''ZY$ to be an allocation matrix, and are important in checking correct computation.

THE USUAL SCHEME [4]

Let us consider the case of data being available on the composition of exports by producing sectors and on the direct allocation of imports to consuming sectors, both exports and imports to and from k different markets. There are no data available on the origin by producing sectors of imports allocated to each consuming sector.

The open static input-output system including foreign trade can in this case be represented by Figure 11.

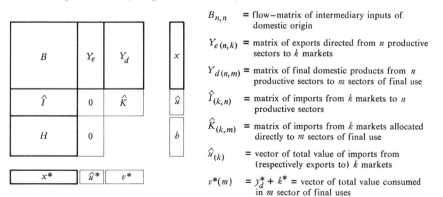

$B_{n,n}$ = flow–matrix of intermediary inputs of domestic origin

$Y_{e\,(n,k)}$ = matrix of exports directed from n productive sectors to k markets

$Y_{d\,(n,m)}$ = matrix of final domestic products from n productive sectors to m sectors of final use

$\hat{I}_{(k,n)}$ = matrix of imports from k markets to n productive sectors

$\hat{K}_{(k,m)}$ = matrix of imports from k markets allocated directly to m sectors of final use

$\hat{u}_{(k)}$ = vector of total value of imports from (respectively exports to) k markets

$v^*_{(m)}$ = $y^*_d + k^*$ = vector of total value consumed in m sector of final uses

Fig. 11. Open static input-output system including foreign trade.

[4] Limited information on imports.

Let us accept that:

$B'' = B <x>^{-1}$ (coefficients of domestic intermediary inputs)

$\hat{I}' = \hat{I} <x>^{-1}$ (coefficients of imports from different markets)

$Q = (E - B'')^{-1}$ (inverse of domestic intersectoral relations)

$y = y_e + y_d$ (end product)

As y stands for the total net output of the domestic productive system, equations (1) and (2) of the abstract scheme hold also for this case, if we substitute Q for Z:

(7) $(E - B'') \, x = y$

(8) $Q \, y = x$

But considering only y_d, the final domestic product for final domestic use, we get:

(9) $(E - B'') \, x - y_e = y_d$

(10) $Q \, y_d = x - Q \, y_e$

Further, instead of equation (3) of the abstract scheme we get

(11) $b'' Q = 1^* - \hat{i}'' Q$

Therefore, an allocation matrix $H'' Q Y_d$ would not satisfy the identity-requirements formulated in equations (5) and (6). In other words, value-added factors cannot in this case be allocated to final uses only, because they are absorbed in exported goods as well; the total value of goods consumed in final use cannot be reduced to value-added factors only, because it includes the value of imported goods as well. For revealing the ultimate relations between primary inputs and final demand in this case, two different methods of computation are employed in Hungary. Both will be formulated, and then it will be briefly shown that under certain conditions (which are usually fulfilled), they lead to the same ultimate results.

The "method of two systems." The elements of this method—not fully formulated—are usually employed, when foreign trade itself is to be investigated, in connection either with the main proportions of the economy, or with foreign trade policy, foreign trade decisions to be taken, and so forth.[5]

[5] Computations were carried out, for example, for the analysis of the statistical data for 1961 by P. Haras, *Divergence Between Price and Value Proportions in the Actual Price System* (Budapest: Közgazdásagi Szemle, 1962), and by A. Racz, *Character of Hungarian Foreign Trade Regarding Inputs of Labor and Fixer Assets* (Budapest: Közgazdásagi Szemle, 1966); for the analysis of

$\hat{I}''QY_e$	$\hat{I}''QY_d$
$H''QY_e$	$H''QY_d$

$\hat{I}''QY_{e\,(k,k)}$ = import−contents of exports

$\left\{\hat{I}''QY_e\right\}_{g,\,j}$ = the amount of imports originating from the gth market, absorbed in exports directed to the jth market

$\hat{I}''QY_{d\,(k,m)}$ = import−contents of final product for domestic final use

$H''QY_{e\,(r,k)}$ = value−added contents of exports

$H''QY_{d\,(r,m)}$ = value−added contents of final product for domestic final use

Fig. 12. Allocation matrix of imports (considered primary) and exports (considered as final use).

As a first step, imports are considered as primary inputs and exports as final uses. The allocation matrix will in this case consist of four different blocks as shown in Figure 12.

The identity requirements hold as follows:

(12) $1^* \; i''QY_e + 1^* \; H''QY_e = y_e^*$

(13) $1^* \; i''QY_d + 1^* \; H''QY_d = y_d^*$

(14) $i''QY_e \, 1 + \hat{I}''QY_d \, 1 = i^*$

(15) $H''QY_e \, 1 + H'''QY_d \, 1 = h$

Each of the allocation matrices and each element of them can be interpreted and are worthy of investigation in themselves; they are of great economic importance for a country which is highly involved in foreign trade.

The allocation matrix $\hat{I}''QY_e$ represents a particular kind of re-export—re-export from different markets to different markets via domestic production. These data can be of exceptional importance in cases where trading or payment conditions are different (for instance, in some of them currencies are convertible, but in others they are not).

Matrices $\hat{I}''QY_e$ and $\hat{I}''QY_d$ describe the allocation of imports used in domestic production, their distribution between exports and final domestic use

the second five-year plan comparing statistical data for 1959 and planned data for 1965, see M. Augustinovics, "Method for Analyzing Planned Economic Proportions: The Case of the Second Hungarian Five-Year Plan" (mimeographed), Budapest, 1963; for computing a realistic rate of exchange, see A. Brody, *A Realistic Rate of Exchange and its Application* (Budapest: Közgazdásagi Szemle, 1964).

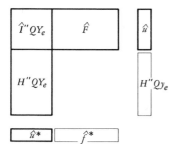

Fig. 13. Foreign trade treated as separately attached input-output system of k sectors.

and, within the latter, the distribution among subsectors. Eventually, matrix $\hat{K}$ may be also drawn into the scope of the analysis. It may be established, for example, whether the imports from various markets serve personal consumption, investment, and so forth, in identical or differing proportions.

Matrices $\hat{I}''QY_e$ and $H''QY_e$ describe the input structure of exports. They show the import content of exports to different markets (and the origin of import content by various markets), and the amount of wages, profits and taxes embodied in exported goods.

After all, the "net outputs" of foreign trade for domestic use are described by the matrix $\hat{I}''QY_d + \hat{K}$, and the "primary inputs" to produce these outputs are given in matrix $H''QY_e$. For connecting outputs with inputs, the "intermediary turnover"—the imports absorbed in exports—have again to be eliminated.[6]

For this purpose, foreign trade may be treated as a separately attached input-output system of k sectors, which can be represented in Figure 13. Let us accept that:

$\hat{F}_{(k,m)} = \hat{I}''QY_d + \hat{K}$ (direct and indirect imports from K markets to m sectors of final domestic use)

$Y_e'' = Y_e < \hat{u} >^{-1}$ (composition of one unit of exports to different markets by domestic producing sectors)

The basic equation of this particular system can be then formulated as follows:

[6] The fact that there was something to be eliminated, was realized with some delay. It was disregarded by Leontief, "Domestic Production and Foreign Trade: The American Capital Position Re-examined," *Proceedings,* American Philosophical Society, 97:4. After having corrected the figures, he formulates an equation for one market (or for one commodity) and points to the fact that in empirical analysis a set of simultaneous linear equations would be necessary. See Leontief, "Factor Proportions and the Structure of American trade: Further Theoretical and Empirical Analysis," *The Review of Economics and Statistics,* November 1956.

(16) $\hat{I}''QY''_e\hat{u} + \hat{f} = \hat{u}$

hence

(17) $(E - \hat{I}''QY''_e)\hat{u} = \hat{f}$

and further

(18) $(E - \hat{I}''QY''_e)^{-1}\hat{f} = \hat{u}$

Let, for the sake of convenience, W stand for $(E - \hat{I}''QY''_e)^{-1}$, then (18) rewritten is

(19) $W\hat{f} = \hat{u}$

The Leontief-type inverse W defines the "gross" amount of exports to different markets, required to "produce" one unit of "net" import—import for final domestic use—on different markets.

$W_{g,j}$ = the amount of goods which will be exported to (imported from) the gth market, if one unit of net import from the jth market is required.

Equation (19) can be for instance employed for planning the total volume of foreign trade, given the final domestic demand in imported goods from each market. But this side of the model will not be discussed in this paper. What we are interested in is the allocation of primary domestic inputs to the net domestic use of imports.

It follows from (19) that the "share" of final domestic consuming sectors in "gross" exports—that is, including exports, covering imports to produce exports—is described by the matrix $W\hat{F}$. On the other hand, domestic primary inputs to one unit of export to different markets, will obviously be described by $H''QY''_e$. Thus, the allocation matrix of this particular system can be given as

(20) $H''QY''_e W\hat{F}_{(\gamma,m)}$

where

$\{H''QY''_e W\hat{F}\}_{g,j}$ = the amount of the gth value-added factor absorbed in goods exported for the net import consumption in the jth sector of final domestic use

(21) $1*H''QY''_e W\hat{F} = \hat{f}*$

(22) $H''QY''_e W\hat{F}1 = H''Qy_e$

The identities (21) and (22) assure that exactly the sum of primary inputs absorbed in exports will be substituted for the value of imported goods consumed in final domestic use.

Thus the "ultimate balance" of the entire system (consisting of the system of domestic production and the separate system of foreign trade) can be described with the sum of two matrices:

(23) $H''QY_d + H''QY''_e W\hat{F}$

where the former defines the allocation of value-added factors to final uses via domestic production and the latter the analogous allocation via domestic production *and* foreign trade. Thus

$\{H''QY_d + H''QY''_e W\hat{F}\}_{g,j} =$ total amount of gth value-added factor directed to the jth sector of final use

Now the following identity requirements hold

(24) $1^* (H''QY_d + H''QY''_e W\hat{F}) = v^*$

(25) $(H''QY_d + H''QY''_e W\hat{F}) 1 = h$

by which the proper allocation of value added to final use is guaranteed.

This "method of the two systems" is obviously very suitable for analyses concerning foreign trade. However, it is often criticized for disregarding the mutual interrelations between the domestic productive system and the separate foreign trade system; the computations based on the "small" inverse W are therefore regarded only as approximate.

The "method of the enlarged system." This method is usually employed when foreign trade is of no particular interest, but the "ultimate balance" of the entire system is aimed at directly. This is the case when, for example, the value-added factor composition of different groups of commodities is investigated, or price indexes, different types of price systems have to be computed.[7]

The k different markets are then included in the domestic production system as k productive sectors. Then the entire system considered can be represented in Figure 14.

The terms applied in this method will be denoted by ^{0}, but for the sake of comparison they are set up here in the terms of the former method.

$$B^0 = \begin{pmatrix} B'' & Y''_e \\ \hat{I}'' & 0 \end{pmatrix} \qquad Y^0 = \begin{pmatrix} Y_d \\ \hat{K} \end{pmatrix} \qquad H^0 = (H'', 0)$$

$$x^0 = \begin{pmatrix} x \\ \hat{u} \end{pmatrix} \qquad y^0 = \begin{pmatrix} y_d \\ \hat{K} \end{pmatrix} \qquad Q^0 = (E - B^0)^{-1}$$

---

[7] The method was applied for computing actual economic proportions expressed in various hypothetical price-systems. See S. Ganczer, *Price Computations, Economic Proportions* (Budapest: Közgazdasági Szemle, 1965).

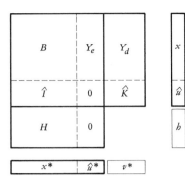

Fig. 14. The domestic production system including k different markets as k productive sectors.

For this system the original equations (1), (2) and (3) hold; by substituting the corresponding notations we get:

(26) $(E - B^0) x^0 = y^0$

(27) $Q^0 y^0 = x^0$

(28) $b^0 Q^0 = 1^*$

Evidently, the identity requirements (5) and (6) also hold and thus need not be repeated for the allocation matrix of this enlarged system:

(29) $H^0 Q^0 Y^0$

In practical computations usually only individual blocks of the above allocation matrix are used.

This method is obviously simple and clearly arranged, very similar to the "abstract scheme" disregarding foreign trade. However, it was criticized exactly for that; that is, for including foreign trade into production which practically amounts to disregarding it, thereby confusing the two and not presenting separate information on foreign trade.

As a matter of fact, this kind of computation gives identical results with the "method of two systems" since the "ultimate balances" are identical:

(30) $H^0 Q^0 Y^0 = H'' Q Y_d + H'' Q Y''_e$

(For proof see Appendix 1.)

This holds on the condition that simple re-export and value added directly used for foreign trade are considered to be zero. In practical computations this is always assumed.

In addition, not only the "ultimate balances" but also parts and blocks correspond with each other as can be seen in the Appendix. It follows that each block relevant for any type of computation or analysis may be set up by any of the two methods. Their advantages and disadvantages seem to be common and they are those of the scheme itself.

The advantages are perhaps obvious: they enable us to trace the final utilization of imports in the economy, to establish the inputs of exports and, finally, considering exports as input of net imports, to establish the ultimate connection between value added and final domestic use—that is, the "ultimate balance."

The disadvantages are equally obvious. The commodity pattern of imports is not known. The diverging flow of various kinds of imported commodities, or the differing ratios of their final allocation, are not traceable. This would be, however, of immense economic importance, particularly for small countries highly involved in foreign trade and especially in cases when various kinds of products are imported under different conditions; for example, from different markets, or from the same market, but with different conditions of payment or delivery.

Further, in this manner the effects of foreign trade on the sectoral pattern of the economy cannot be assessed. To be able to measure this effect, obviously, the pattern of imports should be known not only by markets and domestic using sectors, but according to kinds of products—that is, by potential domestic sectors of origin as well.

The necessary information is already available in the statistical system of several countries and international organizations. The task is then to render the model capable of absorbing and processing this additional information. This should be done again not from purely theoretical interest but in order to insure the correctness and consistency of practical computations.

THE EXTENDED SCHEME [8]

An open static input-output system completed with full information on the composition of imports for each domestic sector from each market by producing sectors, that is, by sectors which *would* produce the same or similar goods, can be illustrated in Figure 15.[9]

[8] Detailed information on imports.

[9] Similar problems were raised for one market only in T. J. Matuszewski, P. R. Pitts, J. A. Sawyer, "Alternative Treatments of Imports in Input-Output Models: A Canadian Study," *Journal of the Royal Statistical Society,* series A, vol. 126, part 3, 1963. The solution seems to be different.

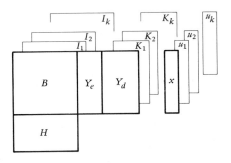

$I_{1(n,n)}, I_{2(n,n)}, \ldots\ldots I_{k(n,n)}$ = flow–matrices of imports for productive sectors from the 1st, 2nd, ... kth market

$K_{1(n,m)}, K_{2(n,m)}, \ldots\ldots K_{k(n,m)}$ = matrices of imports directly for final use from the 1st, 2nd, ... kth market

$u_{1(n)}, u_{2(n)}, \ldots\ldots u_{k(n)}$ = vectors of total imports from the 1st, 2nd, ... kth market

Fig. 15. Open static input-output system with full data on composition of imports by sectors producing same or similar goods.

Let it be assumed that:

$$I = I_1 + I_z + \ldots\ldots + I_k$$

$I''_1 = I_1\langle x\rangle^{-1}$ (coefficients of imports from the 1st market)

$I''_2 = I_2\langle x\rangle^{-1}$ (coefficients of imports from the 2nd market)

.

.

.

$I''_k = I_k\langle x\rangle^{-1}$ (coefficients of imports from the kth market)

$K = K_1 + K_2 + \ldots\ldots\ldots + K_k$

$A = B + I$ (flow-matrix of total—domestic and imported—intermediary inputs)

$A'' = A\langle x\rangle^{-1}$ (coefficients of total intermediary inputs)

$Z = (E - A'')^{-1}$

Again, if we denote by y the total net output of the domestic productive system, that is, $y = y_e + y_d$, for x and y the basic equations (1) and (2) hold:

(31) $(E - B'')\, x = y$

(32) $Q\, y = x$

But this bill of goods denoted by y is neither the real end-product of the system, nor the net final consumption in the system. Even in the "usual scheme" discussed earlier it differed from both these concepts, but there was at that time no possibility of defining the sectoral composition of these two bills of goods, while, in the extended scheme, this possibility already exists.

Following the relations connected with the real end-product, we can describe the *actual system;* tracing the sectoral pattern and volume of gross outputs and primary inputs required for the net final consumption, we can describe a system which *would have to exist,* if final consumption and technology were equal to the actual ones, but goods could not be exchanged on foreign markets.

The actual system. In fact, the real end-product is determined by the gross outputs of the domestic productive system minus total material inputs required for this production:

$$(33) \quad (E - A'') \, x = (E - B'' - I'') \, x = (E - B'') \, x - I''x$$

Substituting from (31) and (32) we get

$$(34) \quad (E - A'') \, x = y - I''Q y = (E - I''Q)y$$

Thus the real end-product of the system is not the bill of goods denoted by y, but only the "domestic part" of it—that is, this bill of goods minus imports consumed in its production.

Thus our first step immediately introduced the product $I''Q$ and the complementary $(E - I''Q)$ matrices. They are key elements of the extended scheme and not as familiar as are the terms and blocks applied earlier. Let us consider them briefly.

The rows of $I''Q$ correspond to the rows of I—that is, they represent the different kinds of imported goods classified by producing sectors. The columns correspond to the columns of Q—representing inputs required for the production of one unit of net output.

Thus

$\{I''Q\}_{g,j} =$ the total amount of imported g^{th} products, required in the entire system to produce one unit of net output of the jth sector.

Obviously, the same interpretation holds for the corresponding

$I''_1 Q, I''_2 Q, \ldots \ldots, I''_k Q$ matrices.

It is equally obvious, that when aiming at the allocation of import and domestic primary inputs to final outputs or final uses in the same detailed

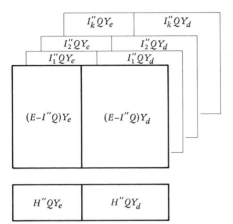

Fig. 16. Matrices illustrating goal of allocation of import and domestic primary inputs to final use.

manner, we now get a series of allocation matrices, which can be illustrated in Figure 16.

For example:

$I''_2QY_e(n,k)$ = imports in sectoral breakdown from the 2nd market, absorbed in exports

$\{I''_2QY_e\}_{g,j}$ = the amount of gth products imported from the 2nd market, absorbed in the total export directed to the jth market

and the similar definitions will not be repeated for each member of the series. The row- and column-sum identities will also be omitted; they seem to be obvious.

There is no need to point out the inexhaustible possibilities of analysis in these allocation matrices. Just consider the case when, for example, certain rows represent "hard" goods, which tend to be in short supply on the market, and their final allocation can be traced, the share of personal consumption and investments can be observed and also compared with the share of these final uses in other, so-called "soft" imported goods, and so forth.

Some remarks should, however, be made on the complementary matrix $(E - I''Q)$. It "cuts out" the domestic part of a vector multiplied by it, as was mentioned in connection with equation (34). But it should be emphasized, that the term "domestic part" does not refer to the individual components of the vector but to the entire bill of goods represented by it. The gth component of vector $I''Qu$ sums up the total amount of imported g^{th}

commodities absorbed in the production of all kinds of commodities in the bill of goods denoted by y. Therefore, the gth component of the "domestic part" $(E - I''Q)y$ will represent the difference or balance between the net domestic output of the gth commodity and the total amount of imported g^{th} commodities consumed anywhere in the productive system. Obviously, the balance can be negative as well as positive. Thus, the very term "domestic part" involves the fact that some exchange of goods takes place.

Nevertheless, the total value of the "domestic part" of a given bill of goods equals the share of domestic value added in its total value; that is:

$$(35)\ 1^*\ (E - I''Q) = 1^*\ H''Q$$

In other words, the allocation matrix $(E - I''Q)Y_d$ simply gives a different arrangement of the very same values as the matrix $H''QY_d$. The former defines the sectoral composition of the bill of goods for different final uses, in which value added is ultimately embodied; while the latter gives the factor composition of the same value added.

After this, digression made necessary by the novelty of the terms introduced, let us return to further definitions of different relations in the "actual system," but only of those which are important for measuring the effects of foreign trade.

From (34) it follows, that

$$(36)\ (E - A'')^{-1}\ (E - I''Q)\ y = x$$

rewritten:

$$(37)\ Z(E - I''Q)\ y = x$$

and applying (32)

$$(38)\ Z(E - I''Q) = Q$$

(See Appendix 2.)

Verbally interpreted: total inputs required to produce the "domestic part" are equal to the domestic inputs necessary to produce the total bill of goods.

From (38) the following relations can be simply derived:

$$(39)\ Z - ZI''Q = Q$$

and thus

$$(40)\ Z = Q + ZI''Q$$

This shows that for computing the matrix of total inputs Z, it is not sufficient to add up total domestic inputs, Q, and total imported inputs,

$I''Q$, as it would be perhaps assumed without investigating the entire logic of the system. One more endless chain of mutual interrelations has to be taken into consideration: the Z factor in $ZI''Q$, representing total inputs required to produce total imported inputs.

As to the problem of ultimate allocation of domestic primary inputs to domestic final uses via foreign trade, nothing can be added to what was said earlier. No matter how much detailed information is available on the sectoral composition of imports, imports and exports when exchanged on the different markets are linked only by their total values and not—at least under normal trading conditions—by the exchange of individual products for individual products. Therefore, the only way to substitute the value-added contents of exports for the value of net imports is the method described earlier. Obviously, there are no practical difficulties when a transition is needed from the "extended scheme" back to the "usual scheme," as

$$(41) \ \hat{I} = \begin{bmatrix} 1^* & I_1 \\ 1^* & I_2 \\ \vdots \\ 1^* & I_k \end{bmatrix}$$

and

$$(42) \ \hat{K} = \begin{bmatrix} 1^* & K_1 \\ 1^* & K_2 \\ \vdots \\ 1^* & K_k \end{bmatrix}$$

The "would be" system. The "would be" system is very simple and familiar. Assume that the country needs the same goods for final domestic uses that it actually uses, that is, the final consumption invariably consists of $Y_d + K$; furthermore, the technological and social conditions described by matrices A'' and H'' are the same, but no foreign trade exists.

Then the gross output denoted by x would be:

$$(43) \ \bar{x} = Z(y_d + k)$$

The amount of primary inputs, denoted by h would be:

$$(44) \ h = H''\bar{x}$$

And the "ultimate balance," that is, the single allocation matrix of the system would be represented by

$$(45) \ H''Z(Y_d + K)$$

Just notice the simple fact that the "would be system" can by no means be outlined without information on matrix A'', that is, without detailed information on imports.

MEASURING THE EFFECTS OF FOREIGN TRADE [10]

An input-output system suitable for measuring the full effects of foreign trade would be an international system. This would have to be a system of input-output tables in the same sectoral breakdown for each country concerned, with the same treatment of every type of activities, and—this is the most difficult problem—at the same prices, separately showing imports from (and exports to) each country concerned.

In a system like this, two things could be done: 1) Actual inputs in country A on exports directed to country B could be compared with actual inputs in country B on exports directed to country A. Thus the actual balance of the exchange could be established. 2) Hypothetical inputs which would be required to produce the goods actually imported could be compared with actual inputs in the country really producing them. Thus, the comparative advantages of the exchange could be measured.

Such a system could probably be represented, illustrated and interpreted in many ways, but statistical data for it are not yet available. The most advanced product of statistics—even on the international level—is at present the system described above. This is what the effects of foreign trade have to be measured with.

Obviously, neither the actual balance nor the comparative effect between two or more countries can be traced in this system. What can be done is to compare a country's hypothetical inputs on imported goods with the very same country's actual inputs on its exports. The result of this comparison— that is, the balance between hypothetical and actual inputs—might be considered as the effect of foreign trade.

One might assume that a further definition is needed. Namely, at least three—seemingly different—interpretations can be given of what has to be considered as exchange of goods, in other words, of what the country has received and what it has given: 1) The most realistic concept would take it for granted that commodities passing frontiers and duties are dealt with— that is, imports are received and exports are given; 2) A more delicate concept would take into consideration that parts of import and export produce adjust to each other and that only the net domestic part of export is

[10] Lack of full information.

given for net import to final domestic use; 3) A generalizing concept would refer instead of separate commodities to the entire system and would insist on measuring the balance with the difference between the "actual system" and the "would be" system.

In the following it will be briefly shown that these three concepts are equivalent in the sense of giving the same result. They define, namely, the very same balance between what the country has received and what it has given and, therefore, the very same balance between hypothetical and actual inputs.

Let s denote the usual concept of the foreign trade balance but with the opposite sign:

$$(46) \ s = u - y_e$$

Further, let g denote the balance between "net domestic" imports and "net domestic" exports:

$$(47) \ g = I''Q y_d + k - (E - I''Q)y_e$$

Now:

$$(48) \ g = I''Q y_d + k - y_e + I''Q y_e$$
$$= I''Q (y_d + y_e) + k - y_e$$
$$= I''Q y + k - y_e$$
$$= i + k - y_e$$

Thus:

$$(49) \ g = u - y_e = s$$

by which the equivalence of the first and the second concept is proved. Let us prove them to be equal to the third.

Let v denote the difference between the real end-product of the actual system and the hypothetical end-product of the "would be" system:

$$(50) \ v = y_d + k - (E - I''Q)y$$

Beyond this:

$$(51) \ v = y_d + k - y + I''Q y$$
$$= I''Q y + k - (y - y_d)$$
$$= i + k - y_e$$

Thus:

$$(52) \ v = u - y_e = s = g$$

(q.e.d.)

From this, it unequivocally follows that the balance of gross output is also identical according to the three concepts, and that the same holds for primary inputs, too. There is still one more point of interest which has to be mentioned.

Balances of gross outputs or of primary inputs are often measured by multiplying both exports and imports by Q representing actual domestic inputs (or respectively by $H''Q$).[11] This does not seem to be quite satisfactory, because the accounting hypothesis of "domestically produced imports" involves the hypothesis that imported inputs would be also produced at home. In this case total inputs are not restricted to actual domestic inputs, but equal actual domestic *plus* imported inputs. In other words, total inputs required to produce any bill of goods (inclusive of imports) would not, in this case, be represented by Q, but by Z.

This is easy to realize if we prove that it is not $(Qu - Qy_e) = Qs$ but exactly $(Zu - Zy_e)$ that corresponds to the difference between actual gross outputs and hypothetical gross outputs of the "would be" system:

$$(53) \quad Zs = Zu - Zy_e = Z\,(I''Qy + k) - Z\,(y - y_d)$$
$$= ZI''Qy + Zk - Zy + Zy_d$$
$$= Z\,(y_d + k) - Qy$$
$$= x - \bar{x}$$

(q.e.d.)

The error caused by using Q instead of Z can be easily determined:

$$(54) \quad (Z - Q)\,(u - y_e) = (Z - Q)\,s$$
$$= ZI''Qs$$

or respectively:

$$(55) \quad H''ZI''Qs$$

where $ZI''Q$ obviously tends to 0 if the components of I'' are small. Thus, the error is probably not significant in the case of a country absorbing relatively little imported material in its own productive system, but it might

---

[11] See Leontief, "Domestic Production and Foreign Trade: The American Capital Position Reexamined," *Proceedings,* American Philosophical Society, 97:4; "Factor Proportions and the Structure of American Trade: Further Theoretical and Empirical Analysis," *The Review of Economics and Statistics,* November 1956; several case studies of various countries not listed individually among References in this paper, and finally A. Racz, *Character of Hungarian Foreign Trade Regarding Inputs of Labor and Fixed Assets* (Budapest: Közgazdasági Szemle, 1966) for Hungary.

grow to a certain importance in a country operating with relatively much imported material.

As a final remark, it should be mentioned that effects of foreign trade in the above sense can also be measured for each market as well as for each domestic sector separately. Naturally, in this case the formulae and computations tend to become somewhat sophisticated, as, for instance, certain identities which hold for the entire system are not likely to hold for separate markets or for separate sectors in such a simple manner. But the additional efforts are worth the trouble in countries highly dependent on foreign trade.

APPENDIX 1. TO EQUATION (30)

It has to be proved, that

$$H^0 Q^0 Y^0 = H'' Q Y_d + H'' Q Y''_e W \hat{F}$$

$$B^0 = \begin{bmatrix} B''_{(n,n)} & Y''_{e(n,k)} \\ \hat{I}''_{(k,n)} & 0_{(k,k)} \end{bmatrix}$$

$$E - B^0 = \begin{bmatrix} (E - B'') & -Y''_e \\ -\hat{I}'' & E \end{bmatrix}$$

$$(E - B^0)^{-1} = Q^0$$

$$(E - B'')^{-1} = Q$$

According to Frobenius-Schur's relation:[12]

$$Q^0 = \begin{bmatrix} Q & 0 \\ 0 & 0 \end{bmatrix} \begin{bmatrix} QY''_e W \hat{I}'' Q & QY''_e W \\ W\hat{I}'' Q & W \end{bmatrix}$$

Where $W = (E - \hat{I} Q Y''_e)^{-1}$

Further on

$$H^0 = [H'' \ 0]$$

thus

$$H^0 Q^0 = [H'' Q, 0] + [H'' Q Y''_e W \hat{I}'' Q, \ H'' Q Y''_e W]$$

and

$$Y^0 = \begin{bmatrix} Y_d \\ \hat{K} \end{bmatrix}$$

[12] For reference, see E. Bodewig, *Matrix Calculus* (Amsterdam: North-Holland Publishing Company, 1959) p. 217; first application to input-output matrices in A. Brody, *A Realistic Rate of Exchange and its Application* (Budapest: Közgazdásgi Szemle, 1964).

thus

$$H^0Q^0Y^0 = H''QY_d + H''QY''_eW\hat{I}''QY_d + H''QY''_eW\hat{K}$$
$$= H''QY_d + H''QY''_eW(\hat{I}''QY_d + \hat{K})$$

$$\hat{I}''QY_d + \hat{H} = \hat{F}$$

$$H^0Q^0Y^0 = H''QY_d + H''QY''_eW\hat{F}$$

(q.e.d.)

APPENDIX 2. TO EQUATION (38)

The identity $Z\,(E - I''Q) = Q$ can also be derived in the following way:

$$Z = (E - A'')^{-1} = [E - (B + I'')]^{-1} = \{[E - I''(E - B)^{-1}](E - B)\}^{-1}$$
$$= (E - B)^{-1}[E - I''(E - B)^{-1}]^{-1} = Q\,(E - I''Q)^{-1}$$

Chapter 25

MATHEMATICS AND THE NATIONAL ECONOMY

EUGENE MATEEV
Bulgarian Academy of Sciences

Interbranch relations are among the most important functional dependences in the system of expanded reproduction. That is why the setting up of the macro-economic models cannot be done without these dependences being somewhat interrelated. At present, the greatest success has been achieved, theoretically and practically, in setting up macro-economic models of the balance of the interbranch relations.

This paper begins by describing briefly the setting up of balances of interbranch relations and about the utilization of these balances for economic analysis and for planning in Bulgaria. The author then presents some of his ideas on improving the system by making it a more perfected apparatus of optimum reaction of economics to the changing exogenic conditions (that is, an apparatus of optimum economic control).

Two statistical balances of the interbranch relations have been worked out in Bulgaria until the present—one for 1960 and the other for 1963.

The nomenclature of the branches in the first quadrant of the 1960 balance includes 69 items; that of the 1963 balance includes 109. Both balances have been drawn up in a number of variants depending on a) the degree of aggregation of the branches and b) the manner of showing the imports in the coefficients.

The balances of both 1960 and 1963 have been expressed in values according to prices for the respective years which are characteristic of the final sales. A higher degree of disaggregation is to be found in the branches of industry. It is the enterprise, and not the separate product, that has been accepted as a qualification unit.

The balances are supplemented by information on volume and structure of basic and turnover funds used in the industrial process and on current working time. All this has served as a basis for calculating the coefficients of the full expenditures of raw materials, semimanufactured goods, power, basic and turnover funds, current working time, and so forth, per unit of final production.

The statistical balances of the interbranch relations have made it possible to make a number of analyses of the economic processes.

Although Bulgaria possesses twenty years' experience in the working out of ordinary state-economic balances drawn up on the basis of thousands of separate products and of the national economy as a whole, in a very extended nomenclature of resources and consumption, the balances of the interbranch relations provided us with the possibility of explaining in greater detail a number of connections and dependences in the economic field—in a unified and integral system. The analyses made in greater detail and in a more harmonious system, based on the balances of the interbranch relations, make it increasingly possible to specify the economic policy with greater precision and to improve the state economic plans.

Planned balances of the interbranch relations have been drawn up in Bulgaria since 1964 on the basis of the statistical balances of interbranch relations. In particular, planned interbranch balances have been drawn up for 1964, 1965, 1966, and 1970. The nomenclature of the branches in the planned balance for 1964 and 1965 consists of 27 items each. The balances for 1966 and 1970 have been drawn up in two variants, with 27 and with 50 branches each. In order to increase the analytical capacities of the balances, they are worked out according to two types of prices, namely: factory prices (which are close to prime cost) and prices of the final sale.

Although the macro-economic plan of the country continues to be drawn up on the classical bases of planning, the balances of interbranch relations are increasingly helpful in planning work. In the first place, a number of indices of the plan are in point of fact drawn up by two methods—by the classical one and by the balances of the interbranch relations which provide for mutual comparisons, specifications, and control. In this manner, it is possible to improve the reciprocal connections among the planned indices, improving their motivation and increasing their precision. In the second place, the planned balances of interbranch relations are increasingly used in planning prices. For instance, calculations have already been made in our country to determine the prime cost of about 160 major products without any elements of profit. This process consists of calculating the prime cost from the materials, power, basic funds, and turnover funds making part of its composition without the elements of the net income (profit in its various forms). In the third place, expanding the scope of the branches, improving the methods of planned correction of the coefficients of expenditure, perfecting the methods of determining final consumption, improving ways of reflecting the imports and exports, and so on, gradually bring us to the drafting of the dynamic model of the balance and to its optimization. Parallel with that runs the process of drafting the macro-economic plan in terms of solving an extreme problem. However clear this trend of perfecting the system of planning may be, there are exceptionally complex economic and mathematical problems that are encountered along the road to its solution.

We would like to draw your attention in the present paper to certain key aspects of the planning problem as a system of economic control in the cybernetic sense of the word.

In view of the fact that the concept of economic control involves a broad circle of problems, beginning with the immediate industrial processes at the lathe and ending with the complex systems of the international division of labor, it is necessary to limit the discussion. The systems of division of labor include the methodological problems of control on the scale of expanded reproduction as a whole or, as usually referred to, on the scale of macro-economic planning (not of factory or branch planning). With regard to the span of time to which the plan targets are related, we distinguish between planning within the framework of one year and planning within five or more years. One more limitation is necessary in view of the essential difference in the problems affecting the two aspects: what we have in mind are the problems of economic cybernetics within the scale of a long period of time—that is, what is known as long-term planning, unlike the current operative planning.

According to the classification given by cyberneticians, social economics belongs to the very complex probability systems. The system of material production is continuously affected by "signals" originating from other spheres of social activities—from the field of demands, of natural environment, and so forth. The system responds to these effects not in a passive manner (as, by way of example, a stone which we may "affect" with a hammer) but after a long and exceptionally complex processing of the input (in the sense referred to) information carried by the signals. The processing depends on the state of the system where it receives the information. The result of this creative work is the new state of the system, a state of response, by which in its turn it affects inversely both the higher spheres of creative work (technology, for example) and the demands of the citizens and society, the natural environment, and so forth. Let us dwell particularly on the relations among the system of material production and other spheres for the purpose of establishing the character of the input information and its processing into output information.

Approaching the problem in a completely inductive manner—that is, from an analysis of empirical facts—we come to the differentiation of two types of quantities which have a bearing on the control of social economy. The characteristic feature of one type is that it is causally conditioned, or, to be more precise, that it is conditioned in a socio-economic manner. These quantities are objective facts to the organs of planning, and the organs must take them into consideration if they want an accurate plan. The organs of planning may affect the objectively determined quantities in an indirect manner, to one degree or another, but, nevertheless, after they have or have not been affected, the quantities of the type examined in this instance constitute an "external" factor with regard to the system of material production. The purpose of planning in regard to them is not one of making "decisions," but rather of establishing the quantities as objective facts. (We would like to repeat that this does not in the least exclude the inverse effect of the plan decisions on these objective facts.) Mathematically, this particularity of the first type of factors is shown in that, upon the formation of the inter-branch relations, they constitute known quantities which are given. Here are a few examples.

The number of the population and its dynamics are, naturally enough, affected by the decisions of the plan (through the birth rate, for instance). Nevertheless, with regard to the decisions to be made by the planning organ, as is the case with the dynamics of production, labor productivity, capital investments, and even the undertakings related to these very birth rates, the population figure (labor resources included) is an objective fact in connection with which the planning center makes no decisions, it must simply take it into consideration.

The planning organ outlines undertakings related to scientific and design work. It exercises its effect primarily by providing material prerequisites for the advance of such work. However, there is a great gap between the material prerequisites for scientific and design work and the actual results. It is obvious at any rate that the results and achievements are not, so to speak, in a state of linear dependence on the expenditures provided for their realization. The dependence is far more complicated. In one way or another, the technical parameters of one particular industrial process are likewise an objective fact for the organs of planning, and they also play the part of known quantities. Examining the technical and the technico-economic parameters as a specific flux of input information, it is necessary to point to their relations with the natural factors and with natural environment. For instance, the technico-economic parameters of a hydro-electric power plant depend on the natural conditions of the alignment and of the cup; the parameters of a mine depend on the quantity of the particular ore and on the conditions of the deposit; in agriculture we have the role of the natural qualities of the soil, the role of the particular climate, and so forth.

In the third place, the coefficients connected with consumption and with the preferences of the citizens should be referred to the same general group of input information. The organs of planning may affect them as well, as is the case of deviating prices from expenditures in one direction or another, by ideological influences, and so forth. However, after the organs of economic and ideological policies have done what is necessary for such an effect, the plan must give the commodity fund not the structure desired by the organs of planning but the one desired by the purchasers. In this case, too, there are objective coefficients which the organs of planning must ascertain and which are not subject to decrees.

In the fourth place, the composition of the quantities that are objective with regard to the organs of planning must also include the proportion of accumulation-consumption. One of the most characteristic features of a Socialist economy is that this proportion takes shape not in a spontaneous manner, behind the backs of the people, as is the case, generally speaking, with a capitalist economy, but is the direct result of the decisions of the central organs of planning. Consequently, what we are faced with is not an objective fact which merely needs to be established by the organs of planning but rather the subject of a planned target. In this respect, the proportion of accumulation-consumption greatly resembles the other type of quantities which represent the output information. Nevertheless, if we also attribute this proportion to the exogenic factors, it is because the proportion is not determined as a function of the other quantities but rather as a synthesis and reflection of the socio-economic factors and principles of the development of society. What is more, after it has been determined by these principles, the proportion of accumulation-consumption becomes one of the decisive factors determining the numerical values of all planned indices and targets and all decisions adopted by the organs of planning.

These four groups of indices constitute input information with regard to the system of material production.

All remaining indices of the plan belong to the second type of quantities involved in planning. Their characteristic feature is that they are the consequence of the four classes of quantities that are objective in regard to the plan. In the case of these quantities, the task of the planning organs is not one of establishing them in a correct manner but rather of deducing them correctly—that is, of calculating them correctly and then of giving them the form of decisions or, in other words, the form of plan targets.

Let us use an example in differentiating between the two types of quantities. We have a certain existing level of productive forces. On the basis of a socio-political analysis, the planning center establishes the possible and necessary proportion of accumulation-consumption which, all other conditions being equal, determines the general rate of expansion, as well as the fund of consumption within a particular period of time. How many motorcycles will it be necessary to "plan for" in the commodity fund? Under the conditions assumed, this depends not on the desire of the organs of planning but on the preferences of the buyers through which they distribute the purchasing power already established by the conditions referred to. The organs of planning must establish this figure correctly. (The problem of the inverse effect on the structure of demand is different.) Let us assume that the finding is correct. From this point on we have only functionally related quantities. If the number of motorcycles must be X_9, then the amount of shaped steel necessary for them must be $a_{89}X_9$, wherein a_{89} is the expenditure quota. If the amount of shaped steel is $a_{89}X_9$, then the amount of steel necessary must be $a_{78}a_{89}X_9$, wherein a_{78} is the expenditure quota of the steel. If this is the amount of the steel, then the amount of cast iron must be $a_{67}a_{78}a_{89}X_9$, wherein a_{67} is the expenditure quota of the cast iron, and so forth. In this manner we obtain $X_6 = a_{67}a_{78}a_{89}X_9$.

As we see, once it has been decided that the output of motorcycles must be 1000 units, and the quotas of expenditure are given, the production of cast iron, steel, shaped steel, and so forth, is determined. With regard to these items, the problem is one of making the calculation and of releasing the figures obtained as decisions. The implementation of these decisions constitutes the realization of the coordination between the numerous production processes situated at various places. In other words, this is the process of controlling production as a system. The function of the planning organ is not one of command (in the narrow and specific meaning of this word). It means that the planner receives the input information (the technical coefficients of the expenditure of materials, the coefficients of fund consumption, the coefficients of elasticity of demand, the accumulation-consumption proportion, and so on), and [he processes] this information not in any arbitrary manner but on the basis of the functional relations, after which it becomes output information and decisions providing for the new state of the system of production.

With the above example, and stressing the economic content of the control of the system of material production, we define one particular mechanism of control. It is the existence of a center which receives information and, after processing it, makes a decision. In other words, coordination is effected by the expedient activities of a certain group of people. It must be pointed out, however, that this mechanism which is convenient for the purpose of showing the meaning and content of coordination (since the latter stands out in its simplest form) is not the sole possible method of control. Besides that, taken by itself (independent of the other possible mechanisms), the one examined is far more complicated than is apparent from our schematic example. In a purely cybernetic sense, the concept of control of the system is within a very broad framework. It involves only the need of obtaining the information and of processing it. What the course of this process will be is a problem which bears not only on the concept of control in general but on its concrete mechanism. That is why the concept of control, particularly as far as the economy is concerned, includes the mechanism of centralized macro-economic planning (of the above type of schematic example) in addition to all and any mechanisms that have existed or can exist, including the law of value and of the mean profit (the market mechanism) in its "classical" form of the period of free competition. As long as we stand on the plane of general definitions, we are not entitled to identify the control, in the cybernetic sense of this term, with one manner or another of coordinating social production.

At the present stage in the development of social production in Socialist countries, the concept of control in the cybernetic sense of the word acquires a more definite content. It is linked in a most direct manner with a specific form of control—planning—as well as with the problems involved in the coordination of the centralized decision with the decentralized ones of the individual economic units.

The characteristic feature of socialism is that of public ownership—with state ownership playing the decisive part. From the point of view of the problem treated here, this signifies that the "decisions" governing the economy are subject to change, compared with uncontrolled economy, in full correspondence with the change in the nature of ownership. As in the case of every other social system, the owner here makes decisions about the process of production and enjoys its economic results by virtue of his being the owner. The difference being, of course, that the owner in this case is society! In other words, the scale of the decisions by necessity reaches the scale of expanded reproduction as a whole. Planning, or in other words the adoption of decisions on a central scale which is necessary and imperative in the case of the fundamental and most important problems of the very development of the productive forces, proves, under socialism, to be a perfectly natural manifestation of the latter's principal characteristic—public ownership.

In this manner, macro-economic planning as a system of decisions by central organs representing society is a form of control which becomes necessary because of the development of the productive forces, and, along with that, it becomes possible and necessary because of the status of public ownership. However, since this system of decisions is necessary and indispensable for a Socialist economy, for the purpose of perfecting this control it becomes necessary to seek methods which will further improve the system of decisions. Without solving this problem, we cannot hope for improvements in the control of the system of social production, regardless of the other useful and necessary corrections that may be introduced.

The system of centralized decisions about the indices of social production under socialism is necessary, though it is by far not the only form of control. In the first place, the very development of the productive forces which leads to centralized decisions on certain indices does not require and does not admit such decisions on other indices. Local and decentralized decisions adopted according to other indices become both possible and necessary on the basis of the primary tasks and of the basic economic indices. From the point of view of the nature of ownership, decentralized decisions are just as possible as are the centralized ones. They signify the delegation of powers by the owner—society in this case—to one of its organs. One form of such delegation is the status of economic autonomy and the indices of value. Value is abstract social labor. That is why the index of value, precisely by virtue of its abstract character, is the only possible and fully satisfactory form of generalized objective. The sphere of decentralized decisions lies within the framework of the generalized objective. In this manner the very system of value indices determines also the powers that the owner—society—grants to its organs.

The fact that a system of decentralized decisions is set up on the basis of direct centralized decisions tends to complicate the "mechanism" of coordination in social production, or of control in the cybernetic sense of the word. Both experience and theoretical considerations indicate that it is precisely this field which contains the most difficult as well as the most important and decisive problems facing economic cybernetics. How should a centralized decision related to a basic economic index be transformed, from a particular point onward, into thousands and tens of thousands of decentralized decisions insuring in their aggregate the implementation of the principal index? How can thousands upon thousands of initiatives and interests of individual citizens and of separate intermediate groups be synthetized in one centralized decision insuring all the necessary conditions for the realization of these initiatives?

It is obvious that the problem facing economic cybernetics cannot be reduced to the restoration of one of the two basic mechanisms of control—that is, the market mechanism in its classical functions and scope. The problem cannot solely be eliminating the decentralized decisions and in establishing the other mechanism in their stead—the system of centralized decisions—because such an objective is unattainable and unnecessary. In the third place, the problem is not limited to simply leaving both mechanisms to operate: they are operating beside each other and through each other, and, thus, to remain at such a solution means to ignore the unsolved problems presented to us by economic reality. The task, therefore, is sufficiently clear. It becomes increasingly apparent that both mechanisms will be operative in the future as they have been operative up to now. The problem calling for further treatment is the establishment of correct relations between them.

The system of public ownership is a major prerequisite for the establishment of correct relations between centralized and decentralized decisions. It makes it possible—at any moment when this becomes necessary—to vary the scope of centralized decisions, and of decentralized ones respectively, in accordance with the requirements of social production (to entrust the competence of making decisions on a certain index to the suitable organ at the particular state of the productive forces and of the interbranch relations). It hardly needs pointing out that precisely this one condition, decisive to the success of economic cybernetics, is highly encumbered under the conditions of capitalism because of the system of private ownership. And we would like to remark that the scope of ownership is the scope of decisions as well.

From this point onward (after the decisive condition of a social and economic character is at hand), the problem of coordination within the system of production and of correctly coordinating the "mechanisms" of control moves toward an analysis of the quantities subject to planning. The organization of the entire complex apparatus making the decisions, the competence of its units, as well as the relations among the units and their decisions—all that depends on the economic character of the information that is subjected to processing.

We are not in a position to dwell in detail here on each of the four fluxes of input information referred to at the beginning of the paper for the purpose of surveying the particular characteristic indicated. We shall confine ourselves to brief characteristics of two of them: the preferences of the buyers on the one hand and the technico-economic parameters of the concrete industrial processes on the other. The problems presented by both fluxes of input information are essentially different.

The information related to the preferences of the buyers involves a very broad manifestation of the law of value. In the process of trade, the commodities pass from one sphere of ownership—the public one—into a plurality of other spheres of ownership—the private economic units of the citizens. The citizens obtain cash income, the equivalent of abstract labor, and this purchasing power is reconverted into concrete use values with the act of purchase depending on millions of decisions on the part of the buyers. In regard to the input information proper—the preferences of the citizens—there appear no novel problems of principle. The whole problem boils down to precise and prompt establishment of these data, as well as to their prognostication. Of course, the further improvement of planning and of economic cybernetics raises many problems in this field which are complicated by themselves, but their general character is clear.

The situation is different in the case of the other flux of input information—the technico-economic parameters of the individual production processes. This is the field with the most complicated problems, and herein lie the roots of the problem of centralization and decentralization of the decisions involved in the plan.

The technical and economic parameters of the individual production processes are the direct result of scientific and technical research. At a lower level of development of the productive forces and of the technical sciences themselves, creative work in this field usually comes from separate individuals and bears the character of "craftmanship" in the realm of science. A process of rapid concentration and centralization is under way in this area today. The organized efforts of large groups of people armed with powerful equipment in scientific research are needed to design a new type of machine, to synthetize a new material, and so forth. Certain schemes of construction call for such a high concentration of design capacity that it becomes necessary to bring together and organize the efforts of all specialists in a particular field. Such schemes usually focus the entire or almost the entire effort of scientific research and the investment policy of the country on a particular goal. However, no matter how fast these trends may develop, the roots of the technico-economic parameters remain, despite the process of concentration, deep in the initiative of the millions of individual citizens, because they are the ones who convert the design indices into actual indices. Technology thrives and becomes practice through the work and creative effort of the citizens.

In this sense the input information about technico-economic parameters is related to the input information about the preferences of the buyers. This means that the joint data reach the millions of citizens in a Socialist society. The one refers to the individual demands and assessments of these citizens, whereas the other refers, though not entirely, to the creative work and initiative of these same citizens—this time, in their capacities as producers.

In the case of the market mechanism, the route followed in coordinating the proposals of the producers is the same as that followed in coordinating the demand of the buyers. Here are the two aspects of one and the same process. However, under conditions of expanded social production, even on the basis of private ownership, the relations between these two aspects become complicated, and the contradiction connected both with the relations of production and, more deeply, with the factor of time which takes matters out of and above the market, acquires an increasingly higher potential. Under the conditions of public ownership, these relations obtain (cannot help but obtain) a qualitatively new character. The problem is two-fold: it is necessary, on the one hand, to take account of the mass character of the initiative which creates and originates the input information, and to constantly expand the sphere of its operation; on the other hand, it is necessary to further improve the integration of all this initiative, since, without this condition, no initiative, no matter how inspired, can be realized in view of the profoundly social character of production.

Almost every concrete production process entering as an element in the system of social production presents the particularity that it can be realized at various technico-economic parameters depending on the technical variant chosen, particularly depending on the type of technology involved, on the level of mechanization and automation, on the degree of concentration and specialization, on the particular location, and so forth. That is why the first processing to which the input information about the technico-economic parameters is subjected is in the selection of one among the many possible variants. This is the task of optimization. As early as this stage, we are faced with the problem of centralization—namely, at what place, in which organ of the apparatus of control can and should the preliminary selection of the input information about the technico-economic parameters be made?

The selection of the optimum technical variant for each one of the tens of thousands of elementary production processes can be successful only if it is backed by abundant information. This prerequisite is to be found "below" —at the elementary production processes. If we proceed from these considerations, we must conclude that decentralization of choice is the only method of successful optimization. The competence of selection must be entrusted to the organs directly in control of the production processes—the considerations being that it is they and precisely they that can be sufficiently well informed. No matter what channels of further processing may lie ahead for the input information about the technico-economic parameters, it must start along these channels after it has been "screened" at the input points— that is, at the very places of work.

These considerations are true, but it is to be regretted that they far from exhaust the problem under discussion. It is a problem much more complicated than can be perceived at first glance. For instance, suffice it to say that this is the problem of a selection demanding comparison, that it is a matter of distributing funds which, taken in their aggregate, are limited, and that it is a matter in which the optimum solution to one problem leads to a nonoptimum solution of another. In other words, there is a difference between the single optimum and the optimum on a social scale. That is why, the very preliminary screening of the input information brings to the fore the need for coordinating the periphery processing of the initial input information with centralized data. In other words, the organization of selection cannot be detached from the organization of the all-round processing of the input information.

The first task related to the optimization of the input data is comparing the minute with the gross amounts of separate technical characteristics of a particular production process and of reducing them to common quantities which can be subjected to a unified quantitative characteristic. The framework of the present report does not allow for a detailed examination of this problem and for sufficient substantiation of the conclusions reached. We shall proceed mainly from those basic considerations which can be taken as more or less generally accepted.

From an economic point of view, the separate technical solutions of a particular problem of production are specifically related to different expenditures of current labor, to means of production, and to different volumes of the production funds—that is, the value of the means permanently engaged in production in their capacity of investments. Consequently, the task of comparative measurement is to reduce to a certain unified quantity the means expended on production, the current labor spent, and the existing funds.

This operation must be carried out in the first place for the means spent on production and for the amount of live labor. It is not necessary to point out in detail that this purpose is achieved through value. The value constitutes the amount of complete labor expenditures on a given product, expressed in a certain unit of price—that is, in a certain price coefficient. With regard to the expenditure of labor, the prices of the entire mass of separate commodities-products make up a system of interrelated equations, namely:

$$P_j = \sum_{i=1}^{n} a_{ij} P_i + \pounds t_j \qquad (j = 1, 2, \ldots n)$$

wherein P_j is the price of the commodity j; a_{ij} are the expenditure coefficients of commodity i for commodity j; P_i is the price for commodity i; t_j is the amount of live labor spent, and $\pounds$ is the full price equivalent of unit of live labor spent. Consequently, if we have prices expressing precisely the over-all expenditures of labor (prices of the value type), we can consider the problem of comparison and of comparative measurement of the expenditure of live labor and the expenditure of various means of production as solved. The reserves, or production funds, in other words—necessary per unit of production—are means of production which are commodities expressed in prices as well. That is why value is also a measure for the third element of the triple relation. If b_{ij} denotes the amount of a certain use value i which is found as production fund per unit of produce j, then $\sum_{i=1}^{n} b_{ij} P_i$ will denote the entire amount, the over-all mass of production funds expressed in price per unit of produce j. In this manner a unified measure is used to express both the current expenditure of working time and means of production, and the mass of production funds—per unit of produce in either case. Nevertheless, we cannot assume that, on the basis of the prices of the value type, we have reduced to one single quantity all three basic elements that are characteristic of a particular technical solution, since in the case of the current expenditure of working time and means of production, it is a matter of value invested at the particular moment, whereas, in the case of the mass of production funds, it is a matter of value possessing an altogether different circulation. That is why all that we could do at this moment is to record a ratio between the value of the commodity P_j and the production funds engaged in its manufacture f_j; in other words we obtain $P_j : f_j$.

Using this ratio, we can compare the economic characteristic of a particular variant for technical solution with the economic characteristic of another variant for technical solution of the same problem—a variant accepted by us as a basis, as is for instance the case with the machinery and equipment available at a particular basic period. Let us denote the variant proposed by 1 and the basic variant by 0. The variant proposed is distinguished by a larger mass of production funds engaged per unit of produce because, by way of example, it provides for a higher degree of mechanization and automation compared with the basic variant. On the other hand, the variant proposed allows for lower current expenditures per unit of produce. We therefore obtain a ratio between economies in the current expenditures (of live labor and means of production) on the one hand and differential fund-consumption on the other which can be expressed in the following manner:

$$\frac{P^{(0)} - P^{(i)}}{f^{(1)} - f^{(0)}} \gtrless 0 \tag{1}$$

The numerator of the ratio shows the total economies in the current expenditures because the value expresses both the direct expenditures of labor and the indirect ones (through the means of production). The denominator, however, shows the direct fund consumption only. Besides that, production in branch j, which needs means of production from branches i $(i = 1, 2, \ldots n)$ results in the engagement of a definite mass of funds in all these branches. These investments would not have been necessary had it not been for the need of producing our output j. Consequently we have an indirect fund consumption, in addition to the direct one. The sum of the two is called total fund consumption which can be defined by the following system of equations:

$$F_j = \sum_{i=1}^{n} a_{ij}F_i + f_j \qquad\qquad (j = 1, 2, \ldots n)$$

wherein F denotes total fund consumption. That is why the full characteristic of two variants for the production of a given commodity j will be obtained by comparing the economies in the current expenditures with the difference between the total fund consumptions—that is, formula (1) becomes the following type:

$$\frac{P^{(0)} - P^{(i)}}{F^{(i)} - F^{(0)}} \gtrless E \qquad\qquad (2)$$

wherein E denotes a certain ratio (coefficient) taken as criterion. This coefficient will be called normative effectiveness.

In the form shown above, the formula of effectiveness is applicable only to such cases in which variant 1 differs from variant 0 by a lower value and, at the same time, by a higher total fund consumption. The formula is not applicable to instances in which variant 1 differs by a lower value and by a lower fund consumption simultaneously. True enough, in such cases the effectiveness of variant 1 is obvious, and it seems to require no measurement. Despite that, the need for a means of economic characterization of all types of variants remains. In order to turn our formula of effectiveness into an instrument of general characterization of any technical variant, it will be sufficient to carry out a minor algebraic transformation. We obtain:

$$P_j^{(0)} + EF_j^{(0)} \gtrless P_j^{(i)} + EF_j^{(1)} \qquad\qquad (3)$$

$$\frac{P^{(0)} + EF^{(0)}}{P_j^{(1)} + EF_j^{(1)}} = E_j \qquad\qquad (4)$$

The quantity E_j will be called coefficient of the relative effectiveness of product j.

It is obvious that the coefficient of the relative effectiveness fully resembles the comparison of the production prices of the commodity j of two variants. In fact, if instead of the full price P we take the cost, and instead of E we take the rate of profit, we shall simply obtain a ratio between two production prices for the commodity j. It must be pointed out, however, that this semblance is only external. The problem lies not only in that we have cost in the one case and total value in the other—the difference related to this characteristic is not great. A more essential aspect is that the coefficient before the production funds at the production price expresses the rate of profit; whereas, in the formula for the relative effectiveness, E stands for a specific quantity—namely, a ratio between current economies and differential fund consumption which we adopt as a criterion, as a minimum limit (or maximum time pattern) below which (or, in other words, at a longer time pattern) we cannot afford to go at the particular moment.

By its economic character, quantity E differs in principle from the profit. The rate of profit depends on the proportion of the primary distribution, whereas quantity E has very little in common with primary distribution. The proportion of primary distribution depends, on the one hand, on the necessary fund of accumulation with regard to the fund of consumption, and, on the other hand, on the size of consumption financed by the state compared with the consumption paid for by the income of the citizens. Also, normative effectiveness E depends, in addition to the relative share of the fund of accumulation, on the relative effectiveness of the entire mass of technical variants available for comparison. That is why the numerical values of the two quantities E and r (r being the rate of profit) can coincide only as a result of rare coincidence. Besides that, they usually move in opposite directions. Thus the higher the economic effectiveness of the technical designs available, the higher the numerical value of the minimum admissible effectiveness E. At the same time, the high effectiveness of the technical solutions makes it possible to achieve the necessary rates of expansion with smaller capital investments and to keep a higher level of consumption because of which the rate of profit at the primary distribution will be lower. Furthermore, if we increase the unpaid forms of consumption, this will compel us to have a higher rate of profit, without in any way affecting the absolute and relative size of the fund of accumulation, as well as the normative effectiveness E.

It is therefore obvious that the criterion of effectiveness is not the rate of profit but a quantity which is absolutely different. The confusion of these two quantities constitutes, in our opinion, the fundamental deficiency of the proposals for pricing systems of the production price type. The principle objective—that is, to obtain an easy and automatic measure of fund consumption, as well as its comparison with the current economies—is not attained precisely because by its very economic nature the production price cannot be a coefficient of reducing the differential fund consumption to the differential current expenditures. On the contrary, we are in a position to obtain, through the apparatus of relative effectiveness, a unified characteristic of the different variants of solving a particular problem of production. And the apparatus of relative effectiveness is based on the price formation of the value type because it constitutes a condition of expressing, through a unified measure, the current economy and differential total fund consumption, as well as to set up a relation between the two.

The coefficient of relative effectiveness of a particular technical variant with regard to the machines and equipment available, which makes up the zero variant, obviously contains two types of quantities, namely: 1) a series of coefficients which are directly characteristic of the concrete technical design and 2) quantities characteristic of the state of the system of material production as a whole. The means of production invested according to a particular technical design as funds in their natural dimension (the coefficients b_{ij}) the direct expenditures of working time (T_j), and the direct expenditure of the means of production (a_{ij}) are indices of the first type. Full information about these quantities is available at the very design level. As we can see, reference is here made to the quantities which were characterized as input information. The prices of the means of production invested as production funds, the prices of the means of production spent as current expenditures, as well as the coefficient of normative effectiveness E are quantities which do not depend on the concrete technical design. They reflect the state of the system of material production at a particular moment —that is, they are information moving in an opposite direction from the center to the periphery.

Consequently, the characteristic which the coefficient of relative effectiveness yields to a particular concrete draft fully corresponds to the conditions of principle about the unity of the input and output information characterized above. If we imagine that at a given moment we know the precise values of the coefficients which are expressive of the state of the system of production, and with these coefficients we determine the relative effectiveness on the spot and for each single production design, this will mean that the conditions are at hand for a preliminary screening of the input information at the enterprises, before it has entered the channels of the system in order to be subjected to processing; in other words, the conditions for evaluating the elementary technical parameters on the background of the state of the system are at hand. These particularities of the apparatus of optimization make it possible to decentralize the preliminary economic evaluation of each individual technical proposal, without this decentralization implying any detachment from the information about the state of the system. On the contrary, the economic characteristic made with such an apparatus is a perfect unity between concrete input information and social criteria.

The draft for the production program of a given branch is obtained as the sum of the proposals by the enterprises making up this branch. The preliminary optimization of the draft program for the branch is an arrangement of the drafts of the separate enterprises whereby the proposals "from below" fill the necessary volume for the branch according to the draft program, provided there is not one single proposal among the unaccepted ones coming from the enterprises for increasing the output which has a higher relative effectiveness than any accepted proposal. In other words, the volume necessary for the branch according to the draft program is filled by the most effective among the proposals of the enterprises. Of course, the reservation must be made that in many cases it may be possible and necessary to abandon a more effective proposal in favor of a less effective one, provided certain considerations of extra-economic nature become involved. In this case, however, we actually have no choice between variants because by virtue of extra-economic considerations we have no right to neglect a certain less effective variant and to adopt a more effective one. That is why, when we speak of optimization, we assume that there exists no extra-economic consideration that could be opposed to the variants selected because of their effectiveness, and vice versa—no such consideration could be adduced in favor of any of the noneffective variants rejected.

From this aggregate of proposals by the individual enterprises—proposals included in the draft for the branch—it is sufficient to take out and find the averages of the coefficients of the expenditure of materials a_{ij}, of new capital investments necessary b_{ij}, and of the manpower necessary t_j, in order to obtain the necessary branch coefficients. The branch coefficients obtained in this manner will comply with the condition of being the result of a preliminary optimization. These branch coefficients are average annual values; consequently, they are constant within the framework of the year. Using them, we are in a position to solve the system of differential equations describing the expanded reproduction, namely:

$$x_i = \sum_j^n a_{ij}x_j + \sum_i^n b_{ij}x_j + y_i \qquad (i = 1, 2, \ldots n)$$

and to obtain the values of the unknown quantities x_i, that is to say, the necessary production program of the separate branches.

The solution can be examined at this stage merely as a preliminary and provisional result. As already pointed out, the coefficients a_{ij}, b_{ij}, and t_j are obtained as average quantities drawn up on the basis of an assumed branch volume of the production program. The solution may indicate another branch volume—that is, another numerical value of x_j at which the branch coefficients, as averaged values, cannot be the same. Further on, in the composition of x_1, x_2 . . . x_n, there may appear values which are technically impossible because there are no conditions prepared for them (for example, there is not a sufficient amount of established reserves of mineral raw materials, not enough incompleted building projects, and so forth). In the third place, the numerical values obtained for x_1, x_2, . . . x_n may be technically possible but at the price of a certain deviation for the order established in the optimization of the input information—that is, only under the condition that the number of drafts included in the branch will also contain such as are contradictory to the normative effectiveness given.

Still more complicated incongruities will be obtained if in the course of the general solution of the system we find more than one positive root of the characteristic equation. This will directly lead to the dissolution of the system. We are not in a position to engage, at this point, in a detailed investigation of the economic basis of such a dissolution. Nevertheless, the superfluous positive roots may, though in a most general manner, be interpreted economically to the effect that the basic structure of the production capacities does not permit such a sharp reconstruction of the proportions within the period planned as is required and imperative in view of the new machinery and equipment represented by the new coefficients a_{ij}, b_{ij}, and t_j.

All this indicates that the first solution of the system of differential equations which gives us the numerical values of the production programs of the branches x_1; x_2; . . . x_n as a passive result of the given input information, though optimized in advance, can be of experimental significance only. The incongruities from the categories referred to are in this sense an exceptionally rich source of information because they show what is possible and what is not possible as a direct result of the initial input information, such as it actually is. In other words, it is not always possible to adopt the proposals coming from the periphery and to integrate them in social economy, even when they have been optimized in advance with the elementary apparatus referred to above.

The adaption of the existing structure of production capacities to the structure of production which becomes necessary with the new technology introduced, or—let us take the mathematical expression of this economic process—the elimination of the roots of the characteristic equation which lead the system to dissolution, constitutes a specific process of secondary optimization, this time from the center to the periphery. Of particular significance in this optimization is the utilization of spare capacities, provided such are available, or the preservation, by way of reserve, of part of the existing capacities which would have proved superfluous.

Under conditions of impossible values for certain of the unknowns x_1, x_2, ... x_n or of such values as do not correspond to the effectiveness given, the problem is reduced to finding an apparatus of receding from the necessary though impossible numerical values at the price of the smallest losses. If the production program of a particular branch, x_j for instance, must reach an impossibly high numerical significance during the subsequent planned period, this is because its produce has proved highly effective. The highly effective variants of the branches—consumers of this produce—included in the list of adopted drafts, have resulted in a high demand of produce j. Obviously, to reduce the value of x_j to the possible level means depriving some of the users of the needed produce—that is, it means a certain recession from their optimum variant. In this case, we are faced with a problem of secondary optimization on the basis of information ensuing from the system already solved (on the basis of output information expressing the state of the system). The best apparatus of this reaction from the center to the periphery is the deviation of the prices from the values in a direction, and size, corresponding to the deficit or surplus shown by the experimental solution for the particular type of produce.

The results obtained from the experimental solution with regard to the labor resources necessary are of a particular character. The system of differential equations, solved on the basis of the coefficients given, may show a greater need for labor power than are the resources available. This result will signify that the scale of intensive expansion (of expansion through the increase of labor productivity) is—at the coefficients given—smaller than required by the system. Such is the diagnosis rendered by the input information processed into output information. If labor resources cannot be increased, a solution of the problem may be sought in changing the technical coefficients, particularly in further economies in direct and indirect labor expenditures per unit of produce.

In what manner is it possible to obtain this correction? The question again leads us to the technical variants. Among the variants diverted, there are those which provide an additional reduction of the direct and indirect labor expenditures—for instance, by further mechanization and automation. If at the particular moment these variants have proved outside the set of the accepted drafts, this is because very large capital investments have proved to be necessary in order to obtain these economies. Multiplied by the coefficient of normative effectiveness, these supplementary capital investments have shown a negative result (proved to be "noneffective"). Obviously, if the coefficient of normative effectiveness E had a lower numerical value, the differential capital investments for technical reconstruction would have likewise belonged to the effective ones. That is why, after the experimental solution had led us to the conclusion that the economies in labor have proved insufficient and that a further rise in labor productivity is necessary, it is possible to obtain balancing by reducing the numerical value of the coefficient of normative effectiveness. The result of this decrease will be an increase in the average branch coefficients of fund consumption and a decrease in the average branch coefficients of the direct and indirect labor expenditures. The former process will lead to a delay in the general rates of expansion because with the new coefficient of normative effectiveness, part of the capital investments will have to go for technical reconstruction, whereas the latter process will lead to reducing the needs of additional labor —until the necessary equilibrium is reached.

In this manner we also obtain a determination of the numerical value of the coefficient of normative effectiveness E. Objectively correct is that numerical value of the coefficient at which a balance is obtained between the needs for and the resources of labor power at a given proportion of accumulation-consumption.

We see that the results of the experimental solution provide us with abundant information about the quantities with which the system must react to the information and affect it as well. The drafting of the plan proves the result of a current and continuous exchange of input and output information within the system of material production.

When we have a single drafting of a plan for one or more forthcoming periods, the solution of the problem appears as a reiterated undulatory movement of such information from the periphery to the center and from the center to the periphery. In point of fact, such an undulatory movement of repeated corrections is a most ordinary fact under current practices of planning which make use of far simpler means. However, if we ensue from another concept of planning—namely, from the concept of planning as an uninterruped process—then also the exchange of information from the periphery to the center and from the center to the periphery stands out in a much more normal light. If at a given moment we possess balanced numerical values of the separate plan quantities, this signifies that we also possess precise data for the prices, as well as a correct numerical value of the coefficient of normative effectiveness E. Let us assume that there are certain changes occurring in the field of technology which the input information from the periphery immediately sends along centripetal channels. The integration of this information takes place on the basis of the quantities available which are characteristic of the system and reflect its state with precision—since we have assumed that there exists a balanced plan at the moment. Under this condition, the input information is rapidly integrated in the system. Of course, it will have an inverse effect on the numerical value of the prices and on the coefficient of normative effectiveness. However, if there is an immediate reaction to each change from without, and not once in three months, once a year, or once in a number of years, then the changes evoked by it also will be relatively small, and we shall not obtain a high-crested wave. On the other hand, such a current maintenance of a current plan will also imply a current and relatively easy adaptation of the information on the state of the system to the changes coming from the periphery.

The description of macro-economic planning by means of mathematical terms seems to be a very bold undertaking at first glance. All these coefficients, systems of algebraic and differential equations, input and output information, dynamic equilibrium, and so forth, bring about too much theory which creates a certain suspicion as to the practical applicability of such mathematical models. What then is the practical significance of this trend of elaborating on the particular problems?

Despite the risk of being considered rude, we would like to use the comparison of Monsieur Jourdain, the familiar hero of Molière. When he began taking lessons in literature, he found, to his great surprise, that he had been talking prose all his life. There is something similar in the traditional method of planning. When the prices are being established in practice, we never think of any systems of equations. Despite that, the establishment of prices in practice implies—though we may not even suspect it—precisely the solution of an enormous system of equations, because the price of coal is dependent on the price of power, while the price of power depends on the price of coal, and so forth. Therefore, if it is a matter of suspicion of the mathematical form, it is obvious that in actual practice we are not "innocent" enough to be entitled to excessive skepticism. The simple fact is that we are dealing, without even realizing it, with systems of equations and are solving them with a high degree of inaccuracy. The problem is one of substituting inaccurate decisions with accurate ones. Accepting one proposal "from below" and rejecting another one, we are in practice comparing two variants, and in this comparison we take careful account of comparative fund consumption, of the amount of the fund of capital investments available, and of the necessary general rates. In this manner, without even being interested in cybernetics and in its terminology, we are in point of fact faced by an instance of repeated exchange of information "from below" toward the center and from the center to the individual projects. The difference is that this exchange is not sufficiently organized; the center interferes too much with the competence of the organs drafting the individual projects; these organs in their turn do not possess regular and well-organized information from the center on the basis of which to find their bearings properly, and in either sphere the information itself is not sufficiently accurate.

Chapter 26

MATHEMATICAL METHODS AND THE USE OF COMPUTERS FOR PLANNING IN THE UNITED STATES[1]

CLOPPER ALMON

University of Maryland

Of the vast number of enterprises to which this title applies, we can here compare only three closely related models. Each of them was designed for a particular sort of planning, and we shall examine how the differences in purposes brought about differences in structure. In the order of increasing complexity these models are: the interagency growth model, designed for manpower planning and the analysis of other government, long-range policies; a consistent forecasting model designed for long-range business planning; and the PARM model, designed for planning recovery from a nuclear attack.

All these models concern the entire economy, involve structural changes rather than cyclical ones, and use input-output tables. Two were built primarily for government planning, one for business planning. For lack of space and lack of competence, I must omit the many interesting planning models concerned with a single product, firm, or region, as well as the numerous annual and quarterly "econometric" models such as the Brookings-

[1] References are: C. Almon, *The American Economy to 1975, an Interindustry Forecast* (New York: Harper & Row, 1966); Marshall K. Wood, "PARM—An Economic Programming Model," *Management Science*, May 1965, pp. 619–680.

SSRC model which, however, has been frequently described at international conferences.

Naturally, we cannot consider total aspects of even three models, but shall concentrate on the basic questions—what makes them go, how are they guided, and how they are used. Perhaps the most striking feature common to them all is that, despite their many simultaneous equations, none of them has that basic simultaneousness which we stress in macro-economics—namely, the simultaneous determination of income and expenditure. This link between income and expenditure, the soul of many short-range forecasting models, has been severed in all three planning models. They work from final demand back to production and employment, but have no feedback from employment and income to consumption. Implicitly or explicitly, it is recognized that taxation or (in the PARM case) stronger means can be used to alter the relation between income and spending.

A model with a fixed relation between income and consumption is like a sailboat with its rudder in a fixed position. The course it will follow can be calculated mechanically, but it is not likely to go where anybody wants to go. Our three models all resemble boats being guided to a desired point. In the interagency model, we are supplied with a chart showing where the boat will be in 1970 and a snapshot of it at that time. It is not, however, really sailing, but is being tugged along by a tiny boat on the other side, so we cannot be sure which way it is actually going. The second model shows the course of its boat ever since it left the mouth of the harbor. It travels under its own sails, and the 1975 picture therefore shows the direction. The only detail lacking is how it got out of the harbor.

The PARM model concerns itself with getting off the mud and out of the harbor. It tells how to set the rudder and the sails, whereas the other two give only the destination or the course, not the sailing instructions.

The interagency growth model comes first, not only because of its relative simplicity, but also because the other two have borrowed from the data it has generated. As its name implies, it is the joint product of several government agencies. The Department of Commerce Office of Business Economics provides the input-output table and some of the foreign trade projections; the Department of Agriculture and the Bureau of Mines contribute in the areas of their expertise; work on consumption and technological change has been contracted to universities; and the Bureau of Labor Statistics (BLS) provides projections of the labor force, of labor productivity, and of the skill composition of employment in the several industries. To the BLS also falls the job of putting together the pieces.

In its workings, the model begins, as do several similar European models, with an aggregate projection (the motorboat of our metaphor); the projection of the labor force is multiplied by a projection of Gross National Product (GNP) per worker to obtain a projection of GNP in the target year, 1970 or 1975. This GNP forecast is then divided into its principal end uses —consumption, investment, government spending—under alternative assumptions about the share of investment. The function of the rest of the model is to divide up these components among the industries, work back to industry outputs, and from them derive the manpower requirements implied by the aggregate forecast. The total growth in consumption is fed through a set of functions to determine consumer demands in the target year for the products of each of the 80 sectors of the input-output table. Government expenditure is split up by function, and the spending by each function is distributed among the various producing industries. Exports and imports are handled similarly. Finally, the assumed total private investment is distributed in an informal manner among the buying industries and then among the producing industries according to the spending patterns of the buying industries. The vector of total final demands found in this way is multiplied by the inverse of the matrix of input-output coefficients projected to the target year. The resulting vector of outputs of each industry is then converted to manpower demands. The employment in various trade and skill categories becomes part of the background for the occupational handbook and other guidance material prepared by the Bureau of Labor Statistics. Other uses in evaluating various policies are anticipated.

The present version of the interagency model does not connect investment with the rate of growth of various industries. The size of GNP and its division among its major components is not determined by the model, but is fed into it. In terms of employment, business-fixed investment is not really very important; and this possibility for inconsistency within the model need not prove embarrassing. It may, indeed, claim the virtue of flexibility; many different possibilities can be readily examined.

In a model meant for business planning, however, investment is far more crucial; because firms interested in other industries' sales—and, therefore, in an interindustry forecast—are chiefly in either the capital goods industries themselves or in the materials industries for which the capital goods industries are major customers. For business forecasting, therefore, simple alternative assumptions about the share of investment in GNP must be replaced by a connection between growth and investment, industry by industry.

Moreover, since the rate of growth in a future year may differ from the average growth between now and then, forecasts must be made for a number of intervening years—not just a single target year. The business forecasting model produced by the author incorporates both these features. Also, rather than relying on an aggregate model for aggregate projections, it produces the aggregate projections as by-product of the detailed projections. It uses much the same input-output table and labor force projections. The consumption functions and labor productivity projections are different but play the same role in the model.

The logic of this model is almost as simple as that of the interagency model but does appear to contain a worthwhile innovation. Instead of starting with a fixed GNP in the final year and trying to divide it up, it starts with only the time paths of government demands, exports and consumption. From these, it generates the investment they require. This investment is then added to the other final demands to yield the GNP forecast. The product-by-product detail of these final demands is worked back through the input-output matrix—projected forward to the year in question—and the industry outputs and employment are found. If the implied total employment is too high relative to the labor force, the assumed growth in consumption is reduced, and vice versa. In the end, the model finds mutually consistent full-employment growth paths for the output, investment, and employment in each industry. Gross National Product, the last thing to be calculated, becomes a by-product instead of a primary input.

This summary of the working of the model glossed over the technically interesting question of how outputs and investments are simultaneously determined. If we have investment, we can calculate output, as just described. Conversely, if we have the course of output for an industry, we can find the expansion investment it requires from capital-output ratios. To this expansion investment, replacements estimated on the basis of past investment and life patterns are added to obtain total investment by industry. Investment implies output, and output implies investment. An iterative procedure is clearly needed. We start by postulating a course of outputs and calculating the investment they imply. This investment is added to other final demands, and the vector total for each year is worked back through that year's input-output matrix to find the outputs. These outputs are then compared with those assumed in the calculation of investment. If there is any appreciable difference, the newly calculated outputs are used as the assumed outputs in a repetition of the entire calculation.

More than a single repetition was seldom necessary to achieve agreement between the assumed and the implied output series. When agreement was reached, employment was calculated and compared to the labor force.

One of the business planning uses of this model involved a large manufacturer who wished to diversify by merger. About a hundred companies had been proposed as possibilities for merger, and proponents of various ones argued that their candidates had particularly good growth prospects. To evaluate the growth potential of the market position of each one of them, estimates were made of the share of each of its product lines in its present sales. Each product line was then assumed to grow at the same rate as one of the following: (a) a particular cell of the interindustry matrix (including the cells of the capital matrix), (b) the sum of several cells, (c) an entire industry. This use of a single cell to indicate a growth rate squeezes much greater product detail out of the model than its 90-industry structure appears to have. For example, paper sales to the printing industry are qualitatively different from paper sales to the paper box industry. "Special Industrial Equipment" sold to textile capital investment—textile machinery—consists of different machines from the same "industry's" sales to automobile capital investment (mostly foundry equipment). Even so, it was felt that the 90-order table caused problems by aggregating activities which are not "in the same line of business." Most of these difficulties, however, could be overcome by a table of about 200 sectors.

These evaluations of the companies against a common background proved useful not only because of the ranking they provided but also as a background against which to discuss particular companies. "So you think the model underrates Company A. In what product line? Why do you think the model does not give a representative growth rate?" and so on. The decisions reached by this method might, by chance, have been reached in other ways. To the management of the company, however, it was worthwhile to know that many alternatives had been carefully compared.

Other business applications in expansion planning, research planning, and regional or locational planning are developing at present.

PARM now stands for *Program Analysis for Resource Management;* but beneath this smooth title, we recognize the stern countenance of the Post-Attack Recovery and Mobilization model. The model is designed to serve in three capacities: first, as a training aid to let post-attack planners practice solving some of the problems with which they would be faced after a nuclear attack; second, as an analytical tool for evaluating various recovery strategies under a variety of post-attack conditions; and third, as an aid in planning if a post-attack situation should ever occur. I should like to add a fourth function, to serve as a raincoat which—as everyone knows—prevents rain better than it keeps one dry once the rain starts.

We can, however, view the PARM model in another role. Its builder, Marshall Wood, has often emphasized that it deals with the same kind of problems that countries face when starting a development program from a small industrial base, for PARM takes the matters of capacity, timing, and substitution very seriously. This emphasis shows up clearly when PARM is compared to the business forecasting model, which assumes that capacity is always flexible enough to meet the desired output. In the forecasting model, investment rises in response to increases in output, but does not have to precede those increases. Since the model starts with present consumption, the consumer goods industries generally have the necessary initial capacity; only the investment goods industries may have discontinuities in their outputs at the beginning of the forecasts and hence the need for more capacity. The discontinuities which have been found in actual practice, however, are well within the range of variation to which these machinery industries are accustomed. For forecasting in the context of present American industry, therefore, the precise capacity constraints do not seem necessary, and neither, therefore, do precise timing constraints.

In a post-attack situation or a rapid development program, on the other hand, we do not start with a going concern which we merely wish to expand at a normal rate. Instead, demands and capacities may be far out of line with one another. All sorts of make-do arrangements, substitutions, and conversions will be called for. Timing becomes crucial, for delays in deliveries can be crippling if not fatal. The problems of making a model to reflect and cope with such a world involve far more complexities than does building a forecasting model. PARM offers many insights into the way such a system can be constructed. To me, its most interesting feature is the *sequence* of the calculations.

PARM begins from damage assessments and determines the initial stock of capacities in various states of usability—usable, contaminated, lightly damaged, heavily damaged, and so on. A trial course of various categories of consumption expenditures is then stipulated by the operator for 24 consecutive periods. The task of the system is then to find a feasible way to meet these requirements. It takes up the industries in triangular order—bread before flour—and makes a complete production and investment plan for one industry for the entire twenty-four periods before going on to the next industry. The process, however, is iterative, and, after the first round, the demands of all industries for each product are considered. We may take, for example, coal mining. Given the production of all other industries in all periods, the model makes a table showing the requirements, production, and capacity of coal mining in each of 24 planning periods. In determining requirements, time-lags play an important role; electrical generation in March may require coal mining in January and transportation in February. The model then looks for ways to make cumulative production plus initial stocks as large as cumulative requirements in each period. Second, it tries to find ways to keep capacity up to production. In its search for capacity, the model has a list of priorities. It will first look for usable capacity; if that is insufficient, it may turn next to decontamination of capacity, then to repair of lightly damaged capacity, then to conversion of capacity from another industry with an excess, then to repair of heavily damaged capacity from another industry with an excess, then to repair of heavily damaged capacity, and finally, to building new capacity, if no other sources are available. (The order of priorities is different in different industries.) Of course, there are time-lags between the beginning of a project to augment capacity and its completion, and the model may be unable to find a way to meet the requirements. It will then try to transfer the deficit to other industries with products which can substitute for the one in question. If deficit transfer is not possible, the model will leave the deficit or shift it forward (give late delivery) and go on to other products. The deficit will, of course, be brought to the attention of the operator of the model, who can then change his stipulations in hopes of finding a feasible program. He may also directly stipulate production floors or ceilings or particular capacity augmentation programs. Once feasibility is found, of course, he can try more demanding stipulations in hopes of improving the program. By considering one industry at a time for all periods rather than all industries at once for a single period (as in the forecasting model), the PARM program is able to exercise considerable ingenuity in finding feasible solutions. This sequence of calculations should be noted by other model builders.

We have several times mentioned the changing stipulations by the operator as if he were an integral part of the PARM system, and indeed he is. For PARM is designed as a system of man-machine iteration. An objection may be that this recourse to the operator in the search for feasibility and optimality is quite unnecessary. Linear, or, in this case, nonlinear programming, could be relied upon to do the whole job at once. In reply, however, it must be pointed out that the computations required would be enormous in comparison with one machine-round in the present man-machine iteration. And this machine iteration already requires some eight to ten hours on a large computer.[2] Most users of computers have noticed that any computing requires considerable man-machine iteration. The first "optimal" answers we get usually reveal only some defect in the model. If we put the entire PARM problem into a vast optimizing program and computed away for a week or so, we would probably find upon examination that something had been overlooked in the formulation of the problem which makes the answers unusable. PARM would probably have found the difficulty long before. Moreover, the operators will want to try various assumptions, even if they know optimal answers for one set of assumptions. PARM is built around such variations. It puts all the levers for trying alternative policies at the operator's fingertips. It is, in short, built to use a computer the way people use computers: try and try again. I expect that this mode of operation, rather than over-all optimization, is going to be necessary for dealing effectively with economic problems of the size and complexity of those faced by PARM. It is less glamorous than over-all optimization, but it is more human.

In summary, this model represents an impressive achievement. It is certainly to be hoped that its builders will succeed in their desires to convert PARM into a tool for studying the impact of various government programs under normal conditions or for assisting in the design of development programs for less industrial countries. Their basic research into capital requirements for expansion points in this direction.

Although there remains plenty of room for refinement and expansion of planning models, it is my own feeling that the basic lines are clear and agreed upon.[3] The real excitement of the next decade is going to come in the applications. While working on the over-all forecasting model, we struggle with the same problems year after year, but each application brings a new challenge. Before we could have any application, we had to have something to apply. Now that we do, an exciting variety of inquiries is pouring in. The demands made by applications make several future developments predictable. There will be more detailed input-output tables available more promptly. There will be models with regional detail as well as industry detail. National forecasts will go into data banks for market research. One such bank has already been announced by IBM; originally,

[2] By comparison, the forecasting model requires about two minutes for a fifteen-year forecast and would require about ten or fifteen minutes if it had an input-output table as large as the 331-industry one used by PARM. This comparison is probably a fairly good measure of the relative complexity of the two programs.

[3] An exception must be made for multiregional models, a field in which there is as yet no danger of dizziness from success.

it is to contain a current input-output table and the Dun and Bradstreet information on the sales pattern of individual firms. It is natural to expect that it will grow in the direction of forecasts as well as present data.

Amid all this proliferation of computerization, however, it is curious and comforting to note a slight inaccuracy in the title of this paper. It speaks of "mathematical methods," but none of the methods discussed uses any mathematics worthy of the name. A more appropriate title might have been "Common-Sense Methods for the Use of Computers in Planning," but who would read a paper with so unfashionable a title? Yet, as I have said, it is the common-sense methods, rather than the elaborate optimization methods, which seem to have a real future in practical applications for national planning. Indeed, common sense may even be staging a come-back today, though only by wearing the Greek mask of "heuristic methods."

Chapter 27

COST-BENEFIT
ANALYSIS AND
ITS APPLICABILITY

ROLAND N. McKEAN
University of California at Los Angeles

In this paper I shall present a brief survey of the nature, shortcomings, and applicability of cost-benefit analysis.[1] Basically, this form of analysis is research intended to provide information about the costs entailed by, and the benefits provided by, alternative courses of action. The reason for providing this information, of course, is to help decision-makers reach better choices. Such activity could be, and often is, called "economic analysis," because from the standpoint of any decision-making unit, it is economical to undertake whatever incremental actions yield greater gains than costs. For example, if a business firm seeks to maximize its wealth, it will compare alternative output programs and expand output as long as marginal gain exceeds marginal cost—that is, it will choose the output that yields the maximum excess of benefits over costs. Like the underlying analysis of the business firm, cost-benefit analysis sometimes compares a continuous spectrum of alternatives, particularly when linear programming techniques are applicable, and seeks to identify the optimum (defined in a particular man-

---

[1] For more detail, see especially A. R. Prest and R. Turvey, "Cost-Benefit Analysis: A Survey," *The Economic Journal*, December 1965, and the bibliography at the end of the article, which cites much of the rather extensive literature that has now developed on this subject.

ner). More frequently, cost-benefit analysis compares a small number of discrete alternatives, such as several specific irrigation projects, and seeks to provide useful information about their consequences.

Examples of cost-benefit analyses include comparisons of alternative urban transportation systems, proposals for utilizing or expanding water supplies, projects producing electric power and flood control, steps to reduce the incidence of tuberculosis, and ways of using school facilities.[2] In the United States, interest in cost-benefit analysis soared with the issuance of an important Bureau of the Budget Bulletin in the autumn of 1965.[3] It directed the eleven federal departments and also eleven special agencies to use such analyses in reaching allocative decisions (as a part of revised budgeting procedures) and urged the other agencies to apply these procedures "to the extent practical." The resulting activity in the federal government has brought increased interest in cost-benefit analysis within universities and proposals to train additional cost-benefit analysts.[4]

Major virtues. The major virtue of cost-benefit analysis is not that it points unambiguously to the correct choice, for in fact it can rarely do this. As will be discussed in the next section, neither chemical analysis nor economic analysis can show what ought to be done. The principal virtue of cost-benefit analysis is simply that it is the right way to look at problems of choice. The central idea is to compare alternatives rather than to advocate some unique requirement or need regardless of the sacrifice entailed. Even by itself this is a significant step forward, because most of us are strongly tempted to distill from our good intentions a belief in unique needs. For instance, if the rat population in a city is such that occupants of houses en-

[2] A small sample of the U.S. literature is: Robert Dorfman, ed., *Measuring Benefits of Government Investments* (Washington: Brookings Institute, 1965); Otto Eckstein, *Water-Resource Development* (Cambridge, Mass.: Harvard University Press, 1958); Jack Hirshleifer, James C. DeHaven, and Jerome W. Milliman, *Water Supply: Economics, Technology, and Policy* (Chicago: University of Chicago Press, 1960); and some items that were not included in the Prest-Turvey bibliography are: Joseph A. Kershaw and Roland N. McKean, *Systems Analysis and Education*, The RAND Corporation, RM-2473-FF, October 1959; Joseph A. Kershaw and Roland N. McKean, *Teacher Shortages and Salary Schedules* (New York: McGraw-Hill Book Company, 1962); Herbert E. Klarman, *The Economics of Health* (New York: Columbia University Press, 1965); Julius Margolis, ed., *The Public Economy of Urban Communities*, Resources for M. Wohl, *The Urban Transportation Problem* (Cambridge, Mass.: Harvard University Press, 1965); Jerome Rothenberg, *Economic Evaluation of Urban Renewal* (forthcoming); Howard G. Schaller, *Public Expenditure Decisions in the Urban Community* (Washington: Resources for the Future, Inc., 1963); Henry Steele, "The Prospects for the Development of a Shale Oil Industry," *Western Economic Journal*, Fall 1963, pp. 60–82.
[3] Bulletin No. 66–3, October 12, 1965.
[4] It might be noted in passing, however, that cost-benefit analysis is not really a new thing. In the early years of the nineteenth century, Albert Gallatin and others produced some remarkably sophisticated analyses of proposed canals and turnpikes.

counter five rats per month, this is deplorable, and one instinctively feels that this phenomenon must be eliminated. Yet in fact the action one advocates should depend upon its cost, that is, the sacrifice of other goods that would be necessitated, and upon the costs and gains from alternative steps. A host of other possible actions should be considered—perhaps lower standards than complete elimination of the rats (such as reducing the encounters to two rats per month) and higher standards, such as eliminating the rats plus otherwise improving the houses. Almost never are there unique needs; with altered costs or gains, the actions or quantities of items that are needed change. And the use of cost-benefit analysis virtually shouts for one to recognize this.

It is the right way to look at problems of choice regardless of one's values. As I shall mention in a moment, people can legitimately disagree about the values to be attached to various effects of an action but not, I think, about the general principle of weighing gains against costs. Cost-benefit analysis does not imply using a particular set of price tags or looking solely at those effects to which market prices can be attached (that is, to what most people would call "economic effects"). Cost-benefit analysis calls for attention to whatever effects have positive or negative value—whether they are traded in markets or not—and whether they are sociological, psychological, cultural, or ethical in nature. This makes good analysis extremely difficult and frequently inconclusive—but not wrong. This also means that one should take into account the prospective costs and gains of making cost-benefit analyses themselves, and for most day-to-day decisions one makes his choices on the basis of hasty almost subconscious evaluations because taking out pencil and paper is too much trouble.

In more important decisions, another reason that cost-benefit analysis is a useful way to look at problems of choice is that the emphasis on the examination of alternatives often leads to the redesign of the alternatives originally visualized or to the invention of entirely new courses of action. In fact this is sometimes said to be the most important contribution of such an analysis to the improvement of decisions. Finally, although such an analysis cannot indicate the actions that are correct in any fundamental sense, it can provide information that most people would agree is relevant and helpful in making choices. Like consumer research (which provides consumers with information about items that they contemplate purchasing), cost-benefit analysis can describe at least part of the relevant consequences of alternative actions.

The reasons cost-benefit analysis cannot indicate "correct" actions in any ultimate sense. There are many difficulties that limit the applicability of such analysis.[5] Here I wish to focus attention on only two. They are so crucial, however, that either one prevents cost-benefit analysis from identifying the *correct* policies. They represent the same difficulties that prevent any positive science—physics, chemistry, or economic analysis—from being able to show what *ought* to be done.

First of all, the set of relationships that the positive sciences have tested and in which we can have confidence is not complete. One cannot predict even the physical consequences of actions with certainty. There are still areas of doubt in physics and chemistry. The direct and side effects of drugs used to treat tuberculosis, the fertility of various soils when irrigated, the effects of weightlessness on the human body, the implications of automobile travel for smog and noise levels—such physical relationships are still not known with a high degree of confidence. When one turns to the social sciences, ignorance is still more impressive. Hypotheses that have been subjected to satisfactory checks in sociology, economics, psychology, and political science are relatively scarce. There are many untested models but few tested ones. One cannot predict with any assurance the impact of a particular housing program on crime rates or on the "ability to get along together" of a particular educational proposal on juvenile delinquency, of a particular institutional arrangement on the behavior of government officials, or the courts.

As a result, one must make personal judgments about many important consequences of alternative proposals. In preparing or interpreting cost-benefit analyses, individuals can legitimately disagree about the magnitude of such consequences. For this reason alone, cost-benefit analyses—while they can aid an official or any other person in his preference—can rarely point conclusively to the *correct* choice.

Second, there is no ultimately "correct" set of value-tags to be attached to the various consequences. Here one completely departs from the realm of positive science, and, of course, there is no set of value-judgments upon which people are logically compelled to agree. The "difficulty," if it is to be so labelled, is simply that individuals are not alike, and they have different values. Perhaps the best way to emphasize the role of value-judgments in cost-benefit analysis is to discuss the reasons that (1) observed market prices

[5] See, for instance, Prest and Turvey, "Cost-Benefit Analysis: A Survey," or Charles J. Hitch and Roland N. McKean, *The Economics of Defense in the Nuclear Age* (Cambridge, Mass.: Harvard University Press, 1960), pp. 105–218.

are not necessarily "correct," and (2) any alternative set of shadow prices is equally hard to defend.[6]

In cost-benefit analyses, value-judgments are embedded in the measures of benefits and the measures of costs—that is, the alternative benefits foregone. To a considerable extent monetary price tags are attached to the consequences of alternative actions. Ideally, prices reflect the substitution ratios that are appropriate if one is to maximize a particular preference function. In reality, however, prices fall short of being appropriate substitution ratios, and, in effect, when one employs a particular set of prices, he is making a judgment that it is more nearly appropriate than alternative sets. Still more important, the substitution ratios or prices that are appropriate depend upon the preference function to be maximized. Thus when one employs a particular set of prices, he is subscribing to the preference function that is implied. (Alternatively, if an objective is specified in physical terms—for example, to provide medical treatment for persons over sixty-five years of age—and if the cost-benefit analysis seeks the least-cost method of carrying out the designated objective, value-judgments are also implied.)

Assume first of all that we agreed on Pareto optimality as the goal—agreed to seek a situation in which each person was as well off as possible, as *he* perceived *his* well-being, without making anyone else worse off, as *he* saw *his* well-being. For a particular initial distribution of wealth, this goal would imply a particular set of prices, and these would be appropriate measures of the values of inputs, intermediate outputs, and end items. For appraising alternative future actions, however, observed prices would fall well short of the ideal set. Some current prices would no doubt be above marginal cost, casting doubt on just what the appropriate substitution ratios should be in seeking "second-best." Some artificial constraints on entry by new firms or workers and on exchange among persons or nations would exist, and there would be questions about whether or not those constraints should be expected to continue indefinitely.

Perhaps even more important, observed *current* prices are by no means perfect substitution ratios for the *future* time-periods to which cost-benefit analyses pertain. Supply and demand conditions are always changing, and if the cost-benefit analyst uses current prices, he is again simply making a judgment that these prices, though imperfect, are better than the practicable alternatives. Finally, observed prices do not reflect the so-called "external effects" of various commodities and production processes—that is,

[6] Roland N. McKean, "The Use of Shadow Prices in Evaluating Federal Expenditure Programs," presented at Brookings Institute Conference, September 1966.

those benefits bestowed or costs inflicted without passing through a market and therefore without having price tags attached to them. Since these effects— for instance, reductions in air pollution—are not marketed, the marginal evaluations of different individuals are not brought into equivalence, and one man's price tag here need have little relationship to another man's price tag.

Next, however, assume that we do *not* agree on Pareto optimality as the goal. Legitimate disagreements about values can then multiply endlessly. And, needless to say, logic does not compel one to accept Pareto optimality as the aim. There is nothing illogical about my *not* wanting individual X to maximize his utility as *he* sees it. I may feel that his consumption of calories or of nightclub entertainment is immoral or unwise. I may wish to take actions or have actions taken without buying the consent of individuals who find these actions objectionable. Indeed all of us demonstrate through our behavior at the polls or in political processes that we do not gladly embrace Pareto optimality as our criterion.

In actuality any government is guided by a complex mixture of rules, constraints, and discretionary authority. There is enormous uncertainty about the preference function that is implied by any such decision-making process. It is certainly not Pareto optimality in its conventional sense that is sought, for the policies will include restrictions on voluntary exchange, deliberate efforts to develop one region at the expense of others, attempts to promote growth more than voluntary decisions would promote it, and so on. All we can feel fairly sure of is that the preferences which are implied make the values and substitution ratios embedded in observed prices somewhat inappropriate for cost-benefit analyses. For instance, if governing officials attach a high value to growth, it presumably means that the price of steel facilities, one form of investment, should rise relative to the price of bowling alleys, another form of investment.

Recognition of the shortcomings of observed prices, however, does not mean that one can derive a more nearly appropriate set of prices. Even with specified preference functions in *relatively simple situations,* finding imputed or "shadow" prices is a difficult task. But without agreement on a preference function, it is impossible to derive an appropriate set of shadow prices. Basically, then, personal value-judgments must be introduced in order to estimate costs and benefits, yet there is no compelling reason for different persons to agree on those values. In summary, cost-benefit analysis cannot point to correct choices in any ultimate sense because people can legitimately disagree about (1) many of the physical and social consequences of alternative actions, and (2) the value-tags that should be attached to those consequences.

Applicability of cost-benefit analysis. Fortunately, economic analysis—like chemistry and medicine—can still serve us well, particularly if we keep in mind the basic limitations noted. Tools do not have to be perfect in order to be helpful. Even a bent rake that reveals nothing about the ultimate value of cultivation can be of great assistance in caring for a garden.

Cost-benefit analysis can be especially helpful in connection with choices that pose relatively minor difficulties of the sort described. That is, cost-benefit analysis can often be applied to choices in connection with which (1) most people do agree on values, and (2) most physical and social consequences of the alternatives considered can be predicted with some confidence. People often agree on values at least in the sense of agreeing to delegate authority or accept a certain decision-making process. Then that process may lead to a decision to carry out a specified task—for example, to provide more water (or an improved allocation of water) in a particular region. Implicitly, voters or at least the governmental leaders to whom authority has been delegated decide that this task is of greater value than alternative tasks. They may also implicitly condone the use of observed prices (or in some instances of imputed prices) as value-tags in tracing out the costs and benefits of alternative ways of carrying out the task. Most individuals accept the situation (at minimum in the sense that they do not find it worthwhile to object). In other words, on certain issues there may in effect exist a working agreement regarding the relevant preferences. There need be nothing illogical about dissenting, and one should not lose sight of the fact that value-judgments are being made, but fortunately there is at times substantial agreement.

Moreover, the alternatives may be ones for which the positive sciences can trace out the major physical and behavioral consequences with a high degree of confidence. In the provision of water to a region, physical scientists may be able to predict rather well what would happen if alternative dams or alternative desalinization plants were constructed, if water were conveyed to the fields by alternative canal systems or alternative underground aquifers and pumping systems, if the water was then applied to various acreages in alternative quantities. Economists may be able to say what would happen if water supplies were reallocated by charging alternative prices to users and to say how individuals would respond to alternative price structures and to consequent agricultural development of the region. Sociologists may be able to predict the effects (perhaps trivial in this instance) of the relocation of families and industries on crime, mental health, and juvenile delinquency. Needless to say, these and the predictions of other sciences would not be completely accurate. Dissent on the basis of one's personal judgments about these things need not be illogical, since the positive sciences still contain many gaps. But again, for some sets of alternatives there may be substantial agreement.

In general, although it is a very loose classification, the broader choices made by higher-level officials pose relatively great difficulties regarding what value-judgments should be made and what the physical and social consequences of alternative actions would be. Consider, for example, the allocation of the U.S. Budget among various departments or ministries or the allocation of funds among such missions as health, education, or better postal service. For making such choices, cost-benefit analysis gives relatively little guidance, for in the end the decision-maker's task is dominated by difficult personal judgments. Cost-benefit analysis can still be useful, for it is the appropriate framework in terms of which to think about these broad choices, and it can usually provide some improved information. When personal judgments must play such a great role, however, the improved information may not be worth much. (At the extreme, if I must choose between two brown bags containing unknown objects, it does not help much to learn that one object is blue while the other is green.)

As other examples of such broad choices, consider the government's allocation of effort between basic research and applied development of immediately useful public goods. To choose between these two alternatives, officials must rely heavily on personal judgment (made in the light of others' views, to be sure) about the consequences and judgments concerning the value of those consequences. Values cannot be taken as given—that is, agreed upon—and physical-sociological effects cannot be predicted with confidence. Quantitative analysis can probably contribute only a little toward the sharpening of intuition here. Or consider the allocation of effort between improved medical care for the aged and for the young. I doubt if one could even predict the physical consequences with much accuracy, particularly the longer-run genetic effects. But suppose one could make extremely good predictions of the effects (which would of course aid decision-makers). The final choice would be dominated in this instance by judgments about the worth of prolonging the lives of elderly persons, the worth of lengthening the lives of persons in great pain, the worth of saving the lives of weakened or physically handicapped children, the worth of different kinds of improvements in health or the relief of different kinds of distress, and so on.

Another broad or high-level choice that brings out these points is the allocation of funds to, or for that matter within, the State Department. In the tasks of diplomacy it is hard to visualize taking a set of value-tags as being clearly stated, let alone agreed upon. And disagreement is quite understandable in predicting the effects of alternative courses of action on the probabilities of various sequences of events. Positive science has provided few tested hypotheses about these relationships.

As one proceeds to "narrower" or "lower-level" problems of choice, these difficulties frequently, though not always, become less severe. There is, of course, a whole spectrum of problems of choice, not just two categories called broad and narrow or high level and low level (though it is often economical to think in terms of such categories). Actual choices vary continuously with respect to the difficulties posed by uncertainties about physical consequences and about appropriate value-tags. Within such tasks as education and health improvement, there are "lower-level" choices for which quantitative analysis may be very helpful, but there are also many "middle-level" choices that are fraught with difficulties. Should more effort be placed on the improvement of mental health even if it means less emphasis on the treatment of conventional ailments? Should effort be reallocated from higher education toward the improvement of elementary school training, or vice versa? (Or should government leave such matters more than at present to the uninfluenced choice of individual families?) Cost-benefit analysis cannot do much to resolve the uncertainties about the consequences and their relative worths.

Within applied research and development, choosing between specific projects might appear to be a "low-level" choice that economic analysis could greatly assist. In such instances, it is true that values can sometimes be taken as agreed upon. In selecting research and development projects pertaining to new fuels, for instance, the values to be attached to various outcomes are not obvious, yet are probably not major sources of divergent views. The principal difficulty is our inability to predict the physical consequences (including "external" or "side-effects") of alternative research activities. Again cost-benefit analysis is destined to play a comparatively small, albeit useful, role.

One can list many problems of choice that seem to fall somewhere in this "middle ground"—that is, where cost-benefit analysis can be helpful, but not enormously so. It would appear, for instance, that the selection of anti-poverty and welfare programs depends heavily on consequences that one cannot predict with confidence and on value-judgments about which there is much disagreement. Choosing among alternative foreign-aid programs is analogous in these respects. Similar statements apply also to the selection of law-enforcement programs—for example, the comparison of widely different methods of curbing the use of narcotics, or of different penal institutions and procedures. In education many decisions that may appear to be "low level" or relatively simple, for instance, the selection among alternative curricula or teaching methods or disciplinary rules, are inevitably dominated by judgments. In most of these instances, to repeat an old refrain, cost-benefit analysis can help. It is the right framework in terms of which to think about alternatives; analysis can often trace out at least some of the consequences of rival courses of action; and just spelling out the monetary costs of these courses of action, even if the benefits and some costs must be entirely matters of judgment, is better than nothing.

It is in connection with comparatively narrow problems of choice, however, that cost-benefit analysis can sometimes play a starring role. In these instances, as might be expected, the alternatives are usually rather close substitutes. In connection with governmental natural-resource investments or choices affecting the utilization of water or land, the sciences can often predict the consequences, and people can often agree on the values at stake—at least to a sufficient extent to render analyses highly useful. Competing irrigation plans, flood-control or power or multi-purpose projects, swamp drainage and land reclamation ventures, acid-mine drainage proposals, and water-pollution control measures are such choices. (One huge specific water-resource suggestion is a $100 billion project to divert water from the Yukon river to Canada, the United States, and thence to Mexico.) Ways to utilize a given water supply better in such areas as California and Pakistan have been convincingly suggested by cost-benefit analyses. Regarding land use, an interesting question that might be answered is the following: is a natural balance of wild game a better use of marginal land in Africa at present than more ambitious schemes would be (in view of such costs as fencing and coping with the tsetse fly)?

Choosing among alternative arrangements for urban renewal and urban development is another problem pertaining to land use. The extent to which cost-benefit analysis can give assistance here remains to be seen. Many sociological and side-effects of alternative policies are still exceedingly difficult to predict, and judgments about values other than those of marketable commodities are involved extensively. Some explorations of the application of cost-benefit analysis here, however, are at least moderately promising.

One of the most important and promising is in the comparison of alternative transportation arrangements. The interdependencies of transportation networks with other aspects of life are formidable, yet with ingenuity extremely useful studies of certain alternatives can be produced.[7] Numerous transportation alternatives have been or are the subject of such studies: highways, urban systems, inland waterways, modified railway networks, utilization of a given amount of sea transport, air transport fleets, and of course many lower-level choices, such as alternative road materials, construction practices, airport facilities, and loading arrangements. In the United States, a good deal of effort is currently being devoted to the examination of certain transportation proposals in the "Northeast Corridor." As one can easily imagine, transportation alternatives that affect an entire region and its development yield chains of consequences that are extremely difficult to trace out.

Similar techniques have been used extensively to aid decision-makers in U.S. defense choices. In this connection, the studies have usually been called cost-effectiveness or systems analyses, but the same methodological points are applicable. Again in higher-level choices the decisions are dominated by value-judgments that people disagree about and judgments about consequences that cannot be predicted accurately. In lower-level choices—whether they pertain to operations, procurement, arms control, or disarmament—quantitative analyses can play a more significant role.

Cost-benefit analysis may prove to be relatively useful in lower-level educational choices, such as scheduling the use of classrooms or substituting local junior colleges for parts of universities' teaching programs. It may be comparatively useful in designing lower-level aspects of health programs—for example, the allocation of effort among alternative treatments of particular diseases or the utilization of hospital and other medical facilities. Cost-benefit comparisons may help in choosing recreational facilities or measures to reduce air pollution. In some of these instances, it might be noted that the difficulties are still awesome. Often positive science has not very fully revealed the relationships between inputs and physical, sociological, and psychological outputs, for instance, the possible impacts of recreation

[7] See especially J. R. Meyer, J. F. Kain, and M. Wohl, *The Urban Transportation Problem* (Cambridge, Mass.: Harvard University Press, 1965) and T. M. Coburn, M. E. Beesley, and D. J. Reynolds, *The London-Birmingham Motorway: Traffic and Economics*, Road Research Laboratory Technical Paper No. 46, DSIR, HMSO, 1960.

or urban crowding on personality adjustment, health, family stability, the probability of maintaining law and order, and so on. In addition the values (plus or minus) of many such effects are crucial but debatable.

Thus, even at best there can be legitimate disagreement about all these policy decisions. Nonetheless, to think systematically about the costs and gains from alternative policies is surely more sensible than to rely on haphazard thought or intuition—at least if we keep in mind these limitations of quantitative exhibits. Such analysis can bring out the areas of disagreement so that people can see where their differences lie. Even with considerable divergence in judgments, it can screen out the absurdly inferior alternatives, focusing the debate on a subset of relatively good alternatives. And for many choices, cost-benefit analysis provides information that can help people select, and agree upon, a preferred course of action.

Chapter 28

A SHORT-TERM MODEL FOR PLANNING IN NORWAY

PER SEVALDSON

Central Bureau of Statistics, Oslo

INTRODUCTION

The Norwegian interindustry-consumption model MODIS II (Model of Disaggregated type, second version[1]) has been developed by the Central Bureau of Statistics for use in economic analysis and planning. The version of this model, which has so far been made operative, is particularly designed for use in the preparation of the annual "national budget," the economic plan for the coming year, which is presented each year in October by the Norwegian government. This version of the model has been formulated in consultations with the Ministry of Finance and the University of Oslo.

The present model, MODIS II, was preceded by a somewhat simpler version (now given the name MODIS I) which has been in regular use since 1960 in various types of economic analysis as well as in government economic planning for one- and four-year periods.[2]

---

[1] Arne Øien of the Central Bureau of Statistics was responsible for the work on MODIS II. The present description is based on Mr. Øien's presentation of the model in a Working Paper from the Central Bureau of Statistics (Series no. IO 66/3).

[2] See Per Sevaldson, *An Interindustry Model of Production and Consumption for Economic Planning in Norway*, Income and Wealth, series X, eds. Colin Clark and Geer Stuvel (London, 1964).

A summary description of the main characteristics of MODIS II may be useful as a background for a formal description of its variables and relationships.

Basic philosophy of the model. The model is based on the following assumptions: 1) Constant price input-output coefficients are fixed. 2) Product prices are the sum of input prices, weighted by the fixed coefficients, plus profit rates, subject to modification by indirect taxation. 3) Incomes are determined by production through the input requirements, by prices for labor which again depend on wage and productivity rates and by profit rates. 4) Private consumption is determined by disposable income and prices.

In order to formulate a model on these assumptions, the following coefficients are needed: input-output coefficients for all production sectors; a set characterizing the relationships between incomes and prices on the one hand and private consumption of goods and services on the other; a number of "transformation" coefficients, needed mainly for the transformation of exogenous estimates to the specifications of the model.

In order to make a model based on these assumptions determinate, the following variables must be given as exogenous estimates: quantity of production or final demand other than private consumption for each sector; the product price or the profit rate for each sector; prices of labor and other non-produced inputs (imports); and tax rates.

The determinate model gives estimates of: production and all deliveries from each sector of production in quantities and values; all items of private consumption in quantities and values; labor requirements, imports and other primary inputs in total and in each sector of production, total value added in fixed prices in each sector and in total; prices and profit rates for all sectors of production, and price indices based on fixed or current weights; income shares and tax revenues.

In MODIS II the following choices have been made in regard to exogenous estimates.

For one group of production sectors, it is assumed that the volume of production can most easily be estimated on the basis of exogenous information. Then, for some sectors in this group, supplementary imports are assumed to fill in a remaining gap between demand and domestic production. For other sectors, at least one item in final demand is determined by the model, and, finally, for some sectors it is assumed that intermediate demand for the products of a sector is determined as the difference between exogenous estimates of production and exogenous estimates of final demand (the assumption of fixed input-output coefficients for the use of these products being abandoned). Sectors for which the volume of production is exogenously estimated are typically those where production levels are relatively independent of short-run shifts in demand (agriculture, for instance), some where production is mainly determined by capacity, and some which are under direct government control.

For the remaining production sectors, it is assumed that production is determined by demand, and that final demand other than private consumption is determined by exogenous etsimates.

For one group of production sectors, defined independently of the above grouping, it is assumed that their prices are given by world market conditions or by policy decisions and thus have to be estimated outside the model. This will be the case for all export sectors, and for many sectors competing with imports in the domestic market, as well as for agriculture, fisheries, and a number of sectors dominated by public enterprises. In these sectors, profit rates will be residually determined.

For the remaining sectors, it is assumed that profit rates per unit produced are determined by conditions in the domestic economy, much in the same way as wage rates. These profit rates must be estimated exogenously. Then input costs, profit rates and indirect taxation will determine product prices.

Data requirements and specifications. The Norwegian model has been formulated in such a way that coefficients of the consumption relationships could be estimated on the basis of national accounts and consumer budget studies for the period 1952–1962.

National accounts and supplementary statistics for a "base year" provide the basis for all other data in the model (except, of course, for the exogenous estimates). Input-output coefficients, for instance, are computed on this basis. (When the model is used in national budgeting, the base year is the year two years before the budget year.)

Model estimates are given in the form of estimated changes a) from the base year to the "current" year and b) from the "current" year to the "budget" year.[3] In order to find the absolute values for the budget year, therefore, account figures for the base year and estimates of exogenous variables both for the "current" year and for the "budget" year are needed.

The model has been programmed on an electronic computer (Univac 1107) in such a way that when national accounts for the base year and, in

---

[3] The terms "current" year and "budget" year here refer to the use of the model in national budgeting. In other uses of the model, any set of "analysis" years may of course be studied, their relevant characteristics given by the particular values chosen for the exogenous estimates, and by the requirement that structural relationships and data from the "base" year be applicable.

addition, up to ten alternative sets of exogenous variables for the current year and the budget year are fed into the machine, the results are produced in an integrated operation in the form of a booklet containing the ordered tables in the form most convenient for the user. Unfortunately, this requires relatively much machine time (ten hours, or seven hours if only one alternative is computed). Nevertheless, results can be produced from one day to the next.

Work on a simplified model for rough "in-between" calculations is in progress. In internal specifications, the model distinguishes between: 165 sectors of production; 30 "import sectors" or groups of import commodities; 9 categories of income shares (depreciation, direct and indirect taxes, subsidies, wages and profit by type of organization). (These income shares can again be specified by sector or by group of sectors.)

The specifications in exogenous estimates in price include: 59 estimates of product prices for Norwegian sectors of production; 2 estimates of the rate of change of profit rates in the remaining Norwegian sectors of production; 29 estimates of import prices; 13 estimates of wage rate changes in groups of Norwegian sectors of production; 12 estimates of productivity changes in groups of Norwegian sectors of production.

In tax rates there are: 20 estimates of indirect tax and subsidy rates; and 6 estimates of rates for direct taxes, social insurance and direct subsidies.

Quantity estimates include: 49 estimates of production volumes in the same number of Norwegian sectors; 380 estimates of final demand for the same number of types of goods. Of these, there are 7 estimates of exogenously determined items of private consumption; 18 estimates of government consumption; 182 estimates of export items; 70 estimates of inventory investments; 103 estimates of other investment items.

When the model is used for planning, the purpose is to obtain a consistent set of estimates of key national accounting variables for the plan (budget) year, irrespective of whether these are endogenously or exogenously estimated. The model therefore produces as its end result a complete set of tables of such variables. These variables are to some extent more aggregated than they would be if the full internal specifications were maintained, and they are not systematically divided into exogenous and endogenous variables. The tables give figures in current and fixed prices, both absolute figures for the base year, the current year and the budget year, and figures for the changes between each pair of years, absolutely and in per cent. Price indices are given for all items.

The main tables of gross national product and its components are: domestic product by category of expenditure (16 items); export by delivering group of sectors (14 items); gross investment by type of capital goods (13 items); government consumption (11 items); private consumption by type of goods (17 items); import by sector (32 items); gross national product by sector of production (72 sectors and sector groups).

Tables of balance of payments and income accounts include: balance of payments (6 items); income accounts: specifications of incomes earned in each of 13 groups of sectors (altogether 120 items).

Tables of disposable incomes and savings give income and savings figures in total as well as separately for persons, corporations, central and local governments and social security.

Price determination in the model. The set of assumptions on which MODIS II is based makes prices independent of market conditions in the product markets: Prices are either exogenously determined, or determined by unit costs together with exogenously given profit rates.

The prices which are not determined entirely outside the model are determined by the exogenous prices through the assumption of fixed input coefficients in production, and by the assumptions about tax, wage and profit rates. The model cannot take care of the possibility that entrepreneurs may vary profit rates in order to change prices in response to changes in demand. (Such a possibility must be handled outside the model—for example, by iterative adjustments in the assumed profit rates.)

Formally, price determination is represented by a submodel, which may be solved separately, independent of the quantity estimates, when the exogenous price estimates and estimates of tax, wage (and productivity) and profit rates are given.

In the model, prices influence the volume and distribution of production and imports through their influence on the volume and distribution of private consumption. Adjustments to prices through substitutions in the production sectors are excluded by the assumption of fixed input-output coefficients.

Prices are also decisive for the level and distribution of private incomes and public revenues.

A simplified model. The system of relationships describing MODIS II is in principle quite simple, since the model is based on a rather simplified representation of a limited number of economic relationships. However, due to the high degree of specifications, and a relatively large number of cases which are given special treatment in the actual formulation of the model, a symbolic representation nevertheless becomes rather cumbersome. The best way of introducing the model therefore seems to be to start from a simplified formulation, representing the basic principles, and then to introduce the complicating features, one by one, as expansions and modifications in the basic model. A simple input-output consumption model could be described by the following set of relationships:

$$x = A_x x + c_x + y_x \tag{1}$$

$$b = A_b x + c_b + y_b \tag{2}$$

$$r = \hat{p}_w W_x \tag{3}$$

$$c = c^0 + D\left(\frac{1}{\pi} r - r^0\right) + N\left(\frac{1}{\pi} p - i_c\right) \tag{4}$$

$$p'_x = p'_x A_x + p'_b A_b + p'_w W \tag{5}$$

$$\pi = p'\frac{1}{\gamma} c^0 \tag{6}$$

$$\gamma = i'_c c^0 \tag{7}$$

$$y = \text{given} \tag{8}$$

$$p_b = \text{given} \tag{9}$$

$$p_w = \text{given} \tag{10}$$

Here:

$x =$ a column vector of production levels measured in constant price values. The dimension n_x of this vector is equal to the number of production sectors (industries) in the model.

$c_x =$ a column vector of sector deliveries to private consumption, measured in constant price values and of dimension n_x.

$y_x =$ a column vector of sector deliveries to final uses other than private consumption (exports, gross investment and government consumption) measured in constant price values and of dimension n_x.

$b =$ a column vector of imports measured in constant price values. The dimension, n_b, of this vector is equal to the number of commodity types in the specification of imports in the model.

$c_b =$ a column vector of import deliveries for private consumption, measured in constant price values and of dimension n_b.

$y_b =$ a column vector of import deliveries to final uses other than private consumption, measured in constant price values and of dimension n_b.

$r =$ a column vector of primary income shares (wages, depreciation, charges, indirect taxes and entrepreneurial incomes) measured in current price values. The dimension n_r of this vector is equal to the number of primary income shares (specified by category and sector groups) in the model.

$A_x =$ a n_x by n_x dimensional matrix of "input-output coefficients," assumed to be constant.

$A_b =$ a n_b by n_x dimensional matrix of "import-coefficients," assumed to be constant.

$W =$ a n_r by n_x dimensional matrix of "income share coefficients," estimated in the base year.

$p_x =$ a column vector of price indices for all production sectors (dimension n_x).

$p_b =$ a column vector of price indices for all import commodity types (dimension n_b).

$p_w =$ a column vector of "price indices" for all income shares (dimension n_r). For each income share, the price index is defined as current income in all sectors of production divided by the sum for all sectors of base year income times the index of production for the sector concerned.

$D =$ a $(n_x + n_b)$ by n_r dimensional matrix of "marginal propensities to consume."

$N =$ a $(n_x + n_b)$ by $(n_x + n_b)$ dimensional matrix of price coefficients for consumption.

$\pi =$ a price index for consumers' goods (a scalar).

$i_c =$ a $(n_x + n_b)$ dimensional column vector with all elements $= 1$.

$c = \begin{pmatrix} c_x \\ c_b \end{pmatrix}$, $p = \begin{pmatrix} p_x \\ p_b \end{pmatrix}$, $y = \begin{pmatrix} y_x \\ y_b \end{pmatrix}$, and so forth.

A "prime" ($'$) denotes transposition.

Superscript 0 denotes base year values.

A "cap" (Λ) denotes that a vector is written as a diagonal matrix. This will also be denoted by a Λ and the symbol of the vector written within parenthesis, that is: $\hat{p}_w = \Lambda(p_w)$.

Here, the first set of equations (1)—later expanded to (1′), (1″), and so forth—gives the levels of production in all production sectors (x), as the sum of deliveries to production sectors $(A_x x)$, deliveries to private consumption (c_x), and deliveries to final uses other than private consumption (y_x). Deliveries to production sectors $(A_x x)$ are assumed to be proportionate to production in the receiving sectors. The elements of A_x can be estimated on the basis of accounts for a base year.

The second set of equations (2) gives the levels of demand for all import commodity types (b) as the sum of deliveries to production sectors $(A_b x)$, deliveries to private consumption (c_b), and deliveries to final uses other than private consumption (y_b). This implies that all imports are treated as "structural." The simple model has no provision for substitution between domestic and imported goods. The elements of A_b can be estimated on the basis of accounts for a base year.

The third set of equations (3) gives the primary income shares in current values as determined by the production volumes in all production sectors. The income shares as fractions of total production in each production sector in a base year, W, can be established on the basis of accounts. Now the wage payment per unit produced in a given sector will change as a result of changes in productivity and wage rates. The indirect tax payment per unit produced in a given sector will change with the change in the tax rate calculated on a per unit basis. The depreciation changes per unit produced are assumed to be constant in volume, and will consequently change in proportion to a price index for these changes. Price indices expressing these types of changes are assumed to be given. If we also assume changes in entrepreneurial income per unit produced in each sector to be known, then we have all the elements of p_w.

The fourth set of equations (4) gives private consumption of products from each sector as the sum of consumption of the same product in the base year plus a set of terms depending on the change from the base year in "real income" $(\frac{1}{\pi} r - r^0)$—real income defined as income deflated by a general price index (π)—plus a set of terms depending on the change from the base year in relative prices. c^0 can be found from accounts for a base year. The elements of D and N must be estimated by statistical studies of consumer behavior.

The fifth set of equations (5) gives the price relationships which must develop in the model. The price index for products from a given production sector equals the weighted sum of the price indices for all inputs and in-

come shares in the sector, the weights being the fraction each element constituted of total production in the base year. These fractions are given in
matrices A_x, A_b and W.

The sixth group of equations (6) and (7) consists of only two. Taken
together they give a formula for computing a general consumers' price
index on the basis of base year weights.

By equations (8), (9), and (10) we assume final demand other than
private consumption (y), import prices (p_b), and "prices" for income
shares (p_w), to be given.

The system is solved by first solving (5) for p_x, then π may be computed
by (6) and (7), and x, r and c are determined by simultaneously solving (1),
(3) and (4). Finally b is computed from (2).

Having solved the equation system (1)–(10) we can also compute the
vectors of current price values: $\hat{p}_x x$, $\hat{p}_b b$, $\hat{p}c$ and $\hat{p}y$.

In order to make it easier to keep track of subsequent partitionings of
variable vectors and coefficient matrices, we may write equations (1)–(3)
in the following form:

$$\begin{pmatrix} x \\ b \\ r \end{pmatrix} = \begin{pmatrix} A_x \\ A_b \\ \hat{p}_w W \end{pmatrix} x + \begin{pmatrix} c_x \\ c_b \\ 0 \end{pmatrix} + \begin{pmatrix} y_x \\ y_b \\ 0 \end{pmatrix}$$

and equations (5) in the following form:

$$p'_x = (p'_x, p'_b, p'_w) \begin{pmatrix} A_x \\ A_b \\ W \end{pmatrix} = (p'_x, p'_b, i'_r) \begin{pmatrix} A_x \\ A_b \\ \hat{p}_u W \end{pmatrix}$$

i_r = a n_r-dimensional column vector with all elements = 1.

The last form of equations (5) illustrates the close relationship between
the production-income-equations (1) to (3) and price equations (5), through
the identity of the coefficient matrices. This identity applies in all but the
last of the following modifications of the model, and even in the last modifications the differences are not very striking.

Specifications of final demand: "commodity converters." We assume all
variables for goods delivered in the model to be measured in (current or
base year) producers' market prices. This implies that trade and transportation margins on all goods delivered are entered as parallel deliveries from
the trade and transportation sectors. The vector c, for instance, contains
deliveries to private consumption from each sector at producers' prices, and
separate items of the trade and transportation margins on these deliveries.

Our first modification of the simple model will be to introduce "commodity converter matrices," which convert a vector of commodity classes demanded for private consumption and a vector of commodity classes demanded for final uses other than private consumption, both specified in (constant) purchasers' prices, into vectors of deliveries in constant producers' prices from production sectors and import classes.

$$x = A_x x + C_x z + F_x u \tag{1'}$$

$$b = A_b x + C_b z + F_b u \tag{2'}$$

$$r = \hat{p}_w W x \tag{3'}$$

$$z = z^0 + D\left(\frac{1}{\pi} r - r^0\right) + N\left(\frac{1}{\pi} p - i_z\right) \tag{4'}$$

$$p'_x = p'_x A_x + p'_b A_b + p'_w W \tag{5'}$$

$$p'_z = p'_x C_x + p'_b C_b \tag{6a'}$$

$$p'_u = p'_x F_x + p'_b F_b \tag{6b'}$$

$$\pi = p'_z \frac{1}{\gamma} z^0 \tag{6c'}$$

$$\gamma = i'_z z^0 \tag{7'}$$

$$u = \text{given} \tag{8'}$$

$$p_b = \text{given} \tag{9'}$$

$$p_w = \text{given} \tag{10'}$$

Here:

$z =$ a column vector of deliveries of consumers' goods measured in constant purchasers' price values. Dimension n_z.

$u =$ a column vector of deliveries of final demand goods other than private consumers' goods, measured in constant purchasers' price values. Dimension n_u.

$c_x =$ a n_x by n_z matrix of coefficients characterizing the composition of each consumers' good in terms of the fractions delivered by each production sector.

$F_x =$ a n_x by n_u matrix of coefficients characterizing the composition of each final good other than consumers' goods in terms of the fractions delivered by each production sector.

$C_b =$ a n_b by n_z matrix of coefficients characterizing the composition of each consumers' good in terms of the fractions delivered from each import commodity type.

$F_b =$ a n_b by n_u matrix of coefficients characterizing the composition of each final good other than consumers' goods in terms of the fractions delivered from each import commodity type.

$i_z =$ a n_z dimensional column vector with all elements $= 1$.

C_x, F_x, C_b and F_b are assumed to be constant and estimated on the basis of base year accounts.

The equation of private consumption (4) must be reformulated in terms of z instead of in terms of c.

The procedure of solution will be the same as for the simplified model: We can first compute prices, p_x, by solving (5′), then p_z, p_u and π can be computed by (6a′), (6b′), and (6c′) and (7′). x, r and z are determined by simultaneously solving (1′), (3′) and (4′), and b is computed by (2′).

Equations (1′–3′) now may be written:

$$\begin{pmatrix} x \\ b \\ r \end{pmatrix} = \begin{pmatrix} A_x & C_x & F_x \\ A_b & C_b & F_b \\ \hat{p}_w W & 0 & 0 \end{pmatrix} \begin{pmatrix} x \\ z \\ u \end{pmatrix}$$

and equations (5′, 6a′, 6b′):

$$(p'_x, p'_z, p'_u) = (p'_x, p'_b, p'_w) \begin{pmatrix} A_x & C_x & F_x \\ A_b & C_b & F_b \\ W & 0 & 0 \end{pmatrix}$$

Indirect taxes. We will then consider in more detail the treatment of indirect taxes in the model. Indirect taxes will be specified as a subvector of r. Since we assume that the sector deliveries are given in producers' market prices, indirect taxes collected from the producers are included in the value of production of each sector, and the amount of each tax collected per unit value produced in the base year is characterized by an element in W. However, indirect taxes collected in trade are not included in the product deliveries from the ordinary production sectors, but will be included in the deliveries from the trade sectors to the receivers of the goods on which the taxes are levied. Thus, a general sales tax on consumers' goods will be represented as deliveries from the trade sectors into private consumers' goods. The revenue from such a tax will be represented in the matrix W by an item giving the revenue as a fraction of the total "deliveries" from the relevant trade sector in the base year. If we subdivide the trade sector functionally in such a way that the collection of each of the types of indirect taxes which are collected in trade is considered a separate subsector of trade, then this fraction must be identically one.

Now, indirect taxes may be collected on a quantity or on a value basis, and some indirect taxes, in particular subsidies, which we may consider as negative taxes, are levied in amounts which are independent both of volume and value of operations. If indirect taxes are collected on a quantity basis, and if all rates for a given tax are changed in the same proportion, then this change may be expressed by an index giving the (average) rate per quantity unit in a given year divided by the (average) rate per quantity unit in the base year. Such indices will then be elements of the vector p_w. They will not make necessary any reformulations in the simple model, neither for the indirect taxes collected from the producers, nor for those collected in trade. If the introduction of a new quantity tax, which was not collected in the base year, is contemplated, then it will be necessary to try to compute what this tax would have amounted to, if it had been collected on base year quantities at the contemplated rate. On this basis, items in an expanded r^0 rector and W matrix can be computed. The price index to be employed on this last element of r will be identically one.

For taxes collected on a value basis the case will be different: these items must be related to price or current value figures and not to quantity (constant price value) figures. In order to account for these taxes we will partition the vector of income shares, r, into three subvectors: r_1, r_2 and r_3, and correspondingly we subdivide p_w into p_{w1}, p_{w2}, and p_{w3}, and W into W_1, W_2 and W_3, in such a way that p_{w1} are the elements of p_w and W_1 are the rows of W corresponding to r_1 a.s.o.

In r_1 we keep all the income shares, which are not the revenues of taxes collected on a value basis. Thus we still have:

$$r_1 = \hat{p}_{w1} W_1 x \tag{3a''}$$

In r_2 we keep the revenues from taxes collected from the production sectors on the basis of the value of production. For r_2 we write:

$$r_2 = \hat{v} W_2 (\hat{p}_x x) \tag{3b''}$$

Here:

v is a vector of "tax rate indices" expressing the relative change in rates from the base year. It replaces the vector p_w in (3′). We will assume v to be given by government decree.[4] Finally the vector x in (3′) is in this subset

[4] A complication occurs when not all the deliveries from a given sector are taxed. In this case the indexes of tax rate changes, v, will not be the actual change in rates for that part of production which is taxed, but have to be derived from these rates. We shall not go into these computations here.

substituted by $(\hat{p}_x x)$—that is, the volume figures are substituted by current price values. (New taxes may be taken into account by expanding the r_2-vector with items for the revenue of the new tax, and by entering the new tax coefficients in the places corresponding to the places of $[\hat{v} W_2]$ in the corresponding equations [3b''].)

In r_3 we collect the revenue from indirect taxes collected on a value basis in trade. We will return to r_3 shortly. With the partitioning of W into W_1, W_2 and W_3 price equations (5') can now be written

$$p'_x = p'_x A_x + p'_b A_b + p'_{w1} W_1 + v' W_2 \hat{p}_x + p'_{\hat{w}3} W_3$$

This may be written

$$p'_x = p'_x A_x + p'_b A_b + p'_{w1} W_1 + p'_x \Lambda(v' W_2) + p'_{\hat{w}3} W_3$$

or

$$p'_x [I - A_x - \Lambda(v' W_2)] = p'_b A_b + p'_{w1} W_1 + p'_{\hat{w}3} W_3$$

Here: I stands for a diagonal unit matrix of appropriate dimension (here n_x by n_x).

Taxes collected in trade on goods delivered to final uses will in the base year be represented by elements of C_x and F_x whether they are collected on a quantity or on a value basis. If they are collected on a value basis, it makes little sense to compute the revenue on a "constant price" basis and to compute "price indices" for these concepts.

In order to be able to form the price equations for final goods, let us instead assume that C_x and F_x can be partitioned horizontally into C_1 and C_2 and F_1 and F_2 respectively by collecting in C_2 and F_2 those rows of the respective matrices which relate to indirect taxes on value. With a corresponding partitioning of p_x we now write instead of the price equations (6a') and (6b').

$$p'_z = p'_1 C_1 + s' C_2 \hat{p}_z + p'_b C_b = p'_1 C_1 + p'_z \Lambda(s' C_2) + p'_b C_b \tag{6a''}$$

$$p'_u = p'_1 F_1 + s' F_2 \hat{p}_u + p'_b F_b = p'_1 F_1 + p'_u \Lambda(s' F_2) + p'_b F_b \tag{6b''}$$

Here s is a vector of indices of changes in the value tax rates. We will assume s to be given, in the same way as v.

Corresponding to the partitioning of C_x and F_x we get a partitioning of x into x_1 and x_2, where x_2 represents the "volume of production" in those functionally defined trade sectors which are charged with the (sole) task of collecting these taxes. Correspondingly, p_x will be partitioned into p_1 and

p_2. Here x_2 and p_2 are of little interest separately, but the current value of the tax revenue will be given by

$$p_2x_2 = \hat{s}C_2(\hat{p}_z z) + \hat{s}F_2(\hat{p}_u u)$$

Since the whole activity in this group of sectors is the collection of the tax, and, since the taxes collected belong to the income share vector, these will also be the remaining elements of r (r_3).

$$r_3 = \hat{s}C_2(\hat{p}_z z) + \hat{s}F_2(\hat{p}_u u) \; (= \hat{p}_{w3}W_3 x) \tag{3c''}$$

Corresponding to the partitioning of x into x_1 and x_2 we may also partition W_1, W_2 and W_3 vertically into W_{11}, W_{12}, W_{21}, W_{22}, W_{31} and W_{32}, to get

$$W_1 x = W_{11}x_1 + W_{12}x_2$$
$$W_2 x = W_{21}x_1 + W_{22}x_2$$
$$W_3 x = W_{31}x_1 + W_{32}x_2$$

Here all the elements of W_{31} must be identically zero, since the collection of taxes belonging to r_3 is by definition restricted to the sectors corresponding to x_2. W_{12} and W_{22} must both be zero matrices, and W_{32} must be the identity matrix, I, since the corresponding sectors are functionally defined to have the sole task of collecting the taxes, r_3.

We have already mentioned that p_2 is without interest, and we can therefore write the price equations:

$$p'_1 = p'_1 A_{x1} + p'_b A_{b1} + p'_{w1}W_{11} + v'W_{21}\hat{p}_1$$
$$p'_1[I - A_{x1} - \Lambda(v'W_{21})] = p'_b A_{b1} + p'_{w1}W_{11} \tag{5''}$$

A_{x1} and A_{b1} are submatrices of A_x and A_b. Partitioning of A_x and A_b in correspondence with the partitioning of x and p_x must give:

$$A_x = \begin{pmatrix} A_{x1}, & 0 \\ 0, & 0 \end{pmatrix} \quad \text{and} \quad A_b = \begin{pmatrix} A_{b1}, & 0 \end{pmatrix}$$

(New taxes on the value of final deliveries and collected in trade can be handled in a way which is quite similar to the treatment of new taxes on the value of production.)

We have not discussed the treatment of value taxes collected in trade, and levied on the use in production of certain raw materials. Since the revenue from such a tax per unit produced in the sector using the taxed raw material would depend only on the quantity of the raw material used per unit of production and the price of the raw material, it might easily have been taken into account. Nevertheless, in MODIS II it was thought more convenient to treat all taxes collected in trade on the use of raw materials as if they were levied on a quantity basis. If this approximation is taken into account when the "price indices" for these taxes are computed, the consequent errors in calculations will be negligible.

Also, subsidies and taxes levied independently of value and volume are roughly recomputed on a per unit basis in the Norwegian model.

Writing out the modified system of equations we now have:

$$x_1 = A_{z1}x_1 + C_1 z + F_1 u \tag{1''}$$

$$b = A_{b1}x_1 + C_b z + F_b u \tag{2''}$$

$$r_1 = \hat{p}_{w1}W_{11}x_1 \tag{3a''}$$

$$r_2 = \hat{v}W_{21}(\hat{p}_1 x_1) \tag{3b''}$$

$$r_3 = \hat{s}C_2(\hat{p}_z z) + \hat{s}F_2(\hat{p}_u u) \tag{3c''}$$

$$z = z^0 + D\left(\frac{1}{\pi}r - r^0\right) + N\left(\frac{1}{\pi}p - i_z\right) \tag{4''}$$

$$p'_1[I - A_{z1} - \Lambda(v'W_{21})] = p'_b A_{b1} + p'_{w1}W_{11} \tag{5''}$$

$$p'_z[I - \Lambda(s'C_2)] = p'_1 C_1 + p'_b C_b \tag{6a''}$$

$$p'_u[I - \Lambda(s'F_2)] = p'_1 F_1 + p'_b F_b \tag{6b''}$$

$$\pi = p'_z \frac{1}{\gamma} z^0 \tag{6c''}$$

$$\gamma = i'_z z^0 \tag{7''}$$

$$u = \text{given} \tag{8''}$$

$$p_b = \text{given} \tag{9''}$$

$$p_{w1} = \text{given} \tag{10a''}$$

$$v = \text{given} \tag{10b''}$$

$$s = \text{given} \tag{10c''}$$

Equations (1'')–(3c'') can be written:

$$\begin{pmatrix} x_1 \\ r_3 \\ b \\ r_1 \\ r_2 \end{pmatrix} = \begin{pmatrix} A_{z1} & C_1 & F_1 \\ 0 & \hat{s}C_2\hat{p}_z & \hat{s}F_2\hat{p}_u \\ A_{b1} & C_b & F_b \\ \hat{p}_{w1}W_{11} & 0 & 0 \\ \hat{v}W_{21}\hat{p}_1 & 0 & 0 \end{pmatrix} \begin{pmatrix} x_1 \\ z \\ u \end{pmatrix}$$

and equations (5'')–(6b''):

$$(p'_1, p'_z, p'_u) = (p'_1, s', p'_b, p'_w, v') \begin{pmatrix} A_{z1} & C_1 & F_1 \\ 0 & C_2\hat{p}_z & F_2\hat{p}_u \\ A_{b1} & C_b & F_b \\ W_{11} & 0 & 0 \\ W_{21}\hat{p}_1 & 0 & 0 \end{pmatrix}$$

Endogenous and exogenous prices. For the next modification in our model we take as a starting point the equation (5''), written in the following form:

$$p'_1 = p'_1A_{z1} + p'_1\Lambda(v'W_{21}) + p'_bA_{b1} + p'_{w1}W_{11}$$

We now partition p_1 into p_I and p_{II}, that is, $p'_1 = (p'_I, p'_{II})$. Correspondingly we partition A_{z1} into $A_{I\,I}$, $A_{I\,II}$, $A_{II\,I}$ and $A_{II\,II}$, A_{b1} into A_{bI} and A_{bII}, W_{11} into W_{1I} and $W_{1\,II}$ and W_{21} into $W_{2\,I}$ and $W_{2\,II}$, that is:

$$A_{z1} = \begin{pmatrix} A_{I\,I} & A_{I\,II} \\ A_{II\,I} & A_{II\,II} \end{pmatrix}$$

$$A_{b1} = (A_{bI}A_{bII})$$

$$\begin{pmatrix} W_{11} \\ W_{21} \end{pmatrix} = \begin{pmatrix} W_{1I} & W_{1II} \\ W_{2I} & W_{2\,II} \end{pmatrix}$$

We can then write:

$$p'_I = p'_IA_{I\,I} + p'_{II}A_{II\,I} + p'_I\Lambda(v'W_{2I}) + p'_bA_{bI} + p'_{w1}W_{1I} \tag{5a'''}$$

$$p'_{II} = p'_IA_{II\,I} + p'_{II}A_{II\,II} + p'_{II}\Lambda(v'W_{2II}) + p'_bA_{bII} + p'_{w1}W_{1II}$$

Finally, we substitute zeroes for the coefficients on the line(s) corresponding to entrepreneurial incomes in $W_{1\,II}$ (but not in $W_{1\,I}$) and add a vector e of the same dimension as p_{II}, in the second equation. Writing $w_{1\,II}$ for the matrix with the zero line(s) we get

$$p'_{II} = p'_{II}A_{I\,II} + p'_{II}A_{II\,II} + p'_{II}\Lambda(v'W_{2II}) + p'_bA_{bII} + p'_{w1}\overline{W}_{1II} + e' \tag{5b'''}$$

The vector e now represents the entrepreneurial incomes per unit produced in each of those production sectors for which the product prices are given by p_{II}.

The income equation (3a'') must now be replaced by:

$$r_1 = \hat{p}_{w1}W_{1I}x_I + \hat{p}_{w1}W_{1II}x_{II} + E\ell x_{II} \tag{3a'''}$$

Here E is a matrix which adds up the elements of $e\,x_{II}$ and puts them into the right category of income shares in r_1. x_I and x_{II} are the subvectors of x_1 resulting from a partitioning of x_1 corresponding to the partitioning of p_1 into p_I and p_{II}.

We will assume p_{II} to be given exogenously:

$$p_{II} = \text{given} \tag{10d'''}$$

The price indices of p_{II} may represent prices of goods that compete on the world market and prices which are determined directly by the government.

p_I will now be determined uniquely by (5a''').

Wages and productivity. We will discuss in some more detail those elements of p_{w1} which represent the indices of labor cost per unit produced. It is obvious that we must have at least as many labor income elements in r_1 as we want to have possibilities for assuming differences in the indices of changes in labor cost per unit produced in the various sectors.

An index of unit labor cost will be determined by the average changes in the wage rate and the average change in labor productivity in the sectors concerned.

Let p_k be the subvector of p_{w1} giving the indices of unit labor costs.

Let k be the vector of wage indices, and let g be the vector of productivity changes, then

$$p_k = (\hat{g})^{-1}k \tag{10e'''}$$

We will assume g and k to be given.

Price index of depreciation charges. In the Norwegian model, entrepreneurial incomes are computed net of depreciation charges. This means that depreciation charges is a separate element in r_1 and that a price index is needed for this element.

The index used is computed on the basis of the prices for investment goods, that is, some of the elements in p_u. We have

$$p_d = d'p_u \tag{6d'''}$$

P_d will be an element of the vector of price indices for income shares, p_{w1}.

The system of price equations. Writing p_{w0} for the remaining vector of p_{w1}, when p_k and p_d are removed, writing W_{kI}, W_{kII} and W_{dI} and W_{dII} for the rows of W_{1I} and $\overline{W}_{1\,II}$ corresponding to p_k and p_d respectively (the "labor coefficients" and the "depreciation coefficients") and writing W_{0I} and W_{0II} for the remaining rows of $W_{1\,I}$ and $\overline{W}_{1\,II}$, we can now write the price equations of the system:

$$\begin{aligned}p'_I = {} & p'_I A_{I\,I} + p'_{II} A_{II\,I} + p'_I \Lambda(v'W_{2I}) + p'_b A_{bI} \\ & + p'_{w0}W_{0I} + p'_k W_{kI} + p_d W_{dI}\end{aligned} \tag{5a^{iv}}$$

$$p'_{II} = p'_I A_{I\ II} + p'_{II} A_{II\ II} + p'_{II} \Lambda(v'W_{2II}) + p'_b A_{bII}$$
$$+ p'_{w0} W_{0II} + p'_k W_{kII} + p_d W_{dII} + e' \tag{5b^{iv}}$$

$$p'_z[I - \Lambda(s'C_2)] = p'_1 C_1 + p'_b C_b \tag{6a^{iv}}$$

$$p'_u[I - \Lambda(s'F_2)] = p'_1 F_1 + p'_b F_b \tag{6b^{iv}}$$

$$\pi = p'_z \frac{1}{\gamma} z^0 \tag{6c^{iv}}$$

$$p_d = d'p_u \tag{6d^{iv}}$$

$$\gamma = i'_z z^0 \tag{7^{iv}}$$

$$p_b = \text{given} \tag{9^{iv}}$$

$$p_{w0} = \text{given} \tag{10a^{iv}}$$

$$v = \text{given} \tag{10b^{iv}}$$

$$s = \text{given} \tag{10c^{iv}}$$

$$p_{II} = \text{given} \tag{10d^{iv}}$$

$$p_k = (\hat{g})^{-1} k \tag{10e^{iv}}$$

$$g = \text{given} \tag{11a^{iv}}$$

$$k = \text{given} \tag{11b^{iv}}$$

$$p_1 = \begin{pmatrix} P_I \\ P_{II} \end{pmatrix} \tag{12^{iv}}$$

This is a determinate subsystem of the entire set of equations. It makes possible the determination of p_I, p_k, p_d, p_z, p_u and π from a set of given price, wage, tax and productivity variables.

This subsystem also gives a representation of the price relationships in the Norwegian model MODIS II.

Using again the matrix form for equations (5a^{iv})–(6b^{iv}) we get:

$$[p'_I, (p_{II} - e)', p'_z, p'_u] =$$

$$= (p'_I, p'_{II}, s', p'_b, p'_{w0}, p'_k, p_d, v') \begin{pmatrix} A_{I\ I} & A_{I\ II} & C_I & F_I \\ A_{II\ I} & A_{II\ II} & C_{II} & F_{II} \\ 0 & 0 & C_2\hat{p}_z & F_2\hat{p}_u \\ A_{bI} & A_{bII} & C_b & F_b \\ W_{0I} & W_{0II} & 0 & 0 \\ W_{kI} & W_{kII} & 0 & 0 \\ W_{dI} & W_{dII} & 0 & 0 \\ W_{21}\hat{p}_I & W_{2II}\hat{p}_{II} & 0 & 0 \end{pmatrix}$$

Exogenous estimates of production levels. In writing out the quantity and income relationships we will now add a new column vector $j = (j'_I, j'_{II})'$, so that we have:

$$x_I = A_{I\,I}x_I + A_{I\,II}x_{II} + C_{I}z + F_{I}u + j_I \tag{1a^{iv}}$$

$$x_{II} = A_{II\,I}x_I + A_{II\,II}x_{II} + C_{II}z + F_{II}u + j_{II} \tag{1b^{iv}}$$

$$b = A_{bI}x_I + A_{bII}x_{II} + C_{b}z + F_{b}u + K_{bI}j_I + K_{bII}j_{II} \tag{2^{iv}}$$

$$r_0 = \hat{p}_{w0}W_{0I}x_I + \hat{p}_{w0}W_{0II}x_{II} + E_{c}x_{II} + K_{0I}\hat{p}_{I}j_I + K_{0II}\hat{p}_{II}j_{II} \tag{3a^{iv}}$$

$$r_k = \hat{p}_k W_{kI}x_I + \hat{p}_k W_{kII}x_{II} \tag{3b^{iv}}$$

$$r_d = p_d W_{dI}x_I + p_d W_{dII}x_{II} \tag{3c^{iv}}$$

$$r_2 = \hat{v}W_{21}\hat{p}_I x_I + \hat{v}W_{2II}\hat{p}_{II}x_{II} \tag{3d^{iv}}$$

$$r_3 = \hat{s}C_2\hat{p}_z z + \hat{s}F_2\hat{p}_u u \tag{3e^{iv}}$$

$$y_I = F_I u + M_I j_I \tag{8a^{iv}}$$

$$y_{II} = F_{II}u + M_{II}j_{II} \tag{8b^{iv}}$$

$$u = \text{given} \tag{8c^{iv}}$$

The elements of j fall into two categories: Either they are identically zero, in which case the equations (1a^{iv}) and (1b^{iv}) are used to determine the corresponding elements of $x = (x'_I, x'_{II})'$, or they are unknowns, to be determined by the equations (1a^{iv}) and (1b^{iv}). The elements of x corresponding to non-zero elements of j must be exogenously given. They are the production levels that are considered to be determined by conditions of nature, or by the availability of factors of production.

The existence of non-zero items of j implies that the remaining terms on the right-hand sides of equations (1a^{iv}) and (1b^{iv}) do not account for the total of domestic production, the balancing items, j, are interpreted in three alternative ways:

1) Some of them are considered to be adjustments in the exogenous estimates of inventory changes. In these cases, final demand other than private consumption is not entirely exogenously determined, as indicated by the equations (8a^{iv}) and (8b^{iv}). (M_I and M_{II} are diagonal matrices with 1's and 0's in the diagonals.)

2) Some non-zero elements of j are considered to represent import substitution, so that a positive element in j represents surplus supply from domestic production which is available for replacement of a corresponding amount of imports, and a negative element in j represents the need for supplementary import in order to cover demand, which, if output could have been further expanded, would have been supplied from domestic production. This interpretation must have consequences for the import estimates. The matrices K_{bI} and K_{bII} in equation (2^{iv}) pick out those elements

of j, which are to be considered as affecting imports, and account for them in the import estimates of the model.

3) The third alternative is to consider the non-zero elements of j to be adjustments to the estimates of demand for inputs in the production sectors implied by the fixed coefficients, A. This interpretation implies that one or more of the production sectors uses more or less of the product in question than it would have done if input-output coefficients were fixed. The corresponding saving or nonsaving in production costs must be reflected in entrepreneurial incomes. Since we do not try to identify the sectors in which the change of coefficients occur, the corresponding adjustment in entrepreneurial income cannot be specified by sector. (If we want to stick to our exogenous estimates of entrepreneurial income per unit produced in sectors with endogenous price determination, we must assume that the adjustments discussed here only affect sectors with exogenous price determination, where entrepreneurial income is residually determined.) The matrices $K_{0I}\hat{p}_I$ and $k_{0II}\hat{p}_{II}$ compute the cost savings and add them to those elements in r_0 which represent entrepreneurial incomes.

Writing out the quantity and income equations in matrix form, we have:

$$
\begin{pmatrix} x_I \\ x_{II} \\ r_3 \\ b \\ r_0 \\ r_k \\ r_d \\ r_2 \end{pmatrix} = \begin{pmatrix} A_{I\,I} & A_{I\,II} & C_I & F_I & I & 0 \\ A_{II\,I} & A_{II\,II} & C_{II} & F_{II} & 0 & I \\ 0 & 0 & \hat{s}C_2\hat{p}_z & \hat{s}F_2\hat{p}_u & 0 & 0 \\ A_{bI} & A_{bII} & C_b & F_b & K_{bI} & K_{bII} \\ \hat{p}_{w0}W_{0I} & (\hat{p}_{w0}W_{0II}+E\hat{e}) & 0 & 0 & K_{0I}\hat{p}_I & K_{0II}\hat{p}_{II} \\ \hat{p}_{wk}W_{kI} & \hat{p}_{wk}W_{kII} & 0 & 0 & 0 & 0 \\ \hat{p}_{wd}W_{dI} & \hat{p}_{wd}W_{dII} & 0 & 0 & 0 & 0 \\ \hat{v}W_{21}\hat{p}_I & \hat{v}W_{2II}\hat{p}_{II} & 0 & 0 & 0 & 0 \end{pmatrix} \begin{pmatrix} x_I \\ x_{II} \\ z \\ u \\ j_I \\ j_{II} \end{pmatrix}
$$

Disposable income. The final modification is in the consumption equation (4, 4', 4'' respectively). Here we now substitute disposable income for gross income. Only wages, r_k, and entrepreneurial incomes, r_0, are used in the consumption function, and we can write:

$$
z = z^0 + D_k\left(\frac{1}{\pi}(r_k - T_k) - (r_k^0 - T_k^0)\right)
$$

$$
+ D_0\left(\frac{1}{\pi}(r_0 - T_0) - (r_0^0 - T_0^0)\right) + N\left(\frac{1}{\pi}p - i_z\right) \tag{4a^{iv}}
$$

$T_k =$ direct taxes on labor income (wages)

$T_0 =$ direct taxes on entrepreneurial incomes

In Norway the tax system is such that taxes on entrepreneurial incomes actually to be collected in the course of a given year are determined by the end of the preceding year, namely as the preliminary "advance tax" for the year plus/minus the adjustments due to final settlements for the preceding year. For wage and salary income, preliminary taxes are depending on the current level of income. We have:

$$T_k = \tau_m \cdot (\hat{k} - I)'(\hat{g})^{-1} W_k x^0$$
$$+ \tau_g [\hat{p}_k W_k (x - x^0) + ([\hat{g}]^{-1} - I) W_k x^0] + T_{kc} \qquad (4b^{iv})$$

Here

$\tau_m =$ an estimate of the marginal tax rate for wage and salary earners (in the "budget year"). It is applied to the increase in wage and salary income which would occur with the assumed changes in wage rates and productivity, if production in all sectors remained unchanged. This may be considered an approximation to the change in wage and salary income due to a change in average income per employed worker.

$\tau_g =$ an estimate of the average tax rate for wage and salary earners (in the "budget year"). It is applied to the remainder of the change in wage and salary incomes, which may be considered an approximation to the income change due to the change in employment.

$T_{kc} =$ the tax revenues that would occur if present rates (for the "budget" year) were applied to realized wage and salary incomes in the base year. T_{kc} can be estimated with a comparatively high degree of accuracy.

Incremental form of the equations. The equation $(4b^{iv})$ is written in incremental form in x.

It is easily seen that the equation $(4a^{iv})$, which is in incremental form in z, can be written in incremental form in x by reformulations of $(3a^{iv})$ and $(3b^{iv})$ and insertion.

Finally $(1a^{iv})$, $(1b^{iv})$ and (2^{iv}) can be written in incremental form in x_I, x_{II}, z, u and b with x_I^0, x_{II}^0, z^0, u^0 and b^0 disappearing if the same equations are assumed to be valid for the base year with j identically zero.

PUBLICATIONS OF THE WERTHEIM COMMITTEE

Published by Harvard University Press

Studies in Labor-Management History

ULMAN   The Rise of the National Trade Union: The Development and Significance of Its Structure, Governing Institutions, and Economic Policies, 1955

GOLDBERG   The Maritime Story: A Study in Labor-Management Relations, 1957, 1958

GALENSON   The CIO Challenge to the AFL: A History of the American Labor Movement, 1935–1941, 1960

HOROWITZ   The New York Hotel Industry: A Labor Relations Study, 1960

PERLMAN   The Machinists: A New Study in Trade Unionism, 1961

MUNSON   Labor Relations in the Lithographic Industry, 1953

MANGUM   The Operating Engineers: The Economic History of a Trade Union, 1964

BRODY   The Butcher Workmen: A Study of Unionization, 1964

MARSHALL   Labor in the South, 1967

TAFT   Politics American Style; The California Federation of Labor, 1968

Published by McGraw-Hill Book Company

ALEXANDER   Labor Relations in Argentina, Brazil, and Chile, 1962

STEVENS   Strategy and Collective Bargaining Negotiation, 1963

DUNLOP AND DIATCHENKO   Labor Productivity, 1964

DUNLOP AND FEDORENKO   Planning and Markets: Modern Trends in Various Economic Systems, 1968

SCOVILLE   The Job Content of the U.S. Economy, 1940–1970

* Out of Print.